THE
GENERAL SEMANTICS
OF WALL STREET

THE
GENERAL SEMANTICS
OF WALL STREET

BY

JOHN MAGEE

WITH ILLUSTRATIONS BY THE AUTHOR

PUBLISHED BY JOHN MAGEE
SPRINGFIELD, MASSACHUSETTS

FIRST EDITION

First Printing, September, 1958
Second Printing, November, 1958
Third Printing, September, 1959
Fourth Printing, May, 1961

Library of Congress Catalog Card Number: 58-11073

Printed in the United States of America

PREFACE

THIS has been a particularly hard book to write. I have found it much harder in some ways than my part of "Technical Analysis of Stock Trends." It has been two years in actual preparation, much longer than that in its preliminary shaping-up.

It is hard because the subject is both so simple and so complicated. It is simple in that there are only a few basic points and these would be almost self-evident to a child if he were not already conditioned to a great many pre-conceptions. It is complicated because these pre-conceptions include a great deal of the teaching that every person receives early in life. Some, perhaps most of this teaching is factual and useful. But mingled with it are the legacies of all the pre-scientific theories, the ancient philosophies, the theologies, that have come down through the ages. And the mixture of custom, ethics, hypothesis, precept, morality, discipline, superstition, directives, etc. includes a good deal that may not jibe with the observed facts today, may even conflict with or contradict itself, and may not be in the best interests of mankind's development as a race nor of a man's individual welfare.

To make things more complicated, these customs, directives, etc. are often clothed in the vestments of High Authority. They are often presented in highly-colored emotional terms, and as Absolutes, not subject to revision or even to re-examination.

Finally, as if to add further difficulties, the structure of language itself tends to contribute to mis-understanding and mis-evaluation; unless that structure and its relation to our thinking is well understood.

v

There have been a good many books written on the subject of General Semantics, some of them far more profound than this one. This particular book was built around the problems of a little cosmos which in many ways provides a good working model of the larger society in which we live. Although the stock market represents only a certain part of the life-activity of a certain part of the population, it presents on its limited stage all of the familiar human emotions, fears, and hopes, and it involves problems which have their counterparts in other domains of business, in social life, in the family, and in the intra-personal world in which each of us lives his own private life.

Some of the thoughts expressed in this book are the outcome of my own experiences in the market and elsewhere. But it hardly seems necessary to add that the background of much of this material rests on the "time-binding" of others; of Alfred Korzybski of course, and Lillian Lieber, Norbert Wiener, John von Neumann, Karen Horney, and many others. I am most particularly indebted to Doctor Daniel R. Wheeler, since the book leans heavily on the philosophy and psychology he has taught and practiced for many years. Doctor Wheeler, in his work as a psychiatrist, has applied the principles of General Semantics in a practical way to the problems of family and job and of living with one's self, which involve the common questions that arise in the lives of most of us. Dan Wheeler feels that if, after we have eliminated so far as possible the probable "physical" sources of "un-sanity," that is, if we find no adequate "physiogenic" cause for maladjustment, we should look at the mind itself, as it has been taught, as it has been shaped and has shaped itself, and discover, if we can, how it is failing to evaluate and deal with the environment successfully. He regards the work of the psychiatrist primarily as that of a teacher engaged in instructing the student not merely in "how to solve problems"; but a teacher who can show the sincere student how to understand the workings of his own mind, and how to shape his further education and/or his re-education so as to make possible a more realistic appreciation of the surroundings in which he lives. After such training the student will not "have to be told" what to do in meeting a particular problem, for he will have developed the ability to do his own thinking and to come up with answers appropriate to the question-at-hand.

This is not, of course, a book on psychiatry, nor is it entirely a book on psychology. It is intended primarily as a guide to help the student of the free market to acquire greater confidence and ability in his contacts with that market; though I hope it may hold some interest, too, for workers in other fields.

I am most earnestly hopeful that Doctor Wheeler will write a book in which he will present the applications of General Semantics with special reference to his own work in the field of psychiatry. Such a book would I believe, go a long way to clear the air of a great deal of misunderstanding and plain nonsense that has been bandied about for years in regard to psychiatry, and not all of it from the lips of laymen.

Of necessity "The General Semantics of Wall Street" touches on a good many different subjects, some of them controversial. I do not make any claim to be "an authority" on any of these subjects. However, in many fields there is such a high degree of specialization that the inner circle becomes more or less cut off from the rest of the world. Thus, in finance, law, politics, religion, sociology, medicine, education, psychiatry, etc. there has come to be a special language used and understood by the initiate. This is probably necessary in order to set up definitions covering the very specialized concepts involved in particular studies. But the "lay public" is not welcome behind this veil, and there is not much communication between the dedicated practitioners and the citizenry at large.

It is not possible to have a really meaningful discussion with the workers in some of the specialized fields, partly because of the barrier interposed by the cant or technical vocabulary of the various trades, as it were; and partly because the professional workers neither have the time to explain, nor has the public the time to listen.

Furthermore, if one attempts to talk seriously about serious things with any of the learned members of the learned professions, these specialists will usually repeat (in simple, easy-to-understand words), the cut-and-dried "official" version of what "should" be told. This avoids wasting a lot of time in fruitless debate with uninformed outsiders. But it also sometimes perpetuates a certain circularity of thinking which makes basic progress impossible.

As a rule professional men will not engage publicly in any debate that might challenge their own premises and conclusions, except to the extent of defending the status quo of their pre-conceived dogma. This may be because, living in a more or less self-contained world of thought, they are not anxious nor able to explore any very different approach. There is the suspicion that some of these learned men, through no fault or intention of their own, are carrying on their labors within a framework of mediaeval philosophy, obsolete science, and pre-historic superstition; in short that they are doing some very fine work considering the tools they are using, but some of these tools may be as dead as the past from which they received them.

Along with all this there is the group defense system which effectively seals off each esoteric guild, whichever it may be, through the organized discipline of the group. No member of a professional group is likely to challenge publicly even the most obvious un-sanity in the credo of his craft. He will "explain" willingly, but always within the limitations of the "party line." If you touch him on some highly controversial matter he will tell you he is "not the spokesman for the group" and would prefer not to become involved. For this you can hardly blame him. You cannot imagine a lawyer speaking openly on a radio program about certain tenets of the law. You cannot imagine a banker appearing on television to discuss frankly certain realities of investment. You cannot imagine a priest facing up to certain questions in theology except in terms of the precise dogma of his church.

In all fairness it should be admitted that the great majority of the sincere, honest, hard-working professional men do subscribe sincerely to the official line of their group. As a matter of fact most of them are far too busy carrying out the important duties of their day-by-day work to have much time for "purposeless research." They are not encouraged to explore scientifically in the light of modern understanding, the underlying sources of their convictions. And it may be, too, that some of them feel that "the end justifies the means." They do not feel a need to probe too deeply into the basic philosophies of their crafts. There is enough hard and useful work to be done at the low level of practical everyday reality. The lawyer must prepare his cases. The banker must deal with practical business problems. The minister must write his sermons, visit the sick, perform the marriages. The teacher must conduct classes as outlined in the curriculum.

But since it is not possible to ask the really "tough" questions and get the kind of answers we need from the men who should know, in their respective fields, and since there is not too much communication between the experts in various specialized fields, we are faced with the prospect of going on very much in the way we have always gone on; and that is no longer good enough. If we are going to survive as a human race, we must establish a genuine "freedom of thought" which will make it possible for men in different fields of study to communicate with one another; to re-examine the very foundation stones of their learning, and if necessary, to change them. Also, to maintain an effective two-way communication with the "lay public" who also have a stake in life, liberty and the pursuit of happiness.

In touching on controversial aspects of some highly specialized professions I do not mean to be presumptuous; and I realize that there are men in these groups, who are well familiar with the problem and who are much concerned about it.

But if the men who should be challenging the past and bringing new education and new light to people who so badly need it, cannot or will not come forward to demand a re-examination of basic methods of evaluation in their own professions, then it may be necessary for members of the "lay public" to speak out. We are fully aware of the great steps that have been made on the mechanical level, and the administrative level, and the research level. But as long as there remains in our learned professions a hard core of pompous archaic nonsense that can lead to hostility, mis-understanding, frustration and unnecessary human misery, we must say what we have to say and hope that more able men, within the ranks of the initiate, will have the courage to challenge the un-sanities that are hurting them and menacing all of us.

JOHN MAGEE

August 27, 1958

A WORD OF CREDIT

IN THE writing of a book, or in any important creative effort for that matter, there are forces "behind the scenes" which are vital to the success of the job. I would like to express here my heartfelt thanks to my wife Elinor, and my three children, John, Louise, and Abigail, for their patience and forebearance during the difficult months while "The General Semantics of Wall Street" was being written, illustrated, and produced.

Also, I would like to give my thanks to our technical staff for "keeping the ball rolling" during this period in the matter of maintaining daily stock charts, the Delta Studies, and the like: To Frank J. Curto, who has worked shoulder-to-shoulder with me for a number of years, and his wife, Marcella, Colonel Harolde N. Searles, Carleen Searles, Harry A. Oltsch, Lottie G. Oltsch, Dr. I. Morgan Levine, Grace Levine, Robert M. Lantry, Henry Larsen, Olen Norris, Sheridan Carey, and John Moriarty.

And to our production and office staff, Flora La Riviere, Alyce Scholz, Charles Curto, and Katherine Quinlan. And to Amy Jones for her help in typing the manuscript.

I want to express my gratitude to Patricia Kelley, my personal secretary, for her encouragement and help in this difficult and sometimes discouraging job.

Most especially I want to thank Muriel Brown, who as General Manager of my business has handled the many difficult problems of a growing organization in an outstanding manner. Her own knowledge of general semantics, plus her unswerving loyalty have given me confidence and inspiration without which the job of producing this book could never have been carried through.

And very importantly, I want to extend my thanks to my brother, Beverly Magee, also a student of general semantics, for his great help in reading proofs and offering constructive suggestions as to necessary changes in the text.

CONTENTS

THE
GENERAL SEMANTICS
OF WALL STREET

INTRODUCTION

WALL STREET is not really a place, you know. Not a narrow little lane squashed between the imposing palisades of the great buildings. Not the Wall Street I am thinking about. On that other Wall Street there are window washers, and typewriter salesmen, and exchange students from Lebanon, and pigeons, and curbstones, and bits of last Monday's Herald Tribune swirling in a dust-devil; street lights and old chewing gum rooted to cracked sidewalks, a professor from Bowdoin College eating peanuts, a small boy from the Bronx going to visit his uncle's office. Fire sirens around the corner; boat whistles in the distance; a real substantial piece of the world, and like any piece of the world, filled with complicated and interesting things. But that is not the Wall Street I mean.

Wall Street, as we use the word, is an abstraction, a symbol. It is real enough, but it isn't the kind of reality that you can go and look at, and take pictures of, and walk around in. It is a metaphor, the first of many we may encounter before we finish our excursions.

The Wall Street we are to consider exists in the minds of people. And the tangible expression of it is not in concrete and steel and plate glass, but in reports, charts, analyses and in the proliferated communications of the tape as its messages are displayed in a thousand board rooms across the country.

And just as we strip the pigeons and the boat whistles and the cracked sidewalk from our picture of the financial world of Wall Street, just as we generalize the activities of the narrow little New York lane to include all the financial interests of everyone who buys the final edition of his home town paper, wherever it is, to check the closing prices for the day, so we again simplify and generalize the financial world of Wall Street. We strip off the superficial and incidental goings-on, and we generalize its basic activities. In short we are trying to see what this thing is, what the essence of it is, and what makes it tick.

More especially, we are trying to see what makes *us* tick. If we really understood what motives press us to the corner news stand to get the earliest possible glimpse of the closing price on General Motors, it might help us to understand why we so frequently buy stocks that subsequently sell much lower, and sell those issues that skyrocket so handsomely.

And, you know, it isn't really Wall Street entirely, either, not even the financial kind of Wall Street. It is purchases and sales, predictions and hunches, profits and losses; the chance to pay off the mortgage on the house, the hope of sending Martha to college, the desire to own a Cadillac.

Nor is that the end of the chain, either. We can carry the abstracting process even further. We can strip away all the symbols of finance and even all the symbols of "what money can buy;" and then perhaps we may stand in the presence of a very generalized abstraction indeed. And this abstraction is not only very general, but at the same time it is very particular and it very specifically concerns you.

I am speaking now of your "self." Not your flesh, blood, teeth and toenails, but the part of you that wishes, and hopes, and fears. The part of you that you must do right by or lose your "self-regard." And when you have abstracted yourself to the level where you can see clearly that the essential objective in paying the mortgage, sending Martha to college, or buying the Cadillac is all of a piece and is concerned with defending and enhancing your self-regard, then you will realize that the roots of the grubby activities of a dirty little lane in New York have their ultimate flowering in the most personal and intimate recesses of the minds of men.

This may explain somewhat why I have related General Semantics and Wall Street. For to understand the strange and often irrational things that people do to themselves in Wall Street, it is necessary to explore the forces that operate on them, largely from within themselves.

And when you have traced these relations and understand them at the levels of high abstraction, you may find when you come down to earth again that some of the puzzling and threatening problems of the market, and of life in all its other aspects, do not seem so puzzling nor so threatening as they used to seem.

THE BIG GAME

STEP right up ladies and gentlemen . . . everybody plays; *every-body* wins. You pick your number, name your prize. It's the Big Game. Hurry, hurry, hurry!

Wall Street. Bright lights and loud music. A new adventure at each concession. Young couples, sharp fellows out on a spree, sophisticated gals on the make, a sailor on shore leave. Hamburgers, cones, fresh roasted peanuts. The Big Game.

Take a ride on the Atomic Fuel Convertibles! Test your strength in the Steels! Try your luck at the Puts and Calls. Do you dare ride high on the Missiles and Aircrafts? If you have a steady hand, try the Arbitrage.

It's the Big Game, folks. And when you've seen all the sights at Luna Park come out back of the fence to the west (to the midwest, rather). Try the Corn Game! Guess your Spread! Swing ten contracts of Lard and win a fine Seegar!

It's the Big Game. Everybody wins. Hurry, hurry, hurry!

The Big Game. How do they rig these rackets? How does the shillaber land three balls right in the buckets and walk off with the Kewpie Doll, but one of mine always bounces out. How come that the wheel always slips by just one or two cogs and misses my number for the box of high grade chawclet creams? It's all pure luck isn't it? Or do these boys know how to gimmick the play? There must be a gimmick. Somehow it's always a shill who gets the Indian blanket, and you and I walk off with a tin whistle for a prize.

Well! It's the Big Game, but maybe it's not your game; and until you can make it your game; at least until you know the gimmicks and where to look for them, maybe you'd better save your quarters for the ice cream cones and the hamburgers.

You'd never think to look for the gimmicks where they really are hidden, anyway. You'd never find them at all unless you knew where to look. Nobody has anything up his sleeves; there are no wires, foot pedals, nothing a policeman or an inspector could put his fingers on.

Oh, there have been some crude jobs. There still are, here and there, and from time to time. But the local police and inspectors have cleaned out most of that sort of thing.

There was a time when Jay Gould and Jim Fisk could rig up a sucker game with the Erie and play it over and over again until the poor crooked wheel was falling to pieces. But that was a century ago. There was a man who made safety matches and was skillful in engraving fine certificates, very impressive and of no value, who stole millions with his fancy game.

And there are right now, as this is written, some floaters and drifters who are making their pitch just about the way their fathers and grandfathers did before them; only instead of peddling Rock Oil it is Uranium or Nuclear Power or something else with a modern streamlined look to it. But the novelties are still the old standbys, except for the names, and if you scratch the gold wash off you'll see the same lead-colored base metal underneath. The word is "slum."

The low pitch with the slum is relatively a minor nuisance. But we would do well to keep away from these sharpers and small confidence men.

Specifically: What do you do when your phone rings some evening just after dinner time, and it is a toll call from New York. And a very well-spoken voice tells you that it belongs to a Mr. Simpson of the Utopian Investment Company. Mr. Simpson has been given your name as one of the forward-looking men in your town, the sort of citizen who will not only have the imagination to visualize a fine opportunity, but also the courage to act without delay. The Utopian Investment Company has acquired a controlling interest in North Manitoba Resources, Ltd., and while it is expected that as soon as the assay reports are published the stock will be worth from $8 to $10 a share, they are holding a few thousand shares for allotment to men of substance who will provide a solid nucleus of shareholders; the type of men, like you, who will in effect constitute a living endorsement of the firm's integrity.   Two hundred shares of U.I.C. are being held in your name at the nominal price of $5.   It is not necessary to send any money.   Just give your O.K. now, and the certificates will be made out to you.   But you must act now; the offer cannot be held open.   Hurry, hurry, hurry!   How can you lose?   Oh, *how* can you lose?

This operation, which you may have observed first-hand, is, of course, simply a matter of larceny.   It is a criminal activity; the promoters have nothing to offer but a bundle of worthless or nearly worthless stock, and they operate from offices known as "boiler rooms," where batteries of phones are manned by expert high-pressure salesmen working from the sucker lists which are the only real assets of the business.

In this sort of operation, which is strictly the back-of-the-fence sneak job, there is no need for any very deep study of general semantics, or of finance.   You would think that anyone who had the sense that God gave to a donkey would know enough not to get roped into "investing" a thousand dollars with a firm he never heard of in a company nobody ever heard of, and on the strength of a call from an utter stranger in another state.

And yet . . . people still try to pick which shell the pea is under. And people still draw their life savings from the bank to buy gold bricks . . . or shares of Utopian Resources, Ltd.

Oh, you'll find all sorts of little games if you have sharp eyes. Slick operators who will set up their tripes back of some tent and take off several scores before the cop or the S.E.C. comes round the corner.

Some of these games are quite legal; but just shoddy.   Postcards of bathing beauties.   Needle threaders and vegetable graters.

Like the ads you will find in some of the financial papers, promising you the names of several stocks that will surely triple in value in a very reasonable time, if you will just send $5.00.   How you can get rich on oil royalties with practically no risk and very little capital. A plan to leverage your investment so that $500 does the work of $5000, and you may make hundreds of thousands of dollars in just a few years and without any effort at all on your part.   Advisory services that will tell you what "the market" is going to do *all year* in advance. Secret and confidential methods now available to you (and others) for only $3.00. But act now. The Big Turn, the Key Period is at hand. Hurry, hurry, hurry!

However, we are not concerned mainly with the shoddy, crooked, and cruel games of the financial swindler and the financial charlatan.

It is true that Wall Street is, in a sense, The Big Game. It is a place where you can find big adventures, great gambles with huge prizes, and every variety of device to test your skill, your luck, or your courage. But, leaving out the nasty little thieves who operate on the sly with their cheap con games, the majority of the operation is surprisingly clean, honest, and open.

For in another sense, Wall Street is not The Big Game at all. It is not a carnival. It is not Luna Park. The business of Wall Street is the business of evaluating and exchanging the securities that represent the country's industrial plant, just as the business of LaSalle Street is the business of evaluating the country's crops. It is an extraordinarily complex business, and in view of this complexity it is extraordinarily well run. The men who work in Wall Street (or it may be LaSalle Street), and this includes all the men whose business is the market, in whatever part of the country they may be, are mostly hard-working, decent people. They operate under elaborate regulatory codes. In addition, they work under the strict rules of their exchanges and associations. And beyond all this, their own ethical standards, on the whole, are as high as those in any other business or profession.

It is the custom between brokers to carry out a contract made and accepted by word or gesture as faithfully as though it had been executed under bond. The majority of brokers will deal with customers on the same basis; and in case of an error or dispute a broker will normally accept proper responsibility for a mistake and will make right any loss to a customer for which he was responsible.

The work of Wall Street is much like the work in any other commercial business. There are bookkeepers, technicians, executives, salesmen, office personnel; the same kinds of people you might find in a bank, or in a department store.

There are schools for Wall Street men. Courses for margin clerks, for registered representatives, and for those who are specializing in some particular kind of security. Thousands of men have taken, and are taking these courses, many of them on their own time, evenings.

And besides this, they are studying, reading, charting, continually learning more about the structure of the financial world.

The men of Wall Street do not, as a rule, look like the prototype of The Capitalist. The vision of the large-stomached gentleman with walrus mustachios, an elk's tooth on a massive gold chain, and a tall silk hat, lives on. But only in the land of the cartoonist and the dream world of the politician. The men of Wall Street today look pretty much like anybody else. They wear about the same kind of clothes, and they drive about the same kind of car as you and your neighbor do. They have a wife and children; and they play golf and swim when they go on vacation; and they like sirloin steak and go to the movies sometimes, and they worry a little about taxes and the cost of living. None of them wear tall silk hats any more except at the Costume Ball, and none of them has horns or a tail.

And the business of Wall Street, that is, the exchange of money for securities and vice versa, is one of the most democratic operations we have. It is much more democratic than our politics, where you have to have certain connections if you expect to get anywhere.

Wall Street doesn't care whether you wear a four-in-hand or a bow tie. It doesn't care whether your bank account runs to six figures or only three. Whether your ancestors came over on the Mayflower in 1620 or in the steerage of the Vulcania in 1925 doesn't matter a bit. You can live in a twenty room mansion on Long Island, or you can rent a furnished room in Brooklyn. Wall Street doesn't care what your religion is, or whether you are black, white, yellow or green with magenta spots. When you buy 100 shares of General Motors you pay the same price that anybody else will pay; and it won't help you a bit if you went to school with the senior senator from the state of New York.

In Wall Street, to an extraordinary degree, a man can still stand on his own feet and be recognized for what he is himself, without regard to social connections, family background, wealth or political pull.

Here, "A man's a man, for a' that." You can stand on your own feet; and the victory, if you achieve it, is yours. And if you fail, you cannot fairly point the accusing finger at the skyline of New York and say, "*They* have robbed me!" For there is no great oval room where the top-hatted, wax mustachioed tycoons gather to plot your destruction. It is all right for the Russian press to draw such a picture, and we can perhaps forgive even the local office-holder who sees a chance to stir up laggard votes with a Hate campaign. But you cannot inject life into the fading Currier and Ives portrait of the villains of Wall Street concocting a network of wash sales, false reports and watered stock to rob you of your savings. You will have to place the blame for losses, if losses you have, somewhere else.

QUESTIONS FOR CONSIDERATION

Do you believe that "insiders" manipulate the prices of such stocks as General Motors, U. S. Steel, Standard Oil of New Jersey? If you do, what are your reasons for believing as you do: on what evidence do you base your opinion?

Do you feel that the profits of a speculator (that is, of a trader in the ordinary sense, not a "manipulator") come out of the pockets of other traders or the general public? What leads you to think this? Have you considered what constitutes the function of a free market? Have you wondered how the values of securities and commodities might be determined without a free speculative market? Would you say that the speculator was a parasite and that his profits were "unearned income"? If you had this attitude how would you feel about your own market gains? Could you buy and sell stocks in the hope of gain if you felt a certain "guilt" about such gains? Would such an attitude give you security and peace of mind? Is it possible that part of the reasons so many market traders do so badly is because they do have such an attitude?

Would you agree that a man who does not feel the market is a useful and necessary part of our economy should not engage in market trading at all?

Where would you place the responsibility for such market losses as are not due to fraud or manipulation?

BLACK MAGIC

THERE are certain situations where you expect to get fooled and where you might even be disappointed if you weren't fooled. You don't really expect to win the bridge lamp and the overgrown teddy bear at Luna Park; in fact, it would be most awkward to lug the damn things home; and what would you do with them when you got home? You expect to lose; and you know that there are certain ways in which the probabilities of your number coming up can be substantially reduced; but that is all right if you're just out for a good time.

When you go to a magic show you expect to be fooled. You see wonderful things taking place. Cards appear in the air, and the very card you chose sticks to the ceiling. A rabbit, two rabbits, a dozen rabbits are taken out of an empty silk hat, the very same kind of silk hat from which Jay Gould produced common stock in the Erie to cover his shorts; but don't forget that was nearly a hundred years ago.

You expect to be fooled. The saying goes, "The hand is quicker than the eye." But don't believe that. The hand is not really quicker than the eye. That is just an easy way for somebody to explain something he doesn't understand.

As a rule the magician is not fooling your eyes. That isn't the way it works. He doesn't need to fool your eyes if he can fool your *mind;* so that you *think* you see something that wasn't really there; or perhaps fail to see what was in plain sight all the time.

It is hard to believe that the twelve rabbits were in plain sight (if you knew where to look) and it is even harder to believe that all the mystery and wonder of the show is going on inside your own head. Girls don't turn into rose bushes, really. A swimming goldfish doesn't suddenly become a pigeon and fly around the room. And you know that. But unless you have studied magic you don't quite understand how it *seems* as if these things happened.

It is a matter of knowing something about how you *perceive* things. And it will surprise you when you find out how much that you perceive can be completely false to fact. Things that, when they are pointed out to you, will seem so simple. And you will say, "How could I have overlooked *that*. Why it was in plain sight all the time." It is sometimes as if we overlooked an elephant blocking our own front door, and squeezed past the animal without seeing him at all.

If you are like most people your earliest experiences in the market were discouraging. There are only a small minority of beginning investors who by luck or by the power of the prevailing trend, make large net profits at the very outset. And they are more to be pitied than congratulated, since for them there is likely to be a day of disillusionment more painful even than for those who took their hard knocks at the start. These lucky beginners are somewhat in the position of the young man who was taken to the race track by an older horse-player; made four successive $2.00 bets, all of which paid off, and turned to this friend all starry-eyed to ask, "Say, how long has this been going on?"

If you are like most of us, the first market adventure is a small one, carefully planned and studied out. One examines the dividend records and the earnings figures for past years as intently as any horse-player scans the form sheets. He weighs "all" the factors and buys the stock that his intelligence and common sense tells him is the logical choice. It cannot go down, not very much; and it must go up in value.

And what happens? Wouldn't you think that just on the basis of sheer luck if you selected any stock at random, the probabilities alone would give you a profit about half the time? "Why do they *always* have to go down?"

Over and over again the novice goes through his evaluative procedure, selects his stock and buys it, and then a few weeks or a few months later, sells out and takes his loss, and prepares to try again.

How can he be wrong all the time?

Who is doing this to him? Who is fooling him? What is the magic, where is the gimmick, how do they do this?

You know, you can go up after the magic show and examine the cards, and the boxes and the wand, and you won't find much. The wand is just an ordinary piece of wood, nicely painted with black enamel. The boxes don't have any false bottoms. The cards are a regular deck, no markings. What happened? How did he do this to me? How did he fool me?

Well; did he really fool me? Or could you say that he just sort of let me fool myself? Yes! The illusion was not in the cards, the boxes, the wand: the illusion was something in my way of looking at these things.

I saw something that was not there. Just as I saw something that was not there when I bought the stock. It seemed to be there. It looked all right. I had good reasons to support my belief. But when the wand was waved, somehow it turned out it wasn't the way I had thought it was at all.

I was fooled. But who fooled me? And how?

QUESTIONS FOR CONSIDERATION

Have you ever been "fooled" into thinking you saw something happen that you knew very well did not happen?

Do you know the mechanisms by which magicians fool the public? Do you realize how many of the illusions are created in the *minds* of the spectators?

Have you ever been "fooled" in the market? Did you ever go back and trace out just how you were fooled?

Would you say there was a similarity between the deceptions of the vaudeville stage and the deceptions you meet in everyday life? Are they all something that is created in the *mind* of the observer?

Isn't it possible that if we understood more about our own minds and how we perceive things we might not be fooled so often?

THE VILLAIN

TAKE down the picture of the Capitalist. He doesn't exist, not like the picture. And tell that magician to step down from the stage. *You* get up there on the stage! If anybody turned girls into rose bushes and made rabbits come out of empty hats, it wasn't the magician. It was you.

And it was you that decided after careful study that Fruehauf Trailer was really worth much more than the $35 you paid for it in 1956. And when you saw it drop mysteriously to $9 in 1957 you cannot quite fairly blame the magician; after all, it was all your own doing. You examined the evidence, and you made the decisions.

Your fault? No, not exactly your fault. Not anybody's *fault* in the sense of blaming anybody. But unless there was deliberate fraud here there must have been some fault; and you were the one who made the decisions.

There must have been some fault because you had arrived at the conclusion that this stock would soon sell for $50 or more; and on that basis you paid $35 for it. And instead of reaching your objective, it collapsed to $9. Your conclusion was mistaken and your prediction was wrong.

Perhaps if you had not been so absolute, so "sure" of what the outcome would be, you might not have been hurt so badly. Perhaps if you had examined more evidence, or looked at the evidence in a different light, it might have helped. Perhaps there were some forces urging you on to buy that stock, forces of which you were not entirely conscious.

13

At any rate, if we look at the records of the average market new-comer the percentage of success is nothing like what you might expect on the basis of any reasonably good evaluation or even on the basis of pure chance. With rare exceptions he loses money with great regularity until either he runs out of capital, gets discouraged and quits the market (with feelings of great hostility toward Wall Street), or ultimately discovers that it is possible to do something to correct some of his most flagrant errors and stop the succession of failures.

It sounds like a very easy thing to change one's method of looking at things so as to see the reality, and not the illusion. It seems such a simple thing.

And it is a simple thing, basically. It is as simple as the fact that the earth is round and rotates on its axis. And yet for thousands of years men believed that the earth was flat and the stars moved around the heavens each night (and some still do believe that).

This business of stumbling over an elephant in your own front hall and never even seeing the beast is fairly common. Science is filled with cases where men searched for years for something which eventually turned up, in plain sight, right in their own front yard.

It is much harder to learn something simple, basic, and quite new to you than to learn something that seems quite complicated. It is harder for a high school student to understand what is meant by the square root of minus one than to learn the list of French irregular verbs.

Ask somebody to imagine a number system based on dozens instead of tens; and if he is not familiar with number concept it may quite throw him.

If you want to see how hard it is for most of us to adapt ourselves to any changes in the concepts we regard as obvious, universal, and eternal, just try, with a few of your friends, leading the conversation around to some hypothetical change in our customs or habits. How would our lives be affected if all present taxes were abolished and we had only a single tax on land values? What would be the ultimate effects of a graduated tax on children, the first-born in a family being exempt, the second subject to a moderate impost, and each successive addition to the family carrying a higher price tag? What would be the result of abolishing all municipal elections and selecting our councilmen and aldermen by lot and by precincts from the list of qualified voters? Suppose we ran our busses free, with the costs carried like schools and streets and parks in the general budget; how would this affect our parking problems?

You may be surprised what confusion it can cause, even amongst reasonably well-educated people, when you suggest the slightest change in the framework of their habitual thinking. Men who will discuss for hours the advisability of continuing or abolishing capital punishment will hardly deign to consider any scheme of preventing homicide by attacking the causes of murder.

When we say, "Don't look at the magician, don't look at the cards or the boxes; look at yourself," that is a very simple, basic suggestion. It sounds so easy. The things you have to look for are so very simple; so simple you will say, "Yes, yes," but you will go right on the way you have gone before. Unless, of course, you realize that these are very serious matters. These are matters that concern much more than making profits in the stock market. The implications here reach into your personal life, your "success," your "happiness," and by extension they concern matters of law and order, and of material prosperity in the community, and of international affairs and of world peace.

These are no trivial points.

QUESTIONS FOR CONSIDERATION

Are you able to evaluate what is going on around you without prejudice, objectively and clearly? (Think several times on this one.)

Where did you get your criteria for evaluation? How can you tell whether these criteria are good?

Suppose the consequences of your judgments are continually disappointing to you? Is there anything you can do about it to avoid so many disappointments in the future?

Do you feel you just have "bad luck" in your market operations? Then why is it that some people have so much "bad luck" all the time, and others very little?

Do you believe that there might be some way by which you could improve your evaluative habits; and that such a step might put you more often "in the path of good luck"?

THE BLIND

YOU may remember a short story by H. G. Wells, a story about a man who strayed accidentally into a mountain-walled valley in South America. The inhabitants, who had a large and prosperous city, with neat houses and carefully laid out walks between them, found their visitor a strange, probably psychotic individual. The visitor, it seems, claimed that he could "see"; that he had some sense which he derived from "light" by means of which he had powers of understanding which (he claimed) they lacked. For the inhabitants of this town were all what we would call "blind." For many generations they had been sightless. They had built their lives around the senses and powers they possessed. This thing called "seeing" seemed to have no place in their lives. It was quite unnecessary to them, since they had adapted their living to ways that did not require sight. And in fact it seemed to them a gross abnormality; and in all kindness and friendship they proposed that of one their great surgeons remove the offending growths the visitor called "eyes" so that he might become a properly adjusted member of the community.

It is not easy to explain to someone a simple, basic concept such as "seeing." It is not easy for anyone to accept something foreign to his habit and cultural environment.

Let me propose a test case for you. I want you to imagine that you could visit a shepherd tending his flocks by night in the hills of Israel 2500 years ago. The simple project I have laid for you is merely to explain to the shepherd that the earth revolves on its axis each day and that the stars remain in relatively fixed positions in the sky.

Mind you, this shepherd has done what you have not done. He has sat on that hillside almost every night for several years. He has sat on the solid rock of the solid mountain on the solid earth, and he has watched, with his own eyes, the stars rising from the eastern horizon, moving across the dome of the sky and sinking to the west.

What language are you going to use to make him understand your crazy theory? Are you going to sketch the earth as a round ball, resting on nothing at all, spinning around in space? Are you going to expect him to accept a dreamer's theory spun out of the imagination, as against the evidence of his eyes? Are you going to win out over "common sense" with your weird story? I would imagine the shepherd would either run for his life, or perhaps get his fellow shepherds to help you back to town for a serious heart-to-heart talk with the rabbi.

Or put yourself in Germany, say around 1938. Go before an audience in any German town and tell them the truth; as you might see it. That Hitler is a dangerous maniac leading their country on a road that must end in ruin. That they are slaves to a cruel and stupid system which is exploiting them and destroying them. If you were not stoned out of the hall at once or taken into custody you would be told that your comments were unsocial, ungrateful, and downright stupid. That Hitler had brought back hope to Germany. That he had promised jobs for all, and there were jobs for all. That he had promised great roads, and new industries and new schools and libraries; and there were all these things. That there were social improvements, aids to the needy, programs of national development, higher standards of living, self-respect and pride, and a sense of great accomplishment. How could you sell your simple theory to these dedicated people? How could you make them see how cruelly they were being deceived, and that much of the deception was of their own making?

It comes hard to see some things. Better to be blind. Yes, really, better not to see at all than to see what hurts too much.

It is easier, is it not, to say that Fruehauf Trailer went down because of a change in "basic demand"; unforeseen conditions in the industry. Nothing that we could do anything about. Nothing in which our thinking was faulty. Simply another bad break to add to the many, many bad breaks already on the books.   This leaves us feeling not-quite-so-hurt.

But it does not help at all in preventing the next disaster.

It may be less painful this one time to be "blind" than to see clearly.   But is it, in the final summing-up, less painful to go through a whole lifetime blind, rather than open one's eyes and face the truth?

It is sometimes hard to face the truth.   You will revolt at some of the things you are going to be asked to look at.   They will seriously conflict with your "common sense."   It may be easier not to look at all; and it certainly will not be easy to look and to see that some of the idols you have served so blindly for so long are only hunks of weathered clay.

But if you want sight you must learn to see.   And you must be able to bear the pain of the unfamiliar sunshine.

QUESTIONS FOR CONSIDERATION

Suppose someone challenged something you had believed in all your life. Would you be able to consider the evidence that your belief was not in line with the facts?

Would you be able to study impartially a statement that seemed to go contrary to "common sense"?   Such as "A triangle may have three right angles," or "It is no more dangerous to sell stocks short than to buy stocks."

If you accepted the evidence of some drastically different point of view, could you utilize it; or would long habit, tradition, and respect for high authority prevent you from actually adopting the new idea?

Do you ever examine the statements of friends, of political speakers, of brokers, or editorial writers to see whether what they say makes sense, or whether they are simply repeating "what everybody knows and accepts"? Would you say this acceptance would be an easy thing for anyone to come by?   Can you see the difficulty in changing habitual life-patterns of long standing?

OUT OF THE DARKNESS

WHAT do you suppose an unborn baby sees? What do you suppose it thinks? How do you suppose it spends its nine months of leisure time before it accepts the irreversible responsibility of entering the world of men?

I wonder if there can be much of anything going on there that you could call thinking? I wonder whether you could properly consider that an unborn baby had anything that we could really call a *mind*?

Mankind, as you know, comes into this world rather imperfectly equipped for unaided survival, as compared, say with a baby chick. Fishes, birds, even some of the mammals seem to arrive with certain built-in instincts, not exactly intelligence as we think of it, but rather a substitute for intelligence, or a nest-egg of mental determinants to which will later be added the products of education and experience.

And with insects, as you know if you have read and enjoyed Fabre, there is really no adequate hook on which to hang intelligence at all. This seems to lie in the mechanics and structure of the insect. Dr. Norbert Wiener of M.I.T. has discussed this in a most interesting commentary. You can't really educate an insect very much. There is practically no learning ability. There isn't anything to work on. The marvellous engineering and social organization, and hunting and home-building techniques we see in the insect world seem to be built on something that is handed down from generation to generation as part of the central nervous system of the insect, built in from birth, complete. Necessary and sufficient.

Not so with man.   You and I needed a good many years of spoon-feeding and cuddling, and teaching and punishing, before we were ready to matriculate at nursery school; and a good many years on top of that before we could drive a car, play poker, or take the bar examinations.

If you want to see how helpless we really are, and how helpless we would remain without the aid of our senses to bring in knowledge from the world around us, read Helen Keller's story of her early years; black, silent, empty years, until by what must have seemed a miracle her teacher, Anne Mansfield Sullivan, re-established communication, and into the nascent soul of Helen Keller began to flow the basic data needed to set up what became her fine intelligence.

I say *became*.   It never would have become.   Not without communication.   Miss Keller undoubtedly had the potential, the capacity to learn.   But without contact with reality she would have remained . . . a blank.

QUESTIONS FOR CONSIDERATION

What is the earliest event you can remember?   How much of your present knowledge do you think you had at that time?

Where did you get your present knowledge?   Where did it come from? Do you think you inherited much knowledge?   What knowledge would you say you were born with?

Suppose you had never been exposed to the world at all; that is, suppose you had been brought up in a dark cell or closet, a small soundproof room, and no one ever spoke to you.   What would you be like?   To what degree could you claim membership in the human race as a human being?

Do you believe that shrewd understanding and sensitive intuition originate entirely spontaneously; or would you say that these things are a product of contact with the outside world?   Do you believe a successful stock trader is "born, not made"?

Is it possible to speak of "a human mind" in any meaningful sense except with reference to what has come into the brain from *outside*?

THE CAMERA

MY DAUGHTER, Abigail, uses one of these box cameras promoted by a mail order concern in Minnesota. The camera comes loaded with film. After you have taken the pictures, you send it back with payment for the film and the developing and printing, and back come the prints with a new camera loaded with blank film.

Blank film. Highly sensitive film, capable of recording in great detail the snowman in the back yard, recess at Washington School, or Pokey and her new kittens.

But the blank film in the camera as it comes to us, has no latent image on it. It is a blind sheet of plastic, showing nothing. Leave it in the camera a month and it will be as blank as it was the first day. The only way that the picture can be registered on the film is to expose the film to the outside world in a suitable light.

Doesn't the first knowledge have to come from outside? The first bright light to follow with the blue eyes. The first sounds, perhaps mother singing to her child. The first sensations of touch, and of taste and of smell. Perhaps all these things are jumbled up and rather meaningless at first; like the coat-room with not enough hooks. There wouldn't be much place to hang and arrange all these sensations at first.

Isn't it remarkable how soon the baby gets the hang of certain things out in the world? Unless you are very careful he will pick up a number of exceedingly stubborn and inconvenient habits in no time at all; and since he has plenty of time and not nearly so many things to think about as you do, he may outmaneuver you in a number of ways if you don't watch out.

Also, he will establish some of the successful maneuvers as habits. He will *learn* (and this is where he begins to lord it over the built-in mentality of the praying mantis) what is most likely to bring him attention or food or warmth or dry diapers or whatever it is that he happens to need.   Long before he is a year old he will have a practical working method for manipulating people, the people nearest at hand, the ones that must be manipulated.

Now at just what stage are you going to say this child has acquired such characteristics as "good judgment," "good taste," "a sense of decency," "a feeling of responsibility," etc., etc.   There have been various attempts to fix the precise time at which these qualities could be assumed to have matured; and there has been discussion of these points by legal and ecclesiastical authorities.

But isn't it more reasonable to suppose that these qualities develop differently in different children, and that in any case they take shape gradually?   And also that there is considerable room for differences of opinion as to whether your child or mine has "good taste," for example.

But you will agree that you and I and everybody else we know evolved from something that was quite blind and quite blank at the start; and for the most part whatever we know we have "acquired." That is to say, we have learned it by observation and experience, it has been taught to us, or we have learned it by combining, abstracting and reasoning from the things we have directly experienced or that we have been taught.

Certainly you and I were not born with an understanding of the English language, or any other language.   We didn't know, at birth, how to figure a margin account, or for that matter how to tie our own shoelaces.   These things, and a million others, were "acquired."

All your life you have been taking in communications from outside.   Not only all the things you see and hear and that you record with other senses as direct experience.   But as soon as you could understand words you were being *told* about other matters outside of your direct experience.   And as soon as you learned to read you began to take in more about matters beyond your personal experience.

In both the learning you received from direct contact, and in that that came from your teaching, you soon found there were "oughts";

there were some "do's" and a great many "don'ts". If you pulled the cat's tail you got scratched. A don't. If you put your hand on the radiator you were burned. Another don't. If you smiled your best smile at Granny you got a peppermint. A do. If you threw snowballs into Mrs. McCarthy's window you were a "dirty little brat." A don't. And so on.

As a matter of survival, or at least as a matter of maximum comfort you soon learned what was expected of you by nature and by your elders and by the domestic animals. You acquired a place in the household peck-order; at any rate, you knew that it was safe to pull Prince's tail, but not Felix's. You could get away with certain things any time with Granny, sometimes with Mommy, and never with Daddy. You acquired a value system, in fact in a certain sense you *were* a value system. That is, the thing that made you really "you" as an individual was this complex structure built up out of your stored-up perceptions.

And, of course, you know that what you learn young sticks by you. That is how we get some of our good thinking habits that help us later in life. Unfortunately, it is also how we get some very bad thinking habits.

Because, if you will think of the good, simple, straight-thinking shepherds and their bafflement at your theory of a round whirling world, you will see that it is going to be rather hard for anyone to change the common-sense views that have met the test of experience and acceptance by others during a whole lifetime. It is particularly hard if the concept in question is so firmly built into one's value system that it seems, as we said before, to be obvious, universal, and eternal.

To challenge one of these basic simple concepts means digging up deep roots. And like any deeply rooted organism, like the tree roots you dig up in your garden, they keep growing back. They are hard to kill. In fact, even when your intellect accepts a new view and you have intellectually rooted out the faulty concept, you will find it keeps creeping back. It sometimes takes a long time to kill off the old root structure.

It isn't necessary to get into very abstruse and obscure philosophy to see how often our preconceived ideas run smack into facts that don't fit. When you were in second grade you were taught that the world was round. That there wasn't really any "up" or "down" in

Space. That there were people living in Tasmania and in China on the other side of the earth. You were taught that, and you could repeat that clearly before the class. But this new knowledge clashed with what you had learned about "up" and "down" before you ever went to school. Didn't it come hard to think of the Australians living on the "bottom" of the earth? Didn't you use to wonder, when you were quite small, why they didn't fall off? And whether they had to walk on their heads? It wasn't until much later that you could really accept a space without "up" or "down," so that you could see all the peoples of all parts of the world, all oriented to different "verticals" and "horizontals" but all experiencing the same sensations of walking, climbing, falling, etc. in about the same way. Or do you really accept that even now? For some quite grownup people their own "up" is much more correctly "up" than that of citizens in Terra Del Fuego or the Cape of Good Hope.

Frank Stockton wrote a story about a little girl who lived in a town called Rondaine. She had a very fine and very elaborate clock by her bed, of which she was very proud. And it bothered her that other people were not sufficiently interested in the correct time to keep their clocks adjusted and set correctly. For she noticed that the big town clock and the clock in the church tower and the two clocks at either end of the bridge all struck the hour a few minutes earlier or a few minutes later than her own clock. In the end, to her amazement and sorrow, she discovered that perhaps none of the clocks struck precisely the right time. And her own poor little timepiece was seriously out of adjustment and several minutes in error.

Of course, that story was merely fiction, though it was, like many of Stockton's tales, fiction with a hard, sharp point. It was written a number of years before Albert Einstein raised some much harder, much sharper points about trying to tell absolute time with clocks or in any other way.

Going back, for a moment, to the "up" and "down" ideas that we get so early in life, and which become so much a part of our perceptive system that we cannot easily change or dislodge them: This chapter is headed, "The Camera." In a sense, you, or any other human being is like a camera, in that you continually record sensations from outside, through your senses, and preserve them for later reference.

This is especially true of your sight. Your eye is, in a very real sense, a camera; or, to put it more accurately, a camera is a rather crude working model of a human eye. The iris diaphragm controls the amount of light admitted, just as the diaphragm of your camera does. The muscles of the eye focus the image on the retina just as you focus your camera. And the convex lens gathers the light from the scene before you to invert it and present it in miniature on the retina in exactly the same way the lens of your camera gathers the light, inverts it, and presents it on the film or plate.

Did we say "invert"? Yes. The image is inverted. And here is one of those disturbing encounters with the "up" and "down" words. For this suggests that then we are seeing everything upside down! It is almost as alarming as the thought of those poor Australians walking on their heads and occasionally falling down into Lower Space.

How can we get around the house or do our work if we see everything "inverted." Well, of course, we don't. The image on the retina is inverted, yes. The picture is actually, "visibly" formed on the retina by the light projected from outside; and it is inverted.

But we do not "see" with the image on the retina. The conscious perception, what we call "sight," occurs in the brain. Sever the optic nerve leading to your brain, and you may still have an image on the retina; but it is not "seen"; for you are then "blind."

"Sight" occurs in the brain. And the brain lies in darkness, encased in the skull. No light comes into your brain, any more than light comes in through the antenna lead of your television set. The perception of light is something that is generated in the dark recesses of your brain.

What difference does it make, then, whether the reception is from left to right or right to left; whether "up" is at the "top" or at the "bottom"? The process of learning to see is a matter of relating what impulses come in from the retina with what experience teaches us is "out there."

And if you think that "up" (as you see it) is absolutely "up"; one of the absolute, universal, and eternal truths, you should study the various experiments in which the messages coming into the eye have been deliberately distorted. Research students have staggered around in glasses which reverse the images of right and left eye, or which invert the inverted image on the retina. They have staggered around for a day or so, their perception revolting at the now-meaningless and paradoxical messages that come in through their optic nerves. Eventually, though, new patterns of perception are formed; and these students have found that it is possible to learn a new way of seeing things. What makes it all so hard, in these cases, at the start, is the need to unlearn what was so deeply learned before.

At this point I am going to plunge into Wall Street for a moment; just for a moment, in order to point a relation. Do you know people who have "learned" certain things so well that they can see them in only one way? So well that, for them, there could be no other way to "see," just as you would find it extremely hard to see with reversed or "upside-down" glasses, at first? Do you know some people who "see" clearly that a stock that pays a dividend must be a better investment than one that doesn't? Do you know people who believe it is important to know how to buy stocks; but who cannot understand why it is just as important to know how to sell them? Do you know people who feel that the only way to evaluate a stock is to read and understand the Annual Report? These people have learned to "see" certain things so naturally that any suggestion that someone else might have a different way of seeing makes no sense to them at all, regardless of argument, evidence, or demonstration. We will come back to this, later.

QUESTIONS FOR CONSIDERATION

At what age did you learn "not to point" at things? Can you remember any other directives about good manners and proper conduct you learned at that time? Would you find it easy to change the habits you established in these matters? Could you get along with people who had different ideas of proper conduct?

At what age were you taught that sexual indulgence was "nasty"? Would you find it easy to understand a culture where people had different views on this? What other precepts did you receive at about that time?

How old were you when you acquired a view on religion and your obligations to society? Do you regard these as something inherent in your own nature, or were these things learned? Could you accept some other point of view as valid under certain conditions?

What are some of the things you "know "about finance and the market? Where did these ideas come from? How did they come to you?

THE PRIMARY RECEPTORS

WE HAVE, then, eyes, which are sensitive to light and which transmit messages to our brains which we then translate into the sensation of "seeing." Similarly our ears are sensitive to sound and transmit messages which our brains translate into the sensation of "hearing." And in like manner with our other senses we react to the incoming stimuli with appropriate "sensations."

It is important to understand that our reaction to light or sound or taste, etc. is not the same as the light, sound, taste, etc. itself. To use the good analogy of television, what appears on your screen, that is, the picture you look at, is not the same as the waves which are transmitted by the sending studio and picked up by the antenna on your set, for, as you know, these waves cannot be seen at all but must be picked up and translated into a picture.

Neither are the waves sent out by the transmitting studio the same as what is being televised.

Nothing is known to us directly except the impulses that come in to our brain through our nerves which transmit stimuli from the outside world to the brain. And whatever else we know must be constructed from the bits of information we receive in this way.

In this, to recapitulate, we are quite different from, let us say, an insect. The insect is a wonderful organism, of course, and marvellously designed to cope with its particular environment. But the pattern is fixed, it is "taped in" like the information on a recording machine. The insect has no capacity to "learn" anything new, or at any rate, its capacity for learning is so slight as to be negligible. For all practical purposes you can't teach an insect anything it does not "know" already; and it does not learn very much by its own experience.

On the other hand, mankind is designed for its particular way of life, which is enormously more complicated than that of an insect. And whereas the insect produces offspring in magnificent profusion, to meet the demands of a high mortality, man operates with a lower rate of reproduction, and a higher rate of survival. In man we have a problem of survival of the individual to a much greater degree than in the case of the insect. Man is not nearly so specialized; he is able to master many skills, to meet many different kinds of situations, to live under widely varying conditions.

So it is not so important for man to have a single specialized way of living, such as the insect possesses. Man must be able to change himself, to solve new problems, to make himself different according to the needs of the situation. This is one of the great demarcations that sets man apart from all the rest of the animal world.

One of the great half-truths that have been bandied about for years is the comment, "You can't change human nature." There is no doubt that it is not easy to change well-established habits and ways of thinking and doing things. And it may be true that you cannot change someone else's human nature. But while it may take time and be a very hard process, there is nothing in the book of rules that says that human nature cannot change. You, unlike an insect, can change yourself. It may not be easy, but it is the brightest hope of the human race that it can learn, change, and improve itself by its own efforts.

But before you can change your ways you must change your perceptions, especially those that have become embedded from early childhood in your value system. And before you can do that you must know something about how these perceptive habits originated, and the mechanisms by which they operate.

Unless you have a reasonably clear understanding of what is going on "in here," you will never be able to interpret clearly what is going on "out there."

In short, you will go right on being depressed, angry, lonely, puzzled; and you will continue to make the same mistakes over and over again, not only in the stock market, but in your job and at home.

Which would be too bad, because you are not an insect nor even a donkey. You are a human being, and you have, to a greater degree than any other organism on the earth, a brain which has the ability to build itself, change itself, and solve new problems.

As Alfred Korzybski put it, "We must not behave like animals."

QUESTIONS FOR CONSIDERATION

Do you have any bad habits? Would you say that you are inclined to be careless in putting things away? Do you put off any job that can wait until tomorrow? Are you extravagant? Do you jump to conclusions too fast?

Are these habits, and others, part of your "inheritance"? Is there nothing you can do to change them? Why do you have so much trouble in changing or controlling them? Is it possible that you are trying to do the job by working superficially at the behavior level instead of checking the premises that lie at the roots of some of these?

In your market experience have you made the same kind of mistake over and over again? Do you feel this is because you are "stupid"? Or would you say it is because you operate according to certain habits stemming originally from what you learned somewhere, sometime? If you could learn something new, would you be able to change your earlier "learning"? Do you think this would be enough? Wouldn't it be necessary then to change the habit of thinking and doing the old way?

Haven't you actually changed your thinking and your doing in some ways in the past ten years?

Would you say that you can change human nature: your own?

A STARTING POINT

IT MUST be clear to you if you have considered the foregoing that if the various nerve channels carrying incoming messages to your brain from the outside world, through the medium of your various sense organs, were to be severed, you would not have any way at all of "knowing" what was "out there." And if these nerves were cut off in your earliest childhood, you would never be able to establish any contact with the outside world. You would never "know" anything.

If what we call "knowledge" is one of the ways we are different from the other inhabitants of this earth, then it must be plain that these cables of nerves to our brains are an absolute essential to our humanity. Without them, and the messages they carry, we would not be reduced to the level of the "lower" animals. We would be infinitely worse off than they are. The animals, at least, do have the receptors, that is, the eyes, ears, etc. to enable them to make contact with and maintain continuous communication with the world around them. That is basic not only for mankind, but for all of the animal kingdom.

But, as we have seen, given the primary senses to establish communication with the outside world, man has the capacity to put these impressions to much greater use than any animal.

He can not only "know" what is going on in the world from direct observation; but he can make abstractions. He can deduce and construct, from past observation, and make predictions and decisions

30

to a much greater degree than animals can. This is not to say that animals cannot abstract and reason; for there is plenty of evidence that they do. The question is more a matter of "how much"; and as you know, their reasoning powers are somewhat limited.

We have had a spate of "shaggy dog stories," such as the tale about the hunter who comes across a campsite in a clearing, where there is a tent, a small fire, and a man and his dog playing cribbage on a flat-topped rock. The visitor watches the game for a while thoughtfully, finally remarks, "That's a pretty smart dog you've got there, stranger." And the camper replies, "Oh, he ain't so smart. I just beat him three games in a row."

What makes this, and all the rest of its ilk funny (and I happen to enjoy them all) is that dogs just don't have that much intelligence. We can love and admire Man's Best Friend, as most of us do. We can take off our hats to his courage, his faithfulness, his ingenuity and skill. But when all is said and done, the faithful beast goes just so far and no farther. No dog has ever learned to play cribbage, nor to read a book, nor to extract square root.

So we start with primary contacts we have with the world (which we share with the animals); and on these we can build the wonderful network of "knowing" and "thinking" to which the animals can never aspire.

H. L. Mencken once enumerated various skills and attributes in which the animals exceeded our own capabilities; the vision of the eagle, the sense of smell of the bloodhound, and the keen hearing, swiftness of foot, brute strength, etc. of the various beasts. Apparently it was only in the possession and use of his human mind in which man excelled the beasts; and this advantage he was apparently too magnanimous to put to use.

This was somewhat of an exaggeration, of course; since the most backward moron is, in some respects, far ahead of the smartest animal in the use of his mind.

But none of us, it is safe to say, are fully using the machinery we, as men, and we alone, possess.

Here we are; able to read, and write, and do at least simple computation. We have a vast store of memories and things learned from others. Some of these things have come to us from the past. They represent knowledge that was written down by our forefathers, long dead. It is only through the miracle of writing and reading that we can avail ourselves of this knowledge. We will speak of this later. Meanwhile, we are well-equipped to study and understand and learn. We can take our present understanding and turn it to advantage by studying how we first learned things. This will help us to find out what kinds of learning are useful and which may be damaging to us. And then we can set to work to correct the damaging factors, to our benefit.

This is the starting point for a study of "How we know what we know."

QUESTIONS FOR CONSIDERATION

In a previous chapter we asked some questions as to when and how you acquired certain "knowledge." Did you find it impossible to remember just when or where you learned certain things? Do you agree that they must have been learned somewhere and sometime in your life?

Is it possible that some of your present actions and your present thoughts and beliefs come from learning which came to you very early in life; and that you have forgotten just how or where or when you received it?

Would you say that some of this learning may have been based on incorrect information, or that you may have misinterpreted the information?

Are all of the conditions in the world you live in the same as they were at the time you acquired your earliest learning? Are you the same person at your present age that you were at the age of three or five? Do you have the same needs, do you face the same problems? Are there some problems you face today that you did not have as a child?

Are you operating with the same directives, precepts, premises today that were suitable to you when you were a child?

Would it be worth while to check back and see "how we know what we know" in order to operate more realistically here and now?

Can you trace just where and how you acquired your present ideas about "the market"? Do you ever recheck these to see if they are true and applicable now?

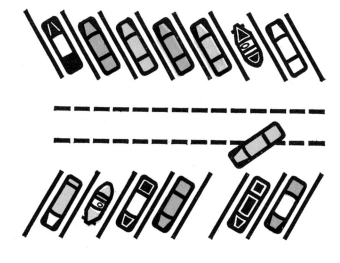

ONE-TO-ONE

LET us simplify the picture of the world outside and the mind within. Let us assume there is just a single impulse that comes in through the skin or the eye or the ear, and registers a stimulus on a nerve. This is not the thing that happens "out there," but something that was *caused by* something out there.

We have a single impression. Soon we receive another impression. And another. And eventually the mind sets up patterns, it provides hooks for these, and begins to organize and give meaning to these various incoming stimuli. Some are tagged as pertaining to "seeing," some to "hearing," some to "taste," etc.

Eventually these patterns assume a certain order and pattern. We are able to "recognize" certain of the patterns as similar to those we have experienced before. We construct something that you can imagine is like a picture; so that when a similar series of impulses come in we can compare the retained picture with the new impressions and say to ourself, "This is very much the same," or, "This is quite different."

It is something like a man making a map. He sets down a pencil dot on the paper to represent the position of the big oak tree. Then he makes another pencil dot to represent the farmhouse. And then he marks the position of the windmill, which lies between the big tree and the farmhouse.

He does not, of course, think that the marks on the paper "are, really" the farm. It is simply a representation of the farm, a sort of

33

symbol to help him know the relation of things on the farm.   For on his map (if it is a good map), there should be a relation between the farm "out there," and the map he is making.

For instance: It may be 150 feet from the farmhouse to the big tree, and this may show on the map as only three inches.   But if the windmill lies between house and tree, its representation on the map must also lie between the marks representing the house and the tree. In fact, if it is a good map, the distance from house to windmill and from windmill to tree should be in roughly the same ratio as the distances between these points on the map.

In other words, each point on the map should correspond with some point in the territory; and the relation of the various points on the map should be approximately the same as that of the real objects seen.

We do not expect to find anything on the map that hasn't some referent actually perceived "out there."

This is the way we make "maps" in our minds; the only way we get to know what is "out there" at all.

It seems childishly simple; and yet people make maps in their minds which have no referents in reality at all.   They sometimes have the strongest belief that they "know" something even without any supporting evidence in external reality or even in the face of contradictory evidence.

If we have a situation where it is possible to check one item against another, in one-to-one correspondence, there can be no real dispute.   If, for instance, there are a certain number of spaces in the parking lot and each space is filled, we do not need to count the number of spaces nor the number of cars to know that the number of spaces equals the number of cars.   This is a one-to-one correspondence. Even a person who had never learned to count could tell you whether the number of cars and spaces was equal, or whether there were more cars than spaces or vice versa.

There are a great many situations where it is possible to make such a check.   Cases where we can verify each disputed point on the map against the external reality.

Let us say, for instance, that you claim there are ten houses on the east side of Sylvan Street between Belmont Avenue and Fountain Street, and I maintain that there are twelve houses.   Evidently I have a different "map" of this territory than you do.

Are we going to settle this argument by a knock-down and drag-out fight? Or are we going to go out to Sylvan Street and count the houses? Which way is more likely to settle the argument? Is there much likelihood that we will disagree as to the number of houses?

The question here concerns how good our own maps really are. And also whether, in the final analysis, *any* map is as good an authority as the territory it represents. The picture cannot be more perfect than the thing itself. Therefore, when we want to know the truth, and a question has been raised, we go to the territory itself to check the facts, if we can.

There can be no dispute as to facts that are verifiable in externality. And the territory is always better evidence than any map.

QUESTIONS FOR CONSIDERATION

Do you feel it is a fair analogy to say that the impressions of things and places in your mind are like "maps" or "photographs"?

Can you see *everything* there is to see in a certain territory by looking at a map? Could you see *everything* even in a photograph?

Would it be reasonable to say that "certain" features show on the map or in the picture? Suppose that your map is inaccurate, due to faulty observation or failure to note certain features. Would you defend your map against the first-hand evidence of the territory itself? Put it another way; if the map and the territory (as observed here and now on the spot) don't agree, which is most likely to be the truth?

Have you ever heard or taken part in arguments in which someone defended his own impression or memory of something against the clear evidence of plain facts?

Do you think people ever defend their views about investments in the face of plain evidence to the contrary? Which has more value; the opinion of an expert or the opinion of a novice? Aren't material facts of more value than either?

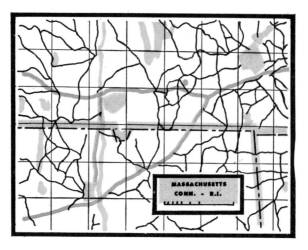

OF MAPS

IN ORDER to understand better how certain things get into our minds, useful things as well as harmful things, we are going to make use of analogies. When we say that our stored-up observations of the world around us, as well as our logical conclusions, our opinions, attitudes, etc. are like "maps," we do not, of course, mean that they are actually the same as printed maps. But these mental images are very much like maps in some ways since they are a lasting record which we consult for guidance, and since they are (or should be) representations of something else, having a certain relation to or correspondence with whatever it is that is represented.

We use the word "map," and sometimes "image." We also use the word "picture" or "photograph" (for a memory is very often so vividly pictorial that we can "see it in our mind's eye"). And we use the word "label" to indicate the names we attach to our mental images just as we might label maps or photographs or files of information.

By using these words we can understand more easily some of the processes by which we understand (and sometimes mis-understand) the world in which we live.

You will agree that a map, unless it is pure make-believe, should be a map *of* something, as we suggested in the previous chapter. Whatever you find on the map should have some corresponding feature in the territory it portrays.

But the reverse is not true. You certainly won't find a representation on the map of every feature in the territory.

You know this is true of some very simplified maps, such as the ones you will find in the little leatherette pocket atlases you can buy at the five and ten cent stores. The map of the United States, for instance, shows the Atlantic and Pacific Oceans and the Gulf of Mexico; and the various states are printed in contrasting colors. You may find the capitals of these states indicated also, and perhaps a few other important cities, New York, Chicago, San Francisco, etc. You can even get an idea of the general shape of the state of Texas. But the little New England States are shown so small that it is hard to see just what shape they really are.

On a map like this you'll find at least something recognizable as Lake Michigan. But you won't find Lake Waramaug. You won't even find your home town if it happens to be Holyoke, or Utica, or Ponca City.

It is true that all the places indicated on the map represent real places in the country in approximately the right place on the map to correspond with the territory. But there is a good deal left out.

Suppose now you get a somewhat larger, somewhat more expensive atlas. Here you will find maps of separate states, and you will be able to pick out, in Massachusetts, not only Boston, but also Worcester and New Bedford, and Springfield. You may also, if it is a good atlas, find Palmer, and Salem, and Newburyport. But you will probably not find Essex or North Wilbraham. This kind of map might show some of the principal highways and railroads; and, of course, it would include the larger bodies of water in the state, such as Quabbin Reservoir. All these things shown are features you can visit by taking a trip, and check that they are really there.

But you will not find Stackpole's farm, nor the lane that runs down to it from the main road, nor the cow pond, nor the wooded ridge along the north boundary; although all these things, too, are part of the territory and can be verified by going and looking at them. In other words, there is still a good deal left out.

If you want to get a better map, one that represents more features of the territory (that is, more detail), get the U. S. Topographic map for this quadrangle. This will show you the Stackpole farm, the lane running to it, the cow pond, and the hill. It is a much more complete map than the one in the little leatherette atlas.

But there is still a lot left out. It will not show you the ell on the house, nor the old well. It does not include the path to the barn. It omits the blackberry patch just north of the barn.

I suppose if you wanted to take the trouble you could survey the Stackpole place and make a map that would show all these things, right down to the rows of blackberry bushes. But it would leave out a lot, still.

You would have to make a map on a very big scale that would show each separate blackberry bush; and then you would need to sketch each bush so as to show every leaf; and then you would need to magnify every leaf to show its exact markings; and ultimately, if you wanted a complete map you would have to work with a microscope to study the precise structure of the cells in the leaves.

And when you arrived at this point you would realize that there was still a lot left out.

In fact, if you carried out this exploration of the sub-microscopic world to its ultimate end you would find that the reality eventually becomes entirely unmappable; a cosmos of particles which cannot be described in ordinary "material" terms, and which are not observable in their individual features since the very act of observation would change the reality, and since the map at this stage would be in such a constant state of change that from one instant to another it would become obsolete.

It is not possible to map a territory completely. The map always includes less than what is "out there." And actually, as you know, it is not necessary to have all the detail. It all depends upon what your particular need for the map happens to be.

If a child comes to you and asks you what the earth looks like, you can get him one of the little ten cent globes, two or three inches in diameter. This will give him a good idea of the shape of the earth, the relative size of the continents and oceans; in other words, a good view of the thing as a whole.

There would be no particular point in showing him a topographic map quadrangle, covering an area say eight miles wide and ten miles long and including one or two villages, a few roads, farmhouses, schools, hills, brooks, etc. as a representation of what the earth looked like. This would be too particular, it would not necessarily be typical of a large part of the earth, and in any case, it would be such a small portion of the earth's surface that it would give the child no help at all in visualizing the planet entire.

On the other hand, if you and your family were looking for a place to picnic, you would get very little help from a three inch globe of the earth; for there is so much necessarily left out on such a globe that the jungles of Africa, the mountains of the antarctic, and the deserts of central Asia would all look very much the same. For choosing a picnic spot you would want a map with more detail, very likely the topographic map showing the general area you had in mind. Such a map would help a great deal in locating a pond, a brook, a hillside, or whatever kind of spot your family might consider suitable for picnicking.

You will understand, of course, that we are talking not only of the kind of maps you can get in stores or at the library, but the kind of maps you carry in your mind; which are also stored up representations of something "out there" (if they are good maps).

They are also, like the paper maps we first considered, incomplete. There is a lot left out, even in the best of them. And the question is not whether they are "complete," for we know they never are; but whether they are good enough for the purpose, some particular purpose of ours.

For instance: In order to walk from your office to your apartment, if you are lucky enough to live within walking distance, you need some sort of "map" to guide you. Your feet are not able by themselves to choose which corners you turn and which streets you follow. Something in your brain must have a pattern; something that corresponds to the route you must take; and you must be able to call forth this pattern in order to find your way from office to apartment. Otherwise, even though it might be only a matter of four or five blocks, you would be "lost," as indeed some people do become lost if they are suffering from some disease or injury that prevents their "re-calling" the direction.

For most of us the "re-calling" of the previously learned "map" is so easy it is done quite unconsciously. We simply walk home. We are following a well-defined and well-understood map, and it is sufficient for our need. But it is not necessarily a very detailed map. You may walk the same route between office and home every day for five years, and still your "map" would not show you some of the obvious features along the way. You would certainly not know how many houses or buildings you passed in your daily walk. You might never have "noticed" a grocery store which you passed every day. You would probably never see the four hydrants you passed at all.

In this case you would be dealing with a very sketchy map, which is all that is required. There are other situations where a much more elaborate one would be needed. Suppose, for example, you were a policeman on this same beat. It would not be enough, merely to know the route from an office to an apartment. You would need to know the location of police telephones, of hydrants, of the principal stores and buildings; and you would probably pick up and store a good deal of other information about the neighborhood, the people that lived in it, and spots where trouble was most likely to break out. In this kind of job you would need considerable detail in your "map" of the precinct.

But, this would still be a matter of *relative* detail. There would still be a lot left out. No matter how long you walked the beat and no matter how carefully you observed the territory and stored up facts, you would never have complete knowledge of those few city blocks.

The late Irving J. Lee of Northwestern University once invited a group of Evanston police officers to study some of these matters; and for a start suggested that each policeman bring in a box of dirt, on which he would write a complete report. Several of the men faithfully dug a box of dirt, examined it and wrote reports. Lee accepted the reports and then pointed out how far from "complete" they really were. Did they include the weight, color, granular texture of the dirt. Chemical nature of its various components. Temperature, moisture content, specific gravity, electrical conductivity . . . this was only a start. It becomes obvious that no one could possibly write a "complete" report on a box of dirt or on anything else. We have to settle for something less than "complete." The expression which mathematicians use is "necessary and sufficient."

What might be necessary and sufficient for one job might not be for another. The measurement of the diameter of a ball bearing may be in tenths of thousandths of an inch. The measurement of a steel girder might have to be exact only to a quarter of an inch. And the distance between New York and Bombay can be given with sufficient accuracy for most purposes if it is expressed to the nearest hundred miles. In estimating the value of the country's wheat crop it may be necessary and sufficient to express it to the nearest million dollars for some purposes. But in weighing a letter for airmail overseas "necessary and sufficient" is "to the nearest half ounce."

It may be getting ahead of things a little to raise the question, here, of what might be considered "necessary and sufficient" information for trading in stocks.   Certainly there are some people who jump into the market with such a glaring insufficiency of knowledge that we can predict with fair accuracy about how long it will take them to lose their capital.   But it may not be so obvious that there are others, hardly any better off, who collect unnecessary and irrelevant facts the way a pack rat collects bits of colored glass, beer bottle tops and buttons.   Too much information of the wrong sort not only adds nothing to clarifying understanding, it can confuse the issue so hopelessly that it is impossible to see what is going on at all.

This point we will consider in a more specific way later.   For now, it is important to note:

1. That the impressions of things in our minds are not the things themselves.   (The map is not the territory.)
2. That the map is never as detailed and accurate as the reality it represents.
3. That some maps are more detailed than others, and which map is best for a particular purpose depends on what we are trying to do; that is, it depends on the nature of the job at hand.
4. A map that covers too much ground and is too sketchy in the detail may be inadequate for the job; and a map which is too detailed may be crowded with confusing and superfluous data.

QUESTIONS FOR CONSIDERATION

Do you know "all" about anything?   About the market?   About any stock?

Is it necessary to know "all"?   Is it possible for a "map" to be "incomplete" and yet entirely adequate for your needs?

Would you say some purposes call for a more detailed map than others: or perhaps for some needs a map must include certain special information?

Could a map be quite satisfactory for a particular job, and yet not adequate for your own requirements?

Do you consider the needs of a job in preparing your own mental "maps"? Do you get enough information from sources as close to reality as possible? Do you get the latest information possible?   Do you verify information from others or from past records where possible?   Do you clutter up your mental maps with a lot of unnecessary and irrelevant material, that is, data which is not essential to your particular need?

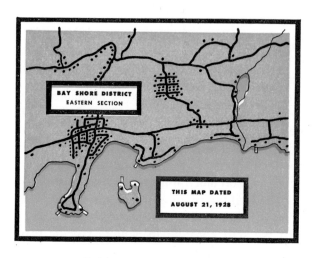

BAY SHORE DISTRICT
EASTERN SECTION

THIS MAP DATED
AUGUST 21, 1928

DATING THE MAP

IF WE use the word "map" to cover any diagram, photograph, plan, description, or mental image which represents something else and which has a one-for-one correspondence with certain features of the something else, you will understand that this includes not only all the snapshots, and blueprints, and specification sheets, etc., but also all the stored-up impressions in our brains that fill this bill. In fact, although we may speak of "maps" at times in the sense of printed sheets of paper, more often we will be considering the kind of maps that are not actually printed except as they are impressed on our memory. While we can't pass these around for our friends to examine, we can take them out for our own private examination whenever we want to; and as you know, you carry a vast number of these maps, a really staggering library of them, in your head all the time. You can, without the slightest effort, re-call the floor layout of Public School #4, or at least those portions of it that you traversed during your servitute in third grade. You know where the coat-room should be and where to look for the door to the hall, and the shortest route to the playground. Also the location of the wash rooms, and how to get to the principal's office. In your own room you can see where Miss McFarland sat, and very likely your map will provide you fair remembrance of just what Miss McFarland looked like. You may also be able to fill in, on the map, the names of various boys and girls down the rows of seats; at least there may be a few you can bring to mind.

42

You have maps covering your own home; probably in very great detail; maps of the streets and stores in the neighborhood of your home. Of the camp where you went one summer, and the cottage your family had at Birchwood Lake. Think of all the houses you have visited, the picnics you went on; look into your memory, and you will find a vast multitude of rather amazingly good maps of places you have known. All of these maps are "constructs" of your mind; they are obviously not the places themselves; and they did not come into your mind as "direct experience," but as nerve impulses from your various sensory receptors. The map (or memory) is something you have built out of the various bits of information from outside, which you can then "project" into consciousness almost as if you were again viewing the original scene. As a matter of fact, sometimes if you close your eyes and think of past experiences, you can come very close to "seeing" these things as visual images.

We say "past experiences." If these are memories, based on actual observation, they must be "past"; for they are obviously not of the present nor of the future. They were seen (or mapped, if you will) previously.

It is a sad thing, and all of us have been disturbed by this discovery, to realize that Public School #4 was torn down to make room for the larger Consolidated School, ten years ago. That Miss McFarland died year before last. That little Archie Smith is now a pompous and overweight insurance salesman and alderman from the third ward. That Tomboy Trembley has lost both the Tomboy and the Trembley, is now Mrs. Arthur G. Graham, and has three children all in Junior High School. It is a very hard thing to look at that schoolroom in your "mind's eye" and realize that those children are dead, those familiar faces are gone irrevocably, even though there are some grownup people around town who have the same names.

The picture of the schoolroom is a valid map. But it is not a map of the "here and now."

A friend of mine showed me a map of the part of the country we live in. It was a valid map made by a competent and observant craftsman who was familiar with the territory. There were a number of recognizable features. The Connecticut River. The Holyoke range of mountains. Springfield. The road from Boston.

But on this map there were some rather unfamiliar features. "Indian camp here" is marked at a point which would be, roughly, the center of the town of Palmer.   There are references to springs of drinking water, areas marked "good hunting here," a spot inscribed "Josiah Chapin's cabin."

I haven't the slightest doubt that these markings on the map correctly correspond with the territory as observed.   I might have a question as to whether some of them were pertinent to me in my particular manner of living.   But as to their being an honest record of fact, they ring true.

In other words, the map is a good one.   But it needs one more detail, which in all fairness to the mapmaker I hasten to mention. In the lower right hand corner the map carries its date: 1650.

You will notice that this map is not a false map.   Presumably it was correctly made from accurate observations at the time.   Furthermore, it was probably adequate for the purpose for which it was intended; no doubt, to guide a traveler across the country and provide him with the necessary information to find his way and to take care of his needs.

It might have been an inadequate map, even in 1650, for some other purpose; for a land survey in connection with a colonial charter or an Indian treaty, for example.   As we said, the amount of detail required depends on the job to be done.

Certainly, as a map of the territory today this map is both inaccurate and inadequate.   Certain of its features, such as Chapin's cabin, the Indian camp, and the good hunting country, are no longer correct.

Other important aspects of the countryside are not to be seen on the old map.   There is no Turnpike, Westover Field does not appear, nor can we find the line of either the Boston and Albany nor the New Haven railroad.

But (and note this), the map is not entirely false.   The Connecticut River is still correctly represented, and the mountains of the Holyoke range are still in the same relative position.   Springfield is still properly indicated.

The important things, of course, in studying this map, or any other map, are to know whether the map was a good one in the first place, whether it was adequate for our particular purposes; and what essential changes have occurred since the map was made.

In other words, we must *date* the map.   And generally speaking, taking one map against another of approximately equal and similar detail, the map carrying the most recent date will most correctly represent the territory as it exists *now*.

CASE IN POINT—A DATED MAP

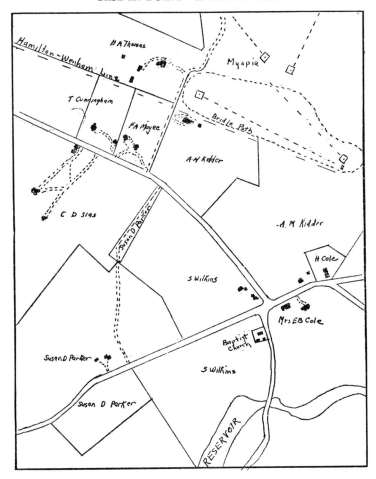

The foregoing was written in March, 1958. A few weeks later, early in April, a very fortunate example fell into my hands. I received from a friend and customer whom I had never met personally, a blue-print of a map copied from an old atlas of Essex County. My friend, Mr. Frederick C. Batchelder, who lives in Wenham, Massachusetts, sent me the print since it covered a certain part of the town where my grandparents had their home. The date of the map was 1910.

Mr. Batchelder "thought I might be interested." As a matter of fact I was most deeply interested; and most grateful to him, for this particular map provided an almost perfect example of what we have been discussing here; and it came to my hands at precisely the time when it was needed.

This is a map of typical North of Boston countryside "as it was in 1910." It is a correct map; that is to say, the various features in it correspond to actual, verifiable physical features in that countryside (as it was in 1910).

It provides an especially interesting study and example to me, since I have also a map of this same terrain which is also a correct map in that its various features correspond with features in the external reality (as of 1910).

This latter is the map which exists in my own mind as an abstraction of this same territory at about this same time. My own abstracting was done between the years 1904 and 1913. I have not visited the area since. Therefore, my own "mental map" of this section is dated 1913 in its most recent revision, and is not too far in time from the map shown here. I can designate the two "maps" as "BP" for blue-print, and "JM" for my own mental map or memory.

There are several points here which are important in any study of symbolic representation. In the first place, none of the basic data on either of the maps can be changed in any particular (except by destruction or distortion of the maps). Nothing can be correctly added now to what was originally abstracted without taking new observations of the territory.

Also, neither "BP" nor "JM" map is "complete." You will notice how exceedingly sketchy "BP" is. There is nothing to show the small brooks winding through the meadows, or the wooden bridges over them. Nothing to indicate the Cunningham's spring house, nor the summer house further up the hill. In fact there is nothing to mark the hills at all, nor the valleys, rock outcroppings, trees, nothing to suggest the color of the landscape or of the houses in it. The buildings themselves are sketchy and even under a magnifying glass convey no very accurate idea of their shape or construction. The map, like all maps, and like all abstractions, is merely *part* of the scene, just those things noted and recorded by a particular observer at a particular time in the past.

Map "JM" is somewhat more detailed than "BP." It is also incomplete. It carries nothing to mark the "Reservoir" which is marked, correctly I am sure, on "BP." "JM" does not show the narrow access strip of Susan D. Parker leading to the main road.

This is understandable since the property lines that might be significant to a grown-up map-maker would mean nothing to a small child. "JM" does not take notice of the "Bridle Path" on the Myopia Club property.

In other words we have two maps, both valid representations of a territory dated about 1910. Both good maps. But they are not the same. They do not *disagree*, for many of the features will correspond, and none conflict. But many features that were abstracted in one map did not appear in the other, and vice versa.

Thus, if points A, B, C, D, E, F, and G represented features in a territory at a particular time, it is quite possible that one map of this territory (as of that time) might show points A, D, and G, while another map might show points A, C, D, and F. Points A and D would show on both maps, point G would show only on the first map, and points C and F only on the second. The points B and E, not having been abstracted in either map would be lost.

Notice that two valid maps do not necessarily show a one-to-one correspondence in all points. Notice that where they show the same points they will agree as to these points. Notice that the sum of the information on the two maps is no less, and usually greater, than that on either alone, but in no case can it equal the "total information" available in the territory itself.

Mr. Batchelder tells me that this territory "has not changed much." "Much" is a broad word. I am quite sure that Frank A. Magee no longer lives at the bottom of the Thomas' hill next to Tom Cunningham. Both Frank and his wife Genevieve, and Tom Cunningham, and old Mrs. Kidder, have long since passed from this world. It is possible that some of the "same" people still live in the "same" area. But you know that after all these years they are not the "same" people; nor is it the "same" territory. As Heraclitus put it many centuries ago, "You cannot put your foot in the same river twice."

There are, no doubt, turtles still swimming in the Miles River, down the hill just to the left of the map. But they are not the "same" turtles. The most one could say is that one turtle looks remarkably like another. There are still, I am sure, mushrooms growing on the rocky pastures back of the Sias place and down by the ruins of the Pingrey house that burned down. But not the "same" mushrooms.

When we say "the same" don't we really mean "so similar that the differences don't make much difference?" And what kind of differences would or would not make a difference would depend on our particular purpose. If the purpose were to paint a picture of a New England countryside it might be true that "map 1958" would be substantially "the same," that is, closely similar in appearance to "map 1910." But if the purpose were to have a tea-party with Marjorie Thomas in her play house, "map 1910" would be entirely obsolete and useless; for if the play house is still standing it will be (1958) Marjorie's grandchildren who are spilling the strawberry jam on their dress fronts.

It should be noted every now and then that there is no "identity" in the world of reality. Resemblances, yes. Similarities, yes. But since we perceive through what we abstract and since we abstract only a very small part of "all" the facts in any external reality, the "identity" we sometimes assume is an illusion based merely on the fact that our rather sketchy maps may have shown only certain features we have noted. We must keep in mind that there is always a great deal more which we have "overlooked."

Notice one other thing. Both map "BP" and the mental map "JM" were based on someone's *perception* of reality. It could be argued that since all we know about anything is based on what we perceive, then if we have perceived nothing we know nothing about it. And if we know nothing about it we cannot very well prove that it exists at all. And therefore it could be asserted there is no basis for claiming that it exists at all, apart from the images we carry in our own mind. This was the substance of a famous argument of George Berkeley, bishop of Cloyne in Ireland in the eighteenth century.

In so much of our work we will be dealing with "maps" which are abstractions based on perceived features of reality. We can deal with these maps and they can be useful to us just so long as we bear in mind that they are symbolic representations, and that we can set up one-to-one correspondences between them and the "perceived" reality. Whether the "reality" itself is "real" is not a question we have to consider in this study.

In this case we are concerned with what we will accept as an external reality, as of 1910, and maps "BP" and "JM." We know, or should know by now, the limitations of such maps. We know that we cannot properly ascribe to the maps any features not specifically comprehended in them. We cannot assume that we know "all" about the territory, then or now. We cannot assume that the territory is now what the 1910 map showed it to be. When we are dealing with symbolic representations, (and all of our thinking comes into this category), we must recognize the limits that apply to it and not try to fill in the gaps out of pure fancy.

QUESTIONS FOR CONSIDERATION

Let us say you find in the attic some prints and papers including a map of the world as drawn in 1450. Would you assume that this was probably a "valid" map? Would you find it a "true" map of the world as you know it today? If it is valid why is it not true? Has the world changed in some respects? Has our knowledge of the world changed in some respects? If you were planning a trip around the world would you prefer to have a map dated 1450, or 1958? Is the date of a map important?

Suppose you picked up a report by a well-known and well respected financial analyst concerning a certain stock; and suppose that this report gave in some detail the facts supporting a conclusion that the stock was a "good investment." What absolutely essential piece of information will you need before you can act on the advice?

Do you carry a great many undated maps in your own mind? Do you believe that South American countries are "always having revolutions"? Do you believe that a boy with good mechanical ability can become a "great inventor"? Do you believe that Standard Oil of New Jersey is always "a good investment"?

BRINGING DATA UP-TO-DATE

I HAVE been trying to build rather carefully, a picture of how all this map-making comes about; and what it means. No doubt this has made the reading dull, and your own quick mind has leaped ahead of the text. You must already have realized that the "map" of Room 12 in Public School No. 4 with Miss McFarland sitting up front and smirking at the class, carries also an element of judgment; perhaps, in this case, that Miss McFarland was rather a nasty old witch. Maps can carry more than geographical data.

You may have had a picture of the New Haven railroad (a map) in your head, dated, say June, 1955. The map might include a judgment as to the value of New Haven stock; and this value might carry the price ticket, $39 per share.

Be sure you have your mental map dated, and be sure you look at the date! If you re-called this map, say in December, 1957, many features of the railroad would look the same. The same remembered stations with the same news stands and dingy ticket windows. The same tracks curving away out of the station into the distance; in fact, a most familiar picture. But be sure you look at the date. For the value you have placed on New Haven stock is still to be seen, at $39 per share, *unless you have revised and up-dated this map.* And the June, 1955 map is not now correct in this feature; for in December, 1957 the ticket should read $5. As a matter of fact, if you want this part of your map to have a close correspondence with its "territory," in this case the price of the stock, you will have to revise the map continuously to adjust to every fluctuation.

And we do have to adjust, revise, and correct maps to bring them up-to-date. But this does not mean that we have to tear up the old maps entirely. All that is necessary is to change those features which are pertinent to our needs, where there have been significant changes in those features.

The constructs we have been calling maps, include rather more than lines and surfaces and visual elements. They can include things we hear. We can re-call the tune of a song, just as though we had a musical score or "map" of the song written out somewhere in our head. Our maps can also include, at least to some degree, odors and tastes and touch sensations; for these things can be somewhat remembered and re-experienced, too.

For the most part the "maps" we have been speaking of so far could be referred to as "descriptions." For whether they outline a a school yard, a familiar street, a favorite tune or the odor of hyacinths and brown earth in early spring, they are descriptive of something we perceive as "out there" or as "having been out there once upon a time."

Now all the data from which these maps were made came in through the senses; that is, the original data. It was all based originally on some experiences or contacts with the world "out there." But not necessarily from our own personal experience with the particular place or thing or tune or odor, and not necessarily "here and now." For some of your knowledge has come to you by word of mouth from someone else—and some you have learned by reading it in a book.

QUESTIONS FOR CONSIDERATION

Do you ever check up on your own maps? Do you ask yourself questions as to how and when you learned certain things, and whether these are still true? Do you go back to the "territory" and re-examine the facts? Do you revise your maps to agree with changes that have occurred?

Would you find it easy to change your opinion on points which you have accepted as "true" for many years; even in the face of strong evidence that the facts call for a change of view?

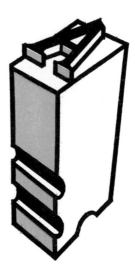

THE TWENTY-SIX LEAD SOLDIERS

I AM not sure how much study has been made of animals' response to "once-removed" experience, by which I mean a picture instead of a real landscape, a recording instead of a voice, a stimulation of a taste bud artificially instead of by a certain quality in the food, etc. I am reasonably sure that the recorded voice of the master would be recognized by a dog, and recorded commands would be obeyed. And no doubt animals can be presented with visual scenes that their eyes will accept as valid, and which they would "recognize."

If we call the descriptive construct built from direct experience an "abstraction," then the descriptive construct we (or an animal) gets from a picture, recorded voice, etc. is an abstraction *of* an abstraction; a map of a map.

But the animals' ability to abstract is rather limited. The very smartest animal cannot abstract as far as the stupidest man. And mankind has developed a very wonderful device which is, perhaps, the great distinctive characteristic that sets him apart from all the rest of the animal kingdom.

Whereas the animal can abstract, that is, it can "see" and "hear" and use its other senses, and can store these abstractions away and re-call them for later use (the animal can remember the way to the store, it can recognize its master, it can identify the mailman's whistle), it has no great powers of communication with its fellow-animals, and so far as these descriptive abstractions are concerned, you can say it has virtually no power to communicate them to another.

Also, it has no way of setting down these abstractions in any symbolic form so that the knowledge, perhaps forgotten, can later be re-stored in the mind.

The wonderful device that man has invented, is language, in its broadest sense. Through language, the use of symbols, it is possible to transmit from one mind to another, the descriptive maps. By talking, one man is able to convey to another man the details of how to get to Westfield, or what the facade of the Natural History Museum looks like. He can, by making certain sounds, send out data which another man can "hear", and can translate in "pictures" in his mind, which can be good and useful descriptive maps of a "territory."

This is a miracle, when you come to think of it. It is much more of a miracle than television, for this is a process of transmitting pictures, floor plans, diagrams, etc. without any visual aids, through the medium of sound alone, without any man-made mechanical equipment whatever; and it has been going on for thousands of years!

Not only that. It is not only possible to invent sound signals for "talking." It is possible to invent visual signals for "writing." Symbols that can be drawn on paper or scratched in clay can be worked out so as to have a correspondence either with the "sounds" of talking; or with the objects represented, such as hammer, house, dog, etc.

This further extension of language makes it possible not only for man to communicate "here and now"; but "not here" and "not now." A spoken word, whisper, shout can only be heard so far, a few feet or a few hundred feet at the most. Its dying echoes fade away in fractions of a second. The voice must be immediate and proximate unless it is relayed by some device such as telephone or radio.

But the invention of a written language opens up an enormously larger world. Man cannot only talk to a man "here"; he can write a letter to a man a thousand miles away, and the thoughts in his head will be unfolded and disclosed to that distant communicant when the messenger delivers a scroll of paper or an inscribed brick of clay.

More than that. By means of the map system we call "language" man can leap forward across the centuries and communicate with his own great-great-great-great-grandchildren, or backward to share the thoughts of his great-great-great-great-grandfather. No animal can do that. Man can, to express it inelegantly, pick his great-grandfather's brains. With the written language the recorded experience of every man becomes the heritage of all mankind.

Do you realize how big a heritage this is? It is the secret of how and why you are a member of the dominant race of creatures on this earth.

For the written language is the transmission belt for the "time binding." Without language whatever knowledge an individual might grasp would endure only as long as he himself lived. While he might be able to pass on by word of mouth some of this knowledge to his offspring, (and this was the usual way of passing on knowledge for thousands of years, and still is in some parts of the world) such knowledge was bound to be limited in extent; and over the years it would tend to become twisted, garbled.

Even where such knowledge was passed on verbally without distortion or loss, it would be likely to become ritualized, and to lose its meaning in the monotonous, sterile repetition.

But when it is written down, it stays there, exactly as it was set forth by the author. The material can be accumulated. There is no need for memorizing, or repetition. And there is no limit to the amount of material that can be preserved in written form.

This written knowledge does not stop with the passing on by rote of a fixed body of information. Successive generations add their contributions, building on the experience of their forebears and using the material gathered by previous generations. With the invention of printing the "twenty-six lead soldiers" of the alphabet opened the whole world of books so that all who would might read.

This points the way to at least the possibility of a much broader "freedom of thought," for, since the scholars are no longer chained to the necessary job of memorizing and passing on a body of ancient lore, there is time to digest the previous material at leisure, to re-examine the evidence in the external world, that is to say, to compare the "maps" as described in the writings, with the "here and now" observed facts in the external world.

Under these conditions, knowledge no longer remains the dread esoteric property of the temple priests and magicians, but becomes the common property of everybody. Also, it becomes enormously more flexible, enormously more adaptable, and enormously more useful.

Written language makes it possible for us to take advantage of the wisdom of dead men, to have communication with thinkers in each period of history; and yet leaves us free to accept, adapt, or reject any or all of the material depending on whether it appears to fit our present needs.

QUESTIONS FOR CONSIDERATION

How much of "what you know" would you say has come to you from teachers and books, that is, through spoken and written language? How much of this knowledge came down from men who died before you were born?

Would you be able to hold your present job or to take part in your family and social life if you had none of this inherited knowledge that has come from the past?

Would you say that this kind of knowledge was like a library of "maps"? Is it important to keep in mind the dates applying to them?

Is it possible that some of the features of these maps do not correspond with the realities we know: either because the territory has changed, or because we have learned more about the territory?

If you call into question some feature of an old map and insist on comparing it with the present territory does that mean that you reject the old map entirely or give it no value at all?

Do you feel that in order to be in the closest touch with reality it is necessary to be free to question any map, or check its features, to alter it if necessary, and to reject it if it does not fit the facts at all?

In your study of finance or any other subject do you place a higher value on the precepts and directives of past authority, or on your own observations and experience?

How much of your efforts in financial study is given to reading the opinions and advice of others, and how much, if any, to your own observations?

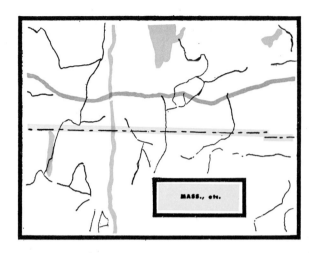

MAPS OF MAPS

WHEN we read a story about a young prospector riding his burro up the dusty canyon we have a picture in our minds. We can see the gray cliffs rising sheer on the left. We can see the clear mountain stream swirling and tumbling over its rocky bed to our right; and we can hear the splash of the water; and our throats are parched from the alkali dust; and we become thirsty.

We have probably stirred into this picture all sorts of bits of abstracted information; the sights and sounds of western canyons as we have learned to know them from the westerns in movies and television, from other stories we have read, and, who knows, perhaps from our own memories of visits to these western areas.

But we are experiencing, too, the particular topography of the particular canyon our author was describing. He had abstracted a canyon. He had set down some details of this abstraction symbolically (by writing words on paper), and now his words suggest to us the bits of information we have stored away in our own mind. We re-call our own mental images. We "see" a canyon; we "hear" the water in the brook; we may even react to the picture by feeling thirsty. It may be a very realistic scene that lies before us in our "mind's eye."

In this case we are abstracting, not from external reality, but from another abstraction, that is, the story we are reading. It is like abstracting from a picture except that in this case we are dealing with verbal symbols instead of pictorial representations. And, of course, since our own memories are not the same as those of the author of the story, the mental image of the canyon that you may create in your mind may be quite different in a great number of details from the canyon envisaged by the author.   In fact, since each reader is free to "make up his own picture," you may consider that there are as many different perceptions of that canyon in the story as there are readers.

If we call our perception of external reality "a map," then we could properly call our perception of the situation and the surroundings in a story we read, "a map of a map."   It is one step further away from the external reality.

And you realize, of course, that it is only because we can make these "maps of maps" that we are able to pass on to others, as we do verbally in a short story or a novel, some part of what we have abstracted ourselves.

Now when we have observed a number of similar features in several different objects we usually attach a verbal label that means to us "anything that has these common features."   It is only by using some of these "label-names" that a writer can write understandably at all.   For while we may not know his particular canyon we do have some idea of what "a canyon" should be like.

There may be many somewhat different things under one label. We know very well that the Third National Bank Building is not the Whitney Building.   But they both have a certain number of floors with wide corridors and offices along them; they both have elevators and mail chutes, etc., so we call them by the same name, "office buildings," along with other structures of this general type.

When we speak of "office buildings" to someone, we expect that he also will have a generalized picture of a structure with these features.

But it is very important to realize that the label "office building" does not describe or designate any *particular* office building.   It could refer to any office building whatever, anywhere, and any time. Therefore, when we say "office building," we cannot expect that our friend will have a very precise idea of just how a certain building looks.   We would have to specify the details at a lower level of abstraction.   We would have to describe the building, name how many floors it had, what color it was, and many other features; and to make ourselves perfectly plain we might want to include the street address.

If we talk and think mainly in high order abstractions (generalities) we may be unable to communicate just what we mean. People who refer to Bull Markets and Bear Markets, or to Negroes, or to "egg heads," are using words that are so "wide" that they can mean many different things to different people. It is no wonder we cannot agree on the facts of a case if we talk only about the high order generalities.

Of course the most serious danger is that we ourselves will fail to discriminate. We will often act on the generality, for instance, that "dogs are friendly," and get bitten because we looked only at the label "dogs: friendly" and not at the atypical beast that charged out of the house at us.

Dogs *are* friendly as a rule and as a broad generality. But this does not mean that we can project that idea to cover each and every dog. In reality it is always a particular, individual dog that we have to deal with, not the generality. It is also true that we have to deal with a particular individual woman, not "women" as a class. And we have to buy or sell a particular stock, not "stocks" in general.

You will realize that we build our "mental files" in stages or levels of abstraction. First we observe Bozo and Zorro as individuals. Then we classify them as "dogs." At this stage we have a broader picture of the common characteristics of "the class dog," but the word "dog" leaves out some of the particular details. The label points to similarities between Bozo and Zorro, but not the differences. If we recognize that there are some similarities between all dogs and all goats and all lions we can group these creatures all together under a higher order label "quadrupeds." We have now included more "territory," but again we have lost some detail. And we can move up from "quadrupeds" to "mammals," in which case the label is of a higher order yet, and includes whales, platypuses, and your sister-in-law. And if I say, "Bring me a *mammal*," you would be able to fill the bill by bringing me a whale, a cow, a giraffe, or any other creature you include under this label. You would not be able to tell the difference between one and another, nor to know which one I really wanted, just from the label alone.

This is one of the drawbacks of using "groups" in studying stocks. It may be useful to know what the "Rails" are doing, as a class. But you must ultimately deal with a particular stock, and the term

"Rail" leaves out all the differences between, say, Canadian Pacific and Western Maryland (and there are many important differences).

Of course you can carry the abstracting and labelling process higher and higher to any level you want. If "mammals" does not cover enough ground you can set up a very large category of "animals." And so on. In the market this would be like lumping bonds, warrants, stocks, debentures, etc., all under the one label "securities." It covers a lot of ground all right, but it doesn't give you much specific information.

What we are talking about here is like using your camera. The close-up view shows a great deal of detail. When you stand back to get in more of the group you lose some of the details. And if you stand way back, so as to include the entire 2nd Battalion of the State Guard, you will hardly be able to pick out Jim Stowell at all because you cannot see the details of the individual men. They will all look very much alike.

QUESTIONS FOR CONSIDERATION

Do you understand how we use "labels" to refer to "things"? Are you thoroughly aware that the label we attach to a single individual thing is different from the label we use to designate a "class" of things?

When we proceed from the "thing itself" to our perception of it, we call that an abstraction. When we give it a name (a label) we call that a higher abstraction. As we proceed to classes of things, and broader classes, we call these higher abstractions. There are many stages of abstraction. Which is closer to external reality, a "high" abstraction or a "low abstraction"?

If we want to know the details of a single individual, which is more useful, a high abstraction or a low abstraction?

If we want to see the common factors and relations between individuals (similarities) which is more useful, a high abstraction or a low abstraction?

Would you say that high abstractions or low abstractions are "better"? Would you say it depended on what you were trying to do at a certain time?

Is it important to be aware of the differences in abstractive level? Would you say that serious mis-understanding can come about if one confuses the levels of abstraction?

From where do you get the broadest view of the city; from the top of the municipal campanile or standing in the crowd at the corner of State and Main Streets?

From where do you get the best idea of what the local people are like: from the top of the municipal campanile or the corner of State and Main?

Would you say high abstractions cover a lot of ground, but at the sacrifice of detail?

Do we usually derive our high abstractions step-by-step on the basis of lower abstractions? Can we then apply the "generalized" conclusions we reach at high abstractive levels to a study of the low abstractions? Can we assume that the high abstractions will include all the details of external reality, or is it necessary to keep in mind that some of the details have been left out?

Would you pick a wife on the basis of what you know about "women"? How do you feel about buying individual stocks on the basis of what "the market" is doing?

THE PIGEONHOLES

TO REPEAT: the name you call something is not the thing itself. What volumes of police records involving assault and battery might be avoided if citizens fully realized that. Whether the name is shouted across the bar room or silently projected from the mind, the obvious fact remains, that "The name is not the thing."

Obvious, like an elephant in your front hall. But like many elephants of one sort or another, frequently overlooked.

No doubt there are some of your acquaintances who think of you as "wise and noble friend." There are others who regard you as "an odd fish, but a fairly intelligent sort," and there may well be a few who look on you as "a stupid fool." Since these labels do not exactly agree, it is a fair conclusion that you are not *all* of these things, at least that they do not fully and accurately describe you. For if the maps (any maps) conflict with one another they cannot all be correct; and if a map conflicts with the territory, that is, if it does not correspond with the facts, then *it* must be in error, not the territory.

Of course, it is quite possible that these various opinions of you may be correct from various points of view and with respect to certain activities. You might be quite wise in your law practice, for example, but quite stupid when it came to buying stocks. Or, you might have appeared quite smart on one occasion, but quite stupid on another (this would be a matter of dating the maps, in which case there would be no conflict).

And since the words we use to ticket things are only symbols, short-hand maps, so to speak, several people might use different words to indicate similar objects. In New York we speak of "the elevator"; in London, "the lift." We use a different label. In other countries other labels are used; we have "different languages." And right in our own country there are sectional idioms. Men in various trades and professions have technical terms that have a special meaning to them in a particular line of work. It sometimes becomes difficult when men from different crafts encounter misunderstandings that arise on account of the different use of words.

Even in ordinary conversation the labels can get us into trouble. When your father was a boy it was a tribute to a man's integrity to say that he was "absolutely square." In current teen-age talk to refer to someone as "absolutely square" would amount to a declaration of social ostracism.

But since the map, name, symbol, or whatever we use to represent reality cannot directly change the physical character of what is being represented, but merely stands for it, we should keep in mind always the superiority of the thing itself whenever there is a conflict.

Thus, we can put Robinson's contract in the folder marked "Contracts—Smith," but this does not change the contents of the Robinson contract. We could call all cows pigs, and if everyone understood that "pig" meant a large brown and black creature with horns, that mooed and gave milk, there would be no real conflict.

All that is necessary is to know, that is understand, what we are talking about. And this applies whether we are talking to someone else, or "talking" silently to our own self.

When we begin to set up symbolic maps, whether they are verbal or otherwise, that conflict with each other or that do not correspond with the facts in a territory, or which do not correspond with *any* demonstrable territory; and where we act on the basis of such maps as if we were dealing with a real and valid map of "something" or "somewhere," then we may be headed for serious confusion.

Now in a great many cases it is possible to get rid of the confusion very easily. It is really wonderful how many arguments and misunderstandings could be settled quickly and painlessly if we only took the obvious step. And sometimes one wonders how it is possible that people can go on being confused or hostile when the answer is so simple and so ready to hand.

All that is necessary is to go and have a look at the territory. Joe says Al's house has three brick chimneys. Sam says it only has two brick chimneys. Before it is necessary to call the police or the hospital, why not all go out together and count the number of brick chimneys on the house? If Joe's map and Sam's map of this situation don't agree, examine the territory.

There cannot be any conflict "out there." It may be that Joe and Sam did have some reasons for defending their maps. They had seen the house, or looked at a picture of it, or someone had told them about it. Perhaps Joe had seen it. But he may not have observed the chimneys carefully, and may be confusing it with another house he saw last week. Perhaps he did see and count correctly, but one of the chimneys has been torn down (this, by the way, would be a matter of dating, since his "map" is obsolete). Perhaps he misunderstood what house was meant, and has re-called another house entirely (wrong map). Or there may be two Al's, and Joe is thinking of Al Brown's house while Sam is thinking about Al Thompson's house (they are not referring to the same territory).

But regardless of what maps they have, if Joe and Sam go out together and count how many brick chimneys Al Thompson's house has *now*, they are not likely to continue their dispute. Their "maps" will be in agreement.

Unfortunately, in too many cases, men will continue to argue a point far into the night, and perhaps come to blows over it, without taking the one easy, direct, and conclusive step of taking a look at the territory.

QUESTIONS FOR CONSIDERATION

Do you feel that an awareness of the various abstractive levels would help you to "arrange" your mind in a more orderly way?

Would you agree that the labels we use to designate things do not affect the nature of the things themselves, but only provide us with a marker for the pigeonhole?

Did you ever put something in a wrong pigeonhole?

At one time there was a stock called "Standard Gas and Electric 4% Cumulative Preferred." This would go in the pigeonhole marked "Preferred Stocks," or "Utilities." Most preferred utilities are very conservative. Would this label necessarily denote conservative habits in "SG PR"?

(Note: In case you are not familiar with the issue, this was one of the most wildly speculative stocks listed on the New York Stock Exchange).

Would a label such as "Doctor" or "Professor" lead you to certain conclusions about a man? Would you verify your conclusions? Do you know that many swindlers have taken advantage of the habit of people to attribute qualities according to a title? If an object were labelled "Guaranteed Solid Gold," would you accept the claim; or would you insist that the gold brick be tested in your presence before you paid for it?

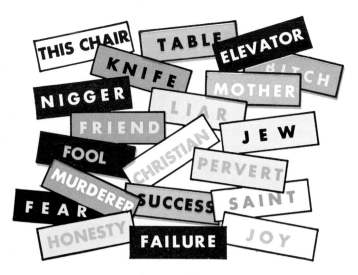

THE LABELS

AS WE have seen, you are not very likely to get badly confused when it is possible to verify a simple fact by counting or checking the territory by observation. People can get into plenty of trouble by *not* taking these simple precautions.

Unfortunately, it is not possible in all cases to make such a simple checkup. One of the big causes of misunderstanding is the use of a high order label as if it were a low order label.

You understand, of course, that by low order we mean something very specific. For example, Bessie (referring to a single, particular cow). Or James Edward MacPhee, Jr. who lives at 24 Sheridan Avenue. These are references to a particular, definite thing, as when we say "The Jones Corporation contract No. A-15-62-X, dated March 5, 1958."

There are all sorts of higher order abstractions, for which we often have verbal labels. The word "cow" is one of these. It doesn't tell us anything about the particular markings, physique, or disposition of Bessie; in fact, the word leaves out all differences between all cows, so that if I asked you to bring me a cow, you could bring any one of millions (of various sizes, colors, and shapes), and each one would accurately come under the label "cow." What this means is that "cow" doesn't describe in very much detail. About all it does is to differentiate between the world of cows and all other animals and things.

In the same way the name "James Edward MacPhee, Jr. who lives at 24 Sheridan Avenue" points out a particular man (except, of course, in the rare circumstance that there might be another James Edward MacPhee, Jr. living at 24 Sheridan Avenue). But the word "man" leaves it wide open to include every adult male member of the human race. If I am looking for "a man" my search will be very easy. I won't have to look far. And any man whatever is equally good, because the word "man" covers any one of them. This will not, I grant, help you very much in locating your brother-in-law at the railway station, nor in picking out a good operator for an overhead crane, nor in capturing the person who held up the Second National Bank last night.

You see, we have put everything you could call "man" into one of the pigeonholes. So far as the label on the pigeonhole is concerned, they are all the same.

And if you have ever worked in an office you know that it may be quite a job to locate the "Jones Corporation contract No. A-15-62-X" if you have to go through the entire file labelled "Contracts."

Where we really get into trouble is where we forget that the higher order abstraction is only a label designating a whole group of pigeonholes into which we are putting several different kinds of things, perhaps *many* different kinds of things.

If we fail to specify which particular cow is going to be delivered, even though we have in mind Bessie, we may find that we have purchased Bossie, who is just as much of a cow as Bessie, but not nearly the milk producer.

And if we confuse one man with another man; well, half the literature of the world, from William Shakespeare on, owes its plots to this particular kind of confusion.

And if we do not tell our secretary very carefully just *which* contract we want, and describe it very precisely in "low order" terms so that it couldn't possibly be any other one, she is very likely to send the wrong one entirely and we may lose a valuable client.

That sounds simple enough. You can't say "send any cow" and expect the cow you get to be exactly like Bessie. You can't employ (or marry) "any man" and expect him to come out exactly like some other man you knew somewhere once, (or possibly dreamed up out of your imagination). And you can't reach into the file marked "Contracts" and send off the first paper you grab, and expect that it will be the one document you need in the Jones Corporation matter.

It is so simple to keep things straight, and in their proper places. And yet people confuse them, and then seem quite surprised when the results are unsatisfactory. They confuse big, wide, general, high-order words, with precise, narrow, specific low-order words. And the confusion may be tragic.

I had written several pages outlining some of the tragedies, some of the disasters that have come about because someone confused a high-order symbol with a low one. Where pure hate, distilled and concentrated, was crystalized into a word, a name; and then that name projected against innocent men and women and children, as it has happened through history and in our own generation. But my wife urged me not to detail again what has been set down by others so many times and in so many ways. However, if you think that the things I am struggling to set down clearly and plainly are trivial, consider the price the world has paid for prejudice and racial and religious persecution. None of the murders, pogroms, lynchings, and campaigns of extermination resulting from these projected hates could have occurred were it not for the confusion of levels of abstraction.

You know how often the projecting of labels as if they were detailed descriptions has resulted in expensive errors in the market. When, for instance, an investor projects images of "safety," "stability," etc. to securities which he labels "bonds" and which he associates with conservative investment policy, he may find himself loaded with highly speculative "bonds" which are quite different from what he had expected.

If we project a name and treat it as if it were a description of reality, we should make sure that we know just how far the name describes that reality and in what detail. We should not ascribe more detail to the reality than is covered by the definition. Wherever possible we should check the reality to see whether the facts are what the definition says or implies. Most of us fail repeatedly to do this. We fail to look at "the thing" at all (even when it is so easy to do so), and fall victim to a misconception resulting from regarding "the name" as if it were, in fact, "the thing."

If men took these simple steps there would not be so many bankruptcies, nor so many fist-fights, nor so many stinking pages of history detailing the persecutions, massacres, and extermination of men and women and little children.

Perhaps a thought has come to you, as it has to many of us at various times. If men have turned against categories of men whom they regard as different from themselves and inferior and intolerable, could we not solve the problem by moving to a still higher abstraction?

Couldn't we quite properly say "All of these groups, including ourselves, are 'men.' Let us forget our differences."

This is the great plea of many humanitarian movements. "Forget your differences! Recognize that we are all 'men'! Let us be tolerant, and kindly, and cooperative in view of our *common humanity!*"

This is plausible enough when you first hear it. It is greatly to be desired that all "men" can live in "One World" in peace and friendship. By putting all "men" into one pigeon-hole we have wiped out the differences and settled all problems.

Unfortunately, this is not a very practical answer any more than it is a good answer in stock trading to "forget the differences" and pretend that all stocks are the same and identical with an average.

It doesn't work to dump everybody in the same bin and put the same label on it. It wouldn't make your filing any easier if you put all the files in one big box labelled "Office Papers." The label is all right, but like all labels it leaves out details. And these particular labels are very high-order ones. They leave out so much it isn't possible to see the facts at all.

Putting a label like "Office papers" on all the memos, contracts, bills, letters, checks, etc. leaves out the details by which we can tell them apart.

It is the old story of the camera. Get far enough back to include the entire cadet regiment, and you can't tell which fellow is which. They all look alike. But that doesn't make them all alike.

And it doesn't make humanity all alike to put it all in one bin. We don't even get very good results by putting the label "Christian" on a category of our population. Changing the map doesn't change the territory, and this business of labelling does not resolve the differences between Baptists, and Roman Catholics, and Episcopalians.

It is my feeling that the best hope of understanding reality, whether it is the stock market, the religious community, or the races of mankind, is to move closer to reality, not to retreat farther and farther into higher and higher order labels. "James Edward MacPhee, Jr. who lives at 24 Sheridan Avenue" we can go and talk to. We can take pictures of him, we can get to know him, and his children and his neighbors, and we can make a pretty good and pretty detailed and pretty useful map of him; one that will tell us a lot about what he is like, and how he lives, what he thinks, and what sort of guy he is.

If we describe him as a "Bostonian", then the detailed picture fades. He merges with all the other Bostonians in that pigeonhole. And if we say he is a citizen of Massachusetts, that gives us a larger and vaguer picture. If we classify him as "an American" it becomes vaguer yet. And if we ultimately lump him in with all humanity under the index "man," then he loses all detail and has no distinguishing characteristics at all, as compared with other adult human males.

If we did this we would have gained a fine broad map, but we would have lost most of the reality. We would be so far away from it.

I have seen how far astray investors can go when they begin to attribute details to individual stocks on the basis of characteristics they assign to the averages. I would feel that just as you would go and take a look at a particular man if you want to know something about that man, so you should go and take a look at a particular stock if you want to know how that stock is acting.

We cannot obliterate differences between stocks (or between people) just by putting generalized labels on them. We cannot make them all the same (except verbally).

And as regards people having different needs, and problems, and ways of life, if I wanted to establish a more brotherly way of living for all mankind, I would not try to gloss over these differences by words, which can do nothing but cover up the real problems still there in reality. Instead I would want to examine the differences very carefully and see which could be reconciled, which could be compromised, which could be eliminated (in reality and not just in words), and which ones could not be changed in reality but must be faced and settled.

What I am speaking of here has its counterparts in other areas. You will find the same kind of problem in religion. In the economic clashes between various individuals and groups. And, in smaller scale, but of no less importance, within family and social, groups.

Someone might object at this point, "Are you trying to under-

stand the stock market, or save the world?" Perhaps the best answer
to that would be to point out that we all need all the understanding
we can get in every department of life. If understanding the forces
that operate in the market helps us to understand ourselves and to
see more clearly the sources of family strife, racial and religious tension, and world conflict, this would be a net gain. And if understanding the forces that operate in human affairs and the principles
that govern them helps us in our investment program, that also
would be a net gain. We are interested in personal survival and
progress. But we also have a very real stake in world peace and
better human relations. It seems to me that helping to save the
world is part of everybody's job, and worth whatever thought and
effort he puts into it.

QUESTIONS FOR CONSIDERATION

If you like golf and your friend Joe likes pinochle, do you think it is
going to bring you much closer together to say you "both like games"?

If you are a Republican and I am a Democrat are we going to settle the
issues between us by deciding that we are "both interested in the welfare
of America"?

Is it possible to realize that people do have common interests in many
areas and still recognize that there are differences that should be stated
clearly?

Could a man make a serious error if he confused things that are quite
different simply by putting them under a "group" label? Is it necessary to
discriminate between stocks in the same "group"?

NOT QUITE THE SAME

WE HAVE played a game at our house; a game about things. It all started with one of the routine outbreaks of sibling hostility between Johnny, Louisy, and Abigail. The particular bones of contention in the case at hand were three yellow pencils, one of which belonged to each of the children. Through some chance the three were put into the same drawer in the kitchen table, at which they ate, played, and fought their battles.

Johnny claimed that Louisy had his pencil. Louisy loudly denied this, and said that anyway, they were "all the same."

Eventually the issue came up before a sort of drumhead family council. Obviously, the root of the contention was whether or not the pencils were "all the same."

It took only a few moments to show that one of the pencils had been sharpened down a little shorter than the other two; and that one of them had been chewed a little, just back of the eraser. There could be no question about the fact that the pencils were not the same. I ventured the opinion that no thing was "the same" as any other thing.

Two same-looking marbles were produced. A little study showed that the interior convolutions of color were quite different. Two flowers were produced from an African violet plant on the kitchen window sill. It took a rather close examination to discover that the petals of one were definitely longer than those of the other. Also, that the color was a shade different. Two coffee beans appeared

71

much the same; but after study everyone admitted that there were slight differences which could be observed under the magnifying glass.

Wherever we looked we could not find two things "the same." To point up the moral or point of the study as applied to the human race, I offered the thought that there had never been a child exactly like Johnny Magee, nor one like Louisy, nor one like Abigail, before; not in the whole history of the human race.

I did not press the further idea that none of these children was the same at any two times. Not the same last year as this year. Not the same yesterday as today. Not the same a hundredth of a second ago as now.

But it is a fact, and perfectly obvious when you come to think of it, that nothing is "the same" as something else; and nothing is identical with itself from one measurable moment to the next. Whereas the ancient philosophers took it for granted as an obvious truth that "A is A," a good many people recognize today that what may be valid in the purely abstract, purely symbolic field of mathematics is not necessarily true in the world of "real things."

As a matter of fact, one of the great minds of our century, Albert Einstein, commented on this very point. In effect, what he said was that insofar as a statement was "valid" in a theoretical, abstract, mathematical sense, it was not "true" in a down-to-earth, specific and "real" sense; and that insofar as it was "true" at the low order of observed reality, it was not "valid" in the strict and absolute sense of a mathematical formula.

QUESTIONS FOR CONSIDERATION

Would you say the statement, "A is identical with A" is: (1) a convenient method of treating abstract mathematical symbols; or (2) a statement of fact about the world of reality? (Note: In order to give this any real meaning we would have to designate the two parts of the equation, as "A^1 is identical with A^2", keeping in mind that no two things are identical and no thing is the same from moment to moment.)

Can we deal usefully with abstract mathematical symbols that do not have any exact counterpart in reality? Is it important at times to understand this difference? Are all "horsepower" (as engineers use the word) identical? Is the power of one horse precisely identical with the power of another horse? Is the power of a horse the same this afternoon as it was this morning?

How can you use the word "identical" in connection with persons, places, stocks, commodities or any tangible things at all? Doesn't it normally and properly imply "nearly identical" that is to say, "similar?"

If we ride roughshod over small differences that may not matter, isn't it possible we may ride over something that matters very much?

Wouldn't it be a good idea to keep a small reservation on the word "identical"? Wouldn't it be better, safer, to think of "identical" things as "very much alike"?

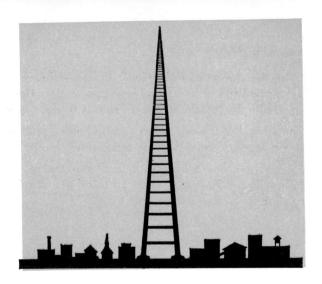

UP AND DOWN THE LADDER

AND this brings us to a question which must have already formed itself in your mind. Is it "better" to look at things specifically, close-up, as they are in the external world of reality; or is it "better" to see the broad outlines of classes and categories in their entirety.

We know that the close-up view shows more detail. And we know that the broad panorama covers a greater scope. In the first case, we lose perspective; in the second, we lose detail.

But there is no rule that we must look only at close-ups, or exclusively at panoramas. Since we have the means for seeing things from many points of view, why not use all of them?

There are times when it is most useful to have a detailed map of a small piece of territory, as when we are looking for a good picnic site. And there are other times when we need a view of the entire country, as when we are planning a system of continental highways.

The important thing is to know exactly what kind of a map or word or other symbol we are using, and not to attribute to it meanings that it does not have.

For example, it is a very good way to study nature to take a particular animal, say a raccoon, and study its habits, its growth, its way of living. By a close-up study of this sort you can learn first-hand the facts as they are in reality for this individual raccoon.

But we could make some serious errors if we attributed all of the observed facts about this raccoon to "raccoons" in general.

On the other hand, we might have collected a good deal of knowledge about *many* raccoons; facts which seem to be more or less characteristic of the entire breed. It is a good thing to have a broad, higher abstraction.

However, we could make serious errors, too, if we regarded this panorama of "raccoons" as a close-up, and expected every raccoon to look like and act like the "generalized" raccoon in every respect.

You see, if you studied only *one* raccoon you would not know very much about the life of raccoons collectively. And if you had abstracted only the common factors in the raccoon tribe you would not know the special features of "this particular raccoon." You need both maps; and you need to know which is which.

There is a place for speaking of "men" in the broad sense; and a place for "Harold W. Ericson" in the specific sense. But it is very important to know whether you are speaking of the "class" or the "individual."

We can go up and down the scale of abstractions, using a symbol or map as broad or as detailed as we need for our purpose in the case at hand. We will not have any confusion so long as we keep clearly in mind just what we are talking about or thinking about, and so long as we realize that we are using symbols, words, maps, which are not the things they represent.

QUESTIONS FOR CONSIDERATION

When you enter a discussion do you know at approximately what abstractive level you are talking? Do you consider what levels the others are using?

Is it possible for serious disagreements to arise when one person is thinking of something concrete and definite, and someone else is referring to high order concepts and principles? Consider the statement: "Lone Star Cement stock advanced two points today." Is this a matter of record? Can it be verified?

Consider the statement: "The Cement stocks as a group have advanced this past week." Is this also a matter or record? Can it be verified if we have a list of stocks included in the Cement group and their prices through the week?

Would you consider the first statement of a "lower order" or a "higher order" than the second in the sense we have been using these terms?

Does the action of Lone Star Cement stock alone give us a good basis for making conclusions and predictions about all the Cement stocks in the group?

Does the action of the group of Cement stocks give us enough detailed information to make very specific conclusions and predictions about Lone Star Cement stock?

Is it important to know just what we are talking about or what we are thinking about?

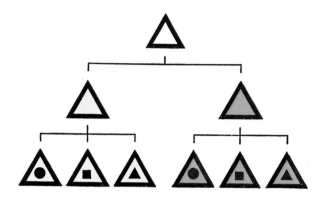

SIMILARITIES — AND DIFFERENCES

SOME pages back we noted that the broad panoramic view of the student regiment showed all the cadets looking very alike. As a matter of fact, as we know, they were all wearing similar uniforms, were about the same age, and for the most part shared the same interests. There were, in other words, a good many genuine similarities.

That is why it is so important to keep in mind at all times, that this *is* a broad picture, not a very detailed one. It would be very easy to confuse Cadet Sanderson with Cadet Jamison; they look so very much alike in the picture. But we know that Cadet Sanderson is very different from Cadet Jamison. Jamison has dark hair, a rather long nose and flat ears. Sanderson is a blond, has snub nose and his ears stick out. None of these differences can be seen in the group picture.

The broad picture, the higher abstraction, calls attention to similarities but does not show differences.

Large size cabinet photographs of Jamison and of Sanderson, on the other hand would show clearly the differences; but they would not point up the similarities.

It is this way with maps, as you know. A map of a considerable area of countryside will show the general shape of the terrain. It will not, however, show the special features of a particular spot and the differences between one spot and another.

The same thing is true of words. Like photographs, like maps,

77

they can describe single things, in which case the various descriptions will emphasize the *differences* (as: "This six-inch yellow 2B El Dorado pencil" and "that eight-inch, green 4-H Dixon pencil.")

Or they can refer, at a higher level of abstraction to "pencils", in which case they call attention to the similarities of these two objects.

Where things are so much alike that one is substantially as good as another for our purpose there is no need to be too specific. "Gimme a cigarette" means any cigarette in the package. They are all very similar, and for all practical purposes they are equivalent. So long as we understand that they are not really identical, it is more convenient to consider them all alike.

It all depends on whether the differences are important or not. Very often they are not. If you were to buy 100 shares of Reynolds Tobacco stock it would make no particular difference to you whether you received certificate number A-4637-WR or number A-3851-XB. On the other hand it would make a great deal of difference whether you received a certificate for 100 shares of Reynolds Tobacco or 100 shares of Reynolds Metals. But there is a verbal similarity here which could result in a faulty identification.

Most of the mistakes in the world, the funny ones and the sad ones, come about because of confusion of one thing with another.

These confusions are not very likely to occur at the levels of direct observation of reality, nor at the level of low abstraction, since here the maps (or the words) are usually very detailed and specific.

The confusions happen at the higher levels of abstraction. For, as you know, it is at these levels that we begin to move back, away from the close reality, and we lose detail. Rather different things begin to look more alike. If we go far enough, very different things will look the same, and we will have the feeling they are identical.

In other words, we can very easily mistake something for something else because of the similarities.

That is what happens when you rush up to a familiar figure on Main Street and slap him on the back and greet him, "Hi, Charlie. I didn't know you were back in town," only to slink away in embarrassment when the supposed friend turns around, and is clearly not Charlie at all but a total stranger.

You had, of course, noticed, perhaps quite unconsciously, some features of this stranger that you linked with Charlie. Perhaps the suit he wore, or the way he walked. You *identified* the figure walking down Main Street with Charlie. You disregarded all differences and acted impulsively on the similarities. And so you confused an utter stranger with Charlie, and your own confusion was the most distressing of all.

If, instead of using the sketchy, loosely drawn "map" of Charlie, you had moved down to lower, more particular levels, and had observed the figure on Main Street more closely, comparing it with more detailed "maps" of Charlie's appearance from your memory, you would not have been tricked by the similarities into establishing a false identity.

It is the same in every department of life, and the confusions result from the same kind of error. The Captain orders the private to have his horse "shod." Some minutes later an echoing report tells the sad story; the private had confused two similar-sounding words. A sleepy nurse reaches for the tall brown medicine bottle and kills a patient with the caustic contents of another tall brown bottle which looks very similar.

Words can often lead to faulty identifications. If you tell me your nephew is a conductor I may think of him as presiding over the Boston Symphony, whereas, as a matter of fact, he is collecting tickets on the Boston and Maine. In this case, you will note, the words do not even refer to the same "class" of thing. There is a similarity that leads to confusion, but it is merely a verbal similarity and has no basis whatever in fact. In other words there is no similarity in external reality that relates closely the occupation of musical director with collecting train tickets.

You may have had some heated arguments with friends about the merits of General Motors. You may feel that General Motors is weak, has broken support, and is headed for much lower levels. Your friends may insist that General Motors has increased its production, is bringing out new and greatly improved models, and is developing a line of light-weight locomotives that will revolutionize rail travel.

Here is a confusion, and a confusion at the verbal level. The term "General Motors" is a name, a map, a symbol. It is not a "thing." We must not confuse names with things.

Actually "General Motors" can and does refer to more than one "reality." The reality of the stock market is an equity, an undivided beneficial interest in the earnings and "book value" of the company. And this reality is itself an abstraction, not a tangible "thing." The reality of the high production and the new products does concern tangible "things."

When you and your friends, then, engage in an argument about the showing of the stock as compared with the physical features of the company or with its activities, you are comparing two quite dis-similar entities.

In fact they are so dis-similar that it is hard to see how anybody could confuse them. They are, to be sure, related in some ways; the stock and the operations of the company. But they are not the same.

What is the same is the term "General Motors." Both the activities of the company, and the performance of the stock of the company are referred to as "General Motors." The similarity (which some people treat as if it were identity) exists *only* in the words.

If "things equal to the same thing are equal to each other," then "General Motors" (the stock) is the same as "General Motors" (the corporate affairs).

But what is valid as mathematical theory is a matter of symbolic relations. Mathematics is not necessarily true by analogy in the world of "things."

And so, by jumping to the "faulty conclusion" that "the stock is the company," we have again confused abstraction with reality, one level of abstraction with another; and, in short, we have made a "mistake."

You will understand that there are many, many kinds of errors that result from identifying things on the basis of "seen," "heard," "touched," "smelled," or "tasted" similarities.

I might, for instance, take a quick glance at my watch, note the time as 3 :20, and go back to my work for another half hour. And if the hands had actually stood at 4:15, which would have a very similar appearance, I might miss a 4:30 appointment entirely. This confusion would not be verbal, for the similarity is not one of words, but of visual appearance. But it could be avoided, like all confusions based on similarities, by a closer examination of the territory, in this case the face of the watch.

Perhaps you yourself have made mistakes on the basis of similarities that are entirely non-verbal. For instance, you may have rushed to answer the front door when actually the telephone was ringing.

James Thurber in one of his collections of short stories and essays speaks of non-verbal confusion of the basis of similar appearances. In an article titled "The Admiral on a Bicycle" he tells how his near-sightedness has given him a world of wonders, in which a wind-blown swirl of old newspapers takes on the appearance of a little old man in an admiral's uniform pedalling a bicycle down the street; and a number of other illusions . . . all based on at least superficial similarities . . . and all of which could be resolved if one were able to have a better look.

Edgar Allen Poe wrote a short story about a man who was startled when he looked up from his reading and saw a great monster crawling down the side of a hillside about a mile away, and approaching the valley at a terrifying rate. It was only on taking off the reading glasses that the monster could be seen as a moderate size insect creeping down the window pane a few inches away. In this case the non-verbal mistake was simply a matter of not "scaling" the map correctly; and something small was perceived as being something big. While this particular confusion is not likely to deceive many people, there are many many life situations where a small thing is "seen" out of scale; in fact we know people who habitually "make mountains out of mole hills."

QUESTIONS FOR CONSIDERATION

How would you say most confusions arise: from overlooking similarities, or from overlooking differences?

Does this mean we should look *only* for differences and pay no attention to similarities? Or should we look for both and realize that both are important in understanding the world around us?

Do gentlemen prefer blondes? Do *you* prefer blondes? Does "blondes" cover a good deal of ground? Does "blondes" neglect to take account of a great many individual differences? Do you consider all blondes alike in all respects? In what single respect could you say that all blondes are alike?

Do you "like the aircrafts"? Does this question leave out some rather important differences? Would you say all aircrafts are alike in all respects? Does the label "aircraft" by itself give you enough information to justify buying the stock of one of these companies. In what single respect could you say all the companies labelled "Aircraft" are alike?

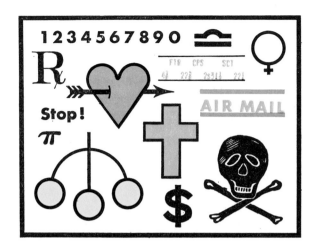

BEYOND THE WORLD OF THINGS

UP TO this point we have been considering maps of places, labels of things, words that are symbols of something tangible "out there" that we can point to, or count, or weigh. Even the "higher abstractions" we have mentioned represent groups or classes of "real things." If we say "Bessie" we can take you out in the pasture and show you what we mean by Bessie. You can admire her, listen to her moo, and pat her smooth broad sides. And if we say "house," while it does not, to be sure, tell you what particular house or kind of house we have in mind, we can take you out and show you a number of houses of various sorts, so that you will know what we mean by the generalized symbol, the word "house."

In other words, for the very low order abstraction denoting a single individual thing, place, animal or event, there is a corresponding "reality" which can be produced and examined. And for all the various stages of higher order abstractions relating to these things, etc., there are realities "out there" which correspond.

But there are other high order abstractions which refer to a reality that is not tangible and cannot be touched, tasted or inspected directly by the senses at all.

And if there are dozens of ways of becoming confused and deluded in our perception of the solid, tangible "things" of the world, there are hundreds of traps that lurk in the tenuous upper reaches of the abstractions we are going to investigate now.

It is very easy to mistake the sound of a doorbell for the somewhat similar ring of the phone. Or to confuse "this dog" with "that dog," or to make any of the other faulty identifications we make in everyday life in dealing with such ordinary things as keys and eye-glasses, medicine bottles, and the like.

But in all these cases we are referring to something that can be sensed directly "out there," and even the higher order abstractions, that is, the names we use to call things by, refer to classes of "real things."

Animals abstract in this way. Some dogs, for instance, react with enthusiasm and agility to the sight of a running cat; any cat, all cats. Animals respond to calls to food and visual or audible signals that dinner is ready. They can learn to understand and relate the original signals; they can establish chains of abstractions with symbols representing other symbols. Very much as a human child might learn that when the clock strikes five we may shortly expect to hear Father's car drive into the garage; and when the car drives in Mother starts to get dinner off the stove.

There used to be great arguments among pseudo-scientific people as to "whether animals could think." If by thinking we mean the power to abstract, to generalize classes of things, to recognize symbols that represent and correspond with parts of reality, and to establish chains of abstraction, then of course animals can think and think very well, some of them. Well enough to serve their needs and secure their survival.

But there is a vast gulf between the abstractive ability of the smartest dog or horse or chimpanzee and the stupidest man able to live as a member of a human community.

And the difference between man and animal is not merely the fact that mankind has enormously greater powers of abstraction, covering much greater scope and variety and involving much greater complexity.

But there are types of abstraction that are not possible at all to the animals.

This is because so much of our abstracting is done in language, whether we speak the words or merely "think" them. The invention of language is man's greatest discovery, and his ability to use language intelligently is the great difference that marks him from all other living things on the earth.

When we build a chain of abstraction, we have "names" to give to the pigeonholes. We can observe the thing, name it (chair), classify it (furniture), put it into a higher order class (household equipment), generalize that class into a still higher order (personal property), etc. We can set up verbal maps to give us much detail or little detail, to cover a particular thing, or to include various categories.

This, an animal cannot do. He cannot do it because he doesn't have the machinery to do it. He lacks the mechanism of language.

We can speculate on whether some animals *might* be able to develop greater "intelligence," "reasoning power," etc. if they could communicate in language as we do. But so long as they do not and cannot, this is merely an amusing pastime. The language barrier puts a full stop to the development of the animal.

We have already seen how language sets the pattern for our pigeon-holing of information. Using words as symbols we can store up almost unlimited files of information in our minds, ready to be re-called and put to use whenever we need them. If we have learned a little about the nature of language as a system of symbols or maps, and have learned not to confuse words with things, nor high order words with low order words, and not to confuse things that are symbolized by the same word or similar words; then we have the basis for a smoothly operating "thinking machine." At least as far as the perception and classifying of "things and events" is concerned.

But there are other words. We have carefully skirted a great mountain of verbal maps up to now, since these non-descriptive words bring with them a whole new set of problems and pitfalls.

When you say "flower" you are using a symbol that calls up all the kinds of things we call "flowers," asters and roses, pansies and petunias, tulips and hyacinths, etc., typical flowers that can be pointed out, touched, and smelled. "Flower" is the name of a class of things.

But when you say "red flower," the word "red" is not the name of a thing, nor of a class of things. You cannot quite establish communication with someone else about redness as easily as you can about the name of a thing.

You can point to something that is "red" to you, that is something which reflects certain wave lengths of light in such a way that you recognize them and call them "red." You can establish in your own mind a concept of "redness," as a fairly high order (broad) abstraction. And you can visualize in your memory various lower orders in this concept of "redness," which you may call "rose," "pink," "scarlet," "vermilion," "maroon," "crimson," etc.

But you may find it difficult to convey to someone else just what you mean by "red" or even what you mean by any of the lower order words that you include in "redness." If you have ever tried to explain to a printer over the telephone just how you want him to change the color in the illustrations for a booklet, to meet your ideas of how they should look, you will appreciate the difference between explaining what you mean by "vermillion" (as you see it in your mind's eye), and explaining what you mean by "carnation" or "petunia."

This idea of "redness" or a certain kind and shade of redness is not too much different from descriptions of "things," since there is, after all a physical referent, certain describable constants that can represent any color or shade in the spectrum. More than a generation ago the language of color was placed on a systematic practical basis for the use of printers, paper manufacturers, commercial artists, etc. by Professor A. H. Munsell. A "Color Atlas" and a "Color Grammar" based on this system were published by The Strathmore Paper Company, and the methods of notation were adopted by various printers, ink makers, and some buyers of printing.

However, for the general public this reasonable and highly useful system had no great appeal. And so today, we still have our troubles trying to match the "beige" stockings for our wives, explaining to the painter what we mean by "magenta," and wondering what the mail order house will send us when we order stationery of "ivory" tint.

It is possible, using electric eyes and various filters, to analyze colors quickly and accurately, and uniformly, so that color-matching data can be transmitted and the color reproduced at another point, or so that the data could be stored and the color produced again at a later time.

But for most of us we are tied to the somewhat imperfect color perception of our own eyes, which for this job are not nearly the equal of electronic devices. We still go on talking about "baby pink" and "orchid" and "powder blue" and go right on bringing home the wrong goods entirely from the department store, as our wives tell us quite frankly and openly.

The fact is that "color" as we perceive it, is not really a "thing" like "book" or "hat." It is an aspect of a thing, or rather our particular response to an aspect of a thing.

You have no way of knowing whether certain light waves reflected from a thing set up the same sensations and feelings in my mind as they do in yours. For all you know I may see "red" quite differently from you. As a matter of fact I do, if you have "normal" color perception, for I am slightly color blind. I cannot show you or explain to you in words or in any other way just how red looks to me, any more than you can communicate your perception of redness to me. But I do know that you are probably more responsive to red, you will notice it more quickly, you will see it more vividly than I do.

Notice that the "redness" is a matter of my "seeing," not a property of the thing. "In the dark all cats are black," and all other things too.

The color is not a property of the thing; nor is it even a property of the light that strikes it. It depends on a combination of the thing, the kind of light being reflected from it, and very importantly, on my perception of it.

In other words "red" is not only a map, or symbol. It is a symbol that is not strictly comparable between one person and another. It has a physical referent in a way and up to a point, but the color as perceived is strictly a personal matter. My red is my own, and your red is your own, and they are not necessarily the same.

What we are getting at here is that color is a much less tangible, much more tenuous kind of perception than "wooden table" or "pile of bricks."

I have spent some time on this point, since it is a bridge, so to speak, at the point of departure as we leave the World of Things and enter the world of "Concepts."

Instead of calling the flower "red," which is what I call the color as I see it, I might have called it a "pretty flower."

What are you going to do with this one?

What is "pretty"? "What does "pretty" look like? Is "pretty" a thing? There have been a few bloody noses and black eyes on this point. I think she is "pretty." You think she is an ugly old bag and say so; and the fight is on.

How are you going to measure "pretty"? What are you going to do when there is a difference of opinion? This is not going to be the kind of argument that can be settled by going out and counting the brick chimneys on somebody's house.

We have already said that there can be no conflict in the world of reality. You feel, and I agree with you, that "pretty" does represent something. It is a map which has a corresponding territory.

But the reality in this case is not a physical reality in the external world. The only reality at stake is our own opinion. When we say something or someone is "pretty," we are not comparing a map to a territory in the sense that we would be if we said "I know that there is a fire hydrant in front of Bill Johnson's house." That statement can be verified by going and having a look, and every reasonable person will abide by the decision.

It is quite different with "pretty." This is a map of a map, and the territory we are checking is *itself* a high order abstraction in our own mind. You can't produce the evidence. You can't prove your point. All you know is whether Miss America as chosen at Atlantic City measures up to the standards of your own "map" of what is "pretty." And that is why "In matters of taste there can be no dispute."

Notice that "pretty" is an adjective. There is a different territory for each one of us. In general adjectives do not denote things, but refer to some quality or property which we attribute to a thing; or, more often than not, to some opinion we may hold about the thing.

In spite of all the committees of experienced judges, in spite of all the expert opinions, definitions, and attempts to set up standards, when they are all done at Atlantic City you and I may feel that Miss America doesn't look "pretty" to us. There is a disagreement.

Since "pretty" is a "good" word, it is associated with "things we like"; and since many of us like very much the same sort of things, we may at times agree on what we feel is "pretty." But it is most important to keep in mind, always, that it is still an entirely personal matter, and what is pretty to me is not necessarily "pretty" to you.

Consider an adjective which you will find bandied about on the front page of your newspaper, in the reports of proceedings in district court, in findings of the Post Office department, and in pronouncements from the pulpit, the lecture platform and the Governor's office.

The word is "obscene." It is, by the way, an adjective.

You are familiar with the all-too-familiar story of the raid at the Starlight Club, where an "obscene" performance was being given.

And along with this hacknied news item is another; the clamping down on the ring that has been distributing "obscene" pictures and magazines throughout the local cigar stores. Ministers exhort us not to visit an "obscene" play at the local theatre. An "obscene" book is banned from public sale. And so on.

This happens to be a "bad" word. But in some ways it is the same *kind* of a word as "pretty." At any rate, if you have followed the legal tangles that have built up around the difficulty of establishing a firm definition for "obscene" you will realize that this word, too, is not a map of a territory in externality, but a map of a map. And a highly personal map which is not necessarily the same for any two persons; not even approximately.

A very interesting discussion of this problem was presented by Mary Ware Dennett some years ago in her book "Who's obscene?", a chronicle of the difficulties she had with this very point, the frustrations she encountered, the hostility she met, and the general lack of comprehension of the nature of the problem.

The difficulty is in writing a firm definition, something that everyone can agree on. This is a wall that lawyers and legislatures have battered their heads against, and without much result. For, in the case of "pretty," or "obscene," it is impossible to write an absolute description that everyone can verify and agree on, since what we are dealing with is not "a thing" but a concept in someone's head, a map in the mind. We have no way of comparing one man's "map in the mind" with another's.

The problem is not made any easier by the fact that it *almost* seems as if we *could*, if we put our heads to it, write such a definition; since, just as most of us agree as to what is "pretty," most of us would agree in certain clear-cut cases, that something was (to us) "obscene," or "not obscene." But this is not because we can compare facts and measure, verify, etc. in a scientific way like counting trees or measuring house lots. The degree of agreement we have is more because of exposure and training in a common culture. But it is only an approximate agreement, and it cannot, in dubious cases, be submitted to any hard-and-fast scientific rules.

Of course we can change the problem. If we can ask the questions in terms that can be answered by observations and measurements in the external world, then we can avoid the impossible task of "comparing mental maps." For instance, as sometimes happens, the judges of a beauty contest may discover that it is going to be impossible to get any sort of agreement on the respective pulchritude of some seventy or eighty damsels. To avoid a deadlock they may resort (possibly in desperation) to setting up standards of "prettiness" which are not really perceptions of beauty at all but are, in fact, measurements of external reality. The whole matter becomes simpler all around when it is possible to compare the girls point by point with some definite standards on which everyone has agreed in advance. Thus, we often see tables of measurements, showing the dimensions of "the ideal woman," or those of the Venus de Milo; and the candidates are submitted to a point-by-point comparison with the standard.

This, of course, is a scientific method and can give a positive answer in terms of degree of correlation with the standard. No one is likely to disagree with the findings, and if he does, it is very easy to check back and verify the figures.

This way leads to no disputes; and when Miss Central Falls is finally selected we all know that she does, in fact and provably, conform most nearly to the standards of beauty set up in advance by the committee.

But whether the selection is going to please you personally or not is another matter. There is no assurance whatever that she will measure up, even approximately, to anybody's "mental map" of what a "pretty girl" or a "beautiful woman" should look like.

And until and unless we are able to condition people in such a way that their opinions, tastes and judgments are precisely the same, we will never quite be able to agree on "what is pretty."

And of course it is the same with any other word of opinion or judgment. You have followed the struggles of the bar and the ministry to define "obscenity," in the sense of an inner awareness of indecency. Probably the most promising efforts, at least the only practical ways open, are to externalize the question, and instead of trying to compare "mental maps," to measure something "out there." If, for example, we agree and pass laws that any photograph of a nude woman is to be considered "obscene," that would define something verifiable. This has been tried, and also a great many other definitions of what may not be done, what must be worn or may not be worn, what can or cannot be said, etc. The cop posted at the back of the burlesque house is following some such rules, and if this is his regular tour of duty, he knows exactly how much leg, and how much body may be exposed and for how long, and what words are taboo, etc., etc.

These are not definitions of any personal attitude or feeling, one way or the other. They refer to specific items to check out there; and if the rules are violated the entire company is packed into the paddy wagon and hauled off to night court. It's as easy as that.

But bear in mind that this is not the essence of the problem, which is trying to measure and compare human perception.

It is so easy to assume that what is "pretty" for you is "pretty" for me; that what is "obscene" for you, is also "obscene" to me. That what is "good," "lazy," "contemptible," "generous," "cruel," "honest," "ugly," etc., to me will coincide with your feelings in any particular case. Very often we will jump to the conclusion that everyone else feels or should feel the same as we do. A conclusion that will not stand up under study.

By way of example let me pass along a little story illustrating how we project our own feelings and assume that something that is really "in here" must be "out there" and observable by everyone.

QUESTIONS FOR CONSIDERATION

Is the word "man" an abstraction? Does it cover a great many very different sorts of people? Is it a label for a large category?

Does the label "man" indicate something rather tangible; that is, could you, by citing a number of examples and describing the characteristic features of "man" make it clear to someone (Man from Mars) what you were talking about? Could you point at an example of what you call "man"?

Is this sharply different from the label "rich man"? Would "rich" necessarily mean the same to you as to someone else? Would it necessarily mean the same to you now as it might have ten years ago?

Would you say that "rich" concerned your opinion or valuation or something? Wouldn't this be true of nearly all adjectives?

How would you classify the adjectives in the expressions "growth stock," "sound investment," "unprecedented opportunity," etc.? Do these adjectives denote or describe something "out there," or do they refer to judgments and opinions in someone's mind?

Would you say that a similar situation prevailed with adverbs; for example, when we say "rapidly expanding," "sharply declining"?

There are certain nouns derived from adjectives which we call "abstract nouns." From "noble" we get "nobility." Is "nobility" something you can touch or point at like "chair," or does it lie in the field of your own evaluation? Consider other abstract nouns: "greed," "success," "happiness," etc. Are these "things"? Or do they indicate opinions and judgments?

Which would be more likely to provoke disagreements: the statement, "That is a table," or "That is a good company"? Is "good" a matter of factual record?

THE MEANINGS WE ATTACH TO MAPS

THERE was this story going around about the psychiatrist and the new patient: At the very first interview the doctor found it necessary to interrupt the patient's recitation of his symptoms in order to get a little psychological background. He explained that he was making a simple test in which he wanted the patient to describe the situation suggested by several sketches, which the doctor drew on his desk pad.

To the first of these the patient responded that it could be a bedroom; with perhaps a double bed and a man and a woman in it having sexual intercourse.

When the doctor drew a second sketch the patient reckoned that it might be *three* bedrooms; each containing a double bed with a couple enjoying sexual relations.

93

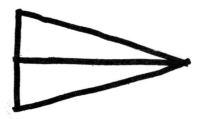

To a third sketch the patient's reaction was puzzlement. However, after some thought he reported that it looked like two bedrooms of peculiar shape, each with a double bed. In one was a couple engaged in rather perverse dalliance; and in the other, two men, carrying on, as the patient put it, "like crazy."

"Well, my friend," said the doctor, "Before we go any further into discussing your symptoms, I think I should tell you that you are oversexed. In fact you are obsessed with sex."

"Oh, yeah?" The patient fixed the psychiatrist with a cold and reproachful glare, "And who, may I ask, has been drawing all the dirty pictures?"

You see, when we are talking about words which represent an opinion or a judgment, that is to say, how we feel about something, we can't point to anything "out there," since what we mean isn't out there at all. When we say "dirty picture," or "brave warrior," the "dirty" and the "brave" don't have the same kind of solid reality as "picture" or "warrior." Common nouns name things, but adjectives are symbols that represent values we have come to attach to things either as a result of experience or, very often, because of what we have been taught. We may have a fairly good idea of what we mean by "awkward," or "brilliant," or "generous," but these are still maps of maps, and they are several or many steps of abstraction away from external reality. And because of this, although we may concur with other people who have been exposed to the common teaching and preaching of the community on many "matters of opinion," the fact remains that when it comes to a really close decision there is no ultimate and decisive way of deciding which opinion is "right."

The point here is that common nouns in general refer to "things out there," while adjectives and adverbs and abstract nouns in general refer to "concepts in here."

What one must keep in mind concerning his own understanding

and communication with others is that when one uses an adjective or adverb, or an abstract noun, he is expressing how something seems to himself; not necessarily to the man next door.

Notice that we use the word "is" or its variants such as "am," "be," "are," etc., to equate our opinion with some "thing." When we say, "Rover *is* a brown dog," we are *saying* that "Rover" and "brown dog" are equal and identical. We have already seen that this is not precisely true, since a symbol or map is not the same as the thing it represents. But in this case we are also including an adjective in the identity. Rover "*is brown*" "to me." More than that I cannot really say; since I cannot surely say that he *is* brown to you; you may not see him exactly the same way I do. And if I were to say that Charles Wilson *is* a *handsome* man, I should be aware that I am comparing Charles Wilson to my mental "map" of what is handsome in a man, and find that Mr. Wilson fills the bill. He is handsome "to me." And if somebody else thinks that Charles Wilson has a rather ugly-looking face; well that is because Mr. Wilson doesn't match up with *his* mental map of handsomeness. "To him" Wilson is ugly, or at least "not handsome." I do not know of any way you can challenge his contrary view and "prove" your own.

The standard method, of course, of arriving at some sort of working agreement so that roughly we can know what our neighbor means, is to take the views of a number of people, and accept the consensus as the standard.

Thus, where nine hundred and ninety-nine people will agree (that is, will have similar "maps" of "handsomeness") that Charles Wilson is handsome, we will probably accept the idea that a certain appearance such as his, in our culture, may be considered by tacit mutual agreement to "be" handsome. This is a sort of extensional bargain.

And this is perfectly all right so long as we understand that we are not dealing with an external reality alone, but with a judgment or opinion about it. If you think this is a matter of splitting hairs just consider the types that we consider "handsome" among men, or "beautiful" among women; and then compare them with the typical choices representing these qualities by Eskimos, or Central Africans, or Chinese! You will see that the opinions most people hold are not necessarily the same in other places or other cultures. Nor would they necessarily be the same in other times.

Most importantly, you will realize that these other and contrary opinions have as much "validity" as your own. But some "valid" judgments and opinions may be more useful than others in interpreting external reality and in making dependable predictions. As we have said before, a valid judgment or opinion may be "true" to a degree as it applies to the outside world, or it may be "false to fact." Or it may have no true-or-false aspect, for instance, if it is a matter of "taste." The judgment or opinion which can determine your attitude on a matter (and therefore your behavior with respect to that matter), depends on the premises on which you build. And even a very "unrealistic" attitude may be logically "valid," though it may be constructed on premises that contradict observable reality. To repeat, it may be "valid," yet "false to fact." This, we must continually check and be on guard against. We must know where we got our basic premises and we must check and examine them if we want to avoid a "faulty" or "inadequate" conclusion.

QUESTIONS FOR CONSIDERATION

In reading your daily newspaper do you pause now and then to read carefully the adjectives and adverbs and abstract nouns as they are applied to "news stories"?

Do you realize how powerfully these words can convey or suggest approval or disapproval?

And do you realize that the judgments and opinions thus projected are not "factual reporting" of the news event, but represent the attitudes of the reporter?

If we say, "Jones stupidly dropped the hammer," does "stupidly" describe something "out there," or does it indicate how we feel about it?

If we say, "His earnestness is in his favor," is "earnestness" a fact in external reality, or are we stating a judgment?

In the phrase, "a magnificent painting," is "magnificent" a "territory" or is it a "mental map"?

THE MAPS WITHOUT TERRITORIES

BECAUSE, unlike the animals, mankind has the great tool of language we are able to make these maps and maps of maps, and to abstract not only things and classes of things, but events and classes of events, that is, what happens and what people do. Beyond that we make maps of how we feel about these things, such as the ones we have just been discussing. Most of the abstracting is done verbally; and our maps are verbal maps, our pigeonholes have verbal labels.

But in all these cases, even the "opinions," there is, at least for our own self, a chain of connection to "things real." We can trace the word and the meaning we assign to it, through a chain of learning and experience which rests, ultimately on the solid foundation of events and things that can be demonstrated "in reality."

There are other maps and labels. It is perfectly possible to draw a map that represents no real place at all. We even write stories about events that never happened and never could happen, and we say of the characters in these stories that "any resemblance between them and any real person, living or dead, is purely co-incidental." It is possible, through language, to communicate these imaginary things to others, so that they will, in some degree, experience the same adventures, meet the same fictitious characters, and perhaps express very much the same emotions we feel ourselves.

This is all right, so long as we understand that we are just playing a game, or at most, setting up a map that has some similarity with

97

things and places and events we have known. We might spin a yarn that is thrilling and exciting to our listeners, even though they know it isn't true. And we might tell a story that could point up some principle or idea, so that even though it was not precisely a "true" story, it would help others to solve a problem similar to one in the story.

If I tell you a story about a "ghost," I think I could make it sufficiently blood-curdling to scare you a little, and perhaps to keep you awake an hour later tonight. Of course, unless you are unusually innocent, you would not expect me to "show you" the ghost or "prove" that the story was "true." I think we would both understand that the "ghost" exists only in my mind, and that fortunately, there is no territory "out there" to correspond.

When we speak of "ghosts," by the way, my job is a fairly easy one, since you already know a good deal about "ghosts." I don't need to tell you what a regulation "ghost" looks like, because you know very well. Tall, white and shapeless, probably clanking a heavy chain, and possibly uttering thin wails from time to time. Of course, not all "ghosts" are of the regulation type; but there is no need to get into all the specialties.

The interesting thing is that you have in your own mind a map of "ghost" which is not too different from my own. You have a map which corresponds to *no* reality and yet has a certain one-to-one correspondence with a map in my own head. That is an extraordinary thing when you stop to think about it. I cannot imagine two animals sharing a thought which had no connection with reality. In fact, I don't think such a thing would be possible, except through the medium of language.

"Ghost," technically speaking is a common noun. It has the appearance of a word denoting something tangible like "book" or "frog." We must be very careful in dealing with "ghost" that we do not confuse it with something more tangible.

Now there are other words besides "ghost" that have no clearly demonstrable referent in externality. Some of these words may have a particular meaning to the user, but because they are extremely high abstractions, the final terms of long chains of abstracting, it is not always possible to communicate this inner meaning. In fact, by comparison, "ghost" may seem a very solid and precisely defined entity.

How are you going to get together on the precise meaning of "sacredness"? Just how would you measure "disgrace"? Terms like these are capable of such broad interpretation that they cease to have much value as means of communication. Whatever value they may have must rest on a purely personal understanding.

A friend of mine once suggested that we could iron out certain differences of view if we could establish a common ground of discussion, agreeing on certain broad principles.

If you recall the case of the camera, you will realize that it is always possible to make different things look the same if we will take a broad enough view, and, by moving away from the subjects, get farther from the reality.

In this case my friend suggested that we could agree on certain points, and then establish further agreement step by step.

If he had suggested that the agreements we would start with would be the "low order" observation of reality, I believe we might actually have made a start. If we had started with the "looking at," "counting," "measuring" of solid, familiar things, and then worked up to the logical abstractions from these, we might have hoped for a considerable agreement.

Instead, he suggested that we agree that we believe in "The Great Eternal Verities."

Is this something that can be counted, weighed, pointed at, or directly observed?

I asked him to define the Great Eternal Verities, and he said that I knew what they were as well as he did. When I pressed the point he became angry.

Now I do not want to accuse anyone of treasuring a map which corresponds to no reality whatever. I think it is possible that my friend does have some idea of what he means when he speaks of the Great Eternal Verities.

But apparently he cannot reduce his feeling to a lower abstraction, not even enough to describe and define what he is talking about. He cannot communicate his map at all.

If you have a map, or a concept, that corresponds to reality, it seems as if you should be able to tell something about the territory referred to. If this was a geographical map you would surely be able to tell something about the country represented, the various features of it, and their relative location.

But here, in the case I mentioned, we cannot get beyond "Great Eternal Verities."

Wouldn't it seem to you, if you treasured such a map, that it could not fail to be more useful if you could bring this great label down to earth. It might help you if you could determine precisely what you mean by "Great Eternal Verities" and check how and to what extent they would apply in each specific problem you might encounter in your own affairs.

Please do not misunderstand this. There is a place for high order abstraction. It is just as important to be able to generalize and proceed by logic and inference from facts to conclusions and from conclusions to principles, as it is to observe the down-to-earth reality. But we should not confuse the high order abstraction with the low order observation; and we certainly should not treat a "map" like "Great Eternal Verities" as if it were a "thing."

QUESTIONS FOR CONSIDERATION

Have you ever known a child who was terrified of "The Boogie Man"? Have you ever seen a Boogie Man? Do you know anyone who has actually seen a Boogie Man? Would you say the Boogie Man was "real" to the terrified child? Is "Boogie Man" a "map" or a "territory"? Where are we most likely to find the "truth," in maps or in territories?

I have heard that "They" are "putting up" U. S. Steel. Who do you suppose "They" are? Have you ever seen "They"? Do you know anyone who can name them and point them out to you? Are you sure there is a territory to correspond with this map? Are "They" real to the people who believe in their machinations? Do you feel that everything that has the appearance of a map necessarily portrays a real territory in external reality? When someone tells you something do you "take it on faith" or do you make some effort to establish that it has a basis in observed fact?

Do you believe it is wiser to accept every statement that comes from high authority than to check such statements wherever possible against the facts?

If you were presented with a map which differed very materially from what you saw yourself in the territory, would you follow the map as if it carried more weight?

Do you make a practice of believing what you are told, and do you place more weight on the "maps" given you by others than those you make yourself?

Do you reserve to yourself the right to question any statement or pronouncement from whatever source?

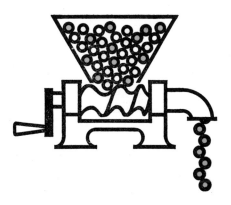

AN EXCEEDINGLY COMPLEX MACHINE

GIVEN the human brain, with its extraordinary tool, language, and we have a marvellous machine; more marvellous than most of us realize.

Some time ago the designer of a rather complex electronic "reasoning machine" explained rather apologetically that he called his creation a "little moron," though in fact the machine was not able even to accomplish the one-thousandth part of the functioning of a human moron. Some of the work that has been done and is being done with electronic computers suggests the ways by which the human mind operates. But no one has even hinted that any such machine is capable of the characteristic human abstracting, reasoning, etc.

Your brain and mine is stored with thousands and tens of thousands of direct observations; a memory covering all the things you have seen, heard, smelt, tasted or otherwise experienced. You have these low order "maps," and then layer after layer of abstraction derived from them, sorting them into categories, sometimes interlocking. Then you have the logical derivatives of these stored impressions, resulting in a further storage of "conclusions" and "inferences," and "opinions," "judgments," etc. You compare maps with maps, maps with new territories. You change maps, that is you change your impression of a reality that has changed or that you have re-examined; and if you are using your abstractive machinery intelligently, you change your judgments and your opinions in line with whatever new evidence appears that may require such changes.

Some of the judgments and opinions could be called your "values," and you may have a very definite scale of values, covering thousands and tens of thousands of items.

Every time you spend a nickel for a newspaper you have to make a value decision. Whether the nickel will be worth more invested in the daily paper or kept for some other purpose. People are continually weighing whether to buy a new television set or a living room table, or whether to take the trip to Florida this winter or have a vacation of fishing in Maine next summer.

There are all kinds of value decisions. We might have to decide whether to stand the toothache or go and see the dentist. It could be a question of whether to enjoy an evening at home, or gain the approval of the P.T.A. committee by attending the meeting. Undoubtedly a murderer must balance the value he places on slaughtering his enemy against the chances of getting caught and punished.

There are some *kinds* of value that are more highly valued than others. Most of us are quite aware of the valuation we place on our homes, our cars, money in the bank. We think of these things as "material" possessions, and if we studied economics in school we have learned to think of these values as inspiring the really important drives in human conduct.

You have, very likely, plodded through the classic books on economics. You are probably familiar with the concepts of "marginal producers," "law of diminishing returns," "supply and demand," and the like. It is possible to figure out pretty well how commerce and industry will develop, which businesses will prosper, which fail, and how humanity will fare under the particular system under study.

There is, no doubt, a great deal of truth in economic theory; and it is sometimes useful to isolate a certain system of forces and study it as if there were nothing else in the world. This is the useful (and valid) method we use in studying mechanism, where gears are considered to fit without the slightest backlash and to operate without any friction at all. We learn, in physics, about the behavior of "rigid bodies," though we know perfectly well there are no such completely rigid bodies in the real world. We set up fictions; we say that this or that behaves "as if" it were like this diagram. So long as we understand that these fictions are merely means of expressing *abstractions* we can use them and arrive at very practical conclusions with their help.

In other words, when we say that for the purpose of studying the relative motion of certain gears, links, levers, etc., we will disregard the weight, structural strength, friction, etc., of the parts, we have a right to do this. We will be making "a map," as it were, of the mechanism, and as you know, a map is never "a thing," and a map never shows *all* about what it represents.

In the same way we can talk about "economic motives" without complicating the problem by talking about some of the *un*-economic forces that also operate in human affairs. We can abstract certain points about the economic behavior of man, and up to a point the abstraction or map we have drawn will have a certain validity. That is, it will have a certain one-to-one correspondence with the facts "out there."

You can show that a hungry man will work hard for a sirloin steak. You can prove that he won't be willing to work quite so hard for a second steak; and that his appetite (and his incentive) will vary inversely with the number of steaks consumed. You can point up a great many of the true situations in life and business by means of economic theory.

But it leaves such a vast amount unexplained! Most of us are conscious of the inadequacy of ordinary economics when we say (without much conviction) that "Money isn't everything."

And yet (here is one of those elephants that is practically blocking the front stoop, which we cannot see at all), we are taught to act "as if" money *were* everything. This "as if" is not quite so valid as some of the others we mentioned before. We say "Money isn't everything," but then if someone we know happens to prefer skin-diving or water color painting to holding down a good job we feel there must be something wrong with him.

Sometimes, you know, people turn down money. It is not the "highest" value in our life.

The chances are you would not be willing to set a price on one of your eyes, in dollars. You would not want to dicker with a cannibal agent for one of your children of tender age. There are a great many things you would not trade for money, and which, although they are of enormous value to you, you could not even express in terms of money.

Suppose that someone offered you a good price to insult and abuse all your friends. How many dollars would it be worth to lose the respect and goodwill of all these friends? What price to make it worthwhile to be an outcast, hated and avoided?

Surely the opinion of others is valuable; and yet it comes quite outside the ordinary laws of economics.

You could, you know, have the respect of many people, and also draw a very good income, say if you were willing to become a spy for some foreign country. For how much would you be willing to sell out your self-respect?

How much of a motive is the preservation and enhancement of your "self"; not your body, but the non-material part of you, the part that does the thinking and the feeling and the abstracting and evaluating.

There are a good many sociologists and psychologists who believe (as I do myself, and as I think you will if you think it over) that this value is at the very top of the heap.

Men will work for money, fight for material gain, plot and struggle to gain the respect of others.

But any man will defend his "self," as he sees it, with his money, his property, his family, his reputation, and the life of his physical body if necessary.

It is the need for survival of this "self," not the physical body, that constitutes the greatest drive that actuates people. This is the highest "value" we have.

You will understand that what makes up "survival" of the self, what enhances it, what preserves it, may not be the same for you as for the man across the street.

What is being defended and enhanced in each case is the particular set of values held by each individual. These values, as we have seen, are derived from long series of abstracting. We see, we hear, etc. We learn. We abstract certain observations. We generalize and group these, and compare them with other groups from other experience.

We notice similarities, and if we are unusually perceptive, we notice the important differences. By logic we arrive at certain conclusions, and these lead to attitudes which express themselves in opinions, judgments, etc. And these very high abstractions are our "values"; collectively, they constitute our "value system"; and indeed they *are* the "self" we have become.

The man across the street may be a pickpocket working out at the race track. It is possible, and even probable, that he may have so directed his abstractive processes that he believes the world is "all crooked," and he is only getting what he is entitled to, and that after all he is supporting a wife and two children. He has made it look pretty good.

He has to make it look pretty good. If he did not, he would have to face the unpleasant truth about his standing in the community and the real nature of his livelihood.

Your neighbor next door, on the other hand, may be a conscientious and dedicated physician, who not only supports a wife and children, but also brings new hope to patients who need his expert help.

He also makes it look pretty good. And he has to, also, for the preservation of his "self" is important to him, too.

Of course, from your own point of view, the physician may be "noble," and the pickpocket "contemptible." But bear in mind that these are simply your own words of judgment, the pigeonholes into which you have thrown these men. You are simply classifying the maps according to your own frame of reference.

We said that these people "have to make it look pretty good." We all know that there is much more, so much more, about anyone than we can abstract in a few contacts or by a few words. ("So much good in the worst of us; so much bad in the best of us, etc.") The pickpocket, if we knew more of the facts, might, even according to our own private set of values appear to be actuated by "noble" motives. And we could, no doubt, find more than one "contemptible" factor in the high-minded medico.

This is not the place to get into a detailed discussion of intrapersonal relations.

But a man will make his "self" look good, even if all rational attempts fail, and he has to "become" the Emperor Napoleon or Jesus Christ to do it.

QUESTIONS FOR CONSIDERATION

When you "jump to a conclusion" do you ever delay taking action until you have studied the steps by which you arrived at that conclusion? Are you aware of the errors that can come about through confusing things on the basis of similarities, or confusing different orders of abstraction, or confusing "opinions" with "facts in external reality," etc.

Have you ever made an investment decision on the basis of "snap judgment" which later turned out to be an unwise one? Where did your "snap judgment" come from? Was it perhaps based on faulty or obsolete premises? Would it have helped if you had delayed action until you had gone over these points? Why do salesmen of worthless stocks always insist that you "act now, without delay"?

Is money "everything" to you? Is money "nothing" to you?

Are there important values in your life which cannot be expressed in money at all? Would you say that these are the most important values of all?

How important is your "self" to you? When you buy stock, or give your wife a present, or quit your job, does your "self-respect" or "self-esteem" come into the picture? To what degree?

Do you tend to overlook or forget your "self" sometimes? Have you been taught that "selflessness" is a "good" thing? Do you often feel "self-reproach"; do you try to "think only of others"; do you regard yourself as "small" or "unimportant"; do you consider yourself "unworthy"? Do these attitudes help you to become more self-confident?

Do you feel that continual disparagement of yourself is likely to lead to your becoming a better citizen, better parent, or better investor?

Do you customarily sell yourself short?

LAYERS OF AWARENESS

IN MOST business offices, the active current correspondence will be found in folders or baskets on the various desks. Letters that have been answered, with the copies of the replies, will go into the regular files. And from time to time the contents of some of these files is carried down to the store-room in transfer cases.

As you know, most of the active work centers around today's mail or at any rate, this week's mail. Now and then we have to refer to the file cabinets. Very, very seldom do we have to trudge down to the storeroom.

And yet, those old papers are important, too. Perhaps the original charter of the company is in a safe in the storeroom. The transfer files contain important records, contracts, communications, etc., which may have to be used at any time.

It is very much that way with your mind. You know this, too, of course. The things that dominate your consciousness are mostly the activities of the day. You think about what you are doing. Sometimes you recall things a few days ago, or plan for next week.

But really there is a lot going on around you, some of which concerns you, of which you are not particularly aware. If your attention is focused on listening to a phonograph record you may be entirely oblivious of a hissing radiator. Oblivious in one sense, and yet, strangely enough, not entirely oblivious either, for if someone jogs your elbow and asks you if you hear the radiator hissing you will realize that you have been hearing it, some part of you has been hearing it, all along.

Perhaps you have had the experience of reading the stock tape on a trans-lux screen. You are particularly interested in some certain stocks. You are checking the prices of these and not watching for any others. In fact if someone asked you to name several other stocks and their prices you might have some difficulty remembering any particular ones. And yet if someone in the board room should suddenly inquire, "Has anybody seen any "XYZ"?, you might startle yourself by popping out with, "I saw 800 shares about ten minutes ago at 43-5/8."

Now where did this come from? How did something you never "saw" break into consciousness on command?

It is almost as if the senses were abstracting information all the time even without our own knowledge.

And actually that seems to be about what happens. While you are reading the book you are picking up peripheral data on comings and goings of the family dog, the gradual changes of light with the approach of evening, the sound of automobile horns outside, the neighbor's telephone ringing; and all these things are being "watched" in a sense, without any effort on your part, and without your even realizing that they are being watched. You would say, for instance, that the miscellaneous sounds around you were "going in one ear and out the other," but that is not quite true. For you may have already discovered, as many of us have, that you can "remember" things not consciously observed if they are later jogged to mind.

There are layers of consciousness, and this is surely not the place to start probing the deep layers of the sub-conscious.

But it is important to keep in mind that down in the transfer files, covered with dust these many years, there may be some vital and important records.

If you have a little time and are interested in trying the experiment, you might select a period of your life about which you "remember" very little (say when you were four or five years old): and take the few little bits of remembered places and people and what you did; and see what else you can connect to them. You may discover a rich and fascinating story buried these many years.

I did this a year or so ago in connection with the time when I was four or five years old. I had only a few sketchy memories of the small Montana town where we lived at that time. I could see the saw mill at Hamilton, the riffles of the Bitter Root River fast-flowing and shallow over piles of rounded stones. The back-waters with the current swirling in circles and finally running again into the main stream; and the quiet pools where black pollywogs wiggled along a yellow-brown bottom. The mill pond and the lumberjacks jumping from log to log, guiding the great trunks to the incline where they would be hauled up slowly to disappear into the whining, screaming mill. The sawdust burner, like a great silo, smouldering gently through a rounded dome. Winter; and skating on the mill pond. The stakes and signs set out where ice was thin; the cold walk home.

And on, and on, and on. The Ravalli Hotel; what it looked like; the arrangement of the dining room; the appearance of the daily menus. Cutting little cardboard sleds out of old menu cards. Main Street. The Marcus Daly Ranch. Walter Gregory's camp; and Dr. Buchann's. The great wall of the Bitter Root Range looming above the valley mile after mile.

How much to recall. I don't know. I have written many pages on just this setting and just this time; always with the feeling that there is so much more to write: not forgotten, not lost, merely stored away in the downstairs transfer files.

And you will find, too, I am sure, if you try it, that there is more in those old files than you realize. You will gradually recall the faces and scenes of many years ago, you will remember the names of friends you played with before you went to kindergarten, you will realize that although you have covered up these old impressions for so long, the perceptions of a young mind are durable; they last a long time.

And just how durable they are you may know if you have a very aged relative. It is a very common experience for old people to "live in the past." My Aunt Esther Putnam couldn't remember whether I had come to visit her yesterday or three weeks ago. As a matter of fact she often confused me with both my Uncle John and my Uncle Howard. She saw and heard what happened today, but her tired old mind did not abstract very much that was new, and what she did take in was not impressed very deeply.

Ask her about her trips into Mexico with her late husband, however! Pick up a little Mexican bowl, or a piece of raw turquoise, or a set of rattlesnake rattles! Aunt Esther could tell you just where she and Professor Putnam found this bowl, about when it was made, and what tribal patterns it carried. She could give you dates and places and a wealth of detail on her treasures. All these things were abstracted at a time when Aunt Esther's mind was very active and very impressionable. What we learn young we learn well. It sticks by us.

And while we have spoken of re-calling times when we were four or five years old and learning fast, you must realize that by the time you were four you had already learned a great deal. You had learned to walk and climb and scrub your own back, and generally make your body do what you wanted it to do. And you had learned to use your eyes, to recognize the faces of people important in your life; and to know who was "with" you and who was "agin" you. You had learned about lollypops, and bean shooters, birds' nests, running through the lawn spray, how to play some games, how to fight, you knew colors, you had learned to like some kinds of music. And very importantly, you had learned to speak and understand the wonderful system of communication we call "language."

Along with all that, we acquired the basis for a good many judgments and opinions. At four years of age we knew what was "funny" and what was "naughty," what was "nasty" and what was "nice." Sometimes we can learn by direct experience, the "burned finger and hot stove" process by which it is recognized that a certain course of action is likely to lead to certain desirable or undesirable results.

As a matter of fact the child of four is perfectly able to make chains of abstraction on matters that concern him. Suppose, for instance, that a rather tough bully from the Third Grade, who usually wore a red coat, cut through the yard every afternoon after school. The four-year-old is quite capable of understanding the threat, and getting out of the way, along with any toys or rolling stock, when this character looms at the side fence. He is also very likely to take refuge if *any* boy wearing a red coat appears suddenly along the fence at about three o'clock. And he might even go so far as to pack up his equipment and move indoors a little while before school lets out, just to be on the safe side.

We are not going to suggest that he would necessarily shy away from red coats for the rest of his life, nor that he would become apprehensive in mid afternoon after he was grown up; since normally as he had broader experience he would learn that "red coat" and "three o'clock" were not the sources of the danger in themselves.

But where an impression has been made, very strongly, on a young mind, and through deliberate teaching and repetition has been etched deeply; and where there has been no word of experience or teaching to modify the original impression; then this will remain unchanged, either conscious or unconscious or deeply sub-conscious.

Many of the concepts we have called "opinions" and "judgments" are taught this way. They are learned and well learned; and never seriously contradicted. They are high-order abstractions, symbols, maps; not "things" at all. But they are as durable as "things," and in fact more durable than most things.

These are the words that often relate very closely to our inter-personal and intra-personal relations. "Good," and "bad," "sneaky," "generous," "evasive," are words of this type, associated with social concepts and usually carrying a very strong aura of approval or disapproval.

One of the most dramatic demonstrations of "early learning" and how it sticks with us, occurs sometimes in connection with the sense of smell. It is too bad, you know, that we do not have any systematic education of the sense of smell; in fact you might almost call it the "neglected" sense. We have no very satisfactory nomenclature for odors. People usually ignore the odors that surround them; and except for politely sniffing a lilac or syringa once or twice a season, we don't go out of our way consciously to use this means of abstracting from the "world of reality."

Smells are generally in disrepute. We think of the stink of chemical labs, of railway station wash rooms, of garbage trucks on a hot day. People avoid a room that is "exposed to cooking odors" over the kitchen. And even perfumes compounded for our delectation are tinged with the pervasive condemnation that we attach to "lusts of the flesh." The sense of smell is treated as a poor relation amongst the senses; not only a poor relation, but a somewhat disreputable one, like a drunken cousin in a family. Smells, generally, are regarded with solid disapproval; and we are not encouraged to train and develop this important sense.

We speak of the sense of smell. You hear a great deal about the "aroma" of coffee, especially the particular brand that is being touted on your TV or radio. Actually, we sell short our sense of smell, we neglect it, it is given very little attention in our culture. And yet, even without cultivation, we do have this sense, and even without training it operates to some extent, and ties into the great perceptive machinery of our minds.

The "aroma" of coffee. If you want to bring back the original connotations, try grinding a few coffee beans in a hand grinder (as we do every morning for breakfast). Put your nose down in the little receptacle where lies the fresh-ground coffee. What kind of a map does this call for?

Remember now, no stimulus can recall anything that was not previously "recorded." And I have no doubt that the rich odor of the ground coffee would call forth in my children a picture of the East Longmeadow Super Market. That would be the map related to that stimulus, for them.

But for me, and perhaps for you, this olfactory stimulus will recall elaborate maps of other stores, in other places, at other times. It will take me into a narrow store each side of whose sawdust sprinkled floor is bordered by long ranges of counters. Back of some of these counters are black japanned bins, lettered in gold, containing coffee and tea of various sorts. And on the counter in front is a large grinding mill, operated by turning a handle on a big wheel at the side. Mr. Van Heule stands there, cheerful and rotund, ready to grind the pound of coffee and pour it from the metal scoop under the grinder, into a paper bag. Nearer the front are boxes of fancy crackers, eighteen-inch cubes open at the top, or perhaps covered with a lid of glass. In a space behind the counter there are barrels of more ordinary crackers, and in front of the counter near the door there are several small kegs containing dried prunes, apricots, etc. Opposite and towards the rear is the meat counter, with its scale and pile of weights, and the butcher ready to suggest, "we have some nice pork chops today, Mrs. Magee. Or would you want some halibut?" Overhead, in the gloom of the high ceiling revolve slowly the enormous fans, like leisurely helicopters. And one knows that, come mid-afternoon, Charlie will be hollering up the back entry, "Grocery boy!" as he lugs the wooden box full of today's provisions.

All this from a whiff of fresh-ground coffee. All this and so much more, from a "map," and an obsolete map at that.

You would think that in the matter of human relations, including your own self-evaluation, it might be important to reduce high order judgments wherever possible, to something as close as possible to reality.

You might tell me that Sam Goodman is "generous." I would know more about him, and would have a better basis for making an intelligent opinion myself if you told me precisely what he did that led you to this opinion. Where and when was he generous? And just exactly what was the action as you observed it at that time and place.

You might say Dave is dishonest, since he told his wife he mailed the gas bill Monday when actually he didn't mail it until Wednesday. And you might consider Mike dishonest since he is a professional safe-blower.

The words are the same: "dishonest." But the situation in reality is nowhere near the same. We have taken two dissimilar events and created an "identity" which is purely verbal.

And yet we all learned these "judgment" words and "opinion" words, and some expressions of approval or disapproval that are not expressed in words, at a very early age. They are drilled into us, and they constitute a major part of our "value system," by which we evaluate the world, the people we meet, and most especially, ourselves.

The saddest part of this is that when it becomes a question of "going by the map" or "checking with the territory," many, possibly most people will choose the map instead of the territory.

And you will probably agree that among the worst offenders (and the word "offenders" is used advisedly) are the well-meaning parents, the priests (including all ministers and rabbis), the teachers, and the lawyers. For these are the moulders of the culture; the custodians of the home, the church, the school, and the state. And they are still, in the main, oriented to a philosophy of high order abstractions.

As we "learn" we become trained to move away from reality toward these higher abstractions. This is all right so long as we also learn that we are making this move. But we are not taught that we are making any move at all.

For instance, in defining any object we learn to put it into higher and higher order categories. If I ask you what "it" is, you tell me "Bozo." And what is "Bozo"? A "Labrador retriever." And a Labrador retriever is a "dog." And a "dog" is a "mammal." And a "mammal" is an "animal." We are not clearly taught that the "is" which suggests identity at each stage is simply throwing "Bozo," "dog," "mammal," etc. into bigger boxes, vaguer categories. Is it any wonder that we confuse things on the basis of similarities, when we are not *taught* to look for the differences. Is it any wonder we cannot see things clearly when we are *taught* to look far away from the reality.

If you have a personal problem, like getting a job or paying your bills, you may be able to solve it by studying your own resources. And if you cannot, you can take it up with your family who may be able to advise you or to provide some material help. If no family help is available, then you can apply to a city agency (we are moving away from you and your particular, immediate problem, are we not?). If the city agency is not able to help, then you can go to the state. This may involve more red tape, and some misunderstandings may arise, and you may feel rather regimented (and why not, for you are moving away from the world of your individual problem). If the state is powerless to aid you, you can write your congressman, and see if some federal agency can lend a hand. And if that, too, fails, you can petition the United Nations. And if nothing is forthcoming there you can "lift up your eyes unto the hills."

Now there is a place for close observation and attention to detail; and there is a place for highly abstract generalities. But in the case of getting a job today so you can pay the landlady for the room and buy some new shoes, which is closer to the reality of your problem: to get out and answer the ads and check the employment agencies; or to lift up your eyes unto the hills?

We are taught that "mammal" is more important than "Bozo"; that "mankind" is more important than "me"; that principles are more important than actions. We are *taught* to move *away* from the evidence in external reality.

QUESTIONS FOR CONSIDERATION

Do you realize how much is going on around you of which you are not, at the moment, conscious?

Do you understand that a great deal of "knowledge" can be assimilated (abstracted) without much conscious awareness, and that a good deal of what was once consciously learned has been put out of consciousness.

Would you say that some of the "unexplainable" actions you have taken may be due to values and attitudes which are not sharply present in your consciousness?

Is it possible that you have made quick decisions on investments, job problems or home matters on the basis of underlying attitudes which you take for granted and which may have become matters of habit with you?

Would it be worth while to stop and examine the decision-making attitudes now and then, especially when they concern important questions? Could some of these attitudes be so out of line with the present facts as to be dangerously misleading?

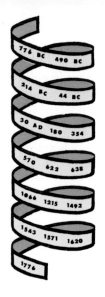

TIME BINDING

THERE is more than one way to learn. As we have already seen, we can learn from direct experience and observation, that is, by looking at things, touching them, smelling them, etc., and we can learn by being "taught," either by a teacher, or from reading in books.

We can also "learn," in a sense, by combining the things we have experienced or observed, or read, or that we have been taught by others, to obtain new ideas and new solutions to problems, and new ways to go about things. We can take the knowledge we have previously abstracted and construct new knowledge through logic, inference, deduction, etc.

However, at the base of such higher order abstractions there must be a solid foundation of lower order information.

And this basic information we could classify roughly as that which we have directly experienced or observed, and that which has been communicated to us from others.

In the first category is all the seeing and listening and trial-and-error "finding out" which must play an enormous part in the learning a child acquires in the first few years.

In the second category is all that is passed on by others. The child gets his share of this through the commands and punishments and expressions of approval or disapproval from his parents. "Don't leave your rubbers in the living room!"; "People won't like you if you go around looking like that!"; "You should *love* your little sister!"; etc.

The child, indeed, is deluged with "don'ts" from dawn to dark, and in the first two or three years he has had knocked into him a good deal of education, a large part of which is in the form of "directives"; the things he should or should not do. The child gets something of a course in "How to Make Friends and Influence People," especially how to make friends with and influence the parents. And eventually the directives that are repeatedly banged into him will assume the character of "values." He will learn that these are the ways one must live in order to win approval and not to get into trouble. He will acquire a sense of "right" and a sense of "wrong." And he will not only judge others by these "values." He will also judge how he will "rate" with other people; and, most particularly, he will tend to "rate" himself, using the same values as a standard.

Along with these "value" elements, the child is also being taught other things. How to count, the letters of the alphabet, the names of the various kinds of flowers and trees and animals, stories, songs, jokes, games, bits of family history, and a thousand and one other things which cannot be directly observed, but must be expressed in language, and which are communicated in words from the parents to the child.

As the child learns to read, he is able to take in these communications from others without the others being present.

It is just at this point that his human-ness breaks off sharply from that of the little beaver or the bear cubs These other creatures learn from direct experience, they are taught and are given directives by their parents (though not in the rich detail possible to mankind with the tool of language).

But there is no animal that ever lived that has been able to accomplish the great miracle of the written language.

With this tool the child can learn from his parents even when they are not in the room. He can read their messages even if they should take a trip a thousand miles away.

Not only that; and here is the greatest miracle of all: The child can learn from men who are *no longer living*. When a smart beaver dies, his mind dies with him. But when a great human thinker dies, his thoughts live on in the pages of his writing, so that a thousand years later a student can have the benefit of that great one's own thinking.

You and I have a pipe-line to the past. We do not have to count entirely on the hard experience of trial and error to learn about life. For we have not only the means of communication with our parents, teachers, and others, but we can reach back ten years, a hundred years, five hundred years, and communicate with the philosophers, and teachers, and law-givers of other times.

This is "time-binding," as Korzybski calls it.

It means that once we have acquired the use of the written language we can literally tap "the wisdom of the ages." It is not necessary for each of us personally to perform the experiment which has been made by someone who came before us. To a very great degree we are freed from the need of "starting from scratch." It is as if, instead of a young man having to earn his way from the start, and painstakingly build up a fund of savings, he was presented at the age of fifteen with a key to the world's treasure.

In our hands, and in our children's hands lies the key to a very great treasure. To the stored-up knowledge and experience of the ages. In books, and scrolls, and papyri, on clay tablets and inscribed on the walls of temples and caves, the thoughts of men have been preserved. They are all ours if we can read them.

What this means, of course, is that we are able to start where others left off. If it was necessary for each of us to work out the theory of mathematics from scratch, we would have no mathematics. It is only because we have the record of the step-by-step development of number concept and mathematical theory over the centuries that we are able in a few years to master mathematics that go far beyond the abilities of the greatest mathematicians in ancient times. We have all this, not only in mathematics, but in every department of human knowledge. It is a wonderful treasure; an unbelievably rich treasure.

And if we are able to start our life work where the greatest minds in human history left off, then we should be able to add something to human knowledge. It is not necessary, and it is not expected, that each of us will revolutionize the sciences. But, with a whole lifetime to live, and with the wisdom of the past handed to us on a silver platter, doesn't it seem possible that some of us might be able to add one crumb of knowledge; to add some little contribution to the mighty mass of humanity's treasure?

This opportunity to add something entirely new is a great challenge. It offers a chance to achieve security, a feeling of success and well-being in our own lifetime, and a chance to pass on to our children a little increment to the most important part of their inheritance.

This opportunity for "time binding" is also a way of immortality. The new discovery, the original theorem that you or I or someone else can add to human knowledge is not just for today. It becomes a part of the body of human knowledge that will remain and be a substantial asset to our children's children's children.

QUESTIONS FOR CONSIDERATION

Do you learn from direct observation of the world around you?

Do animals learn in this way?

Do you learn from books and records representing the observations and thoughts of other men?

Do animals learn in this way?

Is it possible to form opinions on the basis of direct observation or on the basis of what is learned from books, or on both?

What are some of the advantages of our inherited body of learning?

What are some of the disadvantages of adhering solely to it?

In case of a disagreement between the "learning of the past" and what we can observe and check here and now, which would carry the greater authority with you?

If the president of Chase Manhattan bank gave out an opinion which was contrary to your own conclusions based on direct observations of fact would you defer to his "superior knowledge" without question?

Do you make all or most of your decisions on the basis of precepts and directives laid down by others, or to what extent do you try to use these authoritative pronouncements only as a tentative guide subject to your own final evaluation?

To what extent do you tend to assume that the printed word, the statement of high authority, or the opinion of a majority must be "right"?

Do you believe it is wise to reject all the experiences and knowledge of others who have studied a subject? Can you be free to accept whatever part of such knowledge proves useful, and to modify or reject whatever does not fit the present facts as observed by you?

STOP! LOOK! LISTEN!

ALL this about the "time-binding" sounds as if we had something wonderful here. And so we do. Provided that we know exactly what we have and what to do with it.

You will remember, when we were talking about low abstractions and high abstractions, that there were times when it was good to creep up close and take direct observations from a near reality. And other cases where it would be most help to stand away some distance and view the territory in an abstract way. Both ways, and all steps in between, are all right and may be useful in their place. But it is important to be conscious of what order of abstraction we are using, so as not to become confused.

Now there is a similar warning that must apply to this matter of "time-binding."

It is a wonderful thing to be able to reach into the past and learn from great-grandfather, or Benjamin Franklin, or Euclid, or Confucius.

But if we become dazzled by the prospects that open up to us in tapping the wisdom of the ages, we may forget to do any time-binding ourselves.

Notice one or two things about the "time-binding." For one, everything that comes down to us in written form is in the form of symbols, words, that is. Symbols are maps, which are supposed to represent a territory in some significant respects. But because they are abstractions of higher order, they are not as detailed as the territory. They leave out a good deal. They cannot fully represent what they denote.

Again, some of the "verbal maps" that come down to us from the past may be "maps of maps." Where a writer is pursuing a chain of logic or inference, or where he is discussing something that is a matter of "judgment" or "opinion," then it is not possible for him to communicate his meaning even as well or precisely as he might describe an animal, or person. It is none too easy for us to communicate such matters of judgment and opinion even between our contemporary neighbors who have been educated in a common culture and idiom. But in dealing with material that comes from the past and perhaps from another part of the earth, in a greatly different kind of culture, it is more than possible that what the writer means by "rational," or "wicked," or "holy," or "treacherous" may be quite different from what we might mean by the same words today.

This is because we are dealing with a system of symbols that is not necessarily the same as our own in meaning. It is similar to the problem of a translator who finds that it is sometimes impossible to render the meaning of what some author has set down, in another language based on different cultural values. It is also because the concepts of "what is treacherous" or "what is rational," etc. may be different here and now than they were there and then.

And there is another point that we must keep in mind before we open our minds indiscriminately to the inherited writings of times gone by.

The territories may have changed! As you know, one of the vital pieces of data about a map is, "When was it made?" Of two carefully drawn maps representing a particular area, we must choose the most recent; the one that shows the latest changes in the territory. The 1958 road map of Western Massachusetts is a better guide than the 1940 edition. For one thing, the newer map shows the new turnpike, the new South End Bridge at Springfield, and a great many other features that will not show on the 1940 edition.

An ancient historian may describe a city located on an island in a great river. Today, the city may be no more than a monument and walls, and the river may have changed its course by several miles. The description is valid, so long as we assign the correct date to it. But it is not as good a map of this part of the world today as a recent map published by the National Geographic Society.

The territories may have changed! We are familiar with the elaborate "maps" of human conduct presented in the Book of Leviticus; directives and injunctions covering hundreds of aspects of human life; marriage laws, dietary laws, laws relating to property and inheritance, laws relating to hygiene and public health, etc., etc.

The importance laid on these laws and directives suggests that at the time they were first set down they were regarded as of great practical importance, vitally related to the very survival of the Jewish people.

Today many scholars recognize that the conditions that required some of these laws no longer exist or have changed to a degree where they no longer apply as they were originally stated.

In the heritage of science and philosophy that has come down to us we find a good deal that will not stand up; some because it is inadequate and newer discoveries have made revision necessary; some because the hypotheses on which it was based have been supplanted by newer hypotheses which more nearly fit the observed facts; and some (let us face it) because it was sheer nonsense in the first place and never had very much validity at all.

It implies no disrespect to the scholars of years past to suggest that their findings should be brought up-to-date in line with changed conditions, or to include the discoveries of their successors. After all, these pioneer time-binders did the hard work of breaking ground into unknown territory. Chemists worked without formulas, without any knowledge of the elements. Astronomers tried to solve the riddles of immeasurable space without the simplest kind of telescope. Mathematicians labored to solve impossible problems, not having the knowledge to prove that what they sought was not to be found. We must take off our hats to these men who out of a wilderness of ignorance blasted the first narrow trails of understanding. As we travel the broad highway of modern science and philosophy we should not, really, sneer at the wandering, uncertain courses of these ancient trails. For it was over the paths of alchemy and astrology that the pioneer scientists travelled to discover chemistry and astronomy. And in almost every field of thought the early stages were filled with stumbling and error.

A few hundred or a few thousand years ago time-binding was not so easy as it is today. It was not simply that men did not have Linotype machines and high-speed presses, excellently printed books, public libraries in every city and town, and all the machinery of setting down and reproducing knowledge that we have at our command today. But there was also the fact that without the labor-saving devices we take for granted it was not possible for very many men to spend their lives in study, contemplation, or writing. Leisure to learn was a luxury that very few could enjoy.

Under those conditions, it is hardly surprising that when a great teacher or philosopher appeared, his work was valued as something irreplaceable. Such a leader might not come again for generations. It would be most important to preserve the important work of this man, his sayings, teachings, discoveries, so far as it was possible. In the very ancient days, the wisdom of such a sage would be passed on by word of mouth, father telling son and son, in turn, telling *his* son.

Consider the danger here of *losing* the irreplaceable wisdom. Nothing could be added to information; it could only be passed on intact. And any slight alteration might change the original meaning; if a single word were dropped or changed in any way, who could say after a few generations *how much* had been deleted or distorted.

And so, with such knowledge, a certain rigidity was inevitable. The "words" became of paramount importance, and it was not permitted to suggest any revision. The present conditions could not be surveyed in order to bring the ancient knowledge into line with current facts. Changes in custom or in the use of language would not justify tampering with the irreplaceable wisdom.

And so, in the futile hope of preserving alive the living message of the past, men frequently found themselves worshipping the tattered relic of obsolete science, obsolete ethics, and obsolete law.

We are very much concerned with this, because a good deal of our educational process has been rather heavily tinged with this kind of sterile time-binding.

In other words we have an altogether disproportionate and unrealistic respect for the knowledge of the past.

A proper understanding of the real value of what comes down to us from the ages takes account of the errors and losses in transmission, and those of translation. It allows for the changes in conditions, and for the later knowledge which has made obsolete some of the original findings. And it puts to work the great treasure of accumulated knowledge on the practical basis that it will be used where the presumption is strong that it was valid in the first place, and where no later discoveries have nullified it.

We will use as much of the "old" knowledge as will stand up under examination.

And here is the rule for testing: If some theory or proposition from the past is presented to you, see if it is reasonable in the light of other information you have.   If it seems valid in theory, put it to the test of practical experience today and see how it works.   If it still stands up, then use it.   If it does not entirely meet today's conditions, see what changes might bring it into line to make it currently valid.

One of the contributions we can make to time-binding is this process of re-examination and revision.   For we will not be honoring ourselves nor our ancestors if we merely "accept" and stupidly apply the directives and opinions of centuries ago without "checking the map" and making necessary amendments to bring it up-to-date.

QUESTIONS FOR CONSIDERATION

When you are following an old road map do you keep your eyes open for recognizable landmarks? If you find some great discrepancy between the map and the countryside do you stop and check up on the route as it is today?

Do you feel that there has been no progress during the past fifty years in understanding the stock market?

Do you feel that there has been no progress during the past five hundred years in understanding the structure of nature, movements of the planets, growth of plants, chemical elements, etc.?

Do you feel that there has been no progress during the past thousand years in philosophy, ethics, and the social relations of man?

Would you say that mankind was "younger" five hundred years ago or five thousand years ago than it is today? Would you expect that with the "time binding" by which knowledge can be stored and passed on, mankind has more knowledge today, or less, or the same, as it had in "the good old days"?

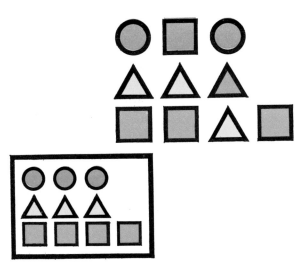

CONTRADICTIONS

SOMETIME very early in life we have, each of us, run up against the problem of the old-time wisdom versus the immediate evidence of our senses. We find ourselves forced to reconcile what we can "see," "hear," and "touch" ourselves, with the weighty pronouncements of ancient wisdom. And if we are quite young, and have been taught to "respect our elders," we are very likely to repudiate what we have learned by direct experience and accept what we read or what we are taught, on the basis that "it would be presumptuous for innocent, unlettered little me to disagree with the great philosopher."

Of course, it is quite possible that you will be selling yourself short unnecessarily. For we can admit Aristotle's "greatness" without accepting every piece of nonsense he ever wrote. After all, Aristotle did not have the instruments and formulas that we have to help him. He did not have so much time-binding back of him to make his way easier. And in many ways the average high school lad today, equipped and trained as he is, may be expected to have more understanding of some of the great problems of mankind and the universe than Aristotle ever possessed; in much the same way and for much the same reasons that the modern jet plane pilot can muster more strength for his attack than Hannibal and all his elephants.

When you hear or read a statement from an ancient authority you can honor it. You do not need to scoff at it or repudiate it out of hand. But you have more than the right to check it and verify it in every possible way; for that is your clear duty if you expect to make any practical use of the information.

But we are not always taught to make these checks and verifications. No; on the contrary, we are often taught *not* to check or verify.

We are taught to accept the ancient authority without question!

We are taught to go by the map rather than the territory!

We are taught that if there is a discrepancy between the map (high authority) and the territory (current observation), that it is "better" to accept the map than the territory it is supposed to represent!

You are familiar with the Hans Christian Anderson story of the Emperor's new clothes. Briefly, two swindlers had convinced the court and the emperor himself that the new suit they were making up for him would be visible only to the pure in heart. Under the fear of disapproval everyone "saw" the fine new clothes; and it was not until a little boy asked why the emperor was marching through the streets stark naked that the people admitted the truth. In other words, if the high authority says the emperor is wearing a fine new suit, and the eyes show that he is naked, a good many people will reject the evidence of observation and cling to the pronouncements of the high authority.

Every child is faced with the conflicts between what he is told or what he reads, and what he actually observes. In civics or social studies he is taught how, in a democracy, the people vote freely and select the best qualified men for public office, abiding loyally by the decision whatever it may be. Perhaps it would be natural for a very young child to accept such statements, for he would have had no opportunity to observe for himself.

But it is hard to understand how grown men can continue to cherish this noble fiction and defend it as if it were the actual truth; even while living in a city where the usual choice of candidates includes men of such obvious ignorance and corrupt association that the discrepancy is glaringly apparent. Anyone who has worked in a municipal election in Massachusetts knows that the usual candidate for any public office could not possibly be described as "the best-fitted man" by any ordinary standards.

But we continue to admire the fine, clean, beautiful map, and to reject the down-to-earth, matter-of-fact reality.

This preference of the "map" for the "territory" is so pronounced, so emphatic that it hardly seems possible anyone could fail to see it in everyday life. Yet . . . it is another of those elephants which so many of us squeeze by, crawl under, climb over, but cannot see at all.

We consider "honesty" a virtue. But there is a great deal more attention paid to whether someone is "honest" than to what he did, at some time, at some place. We speak of "generosity" as though it could be separated from particular incidents and events. We talk of "purity" as if it existed in a vacuum.

We are taught to set principles above specific acts. We are drilled to think in terms of "high aspirations" to a point where it almost seems that the high-level words are more important than how we live and what we do.

In the stock market, the question is always, "What is the market doing?" Not, "What is Southern Pacific doing?" or "What is Jones and Laughlin doing?" But, "the market." If a man asks you, "What do you think of the market?" and you answer, "Just what particular stocks are you interested in?" he will very often become quite irritated with you. He doesn't want any specific information about something we can check and verify. He wants a big, broad generality.

When we deal with the law we cannot consider the case of *this* particular man who has *these* complicated life problems and who has become involved in difficulties as a result. No! We cannot look at the man. We have to look at the label, the map. This man *is* a murderer; or he *is* a rapist. Or he *is* a burglar. Since when do we learn more about human behavior and human suffering and the solution of desperate human problems by staring at a map than we do by searching out the particular details of this one man's experience? Is Burglar "A" the same as Burglar "B"? Do we get a clearer picture of what is causing Burglar "A" to act unsocially by classing him as identical with Burglars "B" and "C" and "D"? Are we likely to arrive at a more practical solution of modern crime by limiting our study to a discussion of verbal maps crystallized into law books, dated, for the most part, before the invention of the first automobile?

Oh! But this is authority. This is precedent. This is the Wisdom of the Ages.

Very well. Credit the Wisdom of the Ages with some value. But if the Wisdom of the Ages conflicts with the facts of a teen-age gang fight on West Madison Street at 11:15 P.M., Saturday, March 29,

1958, which will it be?   Will we back the directives on the ancient map or will we take a hard look at the facts before our eyes today?

When the Voice of Authority says, "Turn the Other Cheek," and the hard facts say, "Fight for Your Life or Die," you are faced with a contradiction.   Perhaps you should follow the directive of ancient wisdom.   Perhaps you should fight for survival.   At any rate, it is necessary, when there is a contradiction, to be able to make a choice. And if your choice is already bound to the ancient wisdom *regardless* of circumstances, through long training and habit, then you cannot weigh the evidence impartially.

On the very day that this page is being written there appeared a feature article in the Sunday magazine supplement, "This Week" by a rather well-known evangelist, entitled "Why I Believe in the Devil."

The reasons given by this person for his belief are: 1. Because the Bible plainly says he exists; 2. Because I see his work everywhere; 3. Because great scholars have recognized his existence.

It seems hardly necessary to ask the question, "Is it necessarily a material fact because the Bible states it?"   We know that the Bible frequently uses metaphor and very high order symbolism.   We know that the men who set down the words in these books were not equipped to understand the external world as we are today.   This is ancient authority; but is it verifiable today?   Was it ever intended to have the material meaning this man attributes to the word "Devil"? Do we know what we are talking about?

And if "great scholars" have recognized the existence of the Devil, we must not forget that great scholars have, in their gropings toward better understanding, held to beliefs that are recognized today as absurd.   The Apostle Paul, referred to in the article as "one of the greatest Christian scholars who ever lived," lived a long time ago. Have we not learned anything about Devils in nearly two thousand years?

Isn't it clear that the writer of this article is confusing a "map" with a "territory."   He is projecting an image of a "real" Devil (that is, having material existence in the external world), and speaks as though we were observing something "out there."   Isn't it clear that "the Devil" is something that exists in men's minds, and is a very high order abstraction representing various unsocial or socially disapproved concepts in our culture.

And when the evangelist says that he sees "the Devil's work" everywhere, what does this mean, if it does not mean that he sees in the world around him various actions of people which do not fit his "maps" of proper and decent human conduct?

How can we expect men to think intelligently about their neighbors, their families, and themselves, when they are deliberately *taught* to think in terms of such high metaphor that there is no way to prove or disprove the assertions except by verbal argument? How can we expect people to cope with international problems of an atomic-age world, or with the economics of today's living, or with the stock market if they are being harangued to look not at the facts at all, but to close their eyes to the world they see before them and set their course on the basis of the mystic writings of pre-scientific sages?

It is all very well to "believe in sin," providing that we understand that we are here comparing what we see with the "map" of our own value system. But to embody "the cause of sin" in a real, tangible, personal Devil (and this evangelist is very specific on this point; he is not consciously speaking in symbols); that is teaching men to value maps more than territories. To value maps more than territories is to move away from reality. And to move away from reality is to move away from sanity.

There is a proper place for high order abstraction, and if we use the word "Devil" in quotes, to represent all that we abhor, that is all right. Just so long as we do not confuse the symbol with the external reality.

As you must know, there are millions of children today who are being taught in school, and millions of adults who are being "instructed" that, among other things, a piece of bread can be and is transformed into a piece of flesh; not as a symbolic or metaphorical representation, but as a matter of substantial fact. People in this modern world and in our own country are being taught that if the evidence of eyes and of taste, yes, and even of laboratory examination were to say "this is bread still," in the material world of external reality, they must reject the evidence of direct observation and accept the directive of ancient ritual. They are taught that it is "better" to accept and believe without question, than to "re-examine" the facts. They are taught to accept the map in preference to the territory, to reject "the world" and accept the "things of the spirit."

They are taught that it is more "blessed" *not* to have seen and yet believe, than to seek the facts in reality.

But would you say that education on a basis of faith alone, and of conformity with ancient doctrine, was a good preparation to meet the problems of a constantly changing modern world? Do you believe that the way toward a peace and brotherhood which have never been even remotely approached in the past by the philosophies of "believe and do not look" will be best served by these now when the problems of human survival have become enormously more complicated?

It is not necessary to reject the aims of high abstraction in moral and spiritual matters. But when we teach people to confuse and identify the immaterial with the material we are educating people in un-sanity, whether it is in the teaching about sex, in the home; or about "the Devil," in church; or in regard to market evaluation, or in any other department of life.

Some readers of this book will remember the to-do about vaccination. Here was a new process, intended to protect mankind from the terrible scourge of smallpox. But to some people it appeared to be in contradiction with some of the ancient wisdom; and for many years there was a concerted effort on the part of sincere objectors to prevent the use of vaccination.

In cities throughout the country, most notably in the city of Northampton, Massachusetts, there has raged a battle between ancient wisdom and modern knowledge in the matter of fluoridation of the water. According to the verbal maps that some people carry, it is contrary to nature, wicked, dangerous, etc. to put "rat poison" in the drinking water. This "map" means so much more than the territory that all the evidence of public records, the opinions of state and federal authorities, the reports of medical and dental societies mean nothing. If we are going to go by the map alone, then no amount of evidence "out there" can affect our opinion.

The world today is faced with a population problem. Where the productive capacities of the earth may be considered to increase, roughly on an arithmetic basis, the population tends to increase on a geometric basis. The weight of evidence seems to show that populations will increase to the survival limit. This is a condition that must result in a world of malnutrition, poverty, and all of the tensions and hostilities that arise in the minds of desperate men.

But how do we look at the problem of world peace and the prevention of war?   Do we examine the evidence impartially?   Do we accept the facts as they appear in the light of modern scientific appraisal? Do we face up to the inexorable problem of "What are we going to do about the birth rate?"

Or do we retreat to the pre-scientific philosophizing of well-meaning theologians who lived centuries before the present crisis had even appeared on the horizon?   Do we take out the old maps and solemnly publish, as "God's law," the old directives to "increase and multiply?"

This is what we mean by valuing a map (and an old and obsolete map at that) more highly than the thing itself.

This is a book about the market; at least it is written around the problems of the market.   In the market, if you accept the old wisdom as you read it and as it comes down through the mouths of traders and board room habitues, you can lose your money.   You can be wiped out if you are not willing and able to look fearlessly at the facts and to revise or even to reject the old wisdom if it does not fit the case.

But in some other departments of life, if you cling to the map and refuse to look at the territory you can lose much more than your money.   You can lose your life, your civilization, and humanity itself.

We have got to stop putting "maps" before "realities"; "symbols" before "facts."

And this does not mean rejecting all of the valid thinking that has been handed down to us.   We have already pointed out that this knowledge is our greatest heritage.

All that we have to do is to re-examine the territory; compare the old directives with the present situation and make doubly and triply sure that the directives still hold; and if they do not, to change them to correspond with present conditions.

I think we could say quite safely that this is exactly what our great thinkers of the past have done.   Moses and Hammurabi, Galen, Newton, Jesus, all presented the accumulated wisdom of their times, revaluated and re-stated to meet the current situation.

And if these sages were with us today, would you expect them *now* merely to repeat what they said in other places, at other times, under other conditions?   Or would you expect them to do what we must do today; take another hard look at the reality and revise our maps to date?

We have spoken of high order maps, symbols, etc., some of which are so far removed from reality that they seem to have no referents in the external world.

A very common example of this sort of symbolism is the word "they" as it is frequently used by those who frequent brokers' board rooms. "They" are putting the market up on account of the election. "They" are selling out now before the annual report comes out. "They" are buying on balance under cover of the decline. And so on.

Reputable brokers, and the New York Exchange itself have been sufficiently disturbed by the loose and misleading use of the word "they" to warn associates and employees against it. In some cases, rather severe punishment has been dealt out. By using a broad, high order word such as "they" it is possible to create a false picture of the secret activities of infinitely wealthy, infinitely smart, and infinitely powerful forces in Wall Street; forces which, it may be assumed by the innocent, are able to manipulate the market to their own design.

Strangely enough, the question is seldom asked, "Just who *are* they?" If it were asked, the ghost might disappear in a wisp of vapor. We have "they" working behind the scenes in politics. We have "they" in matters of public opinion and morals. Many people are vulnerable to a scare technique based on the machinations of a sinister "they."

"They," like any other high order noun is not the same kind of "they" we use when we refer to "the three children," or "the people next door," or even the kind of "they" we mean when we say "Paine, Webber, Jackson & Curtis." The word sounds and looks the same. But in the connection above, "they" is far removed from real people. It is a "long shot" at something or somebody vaguely suspected, moving in the shadows of the far distance. It must be "somebody" that is causing us to fail, to be wrong so often, to lose money so steadily. It must be a "they."

If anyone tells you "they" are doing this or that to the market or to some stock, find out exactly *who* "they" is; and when "they" bought this or sold that, and at what prices. And if your informant cannot produce any evidence, if he cannot point to any territory in external reality, tell him to go to hell. You'd be better off without his advice.

One of the many glittering generalities that is planted in our young minds is the belief that "government" is more honest, more dependable, more ethical generally than "business."

Somehow we acquire the idea that the government of the United States is about the most solid, most incorruptible, and thoroughly admirable institution in the world. And at the same time many of us become indoctrinated with the idea that "private business" is actuated only by greed, corruption and the expediency of the greatest personal gain.

This is the book. This is the way we learn it in civics class, by implication if not by direct statement. This is the way statesmen speak about it. This is the way people seem to regard it all.

Government bonds? Why, they are the "safest investment in the world." The pledged word of the United States of America. A question of business ethics? Who to believe; the tax authorities or the investigating commission, or the subject businessman himself? What is the word of a grubby profit-seeking businessman against the civil servants of our government?

But one does not have to become a traitor to one's country to use his eyes and ears and ordinary intelligence. The securities of government, our own or those of other countries, have been notoriously manipulated, misrepresented, and sometimes repudiated. The bonded pledge of the United States of America was repudiated with respect to the payment in gold of its obligations in the 1930's. The taxability of income from government bonds has been handled evasively, and, some would say, dishonestly; in other words, the large type does not disclose all that is stated in the very small print. Our government has sold its bonds to the people of this country using every device of propaganda and advertising, on the misleading premise that by putting aside $75.00 today, one would receive one-third more principal at the end of ten years. This is true, so far as the number of dollars is concerned; but for a government which has been more or less supporting a program of continuous inflation for many years, it is a misleading statement, and some would say, a deliberately misleading statement by which people have been induced to "invest" their savings now in the hope of a return of greater purchasing power in the future; only to discover that the final payment comes short of buying even as much as the original capital. It is hard, indeed, to believe that these operations have been entirely innocent.

We know that government can and does "reconsider" its contracts, "re-study" or "re-value" former decisions. The pledged word of government is not enforceable in the way the contract of an ordinary business can be enforced. The "sovereign people" can feel great satisfaction in their collective sovereignty and power. They had better enjoy it, for in many ways they have little sovereignty and little power as individuals.

In Wall Street we have had great frauds, deceptions, and all the sorry history of human frailty and dishonesty. But on balance I wonder if we could not match each fraud and each deception on the part of private business with an equivalent fraud or deception on the part of government. And, on the whole, I wonder if business wouldn't come out with a somewhat cleaner record over the long pull. A great deal of our private business is conducted on the basis of personal integrity. A verbal agreement to buy or to sell stock or commodities is regarded normally as binding, even though one of the parties may suffer heavily because of it. There is in Wall Street, and in LaSalle Street, a mutual respect and a self-respect that enforces the proper execution of agreements and the maintenance of confidence between the many persons concerned. For every case of shady dealing or corruption there are hundreds and thousands of transactions which are handled according to the accepted rules and conventions without question.

In government we find an air of suspicion surrounding every operation, as if everyone were potentially crooked at heart. No matter how many thousands of dollars you may spend with the post office, you cannot get credit for a single postage stamp to complete your mailing. Clerks are spied on, and complicated systems of vouchers and double checks are set up to prevent theft and fraud.

You will find the same suspicion, and checking and red tape at City Hall, or in the State House. Whatever the government touches it stains with the smudge of petty politics, the suspicion of small thievery, and all of the hostility toward the "general public" that we associate with customs inspectors, tax collectors, post office clerks, and the like.

Certainly private business has no wings and no halo. But in spite of all the check-ups and vouchers, and the peep-holes and the civil service codes, somehow we still find an amazing number of relatives on the payroll of public officials. There are still great unexplained gaps in the budget items relating to the new voting machines, the storm sewer installation, and the purchase of police motorcycles.

Aside from the hostility and lack of courtesy manifested by our public servants toward the "sovereign people," it seems that our public servants do quite a lot of stealing, directly and indirectly, from these same "sovereign people." Perhaps this stealing (or quasi-stealing such as the outside employment of firemen supposedly on full-time jobs for the city) is necessary to eke out their artificially low wages. For it is true that government and civil service pay is nominally lower than that in private industry.

But why do we act as if the nominal pay was the real pay? Why do we send school children to admire the marble and bronze facade of the post office and not tell them about the slovenly and hostile clerks that grudgingly and inefficiently wait on the line before the one open window? Why do we speak of the indomitable determination that "gets the mail through" under any and all conditions, when the facts, which we know if we receive any mail, are that the slightest train delay, a snow storm, a holiday, or an epidemic of winter colds can seriously impair the mail service?

Why do we do honor to The Mayor, The Governor, the Congressman, etc. as if they were "better" or "more important" than the manager of the local department store or a chemical engineer at one of our factories? No one ever invites a dentist to make a speech before the Graduating Class. And no one ever saw an insurance salesman on the Reviewing Stand.

Just what is it that makes the office of an Alderman or a State Senator more "honorable" than the job of running a hot dog stand on Main Street? What values and measures of human worth are we using? Who is best serving his fellow man? I am not implying that all hot dog stand operators are leading more significant lives than any Senators or Aldermen. I am simply raising the question, "What standards are we to use in judging a man?" We know that there have been some very able and very valuable men who have served in public office intelligently and well. But that is not the point. The question is whether the mere fact that a man is elected to public office, or the fact that a certain security is identified as a "government sponsored issue" should in and of itself clothe the matter in such raiment of purest white that we cannot fairly judge the merits of the case at all. We are regularly presented with faulty, retouched maps; and we are taught to respect the map and not examine the territory.

Why do we set up these pictures of something so fine and so good and so clean that it is not possible? We have made a picture of Our Democracy; a map, if you will. We honor the ideal. We like to think of a cooperative community in which men work together for their own good and for the common good, and will not stoop to robbing their neighbors for personal gain or advancement. We fervently wish our Governor were a great statesman. We would like our Mayor to be a dedicated and able leader. We want a government that is efficient and capable, and honest, and one that respects the individual citizen and treats him fairly.

These are all good ideals. They are goals worth seeking. They are maps of what we *hope* to be true, and what we work to make true. But it does not help matters to act *as if* the map were actually the territory; and to assume that "because we say it is so" that makes it so in very fact.

If we want to cope with the problems pressing us so hard; that is, the practical problems of the high cost of government, the corruption of elections, the parking problem, the school crowding problem, the crime problem, and all the rest, then we should *first* look at the facts, not at the map.

If the Mayor is a former associate of racing interests; and if his record includes various investigations and perhaps criminal accusations, we should recognize all this, and also recognize that this is not an unusual picture in the matter of Governors. We might even look around and see whether our "democratic" method of selecting public officials was, in fact, what we were taught it was in school.

If the Mayor has numerous family connections on the public payroll; and if there is evidence that his personal income as indicated by his manner of living greatly exceeds the legal remuneration of his office, then we might look at the facts, and forget what we learned in Civics or Social Studies.

Perhaps we could at least compare the overall realities of government and business. We could ask such down-to-earth questions as, "If I had to place my trust in somebody in a matter of personal importance, which business men of my acquaintance could I go to with confidence? And which of the politicians that I know would I trust?"

You must know that in certain cities and certain states it is necessary for you to have certain connections in order to expect to be successful in politics, or to serve even in an humble capacity on the

public payroll.   It may be a very definite, though unwritten, require-
ment, that you be of a certain race (or *not* of a certain race), or that
you have certain church affiliations; or that you have certain family
connections.   Imagine a Jewish Mayor of Boston!   Just try to picture
a Negro governor of Alabama!

There may be and no doubt is discrimination in Wall Street.   But
when you go to the broker and deposit your margin and place an
order to "Buy 100 shares of U. S. Steel at the market," or "Sell 5000
bushels of Chicago May Soy Beans," you are not asked what your
social position is, or whether you are a Roman Catholic or an Ortho-
dox Jew.   You may be a man or a woman, well-dressed or shabby,
young or old.   No one can "put in a word for you" to obtain the
advantage of a single eighth.   Your money is as good as the next
customer's and no better.

It is here, in Wall Street, not in City Hall or the State House that
genuine democracy is practiced; and without fanfare or parades.

Isn't it time, then, that we stopped treating "maps" as if they
were "things"?   Isn't it time that we look at the facts first and *then*
make our abstractions.

In other words, isn't it time to stop talking nonsense?

QUESTIONS FOR CONSIDERATION

Do you confuse symbols with tangible reality?   Are you afraid of crowds,
or high places, or caves?   Is this because of a real and present danger "out
there"?   If not, is it because you may be mixing up something intangible
with something tangible?

If I hand you a photograph of your mother would you, for a small reward,
cut out the eyes with a pair of scissors?   Would you, for a modest fee, plunge
the scissors into the picture in the region of the heart?

Is the photograph your mother?   Or is it a piece of paper?   Are you
making a false identification?   Is it the same to cut a piece of paper and to
stab your mother?   Are you confusing the levels of abstraction?

If the certificate is engraved in three colors, and bears the Great Seal of
the Corporation and a vignette of a huge industrial plant does this prove
anything about the value of the stock?

Do you feel that a black sheep is any more wicked than a white one?
Is a black man any more evil than a white one?   Is there a confusion in the
use of symbolic words which could be erroneously identified with external

reality? Do you believe in Devils? Would you say that Devils were symbols or tangible realities? Did you ever see a Devil? Do you know anyone who ever did? Where did you learn about Devils? Where and how and when do you suppose the idea of Devils first originated? Do you accept these sources as authoritive proof that Devils walk around on the earth as "real" people? Would you say there is an apparent contradiction here because of a confusion between symbols and tangible reality?

LET'S NOT BE TOO ANTHROPOCENTRIC

WE HAVE studied the relation of various orders of abstraction. And we have seen that there is a place to count and recognize the individual trees (low order), and a place to view and perceive "the forest" as a collection of trees having some similarities (higher abstraction).

The difficulties most of us get into result from confusion of the levels of abstraction, come when we identify "ghost" as a "thing" or "Devil" as a "person," etc.

Now, in the living of our own lives, and in spite of much that we are taught, our "self" is the center and most important factor. We must learn "to live with ourselves," to "respect ourselves," etc. And we must also learn to live "with others." This is a sort of extension of the self; one identifies his neighbor with himself. We have a Golden Rule which concerns our relations to our neighbors, and which is basic in both the Christian and Jewish religions.

There are a few great philosophers who are able to extend this concept of "common humanity" to "common life." Such men as Albert Schweitzer have a feeling of neighborliness and brotherhood not only toward all men, but toward all living creatures.

It is not specifically important here to consider what it is that shapes Schweitzer's "super-humanity." But it is, perhaps, worth considering why and how it is that most of us attach such overwhelming importance to "mankind."

If we are to be tied to a narrow philosophy that sees man as the center of all creation, we are perhaps making much the same kind of error that the ancients made when they took it for granted that the earth was the center of the universe around which moved, as a matter of course, the sun, the stars, and the remotest galaxies.

It is necessary for us to be able, not only to abstract as a child and see one's own relation to external reality; but to see one's self as related to all humanity and humanity as a perceived higher abstraction. If we can then see the broader relation in which man and the animals are all a part of the still broader manifestation we call "life" we have advanced in our thinking. If we can also see that the trees and ferns and algae are also part of "life" we have extended our map. And if we, ultimately, can see that "I" and "humanity," and "animal life" and "all life," and "all creation" are part and parcel of a single universe, then we have attained a very comprehensive view of the cosmos.

It may help us to understand nature if we see nature as a variety of workings-out of the laws of probability, and of thermodynamics, and of relativity.

Then we will not smugly consider that the deer were put on earth to be shot down by hunters, nor the fish created merely for us to murder in their homes. We will have a proper respect for the universe and appraise ourselves with dignity and honesty without any phony overtones of "special creation," or "delusions of grandeur."

What is important is to be able to see ourselves in our real relation to the rest of the universe. It is not necessary to grovel as "less than the dust"; and to engulf ourselves with self-condemnation as "miserable sinners." Neither is it necessary, if we have a proper understanding of our place in the scheme of things to bolster our sagging egos with self-glorification as "children of God," "created a little lower than the angels," and the like. If we are to achieve sanity we must learn to think sanely, and for this we do not need to don figurative golden crowns and lord it over our less gifted cousins among the lower animals; nor do we need to put on sackcloth and grovel abjectly for being what we are.

The sane man will recognize what he is and how he is related to "the rest of nature." He will learn to make of himself the best-fitted organism to deal with the situation in which he finds himself. This is the goal, not only of general semantics, but of all human effort.

QUESTIONS FOR CONSIDERATION

Would you say that a proper understanding of nature would place mankind in a relation to the animals that would recognize both the differences and the similarities? In order to avoid undue self-humiliation or undue grandiosity, isn't this a rational view? In extending to the animals the respect and understanding we would extend to "cousins," are we not showing a greater respect for all the creation than if we arrogate special status to ourselves? In considering ourselves as "part of nature" are we not likely to be in a better position to understand ourselves and to deal sympathetically with our human neighbors?

Does this "habit" of recognizing "differences" as well as "similarities" seem to you likely to lead to more or to less bitterness and hostility between men?

Do you feel there is a danger in assuming too much glory and special virtue in the human race of which you are a part?

If your own personal accomplishments fall too far short of such exalted images, could that lead to feelings of discouragement, unworthiness, guilt, self-hatred?

Could you connect unbridled greed, ambition, etc. with such feelings of inadequacy?

Do you believe that your "success" in business or in the market lies in the direction of unbridled ambition, greed, etc.?

It is possible that you can serve yourself, your family and the world you live in better if you put yourself realistically in your proper place, rather than to put yourself metaphorically "too high," or also metaphorically, "too low"?

SANITY MUST BE ACHIEVED

WE SPEAK of the "insane." The term calls up pictures of the great gray building on the hill, beyond the edge of town, where howling maniacs are confined in padded cells. You and I, thank God, are sane, like most of our neighbors.

Are we, indeed?

Name ten of your friends who are "sane" in the sense that they are reasonably well-fitted to the environment in which they live. Name ten of your friends who are able to realize their full potentialities in life. Name ten of your friends who are free from all neuroses, alcoholism, domestic maladjustment, phobias, sexual abberations, personality problems.

We take it for granted that everybody is sane unless he has been duly certified as a lunatic and confined in an institution. Oh, if only this were true!

How can we expect people to become adapted to living in the world where they must live when they are taught to *not* look at *it*, but to accept the directives, maxims, proverbs, laws, morals, scripture and superstition accumulated through the ages?

How can we expect people to be sane when they are taught unsanity and *forbidden* even to look at or discuss the facts?

Do you question this? Do you feel that we do have "free thought," and "free speech," and a "free press"? Then consider what would happen if you attempted publicly to discuss sexual behavior, or the existence of God, or birth control, or the Democratic System, or the criminal law, or any of a number of other subjects charged with emotional content. Especially if your conclusions tended to support the view that would be popularly considered the "wrong" view.

You can write or speak on any of these subjects so long as you agree with what has already been stated and accepted as "true." You may not completely express your contrary views on pain of social rejection or worse. You may not express them at all unless you are able to "pull your punches" and soften your arguments to a point where they are relatively innocuous.

And so . . . we are taught to think un-sanely. And we are forbidden to speak entirely sanely on certain subjects.

And we bury some of the real causes of human misery because we are not allowed to talk about them. And then we try to solve the problems in carefully emasculated language, and, if possible, without reference to any basic questions.

Why did Chapin kill the two children? Why did Starkweather spread a path of death across Nebraska? Why are the Russians hostile? Why are prices going up? Why is my wife so cold to me? Why does the market go down?

We cannot answer these questions because our lips are sealed. No newspaper would dare print a forthright answer. The only answers we can make are those derived from the kindergarten-type "education" we have received.

But sanity does not come through faulty and inadequate training. Sanity, meaning the full realization of a man's manhood, or a woman's womanhood, is not something we can take for granted. It must be worked for, it must be won back, to some extent, from the forces of restraint, of "training," of "teaching," of "civilizing."

There is a certain ruthlessness about education for sanity that frightens people who have been coddled behind the walls of aphorism and tradition.

If we are going to achieve sanity in the market or any other aspect of life, we must have the guts to break with tradition, to re-examine and, if necessary, to repudiate the highest authorities.

If we can divest ourselves from the compulsive necessity of following blindly "what we have been taught," we can learn to see what is before our eyes and evaluate it accordingly.

If what we find checks with what we have learned, we can benefit greatly from the experience of the past. But if the evidence does not support the teaching, we must be able to reject the teaching and accept the evidence.

This is the direction of sanity. And this is how we intend to look at the market and at every other aspect of the life around us.

QUESTIONS FOR CONSIDERATION

Would you say that most of us are taught mostly to "think for ourselves," or mainly to "accept what we are told"?

Would you say there is no value to precept and directive?

What would you say when two directives conflict seriously and contradict each other; as, "Many hands make light work," versus "Too many cooks spoil the broth"?

Are you aware that there are many contradictions in the teachings we are subjected to? Do you believe people can adapt themselves to "not seeing" the contradictions? And do you believe this will eliminate conflict when a serious issue has to be faced? How could you reconcile such directives as, "Let profits run," and "A man never went broke taking a profit" (to quote two of the many conflicting precepts of the stock market)?

If you accept without question anything that comes from high authority, isn't it possible that you may be faced with an impossible decision? Can you think of situations in family life, in the law, in religion, in social customs, where such contradictions occur? Where the authoritative wisdom clashes with your present experience, based on your own observations, to which will you assign the greater value? Which would you say comes closer to "external reality"?

Which would more likely result in greater sanity, that is to say, in a greater degree of success in coping with and adapting to the environment: moves in the direction of using data from present observations of external reality, or moves based on ancient precepts, possibly metaphorical and symbolic?

THE THINKING PROCESS

THERE have been a good many magazine articles in the past few years about the relative values of the "classical" or liberal arts education and the "practical" or shop-and-laboratory education.

I wonder if the subject could not be discussed in a little different way, using somewhat different labels with perhaps somewhat different meanings.

We could speak of the tendency of education to look back at "tradition," or to look straight ahead at "the current situation."

The contrast I am thinking of is between the memorizing of dates and speeches and poems and descriptions of battles, etc., and the observation of things and events as they are directly perceived now.

I realize, of course, that "things and events" are not "directly perceived," and that we need not only our own past experience as a means of evaluating the present, but also we need the handed-down experience of others.

But there is a great difference between the young botanist who memorizes the names of 1673 varieties and species and genera of plants, and the young botanist who spends each afternoon watching the growth and development of a bean plant.

To a good many people education is a matter of how much assorted data you can cram into one brain. Some schools seem to be organized along these lines. "Never mind looking! Just listen!" (In other words, "Study the map; throw reality away.")

It is this kind of "education" that leads to arguments such as

"Why a fishbowl with a fish suspended in the water will not weigh more than the same fishbowl if we remove the fish." (Not true, but it has been seriously debated.) Or why men have more teeth than women. Or why a large iron ball will fall faster than a small one. Or how it is impossible for a man to run faster than a turtle. Or, "How many angels can stand on the head of a pin?"

A good deal of our schooling still consists of memorizing a lot of material that could be looked up, if it was ever needed again, in The World Almanac, or Webster, or Kent, or whatever reference book was appropriate. Actually, a good deal of the information is not likely to be called for. In all my life since leaving eighth grade no one has ever asked me the date of the first Olympiad. I do not believe I need to know the order of succession of the French monarchs; and if it should be necessary for me to produce the dates of the principal battles of the American Civil War I could easily find them at the library . . . but I cannot imagine just how this crisis could arise.

The radio and television programs in which a wise-cracking Master of Ceremonies exploits the Prodigy give the impression that education is a matter of how many novelists of the 18th century you can name, or who was the Democratic candidate for vice-president in the election of 1928.

The training and development of an omniverous memory is not the kind of education that leads to creative imagination, nor to an understanding perception of the world around us.

Education, in the sense of understanding life and living and the world we live in, is a much more complicated thing than mastering the atomic weights, the conversion tables, and the lists of irregular verbs.

It must involve direct observation, abstraction, perhaps many stages of abstraction, comparisons with past experience, the recognition of similarities, and also of differences, and the use of whatever material has come from others through teaching and through books.

Of course, in the early stages of childhood one picks up facts from direct observation, and learns through signs and gestures, rewards and punishments that certain things are "approved" and others "disapproved." The child, through language, picks up knowledge from others, not only as regards things and places, but as to opinions, judgments, etc. He accumulates a lot of "do's" and "don'ts" and a "value system."

However, as we have seen, and largely because of the nature of language, he is likely to have a dim understanding of the process by which he learns, that is, by which he abstracts.

It is most important for the child to learn as soon as possible to recognize which of his "thoughts" represent something he knows about material reality, which refer to some conclusion or deduction derived from facts, and, in short, "how he knows what he knows."

If a person was reasonably aware of the process by which some of his most firmly held beliefs, prejudices and judgments got into his head in the first place, he would be able to give them their proper value. The maxim handed down by an aged great-aunt that "an itching palm means you will find money," is not exactly on the same plane as a report from the weather bureau that the precipitation during the past twenty-four hours at Bradley Field was .25 inches. It is one thing to hold to the family opinion that Uncle George is "scatter-brained," and something quite different to consider the fact that Uncle George has held nine different jobs in the past year. The first is a high order judgment; the second is a report as to the facts.

You will notice that the "report as to the facts" may not, necessarily, be a "true" one. Uncle George may have held twelve different jobs in the past year or he may have had no job at all. But this is a question that can be settled by reference to the records in the case. The question of whether Uncle George is "scatter-brained" or not is not referable to any external authority because it is a matter of opinion and exists only as a "map" in someone's head.

Therefore, in learning to think, that is, in learning to think sanely and in an orderly way, the most important foundation stone is to become aware of the *order of abstraction;* to know at all times whether you are considering something close to the object level, or at the high altitude of conjecture and opinion.

Just as in building a house we get a more substantial job if we start with the foundation, rather than with the roof, the first data, and the most basic, is that obtained at the very low levels of observation and personal experience.

To this we can add the communicated observations and experiences of others, checking them directly if possible with the observed facts, and otherwise evaluating them according to the dependability of the source in previous cases. If the facts we read or that we are taught come from a source that is of questionable authenticity, or if the

original fact-finding was a long time ago, or under different conditions, or in a different place, then we should consider these factors
and perhaps discount or modify the information rather than accepting
it in toto at face value.

If we have some idea of at least the approximate level of our further
abstractions, we can avoid some of the most serious semantic traps.
We should know that "maple tree" is a higher abstraction than "this
silver maple tree," and we cannot attribute (project or read back,
that is) everything that applies to "maple tree" in general to the
particular silver maple growing in our back yard.   On the other hand,
we should know that "maple tree" is a lower abstraction than "tree,"
and we should not attribute to all trees the features we find commonly
on maple trees.

Most especially, we must avoid confusing the very high order
concepts with very low order concepts.   "Generosity" is not the
same as "Joe gave fifty cents to a beggar."   "Virtue" is not the same
as "She has never slept with anyone but her husband."   "Success" is
not the same as "making a million dollars."

If we can build a fund of factual information, and then erect on this
foundation a series of abstractions generalizing these facts and deduc-
ing logically certain common features, we can progress to higher
levels where we reach "conclusions"; and from these conclusions we
can form "opinions" and "judgments," which, in turn, will determine our attitudes and these, in turn, our behavior under various
circumstances.

In the processes of logic and deduction we must generalize and
we may quite properly use symbols, metaphor, analogy, or any other
device that helps us to construct useful maps to understand what is
going on "out there," and what it "means" to us.

So long as the symbols, metaphors, analogies, etc. have a verifiable correspondence with something in external reality, these can be
considered useful maps.   It is only necessary that we be aware of
their nature and that we do not set up the map, symbol, etc. as superior to the thing it represents.

Just as an architect manipulates small models and makes drawings
on paper to represent the buildings he plans to construct, and just as
the engineer uses formulas and charts to make it easier to see the relation of more complicated things, so we use high abstractions to engineer our own higher thinking.

There are hardly any limits to what we can attempt and how we can use these devices. The rules are few and simple.

1. We can use a high order abstraction to *represent* some features in lower order reality. But we must not *confuse* and *identify* abstractions at various levels.

2. If we intend to project our abstract thinking to "external" reality, we must be sure that there is actually a territory in external reality to which our maps will apply. There is no reason we cannot construct maps for which we have no corresponding territory. A great deal of philosophical and mathematical speculation has been concerned with purely hypothetical "territories." This is all right so long as we do not then try to force the "theoretical" map onto a "real" territory. There have been cases, especially in the field of chemistry, physics and "pure" mathematics, where a theory built around a "hypothetical" territory has later been applied in a very practical way. These are cases where a territory has actually been discovered such that the previously constructed map does have a verifiable correspondence with the territory. Specifically, here, we are thinking of the discovery of certain elements by spectroscopic analysis before their discovery in nature; the aberrations of light in gravitational fields; and the theoretical development of the non-Euclidean geometries of Riemann and Lobachevsky and their later applications in the world of reality.

3. The observations and conclusions must be consistent with themselves. As you know, there are no "inconsistencies" in external reality. The "inconsistencies" and "contradictions" arise from our faulty perception. Thus, someone may report that there are four houses on a certain block, and someone else reports that there are six. If we have decided, as the second observer did, to include hen-houses and out-houses, then he would be correct. But there is no contradition in what is actually "out there." The contradiction is simply a matter of how we define it and how we speak of it. It is necessary in any orderly system of mathematics or scientific analysis to set up definitions in such a way that there are no internal contradictions in the system.

QUESTIONS FOR CONSIDERATION

When did you close the book on your education? Or are you still "going to school"? Have you acquired some important learning during the past year?

Does part of your "new learning" involve changing or discarding some of what you learned in the past?

Do you implement your new learning by changing your habits?

Are you able to accept new ideas that may conflict with what you learned in elementary school or at your mother's knee?

Do you consider your education to be simply a matter of memorizing facts or abstracting from the thoughts of someone else? How much of your new learning is from your own experience and observation? How much of it consists of new abstractions, that is to say "original thinking" based on the data you previously acquired?

Have you examined the essential steps in education, your own education, that is? Do you have some sort of orderly pattern or structure in developing new knowledge?

In your knowledge of the market do you make use of the same kind of orderly structure you would use to solve a problem in production, in writing a report, or in developing an organization plan? In other words, do you have a systematic method of some kind? Do you use your understanding of the abstracting process (and its pitfalls) to explore some of the statements that come to you about stock market situations? Can you use this understanding to explode nonsense statements, and to probe vague and misleading comments?

THE VAGUENESS OF THE HIGH ABSTRACTIONS

LET us take a further look at the high order abstractions. We have compared them with a "long shot" with a camera, as contrasted with a "close-up." Because they are some steps "away from observed reality," the details are obscure.

In extreme cases the details disappear altogether or become so tenuous that it is hard to assign any precise definition to them; and it is certainly impossible to communicate much meaning about them to someone else.

In religious matters we have such terms as the attainment of "grace." This word, which sounds like a common noun is not quite so precise as "pencil" or "horse." It is not possible to measure "grace," that is to weigh it, ascertain its length or temperature or electrical conductivity.

In the stock market we frequently hear of "good" companies, and "growth" stocks. These are very high order words, so vague in their meaning that it is hardly possible to measure or evaluate them. If, for example, someone says that General Motors is a "good" company, ask him "*How* good?" What is the measure of "goodness?"

There are hundreds, perhaps thousands of terms we use as though they represented tangible realities, which cannot be measured or directly observed because they are of such very high order. "Hope," "love," "envy," "peace," "thoughtlessness," etc., etc.

One such word, which we will discuss further and at some length is "success." It is not impossible to define and measure "success." It is a high order abstraction, a map in your own mind, and you may attach whatever definition you wish to it. You could, if you wanted, decide that "to you" success would mean giving away all your money to the poor. It could mean assassinating the president. It might mean integrating a coast-to-coast system of railroads so that people could have the same uninterrupted ride that a hog may enjoy. Success could mean being chosen Queen of the May, or owning a steam yacht, or getting in the movies, or memorizing the five-place logarithm table.

But if you are going to talk about "success" with someone else, it is rather important that you and he agree as to what you are talking about, and that you have approximately the same values. Otherwise there will be (at this high level) a contradiction, which does not exist in reality.

This matter of making sure that you are actually communicating with someone in terms that have about the same meaning to both of you, is nearly as important as the matter of checking facts extensionally in case of a difference of opinion. Both of these precautions will eliminate disputes; between them they can eliminate most of the disputes that are likely to arise.

QUESTIONS FOR CONSIDERATION

Marjorie says she finds great happiness in her new work. Just how much happiness would that be? Can you tell us? Do you think Marjorie could tell us?

Tom and Joe are artists. They tell us they are moved by noble inspiration. Which, do you think is moved by the most inspiration and the noblest? How would you ever find out? Is it possible to express these high abstractions directly so that another person will know exactly what is meant?

In your own thoughts about yourself do you avoid such terms as "honesty," "bravery," "depravity," "success," etc., unless you have assigned definite and measurable meanings to them?

Have you set some bounds and limits to your various aspirations?

Someone might tell you that he had "a high ambition to succeed." Does this sound as if he had an objective of getting somewhere? Would you feel it was important for him to know just where he was trying to get? Does "high ambition to succeed" in itself tell very much about the goal? Does the map draw a very detailed picture? Are you sure that your friend has a very clear picture of what he wants?

"TO ME"

SEVERAL times we have used the expression "to me" with respect to high order abstractions. You will understand, by now, that when we are referring to a dog, or a table, or a copy of yesterday's newspaper, it is possible to point to the thing, to look at it and abstract some of its features, and to arrive at a good agreement with anyone else who may be present as to what sort of thing we are referring to.

I am assuming here that the parties concerned are of ordinary intelligence and equipped with the usual sensory apparatus. You will recall the story of the several blind men who, abstracting by means of the sense of touch, were unable to concur on the nature of an elephant; one man maintaining that it was "like a wall" (his side), another that he was "like a hose" (his trunk), another that he was "like a rope" (his tail), etc. But we are not thinking of people so severely handicapped.

Most of us can agree on the main gross features of ordinary objects. It is when we get into the realm of highly abstracted concepts, many steps removed from the original factual observations, that we get into trouble.

This is because, as we have seen, it is not possible to point to or touch the high order abstraction; for it exists, like a mental map, only in the mind. We have no way to compare one such concept directly with another's concept in regard to the same matter

When you speak of "your love for Marjorie," how can you tell me "how much" you love Marjorie. You are dealing with something that is very real "to you," but it cannot have the same reality to me, and there is no way you can precisely communicate your concept to me as to your love for Marjorie.

Matters of opinion and judgment, most adjectives, the abstract nouns, all of these partake of the nature of high order abstractions, and to a great degree they are personal and not communicable.

When we say to ourselves, as we leave the house, "This is a beautiful morning this morning," we should, to be strictly accurate add, "to me." It may be a wretched day, a stinking day to someone else, perhaps even to your neighbor next door.

And when I announce, either to myself or to others, "I am a success in life," it is quite important to add the qualifying "to me." After all, one's success must be measured by one's own values; and whatever my standards of success might be, I am sure that there are people who would violently disagree with me.

Even such an apparently factual statement as, "This is a difficult situation," is actually a "to me" problem. It might be very difficult, for instance "to me," to have to explain the operation of the New York Stock Market to a visitor from Japan who had no knowledge of the English language. It might not be a difficult situation at all for someone who spoke Japanese.

An experience which one person will honestly regard as "horrible" may be perceived by another as merely "annoying." It is all a matter of how we think about it, and how we see it.

And how we "see" it is very often how we "say" it. If you are expecting that the extraction of a tooth will be a "horrible" experience, you may well find it "horrible." If you have learned to speak of certain things as "nasty," "beautiful," "awful," etc. you will probably "see" the nastiness, beauty, awfulness, etc. which you are expecting to find.

But it is quite important to keep in mind that the "nastiness," "beauty," "awfulness," or whatever it may be, is not, of itself, "out there," but is strictly related to your perception; and is always to be considered as "to you," not a material attribute of the thing itself, and not necessarily true for any other observer.

It can be dangerous to forget that the higher abstractions we attribute to things are "maps" and not "territories." Your former partner may appear "beastly" "to you," but the beastliness is not something that can be observed and compared and measured factually by anyone interested. The beastliness is actually not something about your former partner at all; it refers to how you feel about him. Your feeling may be entirely justified, or it may be unfair. But it is a matter of how something appears "to you" and this "beastliness" is a symbolic representation of your appraisal of the man.

Suppose that you are evaluating, not your partner's actions, but your own. Suppose that according to your own standards of conduct you have erred very grievously. Then you will feel "guilty."

Now is this "guilt" something factual and observable about you? Or is it the expression of your own judgment? You have framed and focussed the image of your actions and compared them with the projection of your "picture" of proper conduct; and you find that you have not measured up to the standard. Therefore, you appear guilty "to yourself."

It is important to understand the subjective nature of such a concept as "guilt"; for it is such concepts that people are very likely to project "out there" and regard as if they were facts in external reality instead of opinions or judgments.

The amount of damage that has been done through habitual attitudes of self-reproach and self-condemnation is incalculable.

If we can keep our "maps" separate from our "territories" we can avoid confusion that may result in real tragedy. For example, to use the case we have just considered, if we recognize that we have certain standards or values of conduct, and that this is a "map" to guide us, then we need have no compunction about revising the map, bringing it up to date, correcting any errors in it, and generally making it more suitable to the function of guiding us in our living.

We can then recognize that our conduct, in such-and-such a matter, on such-and-such a date did not conform to what we, ourselves, have set as the minimum requirements of "proper conduct." It is not necessary, then, for us to pin the label "guilty" on ourselves as a permanent brand; we simply note the failure and plan to "go, and sin no more."

Very often, in the market, a man will compound his own error or misfortune because he overlooks the fact that his judgments about himself are not "matters of fact" but "matters of opinion." A trader will feel "small," or "sorry for himself," or "guilty." He will hesitate to "make a fool of himself" by admitting his mistakes. He will defend his own wrong tactics rather than change his methods. He will, in short, act as if he were dealing with physical features of himself, instead of with maps and directives concerning his conduct.

If I *am* a "miserable, stupid fool," that does not make me feel very good about myself, and it does not bode very well for my future. But if I understand that I "feel miserable" because I have made what I now realize is a "stupid and foolish mistake," I can look forward to changing my ways and not getting into that particular kind of trouble again. Also, I can preserve, or at least restore, my own self-regard.

One of the first rules we might observe in reading an editorial or listening to a sermon or political commentary, is to question any statement which may have a "to me" character.

When a writer or a speaker tells you the Empire State Building is 1250 feet high, that is a matter of record; it is either verifiably true or provably untrue. But when he speaks of "evil," and "loyalty," and "discontent," and "aspirations," then he should add the important words "to me"; and if he fails to do so (and he will fail to do so), you will do well to add these words yourself; and then you will understand when he is talking about facts and when he is talking about his own personal attitudes.

What you apply to editorial writers, speakers, preachers, etc., you can also apply to yourself. When you express an opinion which is based on how you feel about something rather than about the measurable, factual features of something, then you might well add these important qualifying words, "to me."

QUESTIONS FOR CONSIDERATION

Granny is always complaining the living room is chilly. How could she express herself more clearly and also avoid arguments with the rest of the family?

Jim Benson's wife likes the opera. Jim says grand opera stinks. How could he improve this statement?

A broker tells you that Wildcat Mining and Smelting looks like the best speculative opportunity in years. Would you feel that he ought to add two words to this comment in order to make himself clear?

You decide that Corn looks bearish. To whom does Corn look bearish? You may have good reasons for your opinion, but can you expect everyone you know to share the same view?

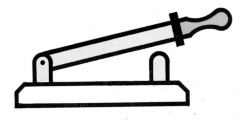

EITHER . . . OR

THERE was a song a few years ago titled "It's Gotta Be This or That."

There are, in life, many situations which we could call "two-valued." That is to say, there are two possibilities, two answers, two ways to act.

You can either get married or stay single. You can then have a child or not have a child. You can go to work or not go to work. You can close the switch to turn the light on, or you can leave it open and sit in the dark. In many elections you can vote either Democratic or Republican. The patient in the accident ward will either live or die. And so on.

The two-valued situations seem so common that some scholars have considered them universal. At least they have acted as if all problems could be reduced to two-valued situations, like the opening or closing of an electric switch.

A basic assumption in classical (Aristotelian) logic is that A is either B or "not B." This is a generalized statement of the two-valued situation.

We are taught to think in a two-valued way. It is "either this," "or that." As though there were two boxes into one of which every statement, opinion, judgment, etc. must be placed.

We say that Jimmy is either "good" or "bad" in school. IIis answer is either "right" or "wrong." He is "honest" or he is "dishonest."

When a man is charged with a crime he is expected, no, he is *required* to plead either "guilty" or "not guilty." There is no opportunity given him to explain that perhaps he is a little guilty, but not *very* guilty. There is no room in an "either . . . or" situation for part-way measures. There are two boxes, two categories and the answer must lie in one or the other. You cannot, for example, turn a simple electric switch on "part way."

And if a man is picked up by the police because he is "acting strangely" he will be examined to determine his sanity. He will be found either "sane" or "insane."

In Wall Street many people recognize only two conditions. It is either a Bull Market . . . or a Bear Market.

Now ask yourself whether the world as you actually know it and experience it, is built entirely on the "either . . . or" plan.

Do you love your work completely and absolutely, at all times? Or do you hate your job entirely and always? Or does the answer lie somewhere in between? You like your work generally, perhaps, but there are times when you abhor it.

Do you consider yourself absolutely honest? Did you never, on any smallest matter, do or say anything that was not completely truthful? Well, then, would you say that you are entirely and absolutely dishonest; that you have never done or said an honest thing in all your life? Well? Then the answer must lie somewhere in between.

A is not entirely, and absolutely, and always B; neither is it entirely, and absolutely, and always "not B."

Have you ever known a time when the market was entirely bullish . . . or entirely bearish? Why, not even in the panic years of 1929 to 1932 were *all* stocks going down in price. And not even in the lush years of the 1954-55 boom were *all* stocks advancing. How can you say the market is either "bullish" or "bearish" when individual stocks can act as differently as they do (or have you never looked to see?)

How? There are ways. We can set up arbitrary standards. We can establish, for instance, certain formal definitions that will establish either "guilt" or innocence. These, however, are "maps"; they are abstractions which we agree to treat "as if" they represented something in external reality. There is a great body of "legal fictions" which can be considered "as if" situations by which it is possible to categorize the law and avoid the embarrassment of actually looking at the facts in individual cases.

We can do something like this with problems of sanity. We can set up definitions of what is "sane" and what is "insane"; and then measure our subject by comparison with these standards. We can say, then, that according to the method used, he is either "sane" or "insane," which merely tells us that he corresponds with the definitions (or maps) we have set up, and that therefore we can put him in one of the two boxes or pigeonholes marked "sane" and "insane."

This, of course, does nothing to clarify the real condition of the subject, helps not at all in understanding his problem, and does nothing whatever toward getting him back into useful life again. It overlooks all of the particular features of the case and lumps the entire problem into two high abstractions representing the "either . . . or" dichotomy.

It is much the same in dealing with the market. We can set up definitions of what we decide to *call* a Bull Market or a Bear Market, and then place any market in either one or the other of these according to how it compares with our own definitions. But this covers up all of the significant action of individual stocks and does nothing to make clearer our view of what is really going on. We can make any definition we want, of course, for the map is not the reality, and your map may be quite different from mine, but we each have an equal right to draw our own maps. You may use the Dow Theory. I may use the Dow Theory with certain variations. Jim may follow the Odd Lot Indexes. And Charles may work with cycles based on the motions of the planetary bodies.

These are all maps and each may provide for categories labelled either "Bull Market" or "Bear Market." But since they are far removed from the reality and are, as you must know by now, high order abstractions, it is hardly any wonder that opinions as to whether "it" is a Bull Market or a Bear Market will often disagree.

One of the hard things about studying the "either . . . or" view, and particularly in seeing its very serious dangers, is that it is not wholly "wrong." As we saw in the early paragraphs of this chapter, there are a great many situations in life where things are "either this . . . or that."

Also, in the very cases we used as examples (and by the way, we could pick a great many more illustrative cases from everyday life), there are many times when there is no problem in making an "either . . . or" choice.

When a man comes into court with a bloody nose, swearing at the police officers and threatening at the top of his lungs to "knock the hell out of that Jerry Mullens," there is a strong presumption that he is guilty of being "drunk and disorderly" as charged.

And if a man were brought in under suspicion of insanity and soberly claimed that God had ordered him to "take possession of the Moon with the title of Emperor and Lord above all the Angels," one might reasonably concur that the gentleman was sufficiently pixilated to qualify him as "insane."

Also, if the Dow Jones Industrial average were to drop to a ten-year low on heavy volume, most reasonable observers would be willing to classify the action as a "Bear Market."

And someone might very well ask, "If many life situations can be represented accurately as 'either . . . or' cases; and if many other situations can be so classified most of the time, then why should we bother about this question? Why not use the 'either . . . or' all the time?"

And, of course, that is just what many people do, and what our teaching tends to lead to.

But it overlooks the fact that "either . . . or" does not apply entirely even in the extreme cases we have mentioned, and that there is a tremendous field that lies in between that cannot be considered "either . . . or." In fact, if we deny that gray exists and stretch everything to be White, or chop it off to be Black, as Procrustes adjusted the dimensions of his visitors to the size of his bed, we are again setting our map at a higher value than the territory it represents. We are not looking at the thing, but at the symbol.

When we call for a plea of either "guilty" or "not guilty," we are overlooking any "degrees" of guilt. When we "find" a man "sane" or "insane," we have deliberately swept under the carpet all the differences that mark his case as unique. On the one hand we may have classified a slightly disoriented person as precisely in the same category as a raving maniac. And on the other hand, we may have given a clear bill of health to a person who can be suffering from depression, irrational fears, delusions, or other symptoms which may become progressively more acute, and possibly dangerous. When we classify a market as "bullish" we tend to overlook the specific action of particular stocks, and we may fall into the error of projecting this "bullishness" (which is not a matter of external reality, but of opinion) onto some stock which is by no means bullish and which may collapse even as "the market" soars to new all-time peaks.

Like all other maps, "either . . . or" must be used with full consciousness of its arbitrary nature. We must recognize that it is not a complete picture of nature, as we will see in the following chapters.

QUESTIONS FOR CONSIDERATION

Can you think of six kinds of situation in your own life where a decision must be made on an either . . . or, two-valued basis?

Can you think of six kinds of situation where two alternative courses were possible, but where in each case one of these was so obviously "unwise," "unworthy," "immoral," or "unthinkable," that in actual fact your decision was limited to one "approved" or "possible" course?

Can you think of six types of situation where many people act and speak "as if" there were only two possible courses, but where, in fact, there are also other intermediate courses?

Do you ever study a problem or question to see if perhaps there are limitations on free choice, or whether there may be other ways of answering besides choosing "the one" or "the other"?

AN EXAMPLE OF THE DANGEROUS NATURE
OF DICHOTOMY

THERE is one particular application of the "either . . . or" orientation that can be especially disastrous. Keep in mind that the
high abstractions are vague, and that the higher we go in the abstracting, the vaguer become the outlines of the reality they represent.
Also, keep in mind that "either . . . or" is a very, *very* high abstraction, since it eliminates all but two possibilities in any situation,

The particularly dangerous case we have in mind is the "success
. . . failure" dichotomy. If we are to apply the two-valued system
to this, also, then there are only two possible eventualities; a clean-
cut and absolute success on the one hand, and an absolute and total
failure on the other.

Since, if we are operating on this basis, any case we consider must
be either "B" or "*not* B," then a man must be either "a success" or
"not a success." And "not a success" is generally regarded as equivalent to "failure."

We are taught, in our culture, to work for "success," to seek
"success," to expect "success." You might almost say that "success" was the great goal of many men.

We are taught to seek it. But we are not taught precisely what
this "success" really is, that we seek. That is left open, undefined.
Success can be regarded as election to the Colony Club, or possession
of two Cadillacs, or the acquisition of an honorary degree from alma
mater. It can be the acquisition of money, or of popular approval;
almost anything, according to one's own definitions.

But there is a further question that certainly bears on the problem. "How much?" How much money to constitute "success?" A thousand dollars? A hundred thousand? A hundred million? How do we *measure* the necessary qualifications of "success"?

And if we cannot measure it, that is, if we have not set any measurable standard to define it, how can we tell when we have attained "success"?

You will understand it is, for many of us, vitally important to be "a success." For if we are not, we automatically, according to our habit of "either . . . or" judgment, fall into that other dreadful category, "failure." And that would be disaster.

We can get into trouble in at least two ways with this one. Sometimes we do not define the term at all, so that no matter what riches, honors, and rewards come our way, we cannot with certainty say that we have reached our goal for we have never set a goal in verifiable terms. And sometimes we may set the goal so high that it is quite impossible to reach. And in some cases both of these factors may be operating.

For example: In the course of a conversation over luncheon one Saturday noon, my companion mentioned a conference he had attended at which he met an important industrialist; a man reputed to own some twenty million dollars in corporate securities. My friend asked, "Why should this guy have twenty million dollars?"

This, of course, was not quite the right way to ask the question. "Why," in this connection is meaningless, for it hardly permits of any definite answer.

Apparently, the question represented not so much a desire to get information as to register a protest at "Oh, the unfairness of it all."

It was such a broad, high order question that it overlooked some details. One of these, quite obviously, was that twenty millions of dollars in securities are not precisely the same as twenty millions of dollars in cash in the pocket. These millions are, in a certain sense, fictitious, or at least artificial and arbitrary. One can go out in the open market and sell ten shares of Westinghouse, or a thousand shares. But you cannot call up your broker and sell a hundred thousand shares at anything like the present market value. Also, from a tax viewpoint, and from a functional viewpoint, the twenty millions invested in business are not actually "consumer spending money." They are more or less "fixed" or frozen in corporate activities, and the accounting of this money is mostly handled as a "business" affair, not as a personal affair.

Furthermore, it is not reasonably possible to consider twenty million dollars as "pocket money" for drinks and dinners, mink coats, sports cars, and the like. Anyone could have such luxuries to meet his most extravagant desires for a small portion of this capital.

I think my friend was using "twenty millions" as a symbol of the success he was vaguely craving. Not that the craving itself was vague; but the particular shape of the goal was not clearly drawn.

The goal was set too high; far beyond the reasonable needs of any-one, and far beyond even the limits of almost unlimited indulgence. Also, the goal was vaguely stated in that there was no clear under-standing of just what this "twenty million" really consisted of.

For a man of sixty to start thinking of success in terms of "twenty million" unless he already has several legs on the prize to begin with, is to make sure of failure. For if one is not "a success," under a two-valued system of evaluation, one *must* be the only other choice: "a failure."

The goal, as stated, is not reasonably possible to attain under the conditions stated. Also, there is the possibility that even, assuming it might be attained, it might be hard to know just when the precise accumulation of twenty million had been accomplished; for the accounting of twenty million invested dollars is not such a simple bookkeeping problem as counting the currency in a bank vault, by any means. When we talk of the "value" of a large amount of in-vested capital we have to consider a number of debatable questions, such as the value to be assigned to patents, to "good will," to land and buildings, machinery, etc., and appraisal of various notes, mort-gages, accounts receivable, etc.

So the goal of "twenty million" is actually both too high to be realistic, and too vague to be determinable.

In other words, the man who sets such a goal is pre-destined to disappointment; he is bound to be "a failure."

Sometimes we can solve a problem by re-stating the proposition in different terms, or by changing the words, or modifying the values.

If, for example, in this case, my friend had looked at his own real needs, he would not have fallen into the trap he did. He would then have realized that what he was complaining about was not the fact that somebody else had twenty million dollars, nor even that he did not have twenty million dollars. What he was feeling was that he "did not have enough." And if he took a realistic view of this, and considered "how much" was "enough," he would surely realize that his immediate and pressing wants did not involve millions of dollars. A new garage. Not more than a thousand dollars. A fur coat and some winter clothes for his wife. Perhaps a new model car. Paint the house. A vacation trip. How much altogether. Five thousand, ten thousand, perhaps twenty thousand; but not twenty *million*.

It might be difficult to meet a goal of accumulating twenty thousand dollars. But at least it would be a definite goal. And at least it would be within the realm of imaginable possibility. Such an objective might be hard to reach; but the project would not be fore-doomed to failure from the start.

The reaching for non-existent, or vaguely defined, or impossible goals is not a trivial matter. It touches the roots of a great deal of the disillusionment and despair of people in every department of life, including, of course, the market.

QUESTIONS FOR CONSIDERATION

Since "Success" as defined in the dictionary is wide-open and can refer to any objective or any degree of attainment in any field, have you ever given thought to what you mean when you think of your own "Success"?

Would you consider that you are likely to reach a satisfactory fulfilment in any effort if you do not have a fairly clear idea of just what it is that you are trying to do?

Have you studied the "Success" idea with the thought of breaking it down into components, perhaps in various areas of your life? Have you considered the possibility of "degrees" of attainment, or do you recognize a full-blown "Success" or a complete "Failure" as the only possible outcomes?

Do you realize that there are similar attitudes in a number of other aspects of your life: That one can reduce many questions to a simple, but misleading dichotomy; Health vs. Illness; Virtue vs. Wickedness; Acceptance vs. Rejection; Ability vs. Incompetence, etc.?

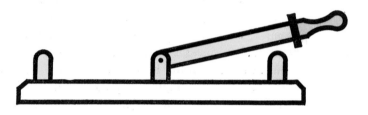

THREE-VALUED ORIENTATIONS

W E HAVE seen how people are taught to think in either . . . or terms about many aspects of life, including some that are much better not regarded in such absolute terms.

And we have seen how this habit of thinking can lead to a single-valued system when one side of an either . . . or situation will lead to self-reproach or public disgrace.

But these are not the only ways of evaluating life situations. There are other systems of evaluation, which in many cases offer a great deal more.

There are three-valued systems. For example, let us suppose I am confronted by an immediate and present danger; let us say this danger is in the form of a lion, escaped from the zoo, which I encounter when I step into a small storage building back of the animal house. Assuming that I do not want to be eaten that day, I must take some definite steps for my protection. I suppose, if I held a heavy whip in one hand and a pistol in the other, and knew how to use both, I could simply advance on the lion and beat him into submission or kill him. In short, I could attack. Or it is conceivable that I might be able to ingratiate the lion, to talk softly to it, to scratch its neck and pat its sides. I could make friends with the lion.

And if I was not "strong" enough to fight the lion to a standstill, and not "sweet" enough to charm the lion, then I could run like hell and slam the heavy door behind me.

In other words, there are two ways in which I could *win* a positive victory; and there is one other way in which I would not lose.

This is basic. People who go through life tied to a one-valued system of evaluation, or those who are limited to a two valued (either . . . or) system should consider the possibilities of the third move; or rather, might well consider the advantage of having three moves instead of only *one* or *two*.

We can lick the gang. We can join the gang. We can keep out of the gang's way. Three courses of action, two positive, and one somewhat negative. But in any case we will not get our head bashed in.

We can consider confronting Russia with overwhelming military power. We can consider a program of conciliation and mutual friendship. Or we can build our defenses and cut ourselves off as far as possible. Not one of these may be a complete or fully effective answer. But they do lay down the patterns along which international strategy must be laid. Three basic moves. Like most of the situations we have been studying you will find this same structure over and over again in many different life situations. Some men dominate women. Some men seduce women. And others avoid women like poison. And in the market, we can buy, we can sell, or we can stay out entirely.

These three basic moves, the move "against," the move "toward," and the move "away," can provide a much greater flexibility than we have in one-valued or two-valued systems. But we have already seen how a two-valued system can become a one-valued system, when one of the two alternatives is suppressed or forbidden. And a somewhat similar limitation often applies to the three-valued system.

Most of us have been trained *not* to be "aggressive." We are forbidden, in many cases, to attack. We cannot move against certain persons (parents, teachers, blind men, nuns, the aged, etc.).

We cannot move "toward" a reconciliation in some cases. We are forbidden to have much friendly feeling toward certain persons (alcoholics, Communists, sex perverts, etc., and it could be, in certain circles, also Jews and Negroes).

Nor can we move freely "away" to protect our interests. It is forbidden or at least disapproved to move conspicuously away from certain persons and groups (family, church, native culture, and all of the social and cultural enclaves in which we move).

Incidentally, we are "forbidden" from acting entirely freely even in the market.   We can "buy"; that has a good sound to it, and enjoys social approval.   But we cannot "sell," certainly not in the sense of selling freely, selling short as readily as buying.   There is a great deal of suspicion and social disapproval connected with short selling; and a good deal of this has penetrated into the value systems of investors, so that they fear to sell, and may actually feel "guilty" in making a short sale.   And while it is not specifically forbidden to stay out of the market (the move "away"), there is such social approval connected with "investing" that it amounts to a definite pressure to "buy sound stocks."   The man who keeps his money in an old sock or in the savings bank does not enjoy great public approbation or self-esteem because of that.

If we could learn to use *three* strategies instead of only one or only two; if we could learn so to evaluate that we could be free to act according to the real needs of a situation instead of reacting to the social pressures which have been built into our own value systems, then we would be able, more often, "not to be eaten by the lion," that is to say, not to be hurt.

QUESTIONS FOR CONSIDERATION

Can you think of six kinds of situation in which you might have a three-valued choice? (Suggestion: I can go to the P.T.A. meeting; I can go to the fights; I can stay home.)

Are there cases which are apparently three-valued, but where, as we saw in either . . . or cases, one or more of the choices is prohibited or impossible?

Are there cases which appear to be three-valued, but where in fact there are a number of possible intermediate choices or combinations?

Can you think of six cases in which the choices to a considerable degree may be considered as "moves toward," "moves away," and "moves against"?

MULTI-VALUED SYSTEMS

B Y THIS time it must be quite clear to you that there are various ways to solve problems. When we say "one-valued," there really are such situations. If you slip on the back steps you grab for the railing. It is the only rational thing to do. There are plenty of "two-valued" situations, where you have two possible courses, and if one is not socially forbidden or suppressed in your value system you can take either course. You can accept the banquet invitation, or you can decline. There are three-valued problems; you vote Republican, you vote Democrat, or you stay home.

But, of course, in some places it is not merely a choice between two parties or staying home, in the election. In France we might find a half a dozen or a dozen parties on the ticket. We could have many choices.

People forget they have many choices. People overlook opportunities as big as elephants.

Joe, for instance, may feel that being half-committed, he must do right by Mary and marry her (one-valued). He may forget, or overlook, or reject the possibility that he could either marry Mary or not (two-valued, either . . . or). He will not give himself the choice that he could marry Mary, or marry Joan, or not marry at all (three-valued). And you could hardly expect a lovesick swain to consider that he could marry Mary, or any of ten other girls, or not marry at all (multi-valued).

Multi-valued strategy would make it unnecessary for the gambler to "go for broke." There may be more to the game than either "shooting the works" or "folding." A man can bet one dollar, five dollars, a hundred, a thousand; he often has a multi-valued choice. And yet, as you know, many card players consider only two courses; to bet the pot, or to quit.

It is hard to believe how strong this impulse to limit choice can be. A majority of commodity traders, for instance, seem to prefer to pick out a single delivery in a single commodity, "the one best," as they see it; and speculate as heavily as possible on the favorable outcome of that one commitment. They will reject quite violently any suggestion that their funds be distributed in a number of commodities so that they will not suffer total loss if any one or any two of their contracts go against them. They do not want a multiple-valued situation. They want to reduce everything to an "either . . . or," which, in the final analysis, means rejecting the "bad" alternative and following a single inflexible choice.

Actually, the world in which we live is filled with multi-valued situations. The telephone book is a directory with many values. We can call up any of thousands of different numbers.

The indicator on an automatic elevator is multi-valued. You are restricted to the choice of definite whole numbers for the floor you want to reach (you cannot ordinarily push a button for the $4\frac{1}{3}$ floor); and you are limited by the number of stories to the building, including perhaps one or two negative integers representing basement and sub-basement. Some automatic alarms are designed to provide a multi-valued choice of rising time, with intervals of fifteen minutes. With a timer like this you can set the clock to turn on the radio at seven o'clock or at seven fifteen, or at seven thirty; but not at three minutes past seven or at seven sixteen.

Stock prices, too, are multi-valued. If a stock is quoted in variations of one-eighth it cannot move up or down less than a full eighth at a time.

When we study the geometry of the circle we learn that by inscribing a multi-sided figure, a regular polygon, either inside or outside of the circle, we approach the form and length of the circumference of the circle closer and closer as we increase the number of sides of the polygon; so that we can say that the "limit" of the sum of the sides of a polygon of many sides, drawn around the outside, or drawn just inside of a circle is the length of the circle itself. Of course, we cannot actually draw a polygon having an "infinite" number of sides; but by using "a great many" sides we can come very close to the figure we want.

In various situations in life it is better to have many points of reference than just one, or two, or three. And in some cases the more points we can set down on our chart, or map, or system of evaluation, the more nearly we can approach an accurate representation of the external reality, and thus our conclusions, based on the map, symbols, etc, will have a better correspondence with the conditions they are supposed to represent. It hardly seems necessary to point out that the closer the map comes to representing the territory, the ·more that map can help you in reaching your objective.

QUESTIONS FOR CONSIDERATION

Can you name six kinds of situation in your own life or experience that you could call "multi-valued"?

Does "multi-valued" mean that the choices are equally possible or desirable? Could it be that some of the apparently possible courses of action might be restricted or forbidden so as make them, in effect, "no choices" at all?

Do you see how it might help you sometimes to re-examine a problem that seems to have only one, two, or three solutions, to see if there might be additional possibilities to be considered?

INFINITE-VALUED SYSTEMS

WE HAVE progressed from single-valued situations where there is no choice at all, through systems offering two choices, three choices, and several or many choices.

It is true that some problems can be expressed only in terms of one, two, three, or some larger number of discrete choices.

But we also have cases which could be called "infinite-valued," or at least "continuous-valued."

When you measure the size of a table top with a tape measure it is true that you call off the size in "inches"; say 40 inches wide and 72 inches long. But this is not quite the same as calling a telephone number or pushing an indicator on an elevator. In these situations you have to make your choice using whole numbers only. But, as you know, when you measure a table, it can be 72-1/2 inches long, or 72-7/16, or if we had a tape accurate enough, 72-19/288. In fact, there is no limit to the number of values we assign to tables having a length of "more than 72 inches" and "less than 73 inches."

Temperature, which we express in degrees, is, of course, not limited to whole numbers of degrees. Temperature is infinite-valued, meaning we can read it as close as our thermometer and our eyesight will permit, and within those limits as close as necessary. For most purposes it is not necessary to know that the temperature outside the kitchen window reads 35.276 degrees Fahrenheit. It is good enough for ordinary purposes to say, "It is 35 degrees."

In determining electrical resistance, potential, etc., and in checking speeds of traffic or machine parts; in reading boiler pressures, light intensities, levels and frequencies of sound waves, in fact, in most of the fact-recording of science we are dealing with infinite-valued functions. And you will keep in mind that "infinite-valued" means simply that we are not limited to "whole numbers," but we can measure the data as closely as our equipment will permit and our needs require. "Measurement" as contrasted to "counting" is the key to the infinite-valued orientation.

And it should be obvious enough that a man is failing to use his entire problem-solving forces if he uses too "coarse" a measure. You would not want to use a scale designed for weighing freight cars in the railroad yard for weighing diamonds, since in the case of coal or sand it would be sufficient to determine the weight within a few pounds and there would be no sense in trying to get the exact number of ounces in a 30,000 pound load. But the difference of a small fraction of a carat (a carat is roughly 1/150th part of an ounce) would be important in the weighing of diamonds.

On the other hand, you would certainly not want to use a jeweler's scale to weigh out a carload of coal.

The matter of "measuring" concerns the choice of a suitable unit, where the choice is "infinite." It would be appropriate to use a steel tape to measure the George Washington Bridge. But for measuring the diameter of a ball bearing we need a micrometer. It is just as stupid to spend time and energy taking unnecessarily accurate measurements as it is to take measurements that are inadequate because they are not sufficiently accurate.

There may be some confusion in your mind unless you are thoroughly familiar with the use of technical and symbolic material, as to the relation of "maps," "symbols," "value systems," etc. To the engineer it is very easy to see a choice of several decisions reduced to so many specific points on a diagram. He can also see the choice of decisions in an "infinite-valued" system as the choice of any point on a smooth curve. The more accurately he measures his data and draws his charts the more precise an answer he can expect to get from the map or diagram. And as we said, it is very important to have a scale and measure that is appropriate to what we are trying to find out.

Another way of putting this, and a way that irritates some people brought up in the "perfectionist" school, is that we follow a rough rule of "least effort." We do the job just as carefully as necessary, but no more so. We never shoot for any greater accuracy than is needed.

This is important. A bank statement has to read to the last penny. But an estimate of the national debt for 1970 does not need to be figured to anything closer than a few millions; in fact, anything expressed more accurately would be misleading, since it is not possible to predict this figure very closely. In the same way it is a waste of time to measure and record the size of a gymnasium in 64ths of an inch; since all we need to know is the size in feet and to the nearest odd inch. Just so long as we keep in mind that the data obtained by physical measurement is not "precise" and does not need to be precise, and *should not be* expressed with any more precision than is needed for the job at hand, we do not need to consider the very small leftover fractions, beyond the tolerances we have set.

So *measuring* is quite different in principle from *counting;* for there are no indefinite leftovers when you say there are six eggs or ten eggs.

In mathematical computation there are two basic methods; and it will not surprise you to know that these are based on the "counting" idea and on the "measuring" idea. The prototype of the "counting" method is the abacus where a certain number of beads represent a certain definite number, exactly, no more and not one bit less. The model for the "measuring" method is the slide rule, which can give you as much accuracy as its scale and your eyesight will permit, but which never expresses a positive, definite result. In other words, with a slide rule, like measuring the size of a room, you can get it as closely as you need it; but you cannot say that the result is "precisely" 172.43908 inches.

Modern computers represent these two basic methods. If they are of the "counting" type, we call them "digital." If they are of the "measuring" type we call them "analogue."

Strangely enough, the differences in the two types of computations are not so vitally important in practice as you might suppose. The apparent "absolute" precision of the digital machine disappears when you begin to run into long calculations involving decimals; for the string of decimal places very quickly runs right off the paper and out of sight, and the very small values at the right hand end of the decimal result become so unimportant as to be entirely negligible. Furthermore, some types of data, which for ordinary purposes we think of as "infinite-valued" are not really unlimited. For instance, we can magnify an object with lenses; we can make it appear bigger yet with microscopes; but eventually we reach a point where the units (the lengths of waves) by which we "see" become so coarse that we cannot "see" any more by further magnification. The image breaks down into "discrete" impressions, like a coarse screen photograph in a newspaper, or like the detail on a television screen.

Most of the data that we treat as "infinite-valued" is, if we carry the argument to the limit, actually "multi-valued." At some point, when we break down our measurements to something very small indeed, we reach a stage where it is simply not possible to go any further because we have reached the point where the data itself is discontinuous and has to be read in "packages" or discrete units; or because our sense organs cannot perceive the stimulus beyond a certain point, except in this manner of separate "packages" or discrete units.

At some point we arrive at the end of the line, where we have broken up the data into the ultimate, smallest "bits." And at that point it is not possible to measure any further; nature has no means of communicating any more detail to us. In the case of counting sheep, this point is reached at the limit of "one sheep." In figuring a bank account the ultimate limit is "one cent." With most stock prices the limit is one-eighth of a point. In various scientific studies we are limited by certain physical constants representing the final breakdown of the data to its ultimate "bits."

The reason we have touched on these questions about "infinite-valued systems" is so that you will understand clearly the nature of what is meant by "infinite-valued." What we really mean is "having a very large (but not necessarily unlimited) number of values."

QUESTIONS FOR CONSIDERATION

In your ordinary daily life how many situations can you think of that involve "counting," where it is possible to give an answer in precise terms?

Now how many situations can you think of that involve "measuring," where it is possible to give only an approximate answer?

Do you see that in dealing with very large numbers of things (such as grains of sand on a beach) "counting" and "measuring" would give approximately the same results for many purposes? Also do you see that in "measuring" situations you are able to make your observations as accurately as your need requires within the limitations of your measuring equipment?

Do you understand how it is possible in "infinite-valued" systems to make very delicate adjustments or shifts, which would not be possible where you were limited to a small number of discrete intervals or units?

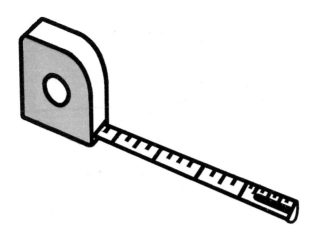

THE GREEKS HAD A PHRASE FOR IT

THE ancient Greeks fell into some colossal blunders in their philosophy and in their science. The "good old days" of two thousand years ago were really "the very young days" of man's understanding. But what is striking about the work they left to us is not what they did not know, or what they knew that was not true. It is how much they were able to discover that was useful and significant and valid especially in view of the limited inheritance of knowledge they received from their predecessors, and the rather primitive equipment they had for making their observations.

We can take the good time-binding they did for us and put it to work today. That is, we can admire and accept whatever part of their architecture, and literature, and mathematics, and logic, etc. we find applicable to the conditions under which we live today in the light of what we know now.

One of the really basic principles of the Greeks can be expressed in the phrase, "Nothing in excess"; and along with this, another phrase, "Measure in all things."

This idea of moderation, of reasonable sufficiency holds the answer to a great many problems that we all have to face every day.

The man who understands this would not be tied to a compulsive need to "hitch his wagon to a star." He would not have to be absolutely successful, absolutely honest, absolutely generous; in short, he would be freed of the one-valued orientation, free to live like a man instead of trying to live like a saint. He would live in reality

177

instead of projecting an image of some high order abstraction and trying to "live up to it."

Of course, to some people, to many people, this drive for perfection is a good thing. As Browning put it, "What I aspired to be, and *was not*, comforts me." We are taught to think this way. We are taught that if we aim very high, if we aim at the very pinnacle, we may still come closer to perfection than those who set their aims very low.

However, if the aims are so high, or so absolute, or so vague that there is no hope of realizing them (a "miss," we are taught, "is as good as a mile") this one-valued orientation may lead to demoralization.

And when the one "right" course to the one "right" objective is contrasted with its "either . . . or" opposite number, the slightest falling short of the goal becomes a complete and utter failure. The man who is frustrated in achieving his impossible aims feels entirely defeated, and is a prey to depression and anxiety.

The Greeks held the key to this problem. But it is as good as lost for many of us, for we have been taught and trained *not to use it*. In our culture we do not put a premium on "measuring in all things." We learn to "go all-out," to make up our minds and then shoot the works. We want the top or nothing. And this oversimplification, where we apply a one-valued or two-valued method to what may be at the very least a three-valued situation, and which may be a multi-valued or infinite-valued one, limits our chances of success.

You will see that these oversimplifications are tied up with the process of abstracting which we discussed earlier. They are not entirely "false," and that is what makes them so dangerous. But they are "faulty," in that they are *inadequate*.

Tell a man that he is making a mistake to set such a high value on "kindness" (a very high order term) that he will feel guilty if he flares up at a child throwing rocks at his car, and he is likely to "hear" you in a two-valued way. If you "don't believe in kindness," then you must believe in unbridled cruelty to children.

In the same way, if he occasionally feels justified in telling a small White Lie, there are some who feel he has thrown honesty to the winds and will stop at nothing. If I say I am not satisfied that all stocks are acting bullishly, there are friends who will take this for a statement that I believe this "is a Bear Market."

But there is something *between* up and down, or black and white, or good and bad. Or between success and failure. It is possible for a man who has learned to "measure in all things" to enjoy a *modicum* of success. He can arrive at the amount of success that for him is "necessary and sufficient."

Engineers know this well. Since all engineering measurements are approximations, the framework of a problem becomes a study in how much accuracy is "necessary and sufficient." It is not at all necessary, nor is it desirable, to shoot for perfection. And failure to achieve the (often impossible) perfection, is not necessarily ruin or failure.

So we can shoot for "*this* goal" *up to a point* (modified one-valued method). We can choose "*this* or *that*, or *something in between*" (modified two-valued system). We can go *this way* or *that way* or *stay where we are*, or *some combination of these choices* (modified three-valued-system). Or we can make our choice *on a scale of many values*, perhaps operating between certain specified limits (multi-valued system).

These last thoughts are not always accepted freely. It is very hard, as we all know, to change the long established habits that were inculcated in us when we were quite young. People will fight to defend old maps and old symbols, regardless of whether they actually represent any territory here and now, and regardless of whether they ever did represent just what we were told they represented.

Even when people will take their map and go to the territory and compare it, and note the changes or corrections it needs, they will *still* cling to the old map. The picture we have in our memory of the old swimmin' hole may be more meaningful to us than the photograph of that spot as it is today. We cling to our ideas about family, and about sex, and about "our country," and about God, and about the ways we feel about ourselves and our neighbors *as if* the maps we hold in our minds were more real than the external realities themselves. So much so that even when these realities have demonstrably changed, or are provably different from the "map," we still tend to deny the external reality and assert the "truth" of the map.

We know that very often it is better to think of something in "degrees" rather than in "absolutes." But the old habits stick by us. We "know" better, but somehow we go right on following the old methods.

In some fields there is no difficulty in thinking according to "degree." No one would think of limiting the temperature of a room to either "hot" or "cold." These words are too broad; for then we would have to assume that if the room is "not hot," it is "cold," and vice versa. That might not be an entirely valueless report, for as between a room at, say, 100 degrees and one at 20 degrees, most people would agree that the former was "hot" and the latter "not hot," and therefore "cold."

But this does not allow for any very fine discrimination. Neither does it allow for any personal choice. Since the concepts "hot" and "cold" are very high order abstractions, they may be different for various individuals, and there is no way to compare these maps directly at the very high levels of abstraction.

But when we measure in multiple or infinite steps, we can assign much closer (and more generally verifiable) values to "hot" and "cold." We can ask "*how* hot?"; "*how* cold?"

This is all very obvious in the case of simple physical measurements such as temperature, voltage, pressure, distance, etc. The principle is not so easy to accept when we are dealing with "love," or "purity," or "success," or even with evaluation of the stock market.

The way we are taught to think, the way almost everyone in our culture has been taught to think, we do not like to see things in terms of "degree." It is almost as though we had been taught to "measure in nothing," or to follow a principle of "everything in excess."

We understand and appreciate the simple, all-out statement much better than we grasp the thoughtful, measured evaluation. This is because the vague, loosely defined generality at a high level of abstraction seems much more significant than the imperfect, measured, observations from reality.

In our enthusiasm over being able to abstract to high principles, which animals cannot do, we forget that the principles, if they have any validity, must derive from roots based on external reality. And so we reject reality which is the source of truth, because it is not so perfect and so all-embracing and so absolute as the fine sparkling abstractions.

We prefer the glorious glittering generality to the little, earthy fact.

And so, speakers will win great audiences orating about "brotherhood," and "holiness," and "loyalty," where the trained observer who is trying to do a job of helping human beings with "necessary and sufficient" solutions to their real problems here and now, stirs no great emotions and wins no great following.

We would not weaken our position if we tried a little *measuring* in making our decisions. Perhaps then we would not inquire whether an employee was "honest," or "not honest"; we might, instead, investigate "how honest" he was. We would not ask ourselves whether we were "a success" or "a failure," but would decide what constituted for us success, and estimate *to what degree* we had achieved it.

But many people don't like "hedgers." They want a leader to speak right out in black-and-white, all-out terms. No compromise. No measuring. Everything "to the limit." If some Jews caused some trouble in Germany, many would not want to know "what Jews," or "to what extent and degree" they made "trouble." Many would (and did) accept the all-out condemnation of *all* Jews as totally "bad"; and the remedy proposed (and used) was simply to *exterminate*, so far as possible, *all* Jews. This is what the "all-out" way of thinking can lead to as it has over and over again in the tragic record of wars, persecutions, massacres, and inquisitions across the pages of history.

People want clean-cut, easy directives in plain loud words like cannon balls. They do not want to hear that "some stocks appear to us to be weak, but about sixty percent still seem to be moving in bullish trends." What they want is a statement that "Yesterday's market confirmed the up trend. The market will make new highs for at least two years to come. Fantastic profits will be secured by those who buy now." Perhaps you have read such statements in the commentaries and the advertisements of financial experts. The public thinks it understands what is meant by a Bull Market. The label does not raise any questions about "how bullish?" or "what stocks are bullish?" It simply indicates, "Buy now!"

And like most absolute directives, such all-out terms carry an unspoken prediction, as though the statement read, "*If* you buy now *you will make fabulous profits.*" This is very similar to the implied promises in other directives. "*If* you honor your father and your mother, your days *will be* long upon the land which the Lord thy God giveth thee." "*If* you are honest, it *will be* the best policy."

We have many of these plain directives, concerning how we regard almost every basic problem of life. You can read them, or hear them any day in the week, and especially on Sunday. They are stated without particularization as to "when," or "where," or "under what conditions." They are stated as absolutes, without limit and without degree. And it is never explained that they represent not reality itself but the outcome of many stages of logic and inference, crystallized as a "judgment" or "opinion."

This is too bad. For many of these directives have a solid center of truth. They are not without value. But they may need verifying, and re-statement in terms of multiple or infinite orientation.

And so, if we really want the most useful answer to a question, we do not go to the mass meeting and listen to a speaker repeating, with gestures, the simplified, generalized wisdom of the ages. We go to the laboratory and study the facts, and we determine to what degree the ancient principles apply today. We measure. We determine what is necessary and what is sufficient, what is valid in the ancient lore and what we can add or change to make it useful for us here and now. We accept the partial, imperfect answer carefully framed to include no more ground than our data will justify us in including. And where we don't know, we say, "I don't know," until we have further facts.

If we look at things in this manner, testing, checking, correcting, accepting only as much from the "directives" as we can reasonably justify, we will be accused of "weakness." Because we cannot or will not come right out and say whether "this" is black or white, therefore we must be "unable to make up our own mind." We must be too ignorant or too timid to take a stand. Unless we can plunk all-out that the Egyptians are "right" and the Sudanese "wrong," then we are vacillating. There is no room for anything in between, no possibility of a "partial" rightness or wrongness. We must endorse a Bull Market or look for a panic. We must pick up one side of the dichotomy and forget the other, and everything between entirely.

Is this the road to better understanding? Is this an approach that is going to help us to understand ourselves and the world around us and how to deal with it?

Is it any wonder that there are contradictions between the views of various statesmen and moralists and stock market analysts, if they are each clinging to a simple all-out view and for all practical purposes ignore anything that does not support the view they hold already? There are no contradictions in reality, you know. When experts declared a Bear Market to be in existence in the summer of 1957, Lorillard did not fit the map. It was true enough that some stocks, many stocks, a great majority of stocks were bearish and fell many points. But Lorillard was pursuing a Bull Market course in every sense of the word, and doubled its value during 1957. This is a contradiction at the high level of "Bear Market." But it is no contradiction at the level of what Lorillard actually did. If we can just look away from the high abstraction long enough to see the facts, we find no contradiction. The only contradiction is in our too-high, too-absolute statement. And if we value the map more than the reality, we must not be surprised to find that the reality doesn't always fit the map. In such a case the reasonable man will change his map; not try to explain away the facts.

Notice that it is not necessary to throw away or burn up the map. Just as we have gone beyond Aristotle in logic, Euclid in geometry, beyond Newton in physics, beyond Freud in psychiatry, we have also gone beyond Dow and Hamilton in understanding the technics of stock trends. But we do not discard all the great work of Aristotle, Euclid, Newton, and Freud. Nor Dow and Hamilton. We simply add the necessary corrections and additions to the maps they left for us, and use these revised and up-to-date maps now.

In some cases this will mean correcting erroneous statements. It may mean developing a new hypothesis better to explain what we perceive in external reality. More often it will mean a slight modification of the terms. For example, a whole family of paradoxes in logic can be eliminated by adding to the words, "This statement is true in all cases," the words, "except in this case." Thus, in order to give any meaning to the all-out statements, "I am a Texan. No Texan ever tells the truth," I must add "except in this case." We could still question whether the statement will hold true, but at least it makes sense, which the first does not. But the biggest, most useful change we can make in the old maps is to add the dimension of "degree." When we specify "how much" or "how many" we will be so much better off than when we say "all" or "everybody," or "forever," or "absolutely."

When we learn to "measure in all things," we will have "nothing in excess."

QUESTIONS FOR CONSIDERATION

Would you agree that in starting out on any venture, whether constructing a temple or building a savings fund, one should have some measurements defining the job to be done?

Would you feel that it was sufficient to decide to build "the most glorious temple" or the "biggest ampitheatre" as a basis for engineering operations?

Wouldn't the same reasoning apply to "building a savings fund" or "seeking happiness"? Isn't it necessary to know at least the rough outlines of what you want?

Is it realistic to set one's goal at the most distant and highest target?

Or would it be more practical to set a more moderate goal and proceed to it one step at a time?

Do you limit your choices to one or two by thinking in "absolute" terms instead of in "degree"? Which seems to you more likely to convey to others (and yourself) just what you mean: an all-out "either . . . or" point of view, or a "multi-valued" point of view?

Do you habitually think of people in high-order categories? Do you regard "women drivers" as a class and judge them accordingly? "Lutherans?" "Koreans?" "Speculators?" "Juvenile delinquents?"

Is there any reason a man should not say, "I don't know," until he has had a chance to examine the current facts of a situation?

Do you consciously try to avoid speaking and thinking in words that cover more ground than you mean to cover? Do you watch for "absolute" words that go farther than you really mean to go?

IMPERFECT INFORMATION

YOU can imagine how unacceptable it would be to a person who has been carefully taught to accept a certain value system, that some of the basic premises of that system would have to be changed. Perhaps you have read Oscar Wilde's story of the Birthday of the Infanta; and wept, as I have wept, at the spectacle of the little princess, brought up to feel that her slightest wish would be met always and always, faced at last with the inexorable fact that Death was not bound to this directive. She, who could command whatever she pleased, had to face the unpleasant fact that Death could claim her, as it could claim any of her subjects.

When we have been brought up to feel that "there is an answer to everything" and that answer, if we only look diligently enough, will explain everything, it is hard to reconcile ourselves to methods that deny the possibility of obtaining perfect information.

It is terribly hard to have to build a way of life around such terms as "I don't know," "maybe," "up to a point," "so far as we can find out at this time," "in all probability," etc. It would be so much easier to have a sure, pat answer, "yes" or "no" to all the questions we have to answer.

We can get those pat answers, too. If we want to close our eyes to reality and work in the ivory tower of high abstractions, we can find the perfection that, alas, is not to be found in the world of reality. But it won't always help us, if we do this; not when we have to deal with the imperfect and the approximate.

You will find, perhaps you have already found, that the law has a great tendency to take the broad directives stated in the ancient wisdom, and apply them to this particular case here and now, as if the map made five hundred years ago told us *all* about this poor devil picked up in Hoboken for obtaining money under false pretenses from his father-in-law. The law, by and large, is not interested and not able to make a particular study of all the factors in this individual case. It is necessary to classify it, that is to convert it into a higher abstraction, and chuck it into the pigeonhole with other cases having *some* similarities.

In every field, especially those concerned with ethics and human relations, we assume that a "perfect" or "ideal" case will serve as a map of all possible cases in present reality. This can lead to a lot of lawsuits, and a lot of other troubles as well.

When you begin to treat "the market" as if it were a single, real thing, instead of the highly complex aggregation of individual cases that it really is, you can delude yourself badly. For instance, if "in the summer of 1957 we had a Bear Market," then we would be justified in selling Parke, Davis short.

Now mark this well! There *was some truth* in the conclusion that "in the summer of 1957 we had a Bear Market." If we had to limit our action to "buying everything" or "selling everything," we would do much better to follow the map and "sell everything." But we can do better by accepting the partial and "imperfect" answer that "most stocks" are bearish, instead of taking the all-out course. If we followed such a plan, we would not have sold Parke, Davis, but would have treated it, on its own merits, for what it was . . . a strongly bullish stock. We might still have sold a majority of stocks, but not this one.

By accepting the imperfect reality instead of the "perfect" ideal, we can often do much better.

The very word "imperfect" suggests that there is something wrong with the information. Really, all it says is that we don't know everything. And unless we have impossibly high standards, which can ruin us in the end, we do not need to seek a "perfect," or "absolute" answer. We can deal with the facts directly, and we do not even need to seek "complete" information about them. All we need is "necessary and sufficient" data, which is something else again.

Considering the market again, if you had been brought up to

believe in "success versus failure," a strictly two-valued orientation, then you are faced all the time with the necessity of classifying "the market" as "strong" or "weak." You cannot very well stay out of it entirely; this is the third choice, the running-away, and nobody likes a quitter, not even you. So you must choose. You must make the all-out choice between black and white. Nothing in between. Either it is a Bull Market, or . . . what else can "it" be. It must be, then, a Bear Market.

But unless you have "a pipeline to the Almighty" as John Brooks expressed it in one of his feature articles on finance in The New Yorker magazine, you are going to be torn by anxiety all the time.

For one thing, not all stocks move together. The case of Parke, Davis is not unique; not even rare. During a series of crashes in early 1953, Pacific Western Oil made new highs, even through a downside late tape.

Ask someone what happened to the market in 1929. He will probably tell you that for several years "the market" had been advancing spectacularly. That it made its high in early fall, 1929. That it crashed in late October, and the crash continued, to become the worst Bear Market in all history.

That is true, in a sense. If we substitute for "the market" the words "Dow-Jones Industrial Average," it is true, Approximately true. It overlooks the big four month rally ending in April, 1930, which many regarded as a resumption of the Bull Market. It overlooks the steady downward trend of dozens of important stocks right through 1924-25-26-27-28-29. It says nothing about the really big stocks, such as Chrysler, which topped out over a year before "the crash," and had lost many, many points in their own private Bear Markets long before "the market" toppled. It sweeps under the rug the fact that many stocks made new Bull Market highs in 1930, and a few stocks made their bottoms in 1929, proceeding from there to start genuine Major Bull Market trends of their own.

Then is the statement that the market advanced to 1929 and then crashed and declined to 1932, a false one?

No. It is not false. It is true to a degree. To a large degree. But we will have a better grasp of the situation if we do not distort and color the picture so as to lose sight of all the contrary action. People get hurt taking things for granted. People get killed because they project a map instead of checking the detail in reality.

My father used to drive an open car from a railroad way station at one end of Morraine Road in Highland Park, Illinois, to the dead end of this road where it terminated at the grounds of the Morraine Hotel.   Along Morraine Road there were just six overhead street lights, spaced rather widely.   On the hotel grounds at the end of the road were a number of trees, and between two of the trees was strung a guy wire at a height of about four feet from the ground.

One evening he and my mother, and two other couples were returning to the hotel down this road.   Father decided to "let the car out" and show what it could do.   He counted the street lights as he came down the Morraine Road, intending to stop before the dead-end at the hotel grounds.   Unfortunately, one of the lights was out that night.   The car tore over the curb, into the hotel park, and it was only by sheerest good luck that some of the passengers did not lose their heads as the car slewed just barely past the heavy steel guy wire.

It was *true*, you will notice, that he had *passed five lights*.   But his information was imperfect; he did not know that one of the lights had burned out.   And he had acted as if his information was perfect and complete.   The data was not false, but inadequate.

When we consider factual, observable events, we can get into a great deal of trouble if we insist on looking at only the high abstractions of these events.   But this is nothing to the troubles we can get into when we are dealing with "uncertainties."

The average man does not like uncertainties.   He is not trained to cope with them.   He will try to "sweep them under the rug." He will use any device that will make it possible for him to feel "more sure," for he is not willing to accept a "maybe" or an "I don't know" as an answer.

And so he will resort to averages, to market indicators, to complicated charts of intersecting lines designed to prove that "it" is either a Bull Market or a Bear Market.   He will accept almost any kind of nonsense if it is stated with enough assurance.   He will buy horoscopes to determine the trend of the market by the position of the planets.   If all else fails, he will look for some authority who will relieve him of using his own intelligence, by making the either . . . or decisions for him.   But he must have a straight, simple answer; otherwise it means nothing to him.

Do you see how this way of looking at things is out of line with the facts?   Do you see how it leads, inevitably, to frustration, anxiety, and demoralization?

It is asking too much of reality. It is setting up a make-believe world, and then crying if the world isn't exactly like the make-believe.

We know, for instance, that trees "in general" are round. But you have seen tree trunks distorted by a cramped location, or by the trunks of adjacent trees, that are not round at all. It is useful to know that "tree trunks are round," only so long as we understand that this is an abstraction, and the reality in any particular case has to be looked at . . . and if it is not round, that is *that*; the territory is the final answer, not our "map."

Suppose we are faced with a more difficult situation. We are going to draw a card out of a well-shuffled deck of fifty-two cards. Which will it be; red or black? A man could go crazy trying to figure this one out. He might consult fortune tellers, astrologers, mystics; but it is questionable whether any of these experts could help him to achieve a significantly accurate naming of the next card to be turned.

What to do? Do we turn our backs on the question, and say (as many do when it comes to the market), "It's all just a gamble." It's a gamble, yes. But not "just" a gamble. It isn't true that we know nothing about the outcome, and it isn't true that we can't cope with the situation. But we cannot name, without fail, always and always, what color the next card will be.

And that hurts. It hurts to be "wrong." We have been taught to be "right." And if not "right," then we must be . . . "wrong."

QUESTIONS FOR CONSIDERATION

Is it possible to know *everything* about *anything*?

When you are engaged in a competitive business can you expect to know *all* about your competitors' plans, their status, and their prospects?

Do you make allowances in domestic, or business, or market situations for the fact that your knowledge of any particular event is "not all" about it?

Do you realize how much has been left out of such maxims as, "A bird in the hand is worth two in the tree," "Red-headed girls have fiery tempers," "You can't go broke taking a profit," "A vote for Finley is a vote for prosperity"? How many different kinds of omissions can you spot in these? Would you say that these are necessarily completely false?

Is it possible to be "sufficiently right for all practical purposes" in some situations where you have only a small amount of data?

Is this a Bull Market now? Or a Bear Market? How could you get into trouble by answering either of these questions "yes" or "no"?

Are you satisfied to be "partly right"; enough right to achieve your purpose? Or do you insist on being "perfect"?

Do you believe a man can operate successfully against a situation that is not fully predictable?

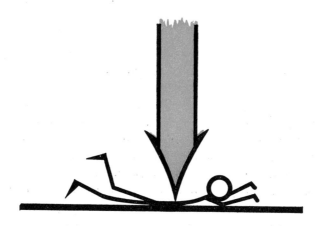

WHY DOES IT HURT SO MUCH?

IF THE non-material part of your "self," that thinks and feels and chooses, is, as we have suggested before, the most important part of your living; and its preservation and enhancement the first objective of survival; the most important value in life; then anything that attacks or threatens to attack this "self" must be avoided, if possible.

How serious any kind of attack must be rated depends on how we perceive the attack. An assault by a gangster armed with a knife might appear rather frightening to me. It would probably be much less alarming to a soldier trained in judo.

Any kind of attack will be perceived according to the nature of the attack itself and also according to our own equipment for coping with it, as we see it. "As we see it" is important, for we all know cases where a big brute of a boy is chivvied around the school yard by a nasty little bully; and we say, "Charles doesn't know his own strength." So long as he doesn't, he is going to be licked by the little bully every afternoon.

Consider the matter of losing money. If the threatened loss is trivial, say a nickel or a dime, we are not going to feel hurt very badly. And if the threatened loss is large, but we have the means of preventing or recovering the loss, we will not be bothered very much, either. But if the threatened loss appears large, inevitable and final, then we are going to worry a good deal about it.

The principle would be similar whether the loss was money, or love, or reputation, or self-regard. If it is trivial, we don't need to bother. If we can avoid the loss we will do so.   And if we actually realize the loss, we all suffer according to the value we have assigned to what was lost.   In other words, the loss of a hundred dollars might be a very serious matter to me, but only a small inconvenience to you.

Naturally, the loss that will hurt the most is the loss of that which has the highest value.   And if you agree that our non-material "self" has the highest value of all to each of us, then a threat against that "self" is the most ominous danger, depending on the degree of the threat and our ability to cope with the attack.

If you have watched children playing, as I have watched my own, you know that a large part of their play revolves around competitive situations, as if the purpose of the game was not the game itself, but a demonstration of which child is strongest, smartest, etc., etc.   The playing often seems to be a contest to determine the "peck order" of the siblings; and very likely that is just what it is.

If the purpose of games and contests is to demonstrate superiority, this suggests that most children (and a good many grownups, too) have such feelings of inferiority that it is necessary for them, continually, to prove how smart or how strong they are.   This reassures the timid one and makes him feel better about himself.   It is probably why so many people like to watch the big TV giveaway programs, for while they cannot win the $64,000 sitting at home and watching, they can, if they are smart enough, name the first governor of the state of Arizona, and give the date of the Dred Scott decision, thus proving to themselves that they are as smart as the fellow before the camera and that they *would* be able to win the $64,000 if they were on the stage.   It does things for their "self-regard."

It would be hard to check this next statement.   One might hazard the guess that (in some cases at least) the public acclaim and recognition, which must in turn lead to a private up-grading of *one's* own self-regard, may be more important to the winners than the cash or mink coats or trips to Hawaii that they receive as material reward.

This is a long way around to repeat the old cliche about money not being everything.   What is everything, or damn near everything, is this matter of self-regard.

Certainly there are many, many times when a man will pass up monetary gain in order to make his "self" look better.   "Let my sister have the inheritance. She needs it more than I do." Why? Because he loves his sister? Yes. But before that love, another. By his generosity he will enhance his "self."

In spite of the classic economists, who had a useful though somewhat inadequate map of human motivation, men and women do not always act according to "dollar wisdom." When the chips are down a man will not do for money profit anything that causes him too serious a loss in self-esteem. What his standards and values are in this matter, of course, depend on his whole background and training; you do not expect the same evaluative abstractions in a dope peddler that you might look for in a bishop.

The question, "Why are you in the market?" seems stupid. If we took a vote on this question in a number of brokers' board rooms, I am sure we would get a fairly uniform answer, "To make money." Like so many simple answers this has some truth in it; also, like so many simple answers, it is grossly inadequate.

For one thing, if the object of being in the market is solely to make money, some of these fellows would do well to get out and get a job in some other line of work, for it is hard to believe that all of the familiar faces that have turned up each morning for fifteen years or more to watch the translux until closing belong to men who have made consistent and substantial profits in the market sufficient to justify the expenditure of all these years of time.

Of course, these board room traders, like others in the market, want to make money. But that is not necessarily the only goal, and there is some evidence to indicate that it is not even the principal goal.

If making money was the only goal, and if these men had used their own powers of observation over a period of, say, the past ten years, they would either have found out enough about the market to be able to take care of their monetary problems, or have decided that the market was not for them.

But, apparently, there are other factors. Social factors. There is congenial and familiar company in the board room. Matters of habit. After a few years one must become very accustomed to the easy-going comradery of the board room. And for some it may represent, too, a welcome shelter away from the problems of home.

Certainly the board room provides a place where one can pit one's self against the forces of "the market," and an audience for whatever victories one achieves.

There is a continual communication of sorts going on in one of these chapels of commerce. Everyone seems to have rather definite ideas about what "it" ("the market") is going to do next. Also, there is a good deal of Monday morning quarterbacking, especially with respect to the recent past action of "it," and of certain stocks.

"Didn't I tell you last Monday, Sam, that we'd get a three-day rally?" "If you'd listened to me you wouldn't have sold Polaroid." "See that 'FGT'? I bought that, the old stock, last year. It's gone up 200 percent."

Somehow these remarks, and many more like them, seem not so much to be directed to the apathetic listeners, who appear to be anxious, mostly, to get in their own two cents' worth; but to be inwardly directed, as though to reassure a timid and uncertain man. The loud, over-assured opinions remind one of the small boy passing the tough gang hangout, and muttering under his breath, "I ain't afraid of *nobody*." Meaning, "I'm scared most to death."

I think we can safely assume that a good part of the board room chatter comes under the head of "talking to one's self," and that it is for the specific purpose of bucking up an apprehensive "self." There is fear and doubt here, not too deeply concealed.

Jones buys 100 shares of Fruehauf Trailer at 24. He will tell you with all the enthusiasm of the true believer what a fine company Fruehauf is, and what excellent prospects they have for the coming twelve months. He will tell you everything he knows that is "good" about the stock; but he will not tell you anything that is "bad." For him there *is* no "bad." His mind is made up. He does not want to be confused with facts. He is not looking for the truth; he has found it. And like a politician or a minister or a trial lawyer, he is not trying to see reality as it is. He is trying to keep himself convinced that his "map" of Fruehauf is actually a good one. He wants to hear nothing that will upset his all-out judgment. He does not want to learn anything different or anything that will require him to change his opinion. What he wants and needs is argument to bolster his shaky judgment and make him feel a little more secure. Therefore, he will not read, or he will forget, anything that appears in the Wall Street Journal which threatens his faith that Fruehauf is "all" good. And he will clip and treasure the favorable comments or reports that tend to show that he was, in fact, "right." The data he collects are no doubt true; but they present a very one-sided picture.

Suppose now, that Fruehauf stock sells off to 18. Will he re-examine the territory and see whether there have been essential changes in the situation "out there"? Or will he, more often than not, cling to the old map of his original opinion and simply go on a search for more evidence to confirm his "rightness" in that opinion? He may even buy another hundred shares of the stock on the basis that if his original conclusion was valid, then this new purchase will "average his cost," or lower the average cost of all the shares he owns, so that even a moderate advance would put him back in the profit column.

What is he doing? Is he making an impartial evaluation of a stock? Or is he defending his obsolete opinion in the face of present facts? Is he acting in a way that is likely to make him profits? Or is he setting a higher value on "being right" than on the money involved?

Let Fruehauf drop to twelve dollars a share. Will this man sell now? No. It would hurt too much to sell. Who would it hurt? Why, it would hurt him, of course. How would it hurt him? Well, it would mean a loss in money. But isn't it clear that the larger loss is not measured in dollars, but in *pride*. It will hurt less to sweep the facts under the rug and delude one's self, and maintain that one was "right" in the beginning and is "right" still, than it will to admit that one was a fool.

To put it another way: if he has decided, "The stock is worth sixty dollars a share," and the market says it is now worth twelve dollars a share, then the market must be wrong. For the sacred map cannot be wrong. It would hurt too much. Call it fantasy, preju-dice, opinion, judgment, what you will, when the high abstraction collides with bare facts, it is the facts that have to give way if your value system places such a high premium on "rightness" that your tender ego cannot suffer the slightest setback.

Many men cannot afford to take monetary losses in the market. Not because of the money itself so much as because of their over-sensitive, poorly trained "selves." The humiliation would be un-bearable. It would hurt too much. The only way that occurs to such men to prevent such painful situations is to strive to be "always right" or nearly always right. If by study and extreme care they could avoid "making mistakes," they would not be exposed to the hard necessity of having to take humiliating losses over and over again.

And so? And so, too often, rather than settle for a relatively minor loss, our friend will stand firmly on the deck of his first judgment, and will go down with the ship. The history of Wall Street (and of LaSalle Street, too) is studded with the stories of men who refused to be wrong; and who ended up ruined, with only the tattered shreds of their false pride left to them for consolation.

How to avoid such unnecessary tragedies? Be "always right"? You know that isn't possible. Keep away from the speculative market entirely? That is one answer, but it is rather like burning down the barn to get rid of the rats.

There are other answers, and they are so simple. They are standing there, right at hand, like elephants in the front hall, if we can only see them.

In the first place, there is no rule that we can't change our minds. It is not necessarily "wrong" or "a mistake" to believe that Fruehauf stock will go up from twenty-four to sixty. What is "wrong" is sticking to the opinion after the evidence clearly shows that the conditions have changed. The rational approach is to be ready at all times to consider new evidence, and to revise the map accordingly.

In the second place, it need not hurt so much to have to change one's mind. Unless we are so wedded to absolute standards that we cannot entertain anything that will conflict with what we decided in the first place, we can alter the map to any degree we want; or completely reverse our position.

If we have a good method of evaluation in which we have confidence on the basis of observed and verified results, we will not have to think of these changes of opinion as "defeats." They are simply part of the process of keeping our maps up-to-date. If we plan to travel to Boston over Route 20, and there is construction work under way on a five-mile section of the route, we don't try to blast our way through anyhow. We take the detour. We go by the territory as it *now* is, not by the old map. And if the road is blocked entirely and no detour possible, we don't shoot ourselves, or run our car over a cliff; we simply turn around and go back home and try it tomorrow.

It is perfectly amazing how many losses you can take in the market and not get hurt very much, providing you are able to cut these losses short as soon as a change of trend appears.

But in order to do that you will have to keep an open mind. Not open just to the favorable things that confirm what you wanted to believe in the first place; but any reports that will have a bearing on the situation, whether "good" or "bad."

The really serious losses come where someone closes his mind and stubbornly refuses to recognize new factors in the situation.

Of course, it is not enough merely to keep losses small. In order to keep solvent one must also have some profits. But profits, too, bring their psychological woes.

QUESTIONS FOR CONSIDERATION

When you sell a stock do you always consider what you paid for it? Is it harder for you to reach a decision to sell if you have a loss than if you have a profit? Why? Do you think the market knows or cares what you paid? Do you think if a stock has been bought at $30 it would be wiser to sell it at $20 if it looked weak, than if you had bought it at $10?

Do you consider each loss in the market as a personal humiliation? Or do you consider your losses as a whole against your gains as a whole? Which would you think might give you a more realistic picture of your operation? Which would be less painful to you?

How much of your interest in the market is involved with your need to feel adequate? To what extent are you seeking to make money, and to what extent is money a symbol for your ego?

Do you symbolize other situations in this way? Do your business successes and your victories in love stand for something else? To what extent do you place the experience of "winning" above the nominal prize?

You have been awarded an honorary degree and $1000. Which is more important to you? Why? Is it "wrong" to value personal honors and tributes? Can it be a mistake to attach to these symbols so much value that nothing else matters?

If the "territory" is clearly black and your map says "white," are you going to die to defend the map in the face of the evident facts?

How "right" do you have to be to feel good about yourself?

With how many thousands of dollars will you back the infallibility of your first decision rather than take a loss of a hundred dollars?

PROFITS CAN BE PAINFUL, TOO

W E HAVE seen how utter ruin can come about when a man perceives any need to alter his opinion as an attack on his ego.

He can also be hurt when he is on the profit side; and for much the same reasons.

Let us say that Ed Smith buys a contract of Soy Beans in 1954 at around $2.90 a bushel. He has put up a deposit of $1,000 against his contract of 5000 bushels. Each cent that Soy Beans advance will therefore mean a gain of $50.00 or 5%.

And let us suppose that Soy Beans *do* advance (as they did at this particular time). What is Ed to do when Beans are selling at $3.00, only a few weeks later? Obviously, bidders have perceived the possibility of a shorter supply of Soy Beans or (you could put it) a greater demand. If Ed sells out now he will have a good profit, in fact he will have 50% on his capital of $1,000.

It is hard to be losing money. But it may well be that sufferings of the trader who has a big profit are more intense than those of a loser.

What to do? To sell the Beans means securing the immediate profit. But if one sells them now, what is to prevent them from going higher. Then one would be left standing on the dock, with a strong feeling of having missed the boat. And then again, if they were not sold, suppose they were to react and end up again at $2.90 . . . or at $2.80.

This is a problem in commodity trading and in money. But it is also, and most importantly, a problem concerning the "self."

Unless one can muster some defenses, it is going to "hurt too much" to see Beans go up after they have been sold, and it will also "hurt too much" to see them go down if one decides to hold.

There are some possible defenses. They will cost some money perhaps, but they may save the ego. One can always argue that the commodity markets are manipulated. Or that the information on which the decision to sell (or not to sell) was inaccurately or dishonestly reported. These defenses make it clear that whatever happens it is "not me" that was at fault. It is somebody else's fault. We do this very often in other life situations. We can keep looking pretty good to ourselves if we can externalize the blame.

We lost the job "because" the boss was looking for a place for his nephew. We lost the girl "because" her mother influenced her against you. We failed in the examination "because" the professor asked some very "unfair" questions. In any case, it was "not me."

And so it appears that some sort of sleight of hand on the part of professional market riggers was to blame.

Of course, this is not the way to correct past errors or improve one's trading methods.

Let us go back to the Soy Beans. Beans, having advanced from $2.90 to $3.00, now run up to $3.15, giving a profit of 125%. If the tension was extreme before, think what it must be now. Consider the ups and downs of the emotional barometer as Beans react to $3.05, advance to $3.30, decline to $3.20, etc. The fact is that on this move Soy Beans eventually advanced a good deal more than $1.00, over 500% gain, in only a few months.

What a wonderful opportunity to take a big profit! Yes; but how many men would have the stamina and assurance to see it through? How many would be able to face the possibility of losing part of the gains?

There are, I believe, many market traders who would find it easier, all things considered, to sell out the Soy Beans when they first reached $3.00, than to let Soy Beans go to $3.50 and then sell out at $3.20. Of course, in this second case one would make a good deal more money. But it is much easier to sell on the way up than to sell after the price has gone "against you" for thirty points. In the first case you can always say, "Well, I got my profit; let the other fellow have his," which leaves the self-esteem looking pretty sharp. But in the second case one is forced to face the fact that one did not "call the turn" at the top.

And you must realize by now that the difference of a few hundred dollars is as nothing compared with the pain of a hurt to the ego.

It all depends on how you measure your values. If you insist on using a fantasy of perfection for a mirror, you are bound to be threatened by the danger that the reality will intrude itself on the pleasant image.

There is no reason you need to regard selling out at something less than "the top" as a defeat. And if you let yourself be worried into premature selling every time you have a small profit, you will find your equity shrinking as the commissions and inevitable losses mount in your trading account.

QUESTIONS FOR CONSIDERATION

Suppose you had bought a stock at $20 a share. It had drifted gradually down to $16, had eventually moved back to $20, and then broke through in a sharp up move on big volume to $22. Would you feel tempted to sell the stock in order to recoup your loss and make a little profit? Are you sure these are good reasons for selling?

Suppose you have bought a stock at $20, and it moves up to $23 within a week or so. Would you probably sell it and make sure of the profit? Why would you be so anxious to sell?

Suppose the stock had made a very big advance, leaping ahead to $25, to $30, to $40, perhaps to $60 a share. Would this present a hard problem to you? How would you decide whether to sell the stock, or to sell part of it, or keep it all, or buy more? Don't you think you should consider these possibilities and have a plan for any contingency before a situation comes to a head?

Would you say that a good many investors and market traders are so worried over the possibility of being "proved wrong" that they are never able to realize their full potentialities in "being profitably right"?

PREDICTING THE FUTURE

W HEN we think of predicting the future we so often think of an old gypsy crone in a screened cubicle at the back of a vacant store. She draws the curtains, decorated with signs of the zodiac, and reads our palm.

Some do it with tea leaves, or by the bumps on your head; and some use horoscopes or examine the entrails of pigeons.

For we all have to predict. And there is no limit on what can be used as a predictive method. I could decide to buy stocks when it rains and sell them when the sun shines. I could go long when the Yankees win, and sell short when they lose.

So far as I know none of the above methods of predicting have any positive value. But you are free to try them, or others.

As a matter of fact you have better ones already. Your own predictions about things in your daily life are pretty good. You predict future events; and they happen with fair regularity. Mr. Tenney is going to meet you at one o'clock for lunch. He usually shows up. The school play is to start at eight P.M. sharp. It will, if you will allow fifteen minutes leeway.

So long as we don't insist on "absolute" predictions, we can do pretty well. Like almost everything in our dealings with reality, we can get along if we are willing to settle for something a bit short of perfection.

It is a matter of degree. "How much" reliability is "necessary and sufficient" for certain predictions, and whether we can expect to attain this degree of dependability. If it is a question of predicting eclipses, we can come very close to the exact time and areas of visibility, with a very high degree of accuracy. If it is a matter of predicting the price of Wheat futures, we must compromise on a very much less dependable prediction.

But the point is simply that prediction of the future is possible, it is not mysterious, it is the carrying out of methods we use all the time without thinking about them.

QUESTIONS FOR CONSIDERATION

If we accept the view that "Benjamin Franklin was an astute and perceptive observer," how would you regard the statement, "Benjamin Franklin said thus-and-so; therefore it is true"? Is it possible that Franklin's opinion may have been valid, and may have been true at the time it was made, but might be quite untrue as of today?

Is it possible for opinions, judgments, precepts, etc. to be "honest" and still be "false to fact"? How come?

How do you predict: The progress of an employee in your office? The weather for tomorrow? The winner of this season's National League pennant? What your wife will have for dinner tomorrow night? The outcome of the next congressional elections? The price of U. S. Steel stock?

Would you bet even money on your predictions in the above cases? Would you take odds of four to one on these predictions? Would you put up one dollar on such a bet? A hundred dollars? Ten thousand dollars?

Do you recognize that there are some situations in which you can make very dependable predictions? That there are other situations where you must allow a great deal of leeway for "chance," "unpredictable new circumstances," "imperfect information," etc.?

Do you realize how basic your predicting activities are in your own life every day and every hour?

THE METHOD OF PREDICTION

IN ORDER to make good predictions we have to have a method.
In order to have confidence in the method we must be able to check
it and see what degree of dependability we can expect from it. Sometimes, of course, you may be faced with a problem which cannot be
repeated, and in which you have to make a prediction and decision.
The ship is on fire. As captain you must decide whether the boilers
will explode, in which case you should order, "Abandon ship," or
whether the boilers will stand up until the fire is under control (in
which case you must not abandon ship). Such dreadful emergencies,
however, are not likely to complicate the lives of most of us. The
kind of predicting we are thinking of is the sort that concerns repetitive situations, situations somewhat like others that have arisen in
the past, and like some expected to arise in the future.

Ruling out all magic and mysticism (though you are free to try
any experiments you wish), all we know about the facts in any case
concerns the past. The future, which we are trying to predict, remains a closed book.

The first thing to do, then, obviously, is to gather some facts
about the past. Some statistics. Then we can study these and see
what sort of patterns these facts seem to make, and whether they
point to the likelihood of certain patterns forming in the future.

For example: old Mrs. Carpenter comes down the front steps of
her house on a Monday morning around ten o'clock and walks down
the street to her daughter's house. And if she does this at about the

same time on Tuesday morning, and on Wednesday, and on Thursday, and every single day for three weeks, I would be willing to make a prediction that tomorrow morning at around ten o'clock Mrs. Carpenter will be coming down the steps of her house to go over to her daughter's.

I might observe that Mrs. Carpenter made this visit every day *except Sunday* when her daughter came to her house; and then I would make my prediction that if tomorrow is any day except Sunday, Mrs. Carpenter will leave for her daughter's house.

Always and always I would be prepared to change my data. Mrs. Carpenter might be taken ill. She might be away for two weeks to visit her other daughter in Kansas. But until I had data of sufficient weight to cause me to change my original view I would feel that the "most probable" outcome would be for Mrs. Carpenter to appear as usual.

Not always would we predict in this "straight-line" fashion. Suppose, for instance, that Don is going to see how many bottles of beer he can drink, with a time limit of ten minutes for each bottle. Knowing a bit about Don's temperament and capacity, I might very well make a uniform series of predictions covering the first, second, third, fourth and fifth ten minute period. However, based on past experience with beer, and perhaps with Don, I realize that a man's thirst will not continue indefinitely to operate on a straight-line basis. He will slow up, and ultimately stop. Therefore, my predictions will have a little less certainty, I will not back them with side-bets so heavily, or I will call for progressively higher odds.

The important thing is to set forth all the relevant facts we can get (leaving out all matters not pertinent to the problem at hand), study what seems to be happening, what seems likely to happen if we move forward in time, and then make a guess.

Some of the guesses we might make are:

The prediction can be represented by a straight line at a uniform level. (Things will continue as they are.)

The prediction can be represented by a straight line at an angle. (Things will advance, speed up, etc. at a uniform rate.)

The prediction can be represented by a curved line having a uniform rate of curvature. (Things will advance or decline with a uniformly increasing, or decreasing, rate of change.)

The prediction can be represented by a curved line having a

changing rate of curvature. (The rate of change will be increasing or decreasing.)

The prediction can be represented by a line going in the opposite direction from the record of past experiences. (The trend will reverse itself.)

At any rate, since we have no direct and certain knowledge of the future, we must study the past, and make the most plausible guess we can as to the future.

Then we see how the guess comes out. If possible, we check the method (the guess) for some time and observe the results.

We note the degree of success or failure in the results of the prediction, and if these appear to be abnormally out of line with what we had expected, we re-check the data. We check the original facts, and perhaps gather more data. We examine the most recent records to see whether there has been a significant change in the patterns; and, if necessary, we make a new guess.

We then check the new guess; and again adjust our method so as to obtain the closest possible "fit"; and once more project a prediction.

We will not ever expect to hit the bulls-eye on every shot with a "perfect" predictive method. Like all engineering studies we are concerned with a good, practical, approximate result, and it is not necessary to try to reach an impossible perfection.

If we find that the best predictive method we can devise will not come close enough to meet what is "necessary and sufficient" to solve our problem, then if possible, we should leave that problem alone. If all our efforts to develop a predictive method for the stock market, or for the grain market, do not, on "test," produce consistently good results to a degree sufficient to pay its own way, then we should stay out of these markets, at least until we have found such a method.

It is not necessary, in the case of market operations, actually to risk dollars in the market. One can usually make "dry runs" by keeping "paper trading accounts," and so test the method before risking capital in it.

Since we are not looking for "perfection," we need to consider losses only to the extent that they may affect the overall net result. If a certain method produces a profit of $800 on one transaction, and losses of $200, $50, and $150, the net result is a gain of $400. If another method, using the same capital, gives four profits of $100 each, and no losses, the net result is the same.

If we can just re-educate our egos to a point where each small loss is not an occasion for the beating of breasts and the tearing out of hair, it will be possible to evaluate the net results as a whole, and in that case the presence or absence of loss items would have no special significance.   We can afford to take losses, and losses do not need to hurt too much if we can operate on a tested and proved method in which we have good reason to have confidence as to the net results.

QUESTIONS FOR CONSIDERATION

On what information and by what line of reasoning would you base a prediction on:

The probable weather in your town for the first two weeks of next July?

Your net income for the coming twelve months?

The chances of an earthquake destroying your home?

The chances of filling a four card flush?

The probability of your going to hell when you die?

The price trend of the stock of New York Central for the next three months?

The production of color television sets this year?

In the preceding questions is there any difference in the nature of the data and the method of evaluation?

Is there any difference in the degree of assurance with which you can answer the questions?   Do you ever check your predictions in various fields?   Do you study the methods by which you arrive at predictions concerning somewhat uncertain events in the future?

Is it often possible to make any prediction with absolute certainty?

Is it necessary to have absolute certainty in order to make practical, workable, and reasonably dependable plans?

Would it be a fair summary to say that you are seeking to predict "the most probable outcome" rather than "the sure consequences"?

HUNTING

I HAVE watched my son out in the rowboat at Bass Pond, weaving a course like a drunken sailor across the water in the general direction of the Indian Village at Camp Wilder. Johnny will take off at a furious clip headed out toward the middle of the pond. After a dozen or so pulls on the oars he will look around, see that he is headed toward the pine grove, and then he will pull harder on the right side. The boat will begin to swing back toward the Indian Village. After another dozen pulls he will look again. By this time the prow has swung too far and he is pointed toward the inlet. He pulls harder on the left oar. The boat swings back and again swings out of course on the other side. Eventually Johnny gets the boat moving in the approximate direction of the Indian Village, but all the way across the lake he is looking around, correcting his course, and swinging first too far to the right, then too far to the left.

The problems of "steersmanship" are familiar enough to anyone who has even taken out a rowboat, paddled stern in a canoe, or handled the tiller of a sailboat.

Even in navigating the placid waters of Bass Pond there will always be steering corrections to be made, and these generally will over-compensate, calling for counter-corrections. And it is not possible, even here, to maintain a "perfect" course for an appreciable time.

But where the problem of steering is complicated by choppy water, gusty wind, and perhaps a tricky current or tidal rip, the difficulties of keeping on course are increased enormously because of the need to adjust continually to new and changing conditions. And the process of steering may involve, too, some predicting . . . an estimate of the size of the next wave or the time of the next-expected gust of wind.

In such waters we do not expect to steer even as close an approximation of a "perfect course" as we might hope to achieve in a quiet pond.

In practice it isn't necessary to expect anything like perfection. If we can keep the boat moving in the general direction of the goal, a certain amount of deviation from "true course" is unavoidable and does not defeat our main purpose.

Naturally we will hold as close as possible to the straightest course. How close this will be will depend partly on our own experience and skill and partly on the winds, currents, and other changing conditions we must allow for in making corrections and compensations as we go along.

Now consider a medium-size black part retriever, answering on occasion to the name "Bozo." Bozo has forebears of sporting stock. His formal training has been entirely neglected, but his instincts still spur him to the chase. Let him out of the car on a picnic and he will take off down the road, nose to the ground, tracking . . . what? A bear, perhaps? A rhinoceros? Who knows? More likely a rabbit. Possibly a cat.

If the quarry is in sight, Bozo will charge off directly. For sheer dynamic frenzy there is hardly anything to touch the furious pursuit and the frenzied flight of a dog-chasing-a-cat. In a straightway run down the road it is simply a matter of speed and endurance. The dog will follow the cat. A linear function.

But if the cat veers sharply and heads across the field, then it is no longer a question of following where the cat *has gone*. Bozo, or any other smart dog, will cut across in a new direction. In short, he will take a course not "where the cat has gone" but toward "where the cat is now." This means abstracting at a "higher level" than merely following.

For example; we have in almost any problem of human activity the factor of the pursuit of a goal. The goal may not be a cat—it may be dollars of profit; it may not be a direct course over water—it could be the improvement of the efficiency of coal-fired boilers. But there is usually a definable objective.

Again, as with the pursuit of the cat or the steering of the boat, we may not hope for perfection in our method, even though we may look for success to a degree in reaching our goal. We are dealing, as a rule, with imperfect or incomplete information. We must make the best use of the information we possess.

And again, the conditions may change. The cat tries a new angle. The wind freshens and swings the bow of the boat off course. We must change our tactics to meet these changes.

And, there is usually an opportunity for prediction. We can, if we have the experience and intelligence, anticipate with some expectation of success, the probable maneuvers of the cat or the set of the tidal rip.

Finally, we have the matter of "hunting," the very important matter of continual overcompensation one way or the other.

The whole principle of adjusting to the "ideal course," which we keep overshooting and undershooting, is based on applying a counterforce to any swing out of line. If the boat swings too far to port or to starboard we apply an opposite or negative correction. If the engine speeds up beyond the constant speed we want, we slow it down. If it slows down below the indicated speed, we accelerate it. We call this process "negative feedback." In such a system of control we are continually applying a negative force to correct a tendency to run out-of-line with what we want. It is never perfect. There is always a certain amount of swinging back and forth, the "hunting" we have spoken of, as we try to hold the never-to-be-exactly-maintained "true course."

This hunting is one of the unavoidable inefficiencies of any steering. It is a loss of efficiency as inexorable as frictional losses in a machine; or perhaps in a better analogy, it is like the back-lash in gears. It is something we can't entirely avoid but something we try to keep as small as possible under any particular set of conditions.

If the hunting swings are too wide, that is, if the negative feedback is too pronounced the goal may be missed entirely. We would say in such a case the boat is "out of control." If the swings are too small, that is, if the corrections are too numerous and too frequent, then we may be paying too high a price in frictional losses, back-lash, and diversion of too much energy to the control mechanism. In such case we may keep headed for the goal, but we may never get there or we may arrive too late.

This discussion must all seem very far removed from the stock or commodity markets.   Actually it is only a short step away if we can now apply our generalized observations to specific cases.

Consider the market for Christmas trees, as you have observed it, trudging through the vacant lot where, for a few days, the air is perfumed with the rich aroma of balsam; strolling through an electric-lighted grove with a couple of starry-eyed moppets in tow.   One year you may find a great scarcity of trees, and the prices uncomfortably high.   This condition will produce a negative feedback in the economics of Christmas tree marketing, for the high prices will suggest a larger stock next year.   And when next year comes you will find such a wealth of Christmas trees in the lot beside every corner store that you can take your pick of the biggest and handsomest at your own price.   And this, too, will set up a negative feedback; oversupply will lead cautious buyers to go slow and in the following year once again trees will be scarce and prices high.

The same principles apply, of course in the big commodity futures markets and in the stock market.   Prices will rise fast on a Minor trend.   Profit-taking will come in; but it will go too far and then a counter-move begins as buyers rush in.   Each move brings its own correction.   And each correction tends to overcompensate somewhat.

In technical studies of stock and commodity movements it is necessary to consider just how much negative feedback to apply in certain situations.   Because of the complexity of the problems this becomes more a matter of experience and judgment than of precise mathematics.   But the basic question must be answered.   Whether to adhere closely to every small fluctuation in the trend, which means making changes in position, paying many commissions, taking small gains and small losses.   Whether to steer a constant course on the Major trend, disregarding all Minor swings and changing the course only when the evidence of a change in that trend is overwhelming, which means risking a rather heavy loss from time to time against the hope of taking a large profit.   Or whether to plan some course between these two extremes, representing an optimum policy.   These are the kinds of questions that arise.

The problem we have just roughly sketched is that of the trader who is weighing the advantages of "short term trading" against "long term," or some compromise or combination of these.   There are other problems involving the steering of a course in market tactics.

And there is always the problem of "how much negative feedback to use." Needless to say the man who has only one course and who uses no feedback but lashes the tiller and goes to sleep is not in a very good position to meet changing conditions of wind and current. But this is exactly what some investors do in their market operation, and if no great changes come about in the economic weather they may and sometimes do bring their craft to port.

Steering and the adaptive and predictive techniques are at the heart of investment and trading policies. It is always necessary to set a course, that is, to work in the direction of a certain goal or objective. It is necessary to take observations relating the actual course and the planned course. And it is necessary to make changes when these two differ too widely.

If you will consider this for a moment you will see that what we are talking about here is simply the re-examination of a territory in order to verify data on a map, and when necessary to change the map to accord with new features in the territory.

QUESTIONS FOR CONSIDERATION

Do you know people whose attitudes on most subjects are like The Laws of the Medes and Persians, which changeth not? You don't happen to be one of these people do you?

Do you believe you can go on deck, take observations, set a course, lash the rudder, and then go down to your cabin and go to sleep, assuming the ship will hold its course without any further attention from you?

Do you believe you can "get an education" in your childhood that will serve you all your life without any checking or revision?

You have heard the expression "You can't change human nature." Do you believe you can't change your own human nature? Do you feel you don't want to change your value system or improve your attitudes?

What is the advantage of taking new observations about things you learned long ago? Is it possible that these things have changed, or that you have changed, or that your own needs are different now?

Who is in the stronger position, would you say: the man who has a fixed and absolute set of values affecting his philosophy, morals, business methods, and way of life; or one who is ready and willing to re-check his course and make corrections if necessary?

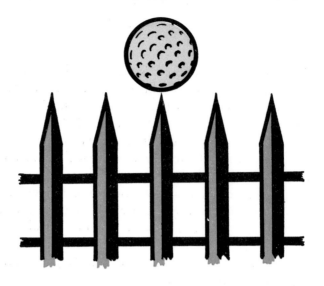

POSITIVE FEEDBACK

IF WE consider some motion, acceleration, torque, trend, habit, or other variable which we want to control between certain limits, we must have a means of correcting the swing as the variable passes the upper or lower limit. The correcting force must be opposite to the movement of the variable.

This has been called "negative feedback." It is never quite perfect in practice. There is always a certain amount of "hunting." And in certain situations the "hunting" tends continually to over-ride the limits by wider margins, setting up wilder and wilder swings until the mechanism simply "shakes itself to pieces."

There is something else that could happen and does happen very often. This is where the feedback is "positive" from the very start, so that instead of *correcting* an overswing it accentuates it. In this case, there is no come-back; the mechanism is out of balance from the word go.

Although this is not what we usually think of when we speak of feedback and controls, it is true that an ordinary pendulum, as it swings wide, gradually encounters an increasing force from gravity which checks its swing and tends to bring it back toward the center. The pendulum, of course, will pass the center and swing out on the other side; gravity again will check it and start it back toward the center. Here we have an object in motion which is held in a stable and controlled situation.

But if we balance a golf ball on a sharp fence spike, although we may set it up very carefully so that it is in balance at the start, we know that this is an unstable sort of balance.   There will be some slight air current or vibration that will move the ball a trifle one side or the other; and as soon as this occurs, the force of gravity becomes stronger *on that side*.   This will not check the imbalance; it will draw the ball further in the same direction, and as this happens, the effect of gravity in that same direction becomes more pronounced. There is a "positive feedback" and the ball comes tumbling down.

This is a long way around to say that you can't keep a golf ball balanced on the point of a fence spike.

We get "positive feedback" all the time in various departments of our lives.   It almost seems as if we were taught this "wrong-way" control method from early childhood.

If there is a real danger that the Puerto Rican kids and the white kids may get into a rumble that might cost some of them a serious injury, we don't use a "negative feedback" attack on the problem. You can't expect the kids to do it by themselves; but parents, teachers, and public authorities might start by checking their own group. The white parents, teachers, etc., might ask, "What are we doing that is obnoxious, hostile, unkind, etc.?"   And the Puerto Rican parents, teachers, etc. might, in the same spirit, look at themselves and their own kids to see where *their* contribution to the trouble lay. Such an approach, or at least an approach in such a spirit, might hold the greatest hope of solving a very nasty social problem.

But if adults on both sides of such a question close their eyes to their own shortcomings and those of their kids; and if they seek out and magnify the faults of the other faction, isn't this exactly the same kind of thing that happened to the golf ball on the spike? They are permitting a "positive feedback" to build up more hostility, which, in turn, will lead to more trouble, which will be perceived as "*their* fault," and so on.   An unstable condition; a vicious circle; or rather, a vicious helix.

Wherever a bad inter-human situation develops, whether it is leading toward divorce, assault, or murder, we are likely to find that as the problem becomes tighter there is more and more of a tendency to see only one side of it; to pile up the "good" forces on our side and the "bad" forces on the other.

As a matter of fact, this is necessary to protect the ego.   No man can maintain a campaign of hate without some justification; and the more unpleasant his own actions become, the more justification he will need. He must continually be able to feel more "righteous indignation," and this requires that he must be able to see how "right" he is and how very "wrong" is his adversary.

This is not exactly the road toward the brotherhood of man.

It seems hardly necessary to add that in spite of inspiring pictures of peaceful souls gathering in friendship at the meeting house to work for the common good, our political system in fact is a matching of hostile forces in which practically no punches are pulled. It is based on the either . . . or principle which permits of no moderation. By and large, the democratic method as it is actually practiced, is a study in organized nastiness, as anyone knows who has taken an intimate part in city politics at the ward or precinct level. The politician not only claims for himself the noblest motives; in many cases, it seems that he actually believes he possesses them. He has trained himself to see nothing but corruption and stupidity in his opponent and his opponent's party. If he were not able to concentrate all the "good" on his side and all the "bad" on the other side, he could hardly get up and roar his speech at the rally with a straight face. This is "positive feedback"; the campaign progresses from debate to accusation, to slander, to stink bombs and bricks tossed through windows.

This is not the way to make democracy work.

Very seriously, one of the great social problems of the next generation (if there is to be a next generation) is to find out how, in human relations, we can put "negative feedback" to work. For we cannot achieve peace in the city by sending our kids to special schools or moving to a better neighborhood, or by drawing lines of discrimination that will keep us from knowing the truth about our neighbors. And we cannot achieve peace in the world by living in a compartmented world, shielding our children from normal contacts so that they will not be "contaminated" by those who think differently, cutting out of our libraries books that tend to show that Germans, or Japanese, or Russians, are also human beings with whom potentially we could enjoy friendship. Somehow, and soon, we must establish *communication*, not with the people who live like us, and think like us, and believe as we do, but with people who have a different view; not so that we can "reform" *them*, but so that we can prevent our own tight little vortex of prejudice and narrowness and hostility from building up explosive pressures.

You know that the attitudes of many sick people are due to the "positive feedback," the same kind of thing we have been discussing. The neurotic, as someone put it, is just like everybody else, only more so. Unfortunately, his controls work in reverse. The very defenses he sets up against the perceived threats of attack intensify his need for aggression, or submission, or isolation; and this, in turn, calls for another round of defenses; the positive feedback or vicious helix.

If our whole social structure is permeated by the kind of perception that tends to make a little problem a big problem and a big problem a tragedy, it is no wonder that people learn to go off on these tangents in almost any field. And when this tendency to see only "our" side of a question has been ingrained in people from the time they were infants, it seems only natural that the same distorted views would apply in the market. And they do.

When we buy a certain stock, we want to see it "go up" in price. We like to read of increased earnings, of higher dividends to be declared, and a wonderful long-term growth outlook. And there is no harm in seeing all the good things about the stock. What can be very dangerous, however, is the habit of closing one eye the moment the purchase is executed, and looking *only* for good news. Instead of allowing the negative feedback of caution and informed pessimism to operate to get us out of the situation if conditions should change (as they certainly can), we tend to overlook or even to deny anything that does not support our original hope.

It could be, you know, that the fault may lie in the weakness underlying that original hope. Maybe we weren't too sure in the first place. But once having made our decision and bought the stock we "cannot afford" to be prey to fear and doubt. And so we bury our fears and close our eyes to the warning signs along the way from that point on.

This is not anything we do consciously or deliberately, you understand. We simply do not read the "bad" commentary on the stock. If it isn't good news we are not interested. (And if you should doubt this, go into a broker's board room some noon time and throw out a few "negative" opinions about some popular favorite among the stocks. You will be as popular as a skunk at a picnic.)

But if you are reasonably sure of your own judgment in the first place and satisfied that your reasons for buying that stock were sound, then you will *not need to be afraid* to know the truth. Since you are secure in your self-confidence you will not need to feel that the stock you bought is "perfect" any more than you need to feel that *you* are perfect. You will expect some bad news along with good news; in fact, if there was *only* good news you might wonder what kind of manipulation or promotion was going on. And if the bad news eventually outweighs the good news, assuming that you are ready, able and willing to evaluate both, then it will be to your own best interest to get rid of this stock at once.

In fact . . . one could almost say the bad news is more important to you than the good; since you are already tipped in the direction of "good" news; so you need the negative, corrective force that can keep your opinion in balance and sound the danger signal when it is time to change your mind.

In reading these paragraphs above, you may wonder whether it is a good thing to buy or sell stocks on "news" at all. Perhaps "news" is not the word. It could be "reports" on the stock, or it could be "technical indications." What is meant here by "news" is the evidence or information of whatever nature, on which one bases his opinion.

QUESTIONS FOR CONSIDERATION

Suppose that you feared you had a serious disease, but several of your friends and a man who had taken two years of medical school told you not to worry; that they felt sure you were all right. Would you seek out other friends or people whom you felt would give you the same reassuring opinion? Would you avoid reading anything or talking to anyone where you felt the opinion might indicate that you did have a dangerous condition? Would you keep away from a qualified diagnostician if you felt his view might upset your comfort? Would all this, in the long run, be likely to help either your peace of mind or your bodily health?

When you cherish an opinion such as, "Dow Chemical is going to advance strongly in the market," (if perhaps you hold some shares of Dow Chemical) do you seek positive information that will confirm your judgment? Do you ignore or avoid anything that might indicate a change in the trend, or new, adverse conditions? By reinforcing your original opinion (which may have been a good one) and excluding any contrary evidence, are you not setting up a "positive feedback"? Is this method likely to keep you well informed for the protection of your own interests?

Do you know many people who hold certain beliefs very strongly and feel that these social, religious, moral, and intellectual "sets" are a comfort and sure guide in a world which they feel is uncertain and insecure? By holding fast to these "eternal truths," and shutting out all evidence that changes and corrections in these views are called for, would you say these people are using "positive feedback" to defend a deceptive and unstable comfort and security?

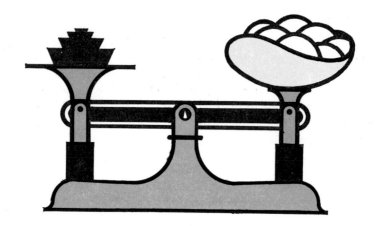

WHAT IS "VALUE"?

FOR eight years I taught at the evening school at Commerce High in Springfield. In my classes in "The General Semantics of Wall Street," I always allowed a full two hour session for a discussion of Value.

I would write the word "Value" on the blackboard and ask the class what it meant to them, as applied to stocks.

There was no shortage of definitions. In fact, before we finished the board would be covered with notes:

Value is what a stock is worth, based on the assets of the company, less the liabilities, divided by the number of shares.

Value is the original cost of all assets less depreciation, and plus the estimated worth of goodwill, patents and other intangibles.

Value is the per-share portion of the company's earnings, times ten. Or times fifteen. Or times five.

Value is the per-share portion of the dividends, times twenty. Or times twenty-five. Or times fifteen. Or name-it-and-you-can-have-it.

Value is the price of the stock in the market.

And so forth. It is not necessary to list all the definitions and all their variations. But one thing was quite clear. There are about as many ideas as to what constitutes "value" as there are investors in the market.

Very well. How do we go about it to find the "true value" of a stock, that is, the "intrinsic value"; not what somebody *says* is the value, but what it *really* is?

218

If you start a discussion on this subject you had best be prepared for an all-out all-night session. There are so many factors to be considered. Assets and liabilities, of course. The intangibles. The items subject to depreciation. The items involving a question of original cost or replacement cost. The long-term prospects for the company, and the trends of earnings, dividends, etc. as well as their present magnitudes. The probable tax liability as foreseen in future years. Development of new products, and the potentials of new markets. And much, much, much more.

And when we get all these facts down, and presumably correct as to the ascertainable facts, then how much will we assume is a "fair" return on capital? How much weight will we give to earnings "plowed back" into development. And who is going to "weight" all these factors and produce a formula that will give us the final answer as to the "real value," the "true value" of the stock of this company?

No matter how factual the reported figures are, it still leaves wide open the question of how to combine these factors. Is a "growth outlook" more important than a steady dividend? Is a new market for a new product worth more than a progressive sales and development program?

These questions cannot be answered positively the way we can answer a question about the amount of last year's dividends. They concern high order abstractions, that is to say, opinions and judgments; and when the experts differ (as they certainly do) there is no external reality to "measure" or "count," so there is actually no final court of appeal. One man's opinion, in a sense, is as good as another's.

Not only that. The facts on which we must base the "true value" are from the records of *past performance*. But people do not buy a stock to get *last* year's dividends. They are thinking about *next* year's dividends. However, the figures in next year's report will concern the future; assets, liabilities, earnings, dividends, and all the rest. We have not seen next year's report. And as you know, we cannot predict the future with absolute precision. The best we can look for is an estimate by qualified experts; and the best estimates will differ rather materially.

These are some reasons why we have no general agreement as to the "real value" of a stock.

We could look at something else. We could examine a half gallon container of water. I have such a container here on the desk before me. It came from the kitchen faucet, and was brought here by pipeline from Cobble Mountain. It is clean, and clear, and cold; and it tests so chemically pure that it can be used, right from the tap, to fill the battery in your car. Our Springfield water is the purest in the east, possibly in the whole country.

What is the "true value" of this half gallon of water? I could try to peddle it from house to house and see what I could get for it, but I *know* what I could get for it. Exactly nothing! Every house on this street has a number of faucets, all connected to the same fine Cobble Mountain water supply. For a negligible water bill each house has what is tantamount to an unlimited supply of this sparkling, delicious water. So its "true value" as economic goods, is so close to zero that we cannot measure it at all.

But last year in certain cities in Texas during a drought, water was being sold in half gallon containers for twenty cents a package. I don't imagine it was as cold, and as clean, and as chemically pure as our Cobble Mountain water, but people were willing and anxious to get it, and apparently they valued it at twenty cents.

Suppose you were driving with your wife and three children along a little-travelled road in Death Valley. And suppose the car gave out on you and left you stranded there in the hot desert for three or four hours. And suppose you had no water.

What would you say was the "true value" of a half gallon of water then? A dollar? Ten dollars? A hundred dollars? A thousand? Everything you've got? It could be.

Don't you see that "value" is not a *thing*? The "value" is not in the water. "Value" is "valuation." It means, how much something is *worth* to you.

"Value" is a transaction between you, and, in this case, the water. You can take a half a gallon of water to the laboratory and you can look at it through microscopes, you can fractionally distil it, you can test it for traces of gold and for radioactivity. You can do anything you want with it. But you will not find the "true value," the "real value," of the water in the water *because it is not there*.

And when you look at the stock of the General Electric Company you will not find its "real value" in the stock certificates. Nor in

Schenectady, nor Lynn, nor any other property of the General Electric Company. The "real value" of that stock is entirely a matter of what it is worth to somebody.

Some chapters back we mentioned one of Frank Stockton's stories. There is another of his stories that applies to this matter of "values." In "The Queen's Museum" a certain queen had assembled the most complete collection in the world of the most interesting things in the world to her: buttonholes. Plain buttonholes, fancy buttonholes, embroidered buttonholes, buttonholes with crocheted edges, leather buttonholes, buttonholes of every sort. And she had built and equipped a magnificent museum so that her subjects could all enjoy this fine collection. When they stayed away in droves she issued a royal edict that they must visit the museum regularly, or go to jail. To a man they chose the jail. And it was only through the timely intervention of a band of outlaws that the poor queen discovered that not everyone values certain things in the same way. Some of her subjects felt that fishing rods were the most important things in the world. The main interest of others was playing cards, or horses, or flowers. And eventually she had to realize that it is not reasonable nor practicable for one person to expect others to have the same value system in all respects as he does.

The term "true value" then, has no specific, definite meaning that can be verified in external reality. Not until and unless we assign particular requirements which we will use as arbitrary criteria of "true value"; and then we are no better off, since the choice of these particular requirements becomes a matter of opinion and judgment.

Value is not "out there." It is "in here." It is a high abstraction, and not a "thing" at all.

But if the market is concerned with "values" and if values are subjective and different for each one of us, how can we deal with the market at all?

Fortunately there is a good answer to that. It involves, as usual, abandoning the "absolute" standards. We must realize that "true value" cannot be precisely established as "real and verifiable." But we can arrive at a good approximation, a consensus.

Here is how we do that. At any time there will be many opinions as to the "value" of General Electric stock. As we have said, it is not possible to settle these differences by appealing to any authoritative source. We each have a valid right to our own opinion. You set a value of $40 a share on your stock. I cannot value it at more than $39. I can order my broker to buy me some General Electric stock at no more than $39 a share. You can instruct your broker to sell your General Electric stock at no less than $40 a share. From all over the country orders funnel in to New York and eventually to the hands of the specialists, specifying the limits of valuation people have set on stocks. You could, if you wanted, set a valuation of $60 on your General Electric stock. And I could make a bid of $25 for the same stock. There is no assurance, of course, that you will sell your stock at $60, nor that I can buy mine at $25. But as the bids and offers accumulate, a certain balance is achieved. Orders to buy that "match" orders to sell can be executed at the price at which both parties agree to sell or buy. Normally we have a situation where there are many orders to sell at various prices "above the market," and many orders to buy at various prices "below the market"; and there will be a small gap just below the lowest offer, and just above the highest bid at any time.

Thus, General Electric may be quoted "Offered at 40: Bid 39¾." This region between 39¾ and 40 is probably the best approximation of the composite valuations of the American people with respect to General Electric stock that we are ever likely to get.

It is not perfect. It may be distorted by some special news item, overhanging supply, or by various minor technical surges in the market. But at a particular moment the best we can say about the value of General Electric stock in any general sense is that on the New York Stock Exchange it is now quoted at 39¾ Bid, 40 Offer. The next sale may be at 39¾, or at 39⅞, or at 40, or even at a higher or lower price. But this "Bid and Offer" for the moment is the only "general" measure of the value that we have.

It is approximate and imperfect and ephemeral. But it is at least something we can all agree on and understand. It is the nearest substitute for a "territory" we can get to correspond with the generalized conception of "real value." In this sense the market is a sort of "synthetic territory."

You will realize that this "market value" which we must use as a "stand-in" for the "true value" will not necessarily, or even usually, correspond with our own personal valuation. In fact, to some people the maps they have constructed in their own heads seem more valid than the whole evaluative mechanism of the market. You have heard people say, "It is selling now at 39⅞, but it is *really worth* at least 60."

Perhaps if these people understood more clearly the subjective nature of such words as "worth" and "value," they might alter the way they stated this. They might then say, "It is selling at 39⅞, but *in my opinion* it *will be worth* $60 before long." This recognizes that the $60 value is a personal opinion and is also a prediction of the future market value. Otherwise, it would mean nothing. It would be like a child who values her favorite doll at a "Million trillion billion dollars." That is a personal valuation, and it has very little importance to the rest of us since nobody is ever going to raise the question, or the million trillion billion dollars, either.

Somewhere in the back of a file case with some of the papers from my father's estate there are several typewritten stock certificates representing fifty thousand shares of the common stock of the Big Blue Lead Mining Co. of California. This corporate property belongs to my brother and me, and our wives. I know that there is gold in this mine. Once, when I was a small boy I saw some samples of pure gold taken from it. I will not bore you with the long history of strikes and flooding, and tax liens and recapitalization. Enough to say that whatever gold might be there is likely to stay there a long time. Nobody is digging for it now, and I doubt whether anyone ever will.

I can place any value I please on this stock. I may be able to convince myself that these fifty thousand shares are worth a hundred dollars apiece, which indeed I believe is the par value. For I do know there is gold in this mine. And I may develop a plan to try again the difficult job of extracting it profitably.

But until such time as someone else shares my enthusiasm and also values the stock at $100 a share, the market value remains where it has been for the past forty years; at precisely zero. And whatever valuation I choose to put on it is strictly a matter of financial solitaire, for it has no referent out there in external reality.

But please; do not feel that the valuation you place on a stock is necessarily worthless. If you have good reasons (better reasons than I might have if I were to try to assign a dollar value to Big Blue Lead) you may be quite right. You may feel that "ABX" will be worth $75 a share when such and such probable developments occur, in spite of the fact that the market now values "ABX" at only $25.

If you are right, that is, if your predictive method is valid, you may see the stock selling at $75 as you expect.

The point here is to avoid *confusing* your opinion with the consensus. They are not the same thing and there is no reason they *should* be the same. But when you express your opinion that "ABX" will be worth $75 right soon, do not forget that the big, free, competitive, speculative market is saying, "We don't think so. We'll sell you all you want of it at around $25."

You buy that stock at your own peril. If you are correct in your opinion you will be richly rewarded. If you are wrong you may lose a good deal of money. You have a right to disagree, but don't feel too contemptuous of "the market." There are other men, some perhaps just as smart as you are, who are also evaluating that stock. And it is possible that some of them may have just as good reasons for valuing it now at only $25 as you do for expecting a value soon of $75.

In a sense you have more than a right to differ with the market. As a speculator (and there are very few investors who are not in some measure speculators) your function is to "speculate"; that is, to observe, to evaluate. It is your actions, along with the actions of many others, that determine the "market value" of the stock, which is, as we have seen, the best general statement of value we can get. When you buy several hundred shares of a stock, it tends to raise the price; if thousands buy it in large quantities it will tend to bring the price of the stock up to their composite valuation. In the same way your selling tends to demonstrate that you feel the stock is likely to be worth less than its present "market value"; and if you and others sell enough, this will force the price down to your composite valuation.

This is the function of the speculator as I see it. For if it is not possible to set an arbitrary "true value" on a stock by formula, nor by government commissioners, nor by any other method we know, then it must be the market itself which sets the "value." The aim of the speculator is profit; and the work of the speculator is evaluation. His rewards will be proportionate to the success of his predictive methods, in other words, in accordance with the general soundness of his evaluation. Furthermore, it is the pressures of speculative opportunity that shape the flow of capital, not according to the dictates of a committee or commissar, but according to the needs of the nation as perceived by the entire investing public.

We do not find "perfection" in the free market, either. Like most things in reality, it falls a good deal short of the ideal. But we have to work with compromises unless we are reconciled to "moving away" to a private ivory tower of fantasy.

And according to Max Eastman, in his 1955 book, "Reflections on the Failure of Socialism," in his opinion, and after years of studying the various economic and social systems, the free market represents the best hope for the future of mankind.

QUESTIONS FOR CONSIDERATION

What do you mean by value? If you attach more than one meaning to the word, what are the various meanings you assign to it?

Does love have any value? How many dollars is love worth? Can you tell in clear terms "how much" you love somebody? Is the value something in the person you love or is it of the nature of your feeling, your opinion of the loved one?

Joe Robinson collects geodes. He has the finest collection of quartz geodes in the state. He has spent many years seeking out rare and beautifully formed geodes. Do you feel that your own valuation of this superb collection would necessarily be the same as Joe's? Do you believe that Joe Robinson would be willing to sell his collection to the highest bidder at a public auction (the highest bid monetary value)? What is the "real" value of Joe's geodes?

You believe that Chrysler will sell down to $10 in the near future. The stock is now selling, let us say, at $58 a share. What is the "real" value of Chrysler stock?

Suppose Chrysler has the exclusive rights on a new atomic automobile engine, but this information has not yet been made public. What is the "real" value of Chrysler stock under these circumstances?

Suppose that General Motors has the exclusive patents on the atomic engine and that this will make obsolete all other types of cars during the next two years. Now what is the "real" value of Chrysler stock?

Is it necessary that your valuations be the same as your next door neighbor's? Is it possible that they will agree in all points? If they do not, which shows a more realistic understanding of the subjective nature of value: To go over and knock some sense into your neighbor's head, or: To realize that, after all the facts are in, your evaluation may be different from his, but both may be equally valid?

Do you consider the free market a good way to resolve the differences of evaluation between people of different opinions?

ASKING THE RIGHT QUESTIONS

YOU will notice that the same *kinds* of problems seem to come up over and over again, not only in the market, but in other areas of life as well. The basic idea of warfare, the contest between the "good" nation and the "bad" nation is simply the either . . . or dichotomy carried to its psychotic limits. The matter of attaining "success" in life is merely a question of softening the "absolute" ideal and recognizing that there are "degrees" of success as with a great many other things. The problem of "value" is repeated in various forms; wherever people confuse a high abstraction with a "thing." We can no more measure "value" directly in communicable terms than we can measure "love," or "hope," or "virtue," or "loyalty."

That is why people get into such terrible conflicts with other people when they try to argue the "absolute" magnitudes of such intangibles. It is also, and perhaps more importantly, why they get into such tragic conflicts with themselves.

It is rather important, when you ask a question, whether of someone else or of yourself, to know what you are talking about.

That seems plain enough. Then why don't we do it more often?

If you have a problem and you want to find the answer, ask some questions. But be sure you ask questions that make sense and that are capable of being answered. Whether you ask yourself or someone else, if you ask a silly question you will get a silly answer.

We might try a few questions, just for size. The sort of questions that people do actually ask. These are just for practice; there won't be any discussion of these particular questions here. Just look them over and see how you would go to work to answer them. In what terms would you answer them? How would you arrive at your conclusions? If there is something the matter with the question, ask yourself, just what is it that is wrong.

"How far is it to the sky?"

"Do animals think?"

"Is it a good movie at the Majestic?"

"If there was a bird named a Wargspan, what color would it probably be?"

"Has Ed Monson any intelligence at all?"

"Do you love me more than Arthur does?"

"The French measure length in centimeters. We measure in inches. Which is better?"

"What would Jesus say about the present policies of the State Department?"

"Will I ever be a success?"

"Which came first; the chicken or the egg?"

"What is the unforgiveable sin?"

"If you were I would you be making more money than I am today?"

There is something the matter with these questions. The truth of the matter is that they are, for the most part, not questions at all. They have the form of questions, but when I ask "How much does a ghost weigh?" or "Who would I be if I hadn't been born myself?", these are just strings of meaningless words, having only the *form* of a question, like a meaningless combination of letters that looks at first glance as if it might be a word.

A question, to have any real meaning, should ask something that is clearly stated in terms that can be understood quite definitely by both the inquirer and the one asked.

If the question refers to something that has no "real" existence, such as "ghost," it is not a "proper" question. There is no possibility of answering it with a meaningful reply. Such a question, like other nonsense questions, is like "dividing by zero." As you know if you have jittered over mathematical puzzles, there is a particularly nasty device by which a perfectly ordinary-looking equation goes haywire before your eyes. The gimmick, sometimes very artfully concealed, is that the denominator of one of the terms, when reduced to its simplest form, turns out to be zero. And dividing by zero is a meaningless operation in our mathematics; so that the result also turns out to be meaningless.

There are a number of possible hidden gimmicks in the form of a question, any one of which will render the question meaningless.

To answer the question may call for supplying data that it is not possible to get. We cannot, for instance give a definite answer to the question of whether John L. Sullivan could lick the present champion. And around this silly question have raged a good many bar-room brawls.

The question may be stated in such absolute terms that any direct answer would be meaningless. For example, "Was Woodrow Wilson a good man or a bad man?"

The question may have implications that distort whatever answer you might make; such as the law-court chestnut, "Do you still beat your wife; answer yes or no?"

The question may involve high abstractions which, because they are subjective and cannot be quantitatively communicated are not capable of comparison or analysis. For instance: "Is your father more patriotic than my father?"

The question may lack definition or sufficient specification to permit an answer. "How long is a piece of string?" would be such a question, or, "Is this piece of wood hard?", or "Is Caroline a superior child?"

The first thing, then, to look for in finding the answer to a question is to take a good hard look at the question itself. Be sure that it means something, and be sure that you know what it means. Also, if you are going to put this question to somebody else, be sure that it will mean something to him.

Decide whether there exists enough evidence to support a logical and rational answer, and whether it is reasonably probable that such evidence can be secured.

Check the question for "too absolute" terms, and, if possible, restate them so that they can be answered as matters of "degree."

Study the question for ambiguous terms, that might mean one thing to you and something quite different to someone else.

Look also for emotionally colored terms in the question. Try to confine the question to matters which can be answered factually, and, if possible, verifiably.

Watch out for words in the question which can be defined only in terms of emotion, opinion, or judgment.

Be sure that the time, place, and conditions of the question are consistent, and consistent with the expected answer. What might hold for ancient Athens may not be true for modern Chicago; and what might apply to Ethiopia may not be valid for the State of Vermont.

And be sure that the question does not, in itself, confuse the levels of abstraction. For instance, "If you were sick would you go to a doctor, or would you hope for recovery?"

Watch out for questions that project to external reality "qualities, as perceived," such as, "Isn't that the reddest apple ever?"

Beware of verbal similarities in a question. The question, "Is Joe democratic?" can easily be confused with "Is Joe Democratic?" with the possibility of misunderstanding all around, especially if Joe is a democratic Republican.

And be careful of faulty identification in the question. The question, "Is Arthur Brown a criminal?" can be asked just as effectively and much more definitely in the form, "Has Arthur Brown performed any act defined by our laws as criminal?" The question, "Is Martha a Methodist?" might require a searching of Martha's very soul to answer; but re-stated as, "Does Martha attend the Methodist church regularly?" it can be answered easily. The question, "Am I a sinner?" is not only so absolute that it permits no degree in the reply, but whatever answer might be given will not help greatly in improving one's behavior. But if the question were re-stated, "What have I done which according to my own values appears wrong?" then I have not only a rational answer, but the start toward taking corrective steps.

This will all seem a great deal of bother, just to ask a question. You may even feel that it isn't worth all the trouble, and sometimes that would be quite true. But if the question is worth asking at all, to use the old bromide, "it is worth asking well." Give the person you are questioning a fair chance and he may give you a mighty good answer. This, by the way, is especially true if you, yourself, happen to be the one you are questioning.

QUESTIONS FOR CONSIDERATION

Do you waste time arguing with people over "nonsense questions" or can you spot the meaningless nature of these questions?

When a question becomes a subject of argument do you study whether your opponent really knows what he is talking about? Do you study whether *you* really know what you are talking about?

Is it possible to make direct observations of how someone in history felt about any situation?

Is it possible to settle an argument (even by assault and battery) relating to matters of taste; as, "Is this wallpaper prettier than that wallpaper?"

Would you say that some disputes could be settled by appeal to the observed facts?

Do you feel that some arguments could be resolved by a restating of too-absolute propositions in more moderate terms?

Is it important in asking a question to state exactly who, when, where, what, etc. if these points are pertinent to the issue?

Have you ever considered the possibility that some conflicts and misunderstandings take place within your own mind? Do you feel it is at least as important to understand your own questions and propositions as those of other people?

TWO VERY PRACTICAL QUESTIONS
FOR EVERYDAY USE

WHEN somebody makes a statement, we can either pay no attention to it (the move *away*), we can accept it sweetly at face
value (the move *toward*), or we can charge in and tear it to pieces (the
move *against*). A neat demonstration of the three-valued orientation.

Naturally, there are many statements we would brush off blandly
without the slightest reaction since they do not concern our lives in
any way. I would not, when sober, question your statement that
Myron B. Northrop was defeated by 27 votes for the Democratic
nomination for Lieutenant Governor in the Rhode Island state primary of 1898. It may or may not be true, and as a matter of fact, it
probably is not true, but it makes no difference to me whatever. I
would not dispute it.

And if you said that the performance of Alicia Markova in "Swan
Lake" was the most graceful you had ever seen, I would accept the
statement politely and pleasantly. In this case I would feel, no
doubt, that your feeling was sincere, and, of course, I would be aware
that there could be no possibility of "proving" how you felt in any
case.

But if you tell me that my new driveway runs eighteen inches
across the boundary onto your lot, then I am going to ask a question.

It is not in itself a very deeply probing question. It is just something to explode in the general vicinity of your statement like a depth
charge, and like a depth charge it may sometimes blow your statement right out of water.

The question is, "*Is that so?*" This is a hard, cynical question, one to be uttered with a twisted leer and a nasty snarl. You have touched on something that does concern me. Your statement is not just a matter of opinion; it is something that can be proved or disproved by reference to external reality. And so I snarl, "Is that so?"

You may be surprised how often this preliminary attack will settle the issue. It forces whoever made the statement to take a second look; and he may find that he had not said just what he intended to say; or that what he said would not really stand up under fire.

We might try a few on this basis, just to check the deadly effectiveness of this preliminary attack.

Statement: "If you give me a ticket, I'm going to report you to the Chief of Police, who is a friend of mine." Reply: "*Is that so?*"

Statement: "It is very easy to make money trading in low-priced stocks." Reply: "*Is that so?*"

Statement: "Just open wide, now. This won't hurt a bit." Reply: "*Is that so?*"

Statement: "I've got you beat, just with what I've got showing on the table." Reply: "*Is that so?*"

Keep in mind, always, that a good part of the time the conversations, arguments, etc. are not between you and some other person, but between you and yourself. They may not be consciously verbal, either. But sometimes by asking the question in verbal form, you can bring yourself up short, and see just where you are headed for trouble.

You say: "I'm going to sell Lukens Steel short. It can't go any higher." Yourself replies, "*Is that so?*"

You say: "I can just pick up the money and walk away. No one will ever know." Yourself replies, "*Is that so?*" *You* will know.

If it is important, challenge the statement. And if you really mean business, follow up the challenge with the second question: "*How do you know that?*"

A neighbor calls you up and tells you that your Johnny smashed his garage window with a baseball. Question: "Is that so?", and the follow-up: "*How do you know that?*" Did the neighbor see Johnny throw the baseball? Did one of the other boys on the block tell him that Johnny broke the window? Did he decide Johnny *must* have broken it because he has broken a lot of windows before?

When somebody sees something with his own eyes, he is abstracting at a low level, from close to reality.   He can be mistaken, it might be some other boy he saw who looked something like Johnny, but the chances are pretty good that he is correct in his statement.   If he got his information from one of the other boys, he is not quite so close to reality.   The other boy might also be mistaken, he might mean another "Johnny," and he might be lying.   And if the statement that Johnny broke the window was based on Johnny's past record, this is not nearly so tight a case; it becomes, then, a matter of inference, of high abstraction, rather than direct observation.

Low level abstractions are more dependable as evidence of facts in external reality than high level abstractions.

Just consider how much trouble people could have saved themselves if they had questioned themselves on certain decisions based on statements expressed or implied in their own minds.

"This gun isn't loaded."   "Is that so?   *How do you know that?*" "Ford stock is a good buy at 65."   "Is that so?   *How do you know that?*"   "Stocks that pay dividends are more profitable than stocks that don't pay dividends."   "Is that so?   *How do you know that?*" "Ball point pens can't leak in the pocket."   "Is that so?   *How do you know that?*"   "One more drink won't interfere with my driving."   "Is that so.   *How do you know that*"   "Selling short is more dangerous than buying stock."   "Is that so?   *How do you know that?*"

And so on.   You could add a hundred, a thousand such statements and questions.

You may think we are laboring a very simple point here.   It seems perfectly clear that anyone will ask the simple questions we have suggested.   And yet . . . they do not.   Very often they do not at all.   They plunge right ahead, sometimes into the jaws of real disaster.

If the statement seems so obvious that it is impossible to conceive that it is wrong, many of us will not even ask the questions.   Such a statement, for the ancients, might well have been, "The earth is generally a flat surface, modified by hills, mountains, etc."   They would not welcome your question as to how they "knew this." They would not see any need to prove what was so perfectly obvious. And feeling this way they would certainly reject any suggestion from you that the world might not be generally a flat surface, but might be, say, more like a sphere.

It seems obvious enough to some people that stocks that pay

dividends regularly must be safer than those that never pay any dividends.   Not always true, but they are so wedded to "what they believe" that their mind is not open to any new idea.   In the same way they will stand firm in the belief that short selling is more dangerous than buying stocks.   And they will defend their faith that "blue chip" stocks are "safer investments" than speculative stocks.   And that commodity trading is foolhardy.   And so forth.

How can a man expect his evaluative equipment to help him and protect him when it is frozen?   How can he put his abstractive ability to work to make him better maps when he will not look at the territory, but simply fumbles with the old maps he has always used?

In short, how can a man see many angles of a situation if he has shut his mind tight against learning anything new?

If you want to improve your judgment and your record of predictive success you have got to go back to the territory of external reality and take a good hard look from time to time.

And if the territory does not match the maps, you have got to *change those maps.*

Why do you suppose it is so hard to take a second look?   Could it be because we value the old maps so much more than the reality that we will deny the reality if it might conflict with the map?

Could it be because these old maps were part of what we learned early in life when the mind was still flexible and receptive; before it had become frozen into a rigid "value system"?

Could it be because we had certain directives pounded into us by precept and by example; by the words of mother and father, and the counsel of grandfather; by the instruction we received at church; by the lessons at school; by the example and custom of all our friends; by the laws and folkways of our culture; and by the words of high authority that were passed down to us from our forefathers?

Could it be that we have been trained *not to look at the facts,* but to accept without question what others tell us?

You know that when the map does not coincide with the territory it is not the territory that is wrong.

It cannot hurt you to know the truth.   Not so much as *not* knowing the truth.

If someone tells you one of your employees is stealing money from the till, it may be very generous and noble of you to show your faith by refusing to entertain the suspicion at all.   But if the employee is, actually, dishonest, it will be better to find it out as soon as possible. And if he is not dishonest, it can do no harm to explode a malicious rumor. In any case, it will not make matters any worse to take a hard look at the facts.

If someone says, "This is a Bear Market," you can hide your head in the sand and deny that it is anything of the sort, because you do not want to believe it is a Bear Market. And you can muster a pile of clippings quoting market experts to prove that it is *not* a Bear Market (rejecting any market experts that think it is). But will all this phony map-making give you a true picture of the territory? Will it help to guide you through the very real problems of the market as it is? Or are you simply using the voices of high authority to shield you against the cold fear you shrink from facing?

The way to cope with the market is to look at the facts! The way to look at *any* problem is to look at the facts! Then you can do your abstracting from current here-and-now data and form opinions and judgments that are, at least, based on the best evidence available.

And all of this, by the way, is not only a method for the market. It is the method of modern science and modern engineering.

QUESTIONS FOR CONSIDERATION

Do you (perhaps silently) make a practice of giving any pompous or pontifical statement (such as some bankers' advice to buy "good sound stocks") the cold and fishy eye? Do you ask yourself, "Is that so?"

Suppose the statement comes to you from such high authority or on the basis of such universal acceptance by "right-thinking" people that it seems obvious, right, and needing no proof. Can you give it the fishy stare and ask "Is that so?"

And suppose the statement (or precept, or directive) was something ingrained in your own value system; something you had learned so early in life and taken so much for granted that it never occurred to you to question it. Could you; would you be able to give it the same treatment? Could you question the laws of the Medes and Persians? Could you doubt the teachings of the great philosophers? Could you stand on your two feet and ask the question, "Is that so?"

Do you believe that it is better to accept what you are taught on faith than to demand the proof, the evidence?

How much of your own knowledge came to you "Because it is in the book," and "Because I say so"? How often do you check any of this knowledge?

Is it a fair question to ask anyone expressing strong or absolute opinions; "How do you know that?" When you have very strong and absolute opinions about something do you ask yourself this same question? Do you make yourself back up your opinions with evidence?

How many of the "obvious truths" of the marketplace are no more than the generalities, wishful thoughts, half-truths, and nonsense collected in the sterile forum of the boardroom for generations? How many of these can you think of now? How many can you explode and clear away out of your mind?

In your market work and in your other affairs do you try to apply a systematic method of evaluation, based on the most reliable or verifiable evidence obtainable?

BALDERDASH, UNLIMITED

TO SOME industrious souls, "getting the facts" means piling up a lot of data including much extraneous junk and irrelevant nonsense, so that the end-result of the fact-gathering is a great bulging mass of data something like the old Collier mansion in New York.

It would be a good idea, before going too deeply into the business of fact-gathering, to set some limits on just what facts are to be collected.

If you are making a study of libraries it is probably irrelevant what kind of chewing gum the assistant librarian chews. It is a fact all right; but it has no particular bearing on the problem at hand unless you happen to be making a merchandising survey for Wrigley.

There are men who collect facts the way a pack rat collects small bright objects. They have clipping files, and reference files, and chart files. They can produce the names of all the directors of a company for the past forty years. They know the terms of the merger completed in 1934. They have copies of the annual reports as well as the analyses of the corporate affairs by various financial commentators.

Some of this data may be important to them. It all depends what they are trying to do.

A research team that is trying to determine natural magnetic fields at various points on the earth's surface might require certain types of data that would be quite superfluous to a group studying the distribution of earthquakes and the principal fault lines. What might be "necessary and sufficient" for one type of study might be "inadequate (in some respects) and superfluous (in other respects)" for another.

In fact, as soon as we have decided exactly what we want to find out, and have framed the question or questions we want to ask (and it does not pay to stint on care at this point, that is, in framing the questions), we must face the next step in the study by deciding just what kind of data we are going to need in order to be able to answer these questions.

In some fields of study, and I would include the market here, the problem is not so much a lack of data, as *too much* data.   You can get plenty of factual information about the market; daily, weekly, and monthly charts, some with volume and ratio comparisons to the averages, dividend and earnings records, percentage advances and declines, etc., etc., etc. almost without end.

It is a matter, very largely, of weeding out the superfluous.

We think of students failing in some research because they have not searched enough.   We blame their failure on lack of information. But isn't it possible that there have been just as many failures because there was *too much* data unrelated to the problem at hand?   Almost always, in any original study, there is a stage of more or less indiscriminate "collecting" of facts.   And then, if the project is going to carry through to success, there comes a time when all this stuff has to be sorted out and organized; and very likely three-fourths of it discarded or thrown away.   This cleaning-out and concentrating is just as much a part of the job as the collecting and observing.

As a matter of fact, a very important part of problem solving today consists in the preliminary work; such things as stating the problem, asking the questions, determining the data to be assembled, and abstracting from this data the essential information bearing on the job at hand.   There has been a good deal of work done just on the method of planning experiments, and on the "programming" of the work to be done by the big electronic computers.   You might say, with some accuracy, that the preliminary work was the most important part of the job, and once it was out of the way the rest was relatively straight sailing.

It is pretty much a matter of determining what is relevant, that is, what is important to the job at hand.   Of course, there is always the remote possibility that something apparently meaningless may turn out to be of vital import.   For instance, there have been some detective stories and some real cases of crime detection that have revolved around exhaustive examination of every little piece of junk that came to hand. But, in general, one is likely to solve more crimes if he looks for something that might have something to do with the crime. If I am trying to find out what is going on in some stock that has suddenly burst into great activity, it seems unlikely that I will find the answers I am looking for by rummaging in the corporate statistics of the past ten years; for the plain reason that the new activity in the stock *itself* suggests that the conditions are now strikingly different from what they have been. New conditions call for a revision of the old maps, or an entirely new map; and you will not find the new toll bridge on the 1952 road map no matter how hard you look for it.

To a great extent, then, the job of analysis, once the data has been collected, is a matter of sorting out this data and throwing away all of it that is irrelevant. Very often this means throwing away most of it, just as a miner, having a great pile of ore, will reduce it to a small amount of a concentrate, and throw away all the rest.

Perhaps I could cite my own experience here by way of example. In my work as a counsellor in stocks and in commodities I follow what is known as the "technical" method, as contrasted with what has been called the "fundamental" method of analysis.

Briefly, the fundamental operator tries to evaluate all of the factors affecting a stock on a sort of "reason why" basis. There have been some outstandingly successful traders who worked on this basis; probably because they knew which factors were important and which were not, and who were therefore able to select the relevant data. And there have been thousands of investors who have attempted to buy and sell according to the "fundamentals" who have failed; perhaps because they did not realize that it is not possible to "know all," and because they were not able to select the really important facts, or to relate these facts one to another.

The technical operator, on the other hand is concerned mainly with the action of the stock in its market behavior. He makes no attempt to find the "reasons why" things happen as they do, but strips the problem to a limited field, namely the observation of the market action alone. This line of attack was opened up by Charles H. Dow and William Peter Hamilton in their discovery that the market averages have a relation to the probable future course of business. Others have carried this work forward, and in the early 1930's Richard W. Schabacker applied the technical principles to the evaluation of individual stocks.   Later, Robert D. Edwards and I elaborated these studies, and, I hope, did some further "time-binding" of our own in our book, "Technical Analysis of Stock Trends."

Now, the technician is still regarded as a strange breed of cat.   He ignores, for the most part, the flood of statistics, reports, rumors, tips, production and earnings records, and most of the "fundamental" information.   He does not do this simply because he is an odd fish, nor because he feels that these facts are not important.   He recognizes as well as the next man that they tell the story of what is behind his charts and diagrams.

The technician has elected to study, not this mass of "fundamentals," but certain abstractions, namely the market data alone.   He is fully aware that this is "not all" and that it does not provide an infallible guide for predicting the future of any stock.   Also he is aware that what he is looking at is indeed a fairly high order abstraction and that back of it lies the whole complicated world of "things" and "events."

But this "technical" view does provide a simplified and more comprehensible picture of what is happening to the price of a stock. It is like a shadow or reflection in which can be seen the broad outline of the whole situation.

Furthermore, it works.   It is not "perfect," but neither is any other way "perfect."   It is easier on the nerves because it can be made quite definite, subject to rules and policies laid down in advance; and these rules and policies can be re-studied and revised whenever it seems necessary.   They are general enough so that it is possible to compare very different kinds of stocks and see the similarities in their behavior.   There is not so much detail involved that one cannot see the forest for the trees.

From my standpoint it is a more realistic and more practical way of dealing with the market than any other method I have known.

The art of analysis is the art of selection; of knowing what is important, refining the nuggets of pure information, and getting all of the immaterial out of the way.

If we call the information we want: "the message," or "the signal"; and the extraneous material that is not for us of any meaning, the "noise"; then what we are trying to do is to get rid of "the noise," and increase the "signal-to-noise" ratio; which is at the heart of many problems of communication and analysis.

QUESTIONS FOR CONSIDERATION

Are you familiar with the type of mind that collects facts the way the junk men collect rubbish, taking everything that comes along without discrimination?

Do you find that after collecting data on a problem it helps clarify the picture to organize the material and eliminate everything that is not relevant to the question-at-hand?

In considering the purchase of Pepsi-Cola stock would you regard the fact that people drink more soft drinks in the summer than in the winter as necessarily relevant?

In evaluating the stock of United Merchants and Manufacturers (who make and sell men's clothing) would you consider the fact that men's clothing is a necessity, and therefore the business is a stable one, to be highly relevant?

Just how important is the picture of the sun setting over the Paducah refinery, in the annual report, as an aid to evaluation of the stock?

Can you evaluate the stocks of various oil companies from a study of their various productive capacities, their interlocking leases and agreements, the prospects of increase or decrease in world oil consumption? Are these matters entirely irrelevant? Are they too complicated to permit evaluation by the average man? Then why bother?

Do you try to strip the unnecessary details from a question or problem so that you will not start out with a load of excess baggage?

WE CAN'T GET IT *ALL*

BACK of the drive some people have for the indiscriminate collection of data, whether the data be useful or irrelevant, rational or nonsense, seems to lie the idea that if only we have "enough" information, any problem will become clear.

That, of course, is true. We must have the "necessary" amount of information. But we stop at a "sufficient" quantity. Otherwise the grain of truth will be lost in the barrow of balderdash.

Sometimes a very little clear light on a problem, if it is not obscured by clouds of ambient gibberish, is all that is needed.

And volumes of statistics will not solve anything until they have been reduced to orderly arrangement so that intelligent abstractions can be made from them.

But some people have the feeling that, if they "know everything about it," all the answers will be clear.

The fact is we don't know everything about *anything*. We don't know *all* about a grain of dust.

It is too bad that children are taught so definitely that mathematics is "the exact science." They are drilled in the mechanics of positive integers until it seems as if two plus two equals four was the very foundation of all truth.

Nobody ever tells these children that they are dealing with some very special situations in the world of figures; and that the figures themselves are high abstractions having significance only according to the particular rules of the game we decide to play with them. They are taught that it is always possible to come out with a "perfect" answer in arithmetic; and by extension, they may (and often do) get the idea that it is always possible to get a perfect answer to any problem if only you work hard enough.

It must come as quite a shock to them to find, even before they are through junior high school, that it is not possible to get perfect answers in many, in fact most, of the problems of mathematics; and that in other fields it isn't even remotely possible to "know it all."

Perhaps that is why children are so bothered and frustrated by math. And why so few adults ever really accept the broader view, the idea of approximations, the "partial" answers. And so they go through life still looking for a "two plus two" that always and precisely equals four.

It is not possible to express exactly the diagonal of a square in integers. Nor in fractions. Nor in any simpler way than as "a function of the square root of two." The ratio of the circumference of a circle to its diameter will not "come out even." You cannot get to the end of it. You cannot "know it all." The base of the natural logarithms, "e," has no end. You cannot "know it all," either.

When you look at a tree, or a cat, or a neighbor, we will realize, if we have moved beyond the "two plus two" stage, that it is not possible to get it *all*.

And this can be another case of the either . . . or dichotomy, unless we can take a more reasonable view. For if we have only two values, and if we can't "know it all," then we must know "nothing," and then we cannot expect to make any practical deal with our environment at all.

Well, of course, it is simply not true that there is no middle ground.

We can not only deal successfully with things we do not fully understand, but we can deal very successfully with things about which we know relatively little; if that little is of the right sort and properly applied.

Some of the Eskimos are said to be very expert mechanics in the repair and maintenance of machinery, such as diesel and gasoline engines in their fishing boats. It seems unlikely that all of these fishermen are trained engineers, familiar with the construction and theory of these engines, and conversant with the chemistry and physics and mathematics involved in their construction. But they know a little, and in the right places.   They have what is necessary; and sufficient.

There are circumstances where it is desirable to know a good deal about the detail of a corporation's structure, and about its production, management, financing, future prospects, etc.   But no one can know *all* about these things.

Also, it is not necessary to know very much about any of them, in order to buy and sell the stock of that corporation successfully in the market.   I know a number of successful investors whose knowledge of the "fundamentals" in such cases is very limited.   They know just what is necessary and sufficient to their technical operations in the market.

In much the same way I know some traders in commodities literally would not know the grains they trade in if they were to see them.   You cannot say they know "nothing" about these grains. But they are not even trying to "know all."   They have developed technical methods that are adequate to meet their requirements. And with their limited knowledge, of the right sort for the purpose, they are successful.

So, along with abandoning the drive for "absolute success," and "complete happiness," and "infallibility," we are going to have to give up the idea of "total knowledge" about anything or any person. And a bit later we will discover that it is necessary to let go of the ideal of "absolute certainty."

It seems as though we were having to let slip some of the things we have been trained all our lives to value very highly.   And that is true.   We have been trained to value these absolutes *too* highly. Until we can see that "ideals" are not "things," and until we are willing and able to scale down our ideals to something within the range of possibility, we will never be able to attain any very great degree of "success," or "happiness," or "rightness," or for that matter, of "understanding."

Let's put it this way.   When our "maps" representing our aspirations are too far above or beyond our "real accomplishments," we are bound to feel defeated, depressed, discouraged, unworthy.

The solution to these problems may be to raise the level of our accomplishments; or to lower somewhat the absolute quality of our "ideals"; or a little of both.   But until we can bring our own picture of what we "should be" into some degree of focus with what we actually are, we cannot expect to feel very much satisfaction or security.

QUESTIONS FOR CONSIDERATION

Outside of the banking and accounting professions and that part of the legal profession which is concerned with these same matters, how many situations can you think of where exact numerical answers are required?

Is the size of your house lot exact? Have you looked at your deed? Do you find the phrase "more or less" after the acreage?

What is the circulation of the Wall Street Journal? Do you think the publisher could give you an absolutely exact answer to that question?

What was the number of riders on the Pennsylvania railroad today? Do you think the directors could tell you, exactly?

What is the distance from New York to Baltimore? Would Rand McNally be able to tell you, precisely? The U. S. Geodetic survey? How many miles to the moon? To Alpha Centauri? To the Companion of Sirius?

How many atoms in a cubic centimeter of water?

Do you take exactly an hour for lunch?

Does a package of bacon marked "Weight One Pound" contain precisely sixteen ounces?

Professor Perkins is one of the smartest men in his field of study? Does he know "all" about it?

Isn't it enough to know "enough," do "enough," have "enough," for the purpose at hand?

THE TRUTH, THE WHOLE TRUTH,
AND NOTHING BUT THE TRUTH

HEAVEN help the man who took the legal oath at face value and attempted to give his testimony strictly in accordance with the oath. If we might quote one Pontius Pilate, "What is truth?" The poor puzzled Pontius was beyond his depth; and unless one realizes that "truth" is one of the abstract nouns of very high abstractive level, one could flounder pitifully trying to explain in terms of "things out there" what properly belongs with "maps, in here."

We know already that "the whole truth" is not possible to comprehend. Not in the literal sense of "all," for we cannot know all about even Tennyson's little "Flower in the Crannied Wall."

We can get a practical grasp on "the whole truth" if we will once again chuck out some excess baggage. This is, if we will stop using words of unlimited or absolute scope, such as "utter" and "complete," etc. Mathematicians do this by attaching limits in their formulas. We may consider a certain function "between the limits X equals zero, and X equals one thousand."

In the same way we can limit "the whole truth" to "that which may reasonably be considered to have a significant bearing on the case at hand."

In this chapter, however, we are not concerned so much with the problem of superfluous truth as with the matter of "lost" or "suppressed" truth.

You may remember the invisible elephant. It may be practically blocking your front door, but you cannot see it unless it is significant to you; and you may not be able to see it even then under certain conditions.

There are conditions in which "selective inattention" can tune out almost anything.   You probably know from your own experience how the pain of a headache can mar your perception of normally enjoyable company at a party.   It is also true that when the dentist's beautiful nurse smiles at you in a tender manner, the grinding of the dental drill seems somewhat less irritating.   In such simple cases you know how much the attention can be shifted, so much so that certain things are not fully and consciously perceived.   Of course the really spectacular cases of selective inattention are those that involve the "self."   We do not like to observe things that make ourselves look small, or cheap, or stupid, or mean, or dirty.   We will go a long way to avoid seeing ourselves (as compared with our own "values") as degraded, guilty, or unworthy.

We will go a long way.   In fact if necessary we will go all the way and deny that what is true "out there" exists at all.   We will escape into a world where we are not rejected and where we do not have to reject ourselves.   Very likely we will be locked up in a state institution then; but we may be happier than we would be if we saw plainly what would hurt us too much.

As always, it is a matter of values that are too high, too vague, too absolute.

And until we can begin to see things somewhat more flexibly, we are likely to be at least a little blind, blind perhaps in the sense that a "color blind" person is not capable of seeing external reality as completely as one who does not suffer this disability.

QUESTIONS FOR CONSIDERATION

Have you ever discovered or been shown some feature of your daily world which had been in plain sight for a long time but which you never "saw" at all?   Have you suddenly discovered that there was a barber shop in the building at the corner, which you had never seen although you have passed its door every day?   Have you suddenly noticed an unusual tree or shrub near your home, which had been there unnoticed for a number of years?

Have you found that it is particularly easy to overlook or "not see" something which might cause you pain if you were to "see" it?   For example, certain shortcomings or faults in your own business or social behavior.

Or again, for example, certain information that might tend to contradict your feeling about a particular stock in which you are interested.

Can you see that in some areas where a matter might affect your own self-regard very seriously (especially if you already feel somewhat insecure) you might be unable to see certain parts of the truth because they could hurt you badly if you recognized them? If you have not been able to observe this in yourself (for obvious reasons), have you noticed how some of your friends can overlook stumbling blocks in their own lives, although to others these stumbling blocks are plainly to be seen?

INTERLUDE

YEARS ago there was a rattling good musical show on Broadway, "The Night Boat." It had one or two unusual wrinkles in it. About ten minutes after the start of the show the curtain came down and a chorus line came out from the wings, spaced themselves across the stage and addressed the audience in unison: "For the benefit of those who came in late, we simply wish to state . . ." and then described the opening scene and outlined the plot setting. The curtain went up and the action continued. Near the end of the second act, the curtain was rung down again and the chorus line again took their places before it and recited: "For the benefit of those who still remain, we simply would explain . . ." and reviewed the situation up to that point in the show. And then the curtain went up and the performance resumed.

This is a brief explanatory interlude of that sort. Up to this point it is quite possible, yes, rather more than possible, that the long-suffering reader has been wondering whether this volume was actually a book on the market, or on general semantics, or on sociology, philosophy, mathematics, or just exactly what. It has been, as in fact we threatened in the preface, a little of all these things, offered humbly by one who is not a master of any of them, in the hope that between his efforts and those of the readers, a little more understanding on a number of matters might take form.

If your interest lies primarily in the marts of trade, you may have been bored stiff with the seemingly wandering trail of these long discourses.

Actually, more than the market is involved, much, much more. The market is important. But it is no more important than certain abstract values that have nothing to do with dollars or shares of stock: Love, peace, security, confidence, joy, wonder, contentment, enthusiasm, in fact all of the concepts implied by the Founding Fathers of this country in the phrase "the pursuit of happiness." All these things are important for they are the salt and flavor of life.

And, as we have tried to show in the previous pages, these subjective satisfactions rest in very large degree on the maintenance of an adequate degree of "self-regard."

Since it is closer to observable reality to deal with matters which can be checked, verified, demonstrated in such a way that we can call them "facts," it is easier to study the mechanisms of general semantics with reference to a specific area of external reality than to speak in purely abstract terms. By using the market as a theater of operations we are able to apply the highly abstract principles to a particular down-to-earth case in point.

But you will understand, it is hoped, that the methods of study and the applications of general semantics are not limited to the market at all. They can be applied in very much the same way to other problems in other areas. They are applicable in home life, and in the complicated domestic tangles that arise within the family constellation. Most especially, they can be used to ease the tensions and conflicts that work inside our "selves." For if we can see wherein we have been taught too much that is obsolete or absolute, or nonsense, and how we have set as our goals the impossible, the indescribable, and the ridiculous, then we can begin to know how to live easier and more comfortably, and how to take care of our "selves" more adequately, and how to realize more fully our own potentialities.

And it should be noted here, that the man who does not adequately satisfy his own "self" is not well fitted to help others, nor likely to do so. The starving man cannot do much to feed the hungry. The sick man cannot do much to help those who suffer. Unless a man has "enough" food, and "enough" approval, and "enough" sex, and "enough" money, approximately to meet his own appraisal of his minimum needs, he will be a weak, insecure, fear-ridden, and possibly criminal or insane menace to his neighbors.

That is why the basic foundation of general semantics is so important. We have used the market as an example, like a little world where we can test the method; and from time to time we have hinted, by examples taken from fields outside the market, that the applications are much broader. But you will understand that the applications are only the end-result of a basic method of evaluation.

And it is the "method of evaluation" that is important, for it applies in every aspect of life.

And now . . . "For the benefit of those who still remain," in the chapters to come we will focus more and more sharply on the specific problems connected with the market. We will see how the "method of evaluation" applies to a number of particular problems that the investor or trader will encounter.

Only remember; these are all examples of something much larger and more important. Namely, a "basic method of evaluation" which, if you master it, can help you in every part of your life. It can literally enrich your entire living. And though we know it is not easy to "change human nature," you may find that it is worth the effort to study your own human nature and make those changes that will be so greatly to your own advantage.

QUESTIONS FOR CONSIDERATION

Does any of this make any sense to you up to this point?

Do you realize how your ability to recognize things and to perceive events in the world around you builds up a file of stored information?

Do you see how, from this storehouse of primary data, you learn to abstract further into categories of various degree?

And do you understand how we build intangible constructs from the basic data, leading to judgments and opinions?

If this is a fair sketch of the way we acquire knowledge and understanding, isn't it important to know what new data is coming in to us, and what supports it; and to re-examine our present judgments and opinions and the data they rest on?

Would such a continual study and re-examination help to prevent some of the misconceptions and mistakes we all make?

Is all of this likely to clarify our thinking and reduce our anxiety in the market?

Is the market the only place it would apply? Would these same methods apply equally to our family relations, our social contacts and evaluations, our aims and efforts in business, our religious and political views, and all other departments of our lives?

DATED DATA

IF YOU impress something on a recording medium, say your own brain, at a time when there is very little material already recorded on it, and when the equipment is sharp and fresh and sensitive, it is likely it will stick with you a long time, as we mentioned earlier.

You have probably had the experience of meeting an old school or college friend after an interval of years, and experiencing a shock, when you are faced with the facts, to find that your "maps" are badly out of date. The roistering, hard-drinking, wise-cracking, gal-chasing boon companion of *then* has become a well-married, respectable vice-president-in-charge-of-research for a Great Corporation, whose idea of a really big evening is to attend a panel discussion on the Future of the Middle East in Relation to the Impact of Western Democracy. As always, when the map does not correspond to the territory, we must be prepared to change the map. If we retain the old map, as we surely want to retain our good memories, we must "date" that map and not confuse what was *then*, with what is *now*.

Perhaps we do not entirely understand Salvador Dali's paintings however much we may admire his techniques. But the *title* of his famous "folded watches" picture, "The Persistence of Memory," surely makes a point.

Consider the dated data many of us have about transportation. We think of electric street cars as something "real" and important, as indeed they were in every city in the country only a few years ago. Perhaps you can remember the great lurching cars, with their

252

destination signs over the front reading "Meadowvale" or "Main Street" in white gothic letters on a green background, and to one side, a huge number. Below the glassed-in front from which the motorman looked out along the track were hung, on each side of the single headlight, signs announcing the wrestling matches at the Arena, and the opening of Luna Park. You can probably remember the elaborate folding doors and the high steps, so difficult for old ladies. The smells of wet rubbers and raincoats during a late winter thaw. Very likely you recall the irritated thumping of the motorman's foot on the clanging bell when some truck or ice wagon blocked the course ahead. Maybe you remember some occasion when a great flash and "bang" in the front of the car proclaimed the blowing of a circuit-breaker, and the silent period of waiting until the motorman was again able to slide the handle of the controller around and ease the car into motion. You have likely watched the conductor, at the end of the line, trundling the trolley around from the back of the car to the other end for the return trip, as the motorman followed with his brake handle and control handle in his hand. You may have seen the great shower of sparks when the trolley came off the overhead wire and had to be eased back by manipulating the rope at its end, an operation much like playing a fish in an upside-down sort of way. And in your memory you may hear the screech of the trolley wheels as they negotiated the curve into Maple Street, late, late at night.

No more. The trolley cars exist, as memories, as mental maps; that is all. Our children do not understand what they were like at all. They have never had the pleasure of racing through an empty car and pulling over the seats to face the other way. For them, the trolleys never did exist at all in external reality.

And when you stop to think that the trolley car did not come in until almost the very end of the nineteenth century, and was well on its way out twenty-five years later, you will realize that this "reality" which was so close and vital a part of the lives of some of us was only a passing phase. In order to have any meaning it has to be referred to a definite period, a period, roughly, of only a matter of twenty-five years.

These maps! These early maps! They stick with us. And they are not all "verbal maps." Language is so important in our lives that some students of general semantics have given practically all

their attention to the *verbal* aspects. But we make maps that are
not verbal at all; they are abstracted from non-verbal sensory data.
And the maps abstracted by means of one sense may be related to
those abstracted by means of other senses; and all of these may be
related to verbal abstractions.

Just be sure you date them!

If such detailed and sharply defined images are projected from a
"map" more or less casually acquired, just think of the likelihood
of other impressions staying with us in matters which were *not*
casually acquired, but were drilled into us by our elders. These maps
stay with us and, where they concern our appraisals of reality, become part of our "value system." Inasmuch as we act and think
and feel according to this "value system," they are, in fact, the thing
that is "ourself."

But if these elements in our value system are not up-to-date and
in line with present reality, we cannot expect them to apply. We
must date the maps. And if we intend to use them we should examine
them, check them, revise them if necessary, and make new maps if
that is required.

There is not space here to take up all the kinds of maps that
may be in greater or less degree obsolete, which many people regard
as "true," without date or specification, absolutely and always.
We have been taught so many things; about how we "should" act,
what we "should" regard as "good" or "bad," as to standards of
success, as to religious views, as to relations with our neighbors, as
to sex, as to the bringing up of children, as to our relations with
wives, husbands, parents; in fact, almost every angle of life is affected
by precepts and directives handed down to us from our elders, or
through them from our forefathers.

These are all what we have called "maps." They are the "time
binding," the process by which wisdom and experience can be preserved and passed along from generation to generation in the human
race as it cannot be in the case of animals.

Many of these precepts and directives are practical and fully as
applicable today as they were when conceived ten years or a thousand
years ago.

But if they *are not dated*, and if one is not willing to re-examine
them and revise them if need be they can do inestimable harm.

A map, to be a safeguard, must apply to "this place here," "under these conditions," and "at this time." Otherwise you may be driving off the end of an embankment where the washed out bridge used to stand.

Of course, too, we have assumed that all of the precepts and directives were, in fact, valid, practicable and honest, when originally conceived. There is also that possibility that some, at least, of them may have been nonsense to start with, or might even have been plain, deliberate deception from the start. This is not a great probability but it must be weighed.

What is more likely is that the precept or directive may have referred to some special or temporary condition, not generally, or always applicable.

Or it could be that the original precept or directive had a "symbolic" meaning, that is to say, that it was not intended to be taken literally but only as an analogy or metaphor. In this case, of course, we are dealing with a confusion of the levels of abstraction. This is what happens when people speak of the action of "the averages" in the market, forgetting that the "averages" are not the real actions of specific stocks, but a high order abstraction. In the case of high order abstractions, as we will see, they can be very useful so long as we label them definitely for what they are and do not try to apply them where they would be meaningless.

Now, let us take a look at a few dated data, things you and I were taught quite early and which we still tend to project onto reality and read back as if they were really "out there."

QUESTIONS FOR CONSIDERATION

When was the last time you saw a big league baseball game? How much can you remember about it?

Think of ten important days in your life when you were about eight years old. Now try to think of ten important days in your life when you were about eighteen. Or twenty-eight. Or thirty-eight. Why do you think the details of certain gala days stand out so much more clearly in the early years?

Why is your first fist fight such a powerful memory? What was there about your first real date with your first real sweetheart? Where was the glamour in your first circus, the glamour you have never been able to recapture? Why is there so much intensity, so much sadness, so much hostility, so much joy, so much despair, so much persistence in memories of these early events? Why do they stand out so sharp and clear after so long a time?

Do you think it would be easier to forget what happened last week: or what happened twenty years ago?

How much of your basic evaluative method have you acquired since you grew old enough to check and examine evidence, and how much of it came to you before you had the experience or maturity to judge what you were taught?

Is there any connection between this situation and your failure "to act as intelligently as you know how to"?

Is it worth the effort to re-examine the obsolete maps and if they need revision, to revise them?

Do you think it will be easy to change the habitual attitudes you have taken for granted most of your life?

"BUY GOOD, SOUND STOCKS"

THERE are so many books on "How to Buy Stocks." You can send in coupons with three dollars or five dollars and get lists of "Stocks to Buy Now." Investment clubs are formed to study "which stocks to buy." Even the New York Stock Exchange (and we can forgive them for not trying to buck a precept that has almost the force of religious authority) publishes brochures and advertisements explaining how to set up an investment program by buying "good" stocks.

Some of us, who were exposed to a "sound" and "conservative" philosophy, take this so much for granted that it goes without saying. "Buy good, sound stocks" seems perfectly obvious and perfectly plain, like saying that "Honesty is the best policy," or "Haste makes waste."

We don't attach any dates to the directive, nor do we ask when, where, or under what conditions it applies.

Nor do we ask even what it means. It could be as meaningless as one of those dead-level abstractions like *"Virtue* is *good,"* where we simply reword the same idea without explaining anything at all. A case in point would be the man who consults his physician about a very sore toe. After his foot has been examined and perhaps X-rayed, the patient may be given instructions for the soaking and bandaging of the ailing member. If he seeks further information and a diagnosis, he may be told that he has acute *"digitus ulcerosus"* which, being looked up later, turns out to be the latin equivalent of "sore toe."

If we mean by "good, sound stocks" those which will probably result in a strengthening of our financial position, and which will give us security and income, then we certainly *do* want "good, sound stocks."

But if we mean, here, "the stocks of good, sound corporations," then we should say just that. The two statements are not identical and may not mean the same thing at all. It is quite possible for a stock to be highly profitable and to provide great security and enormous income, although it may be the stock of a highly speculative development venture in uranium mining. And, as you may know from your experience in recent years, the stock of the most staid and solid company can droop and sag and perhaps collapse utterly in the course of time.

There is a confusion here between "General Manufacturing," the stock, and "General Manufacturing," the company. If it is the stock we are dealing with we can observe its *relation* to corporate affairs; but we should not make a faulty identification.

Back at the start of the century there was a "good, sound stock," which Jesse Livermore tells about in his book, "How to Trade in Stocks." It was the stock of a New England company, financed and operated largely by New England businessmen. It enjoyed a steady commerce, and was a monopoly in its field. The stock was regarded as a "blue chip," and it was widely held by trust funds, insurance companies, wealthy investors, rich widows, etc. Its name was New Haven, and it was the stock of the great network of rail lines throughout New England known as the New York, New Haven and Hartford. It fluctuated somewhat in price, but not widely. It paid regular dividends at a conservative rate. Its earnings were steady. It sold, near the turn of the century, around $250 a share.

Let others speculate in coppers, or textiles, or machinery. For the conservative man New Haven represented security.

Such a man (and his name was legion) did not "speculate." He bought "good, sound stocks." Period. If New Haven advanced in the market he would not sell, for he was not a gambler. If New Haven declined, he would not let it worry him; he might, indeed, call his broker to pick up a few additional shares.

But suppose, as Livermore suggested, New Haven drops off to $150. What does one do then? Why, if this is a "good, sound stock," why should one be disturbed? There is no need to do anything. Let the traders in the market buy and sell; but the physical properties are still there, the rails and cars and engines; stations, tunnels, bridges. The "true value" has not changed.

And what if the stock drops to $100. No matter, the public is simply unaware of "real values."

Do you see what is happening here? Do you see that a "map" *without date* is being treated *as if it were a territory?* And the map is being given greater weight and value than the territory itself. These investors were not only confusing the physical company itself with the "stock" of the company; but they were also attributing a "value" to the stock. Worse, they were quite unaware that this "value" was an abstraction, a matter of opinion, and that the very fact that the market price had dropped 150 points was presumptive evidence that collective opinion had changed with respect to New Haven stock.

And, having the somewhat inflexible value systems of the Proper Bostonian of that period, they were quite unwilling or unable to take another hard look at the territory, but continued smugly to have faith in their obsolete maps.

And if New Haven should drop to 50? It did. And did they change their opinions? They did not.

And when New Haven was selling at 25? And at 10? And at $5 a share?

"At just what point," Livermore asks, "would these investors realize that they like all other investors are, in fact, speculators?" In other words, how far out of line must the reality become before they realize that the old map has to be changed? New Haven, as you know, went to $1.00, and to 50¢. After Livermore's death I saw New Haven quoted in sixteenths; this was just before the stock was de-listed, wiped off the board, pending a reorganization.

Who is going to say that the original valuation of New Haven at $250 a share was "wrong"? At the time, under the conditions then prevailing, it may have been a most reasonable and realistic appraisal. The fault was not in the original map, but in hanging on like grim death to an obsolete map that no longer represented the territory in external reality. Things had changed. And when things change, we have to change opinions.

We said "hang on like grim death." And grim death it was for many. A young man in my adult evening class came up to me one evening during recess, when we were having a smoke back of the

school building.   We had just been discussing this New Haven case.
He told me the true story of how his grandfather, not trusting the
vagaries of the Younger Generation, had left his estate almost entirely in the form of New Haven stock; and had so entailed it that
it was forbidden to sell that stock under any conditions.   This was
in line with the implications of a "map" that showed New Haven
to be a "good, sound stock"; and the purpose of the provision was
to prevent the children and grandchildren from frittering away their
patrimony in "speculation."   The case was taken to court during
the years while New Haven coasted toward total collapse, in a futile
attempt to break the provisions of the will.   But the will could not
be broken, and the family inheritance vanished in thin air.

You know, there is not only an unwillingness to face the fact
that "things are different now."   There are also some factors related
to preservation of the ego.   To some people it is a hurtful thing to
have to change an opinion.   And such people may cling to a faith,
directive, precept, etc. to the very bitter end, rather than make the
supreme sacrifice of going out and taking another look at the facts.

It does not need to hurt that much.   Not *unless* . . . you have such
a rigid conception of "rightness" that an opinion you have once
formed becomes something sacred and eternal, not ever to be questioned or examined again.

There is another way the idea of buying "good, sound stocks"
can hurt us.   There are many angles to our value systems, and they
involve not only matters of ethics and conduct, but how we value
our "selves" in relation to the clothes we wear, the houses we live
in, the kind of cars we drive, and even the stocks we own.   There are
people who feel that it is "better" or at least "more respectable"
to own shares in a "high grade," "conservative" utility, such as
Commonwealth Edison, than to muck around with more speculative
issues, such as Polaroid, which has been expanding and developing
very rapidly in recent years.

They are, perhaps, confusing the fact that there is more "risk" or
"leverage" in certain stocks, with some abstraction connected with
"respectability."   Some writers have noted that unearned or inherited wealth carries more prestige and "snob appeal" than earned
wealth.

Now, admitting that when we look for extraordinary gains we
must expect to take extraordinary risks, it is strange to see how much

"moral" implication is read into the situation, quite unconsciously, by a great many people. Somehow, it is considered more "respectable," at least more "solid," to clip the coupons on 2% bonds, than to speculate in Canadian "penny" stocks.

But this point seems to be more related to social snobbishness than anything else. Naturally, the "have-not" young man will have to get into something with opportunity to increase his capital or he will never be in a position to lounge on the deck of his yacht and clip bond coupons. And conversely the very fact that Mr. Pot Belly is able to sit in the window of the Union League Club and ponder the tax exempt features of certain new debentures, is evidence that he has already "got his." Therefore, by semantic extension, he is higher up the social ladder, is "better" than most of us, and what he does must be "right."

Perhaps this map, which so many of us have held at one time or another, ought to be torn right out of the book. If you are going into the market you should recognize that you are a speculator, both in the original sense of being an observer or evaluator, and in the sense of being, to some extent, a gambler. And while you can strike almost any balance you choose as to the amount of speculative risk you want to assume, this is a matter of *degree*, not of principle.

It is similar to the case of the two men who were arguing over the approachability, or at least the availability of a certain young woman strolling along Fifth Avenue. A bet was concluded between them, and one of the men accosted the girl. "My friend and I have been having an argument about the moral standards of women today. Could I ask you a question, a rather frank question?" "Why, yes, what is the question?" "Would you be willing to sleep with me if I paid you ten thousand dollars?" Pause. "Yes; I think I would, for ten thousand dollars." "Well, would you sleep with me tonight for ten dollars?" "Naturally not! What do you think I am?" "Excuse me, but that really isn't the question. I know what you are. What we are talking about is the price."

Some years ago I visited my father in Connecticut. During the evening he gave me a little fatherly advice on financial planning, investing and the like, and finally said, "What you've got to decide is whether you are an investor . . . or a speculator."

You will notice the "either . . . or" dichotomy here. One apparently is expected to be either an investor . . . or a speculator.

One cannot be both, and one cannot be even a little of each. There is no in-between. Also notice that the words "investor" and "speculator," although they sound like common nouns, actually represent rather high order abstractions. In order to mean anything very specific they have to be defined. And when we use words which we have not clearly defined, even to ourselves, then we are very likely to find ourselves talking nonsense, as indeed I believe my respected parent was on this occasion.

Also, as often happens with these either . . . or situations, you will realize that there was to my father, as there is to many people, a "moral color" to the words. "Investor" not only purports to be the name of a "thing," but it is the name of a "good thing." It calls up pictures of solid citizenry, an honest taxpayer, faithful husband, intelligent parent. "Speculator," on the other hand, suggests a weak-lipped, amoral ne'er-do-well, someone who is dissipating the family fortunes in wine, women, and song. He is the fool who is so soon to be parted from his money. How could it be otherwise? He has appeared in so many newspaper stories, so many sermons, so many lectures on "sound finance" and so many heart-to-heart talks. He is, in the person of poor Uncle William, numbered among the family skeletons. "Investor" is a good word. "Speculator" is a very bad one.

At any rate, on my return from father's, I related our discussion to my wife. She asked, "What did you tell your father? How did you answer him?" And I told her that I couldn't answer that question. For if I had to make an "either . . . or" choice, I had already made it. And, of course, it was the "wrong" one, at least from father's point of view.

QUESTIONS FOR CONSIDERATION

What kind of words are "good" and "sound"? Are they common nouns, adjectives, verbs, adverbs?

Do adjectives denote or describe "things" or do they generally indicate a judgment or opinion we ourselves hold about certain things?

Can you attach a permanent reference such as "good" or "sound" to a stock regardless of what happens to the stock? If we do this, could it be because we are confusing the stock with a corporation or the property of a corporation? Could it be because we are unable or unwilling to change our map to correspond with a change in the status of the stock? Would it be because we feel that to change an opinion represents an admission of error or stupidity so that we lose self-regard?

Does "respectability" have a high value to you? Do you place a good deal of importance in lunching with the "right" people in the "correct" places? Do you tend to choose your home, your books, your hobbies largely on the basis of what is "being done"?

Do you think there are people who feel it is "more respectable" to buy American Telephone and Telegraph stock than to buy Benguet Mining? To hold stocks long rather than sell them short? To seek a return from dividends rather than from speculative gains? To invest in stocks rather than to trade in commodities? How do you feel about these matters?

Might it be profitable to re-examine your definitions of "goodness," "soundness," "respectability," etc.?

"I AM INTERESTED ONLY IN INCOME"

THIS is sort of a footnote to the preceding chapter. It concerns much the same line of thinking we have already discussed, that is to say, rigid opinions about the market, about stocks, and about investment generally, based for the most part on "what grandfather always said," or what has been gleaned from other high authority by way of a substitute for direct inspection of the facts.

The particular shibboleth in this case is, "I am interested only in income." Like several other attitudes we have examined or will examine, this makes it very clear that the speaker is *not* interested in speculative profits, and implies that he has no high opinion of those who make their living, or try to make it, in speculation.

By making it quite clear that one is not interested in the day-by-day or week-by-week fluctuations in the price of a stock, one can underscore the "solid conservative policy" one follows. The impression is given that one's securities are so unimpeachably secure that the waves of market action can beat on them for years without eroding away an iota of the "real value." Whether anyone else is aware of this super-confidence or not, it serves the purpose of making unnecessary any mental efforts on one's own part. All that is necessary to understand the current position is a pencil and paper and the dividend record for the past year.

Out of this frame of mind comes the abhorrence of "dipping into capital," for "capital" becomes something fixed and unchanging in this view, a great defensive structure like the Rock of Gibraltar, in itself the protector and the treasure, not to be violated, not to be chipped away, but to be preserved as a sacred trust and passed on intact to one's children and their children.

As a result of this outlook the descendants of wealthy families have grubbed along for years on the pitifully small and often shrinking returns of the once-handsome family fortune.   Nibbled at by the tax collector on the one hand, and by the administrators, advisors, lawyers, etc. on the other, while all the while the forces of long-term inflation deplete the exchange value of both principal and income, it is small wonder that in the end there is very little left to show for the original inheritance.   In these cases it is not a matter of eating one's cake and having it, too.   It is more a case of not ever getting to eat the cake at all.

G. M. Loeb, a partner in E. F. Hutton & Co., in his excellent book, "The Battle for Investment Survival," takes up this matter of the separation of income and principal.   He feels that it is not possible to maintain income in one category and principal in an entirely separate one.   The two are inextricably related.

For example; when a stock selling, let us say, at $20 goes ex-dividend in the amount of $1, we do not expect to see the stock open the following morning at $20.   The probabilities are that it will open around 19; perhaps at 19-1/8 or at 18-7/8.   The dividend that has been taken out is reflected immediately as a depletion of capital; and this is true whether or not the dividend is "made up" by earnings during the following quarter.

It would be possible for a stock to go on paying dividends for months and years, even while the price continued down, and down, and down.   And this would raise the interesting question of whether "in fact" the dividend was actually coming out of capital so that in drawing out and spending the dividends one would be "dipping into capital" right along.   Of course, this may be stretching things too far; there will be auditors and lawyers who will prove that it is not possible to pay dividends out of capital.

And yet, how about one of my students who told me that he had held an important chemical stock from a purchase price of nearly $60 a share to around $18, over a six-year period.   During that time he had received dividends regularly; some at the rate of $2.00 per year, others at the rate of $1.50 per year; say about $10 per share altogether over the entire period, while the market value of the stock declined some $40. We could say that the decline of the stock had no direct relation to the payment of the dividends, and that may be true. But it is "as if" the dividends had been deducted or taken out of capital along with other decrements. At any rate, the net result was that this man had very considerably less than he started with, even counting in the dividends received; and the stock was a genuine "blue chip" at that.

We cannot abolish the distinction the tax collectors set up between income and principal, that is, we cannot abolish it so far as our tax returns are concerned.

But in all other ways we can consider income and principal as one, if it will help us to a more practical financial philosophy. It is like the higher abstractions we have spoken of so frequently before, in that it wipes out differences, but provides us with a clearer picture of the situation as a whole.

If we do this, we will not be likely to draw out "income" complacently each month while our capital skids down the scale in a Bear Market slide. Neither will we feel that a moderate cash withdrawal from time to time is a quasi-criminal insult to our ancestors and an attack on our descendants.

When we receive "income" we will simply credit it to the account, just as a margin clerk will do in keeping his records. The dividends will simply increase the "equity" by so much. An advance in prices of the stocks held will also increase the equity. Both will be measured in the same account, and in the same way. When money is drawn out of the account, it will be debited, and will decrease the total equity. And a decline in the prices of the stocks in the fund will produce the same effect; a decrease in equity. We have used the word "equity" here, rather than "value" since it has a specific meaning. It is the value in dollars of everything held in the account as of a certain time. It includes, therefore, all additions, whether dividends or deposits from other sources; all withdrawals from the account; and all "accrued" changes in dollar value due to changes in the market prices. (The question of "Accrued" values versus "Realized" will be taken up a few chapters hence.)

In practice, what this means is that we will not try to keep our "capital account" in one place or in one set of books, and our "income account" in another. This is a case where we have nothing to lose, and a good deal to gain, by abstracting at a higher level, that is, by merging these two accounts into one.

The reason this point of view is so hard for some to come by lies probably in our puritanical teaching. It is linked nebulously with the general feeling that "working is good," and with the "acceptance of responsibility" as it concerns capital.

Thus "income" could be regarded as some sort of return for goods delivered or services rendered, while "increment" is likely to be preceded by the word "unearned," and suggests to many people a rather reprehensible "getting something for nothing." It is the old "either . . . or" again. Two values. A "good" one and a "bad" one. We reject the "bad" one and accept the "good" one.

It seems hardly necessary to point out that regardless of whether your 100 shares of "XYZ" were inherited or bought from the proceeds of your hard labor, the return you get on this stock cannot realistically be segregated according to some bookkeeper's formula so far as it concerns you. Whether a stock advances ten points in price and pays no dividends, advances five points and pays five dollars in dividends, or remains at the same price and pays you ten dollars in dividends, the result, outside of taxes, as it touches your financial status, is precisely the same.

QUESTIONS FOR CONSIDERATION

To what extent are you influenced by the feeling that "income" from dividends is "good," and "profits" from speculative changes in a stock's price are "bad"?

Do you know that some studies have shown that a person who gets most of his income from dividends is identified with a "higher stratum" of society, that is, he has more "snob appeal"?

Is it possible that the tendency to seek dividend "income" as distinguished from "speculative gains plus dividend income" is an obsolete or faulty map?

Would it be helpful to consider dividend income and speculative gains as part of a totality without trying to maintain them in separate compartments?

"BUT STILL I INSIST ON MY DIVIDENDS"

IF A man is not used to exercising his mind against new and unfamiliar situations, he is very likely to go through life depending on a whole body of directives and precepts picked up in the family circle, from various teachers, friends, etc., and from books, without ever going out to look at the world and see what it is really like.

The fact is that the good advice and rules for living that he accumulates from others, may be, and probably are, on the whole, pretty good. It may be just because it usually works pretty well that he never bothers to question anything that has come to him from a trusted authority.

But a statement can be an "untruth" without being a "lie." It may be obsolete, vague, inapplicable to a different situation, or it may be mistaken. Also, it may be "partly true," that is, inadequate. And in any of these cases, none of which could be described as "lies," the statement can get one into a peck of trouble if it is acted on without question.

It sounds so cynical to say, "It may be true, but I want to take a look for myself." Some people would resent anyone wanting to verify a statement they had made. You are supposed to keep your eye on the map all the time and never peek at the countryside itself.

They will tell you, "It stands to reason." Meaning, "It isn't necessary to prove it out there; you can prove it right inside your own head."

Case in point: Here are two important, well-known stocks, both listed on the New York Stock Exchange.

In January, 1950, S. S. Kresge, a conservative investment type stock, showed a record of steady earnings, well above $3.00 a share for a number of previous years. It also had a record of steady dividends at the rate of $2.25 to $2.50 a year. The stock was selling at this time for $43 a share.

At this same time, January, 1950, Baltimore and Ohio R.R., a speculative and erratic issue, showed an irregular record of earnings and no dividend payments for a considerable period of years. It sold then for $12 a share.

Which to buy? The "good," "safe," steady-earning, dividend-paying Kresge; or the chancy non-dividend-payer, Baltimore and Ohio?

How many bankers, how many trust administrators, how many "prudent men" would have even considered "BO" as against "KG"? Doesn't the answer seem obvious?

And yet—over the next six years S. S. Kresge moved down in a steady trend, reaching $25 by the end of 1956. While during this same period Baltimore and Ohio climbed to $46. Which turned out to be the better buy?

You could say this is an exception. Perhaps so. But some years ago I made a study of nearly a thousand stocks during a period of several years, comparing the value received in dividends and price increment or decrement at the end of the period, with the price at the start, and separating the stocks into two groups, those that paid steady dividends and those that paid none, omitting entirely those that paid dividends irregularly in certain years.

The results of taking this look at reality were surprising. There was no net advantage in this period to buying the stocks in the "dividend-paying" group. The "non-dividend-payers" did just as well, in fact, a shade better. That is, if we compared the final price plus dividends received in the first case with the original price, it averaged a bit less than the final price in the second group, the non-dividend-payers, compared with its original price.

The vehemence with which some people will defend their feeling that dividends are necessary and are the essence of investment wisdom makes one wonder whether it is really a matter of investment wisdom at all, or merely an opinion related to vague ideas about "common sense," "prestige," "conservatism," etc.

A good friend of mine, a successful paper merchant, practically went into hysterics when it was suggested to him that he might consider buying a stock that did not pay dividends. "I'll tell you one thing," he roared, "I'll never buy a stock that doesn't pay a steady dividend." Would he, do you suppose, sit contentedly and draw his dividends while the market value of his stock drifted down, and down, and down? And would he refuse to buy a stock of some concern engaged in such tremendous development that it might be several years before the fruits of the effort could appear in the form of dividends?

It is simply amazing how the connotations of a word can blind us to the real facts of a situation.

QUESTIONS FOR CONSIDERATION

If two stocks are each selling at $20 a share and one is paying a dividend at the rate of $1.50 a year while the other pays only $.50 what conclusion would most people you know have as to which stock to buy?

Is there another way of looking at this? What other angles can you see?

Suppose that stock "A" was selling at $20 and paying $1.00 dividend while stock "B" was selling at $40 and also paying $1.00 dividend. Is it obvious which stock is the better buy? Why, if both stocks are paying the same is one bid so much higher?

If a stock paid no dividends for several years, does that make it worthless? What would you expect from a stock which showed a very high dividend yield, say 15% or 20%?

Could you say that the dividend yield, and the price-earnings ratio were inadequate criteria on which to base an investment decision?

PUT THEM AWAY IN THE BOX AND FORGET THEM

VERY often you will hear arguments that are just plain silly seriously advanced to support something that someone *already believes*. Motor stocks, you may be told, must be good investments
because the automobile is here to stay. Aircrafts must be good investments because we are entering a new age of air travel. You have
heard these and a thousand like them.

In the first place, such statements are terribly superficial. They
overlook the fact that the price of the stock has already been determined in a highly competitive market, and that the basic character
of the business has already been appraised very thoroughly, long ago.

If a stock must be "good" because the company represented is in
the food business, that was as true ten years ago as it is today; yet
the stock has probably made enormous moves since that time.

Along the same lines, you will often hear that certain stocks or
"all" stocks are seasonal, that is, they are likely to go up in the spring
and decline in the fall. If this is true, it would be worth acting on;
but the evidence to support this is, for most stocks, not convincing.
If any general "seasonal" trends existed, they would be discounted,
and the discounting process itself would smooth out and destroy the
seasonal cycle.

Perhaps a great many people forget what they mean by "good" or
"sound" when they speak of stocks. Probably they are thinking of
certain *kinds of business* as "good" or "sound," but even this is a
matter of opinion and judgment. Certainly the railroads, today,

do not look quite so "good" or quite so "sound" as they did forty years ago before the trucking business took up the work of mass transportation.

But some investors, and some brokers, and a great many bankers, will continue to consider S. S. Kresge a "better" investment than General Cigar, in spite of the fact that Kresge has gone from 45 to 22 in the past eight years, while General Cigar has moved from 14 to 49. Wouldn't you feel that the proof of this particular pudding, that is, enhancement of capital, was an essential part of investment planning? Or do you feel that it is more important to conform to the "prudent man" standards than to look at the real facts?

There is another question involved in this matter of "investment" versus "speculation." It revolves around the conservation of capital as seen by a bank or a court of law. In their eyes the primary objective is to preserve the same value in dollars in an account as were in it at its inception. This is a good objective, as compared with a policy of not caring whether dollar capital was preserved or not. But it is hopelessly inadequate.

Would you consider it a satisfactory performance if a trustee turned back to you the same number of dollars he had originally received, after an interval of twenty years; plus, of course, the two or three or four per cent income received during that period? Is the Almighty Dollar to be so rigidly valued that we overlook the realities in the case?

We like to think of the American dollar as a solid rock amid the raging waters of economic changes. But the dollar, at least in our times, is not strictly defined in terms of gold or any other commodity. It is an abstraction, a map, and like any map it requires a date to make it fully meaningful. If you had put away $10,000 twenty years ago for the purchase of a house now, you would find that these dollars would not buy you anything like the home you could have bought then. You would still have $10,000, the same number of dollars you had in the first place. But this is a case of faulty identification since the dollars today are not "the same" as they were twenty years ago. Even if you had invested these dollars in government bonds and had accumulated all the interest on them for the entire period, you would still not have enough dollars, at their present exchange value, to buy as good a home as you could have bought with the original capital. The promotion of government securities has not been frank in pointing out the rather steady depreciation of dollars, and therefore the substantial losses that buyers may sustain on this account.

The United States government has not been entirely frank, either, about the tax liability of its securities, or about the "real" value (in terms of purchasing power) of the proceeds of its bonds. We have spoken of "partial" truth, that is, truth that is slanted not by falsification, but by concealing or neglecting to state part of the essential information. We have been told that the government bonds are the "safest investment in the world," meaning that the precise number of "dollars" specified will be paid, after, say ten years. This is a lie by implication unless the listener is aware of the speculative risk in the dollars; unless he realizes that an agreement to pay over a certain number of undefined "dollars" means very little unless we have some assurance that these same dollars can be converted into definite quantities of particular commodities. The whole weight of government propaganda has been thrown behind the drive to stress one side of the story; to present a half-truth, a distorted truth, as if it were a complete picture.

We have not had a ruinous runaway inflation. But put yourself in the position of someone who bought German mark bonds just before the post-war inflation of the 1920's. You would have received back precisely the principal and interest agreed upon; but they would be worth nothing. The difference here is only one of degree: the man who overlooks the necessity to increase his dollar capital in line with the march of inflation is simply letting the inflation eat up his life savings. And if he sets a great value on the precepts of high authority, he will not even take a look at the facts. He will value the map, "what he has been told," more than the reality, "what is really happening."

QUESTIONS FOR CONSIDERATION

Is it harder for you to sell a stock you inherited from your father than one you bought yourself last year?

Are there certain stocks, or certain groups of stocks, toward which you have a favorable "set" regardless of market conditions?

Are you "married" to some particular issue to a point where your judgment concerning it may be "prejudiced"?

Are you willing and able to change your evaluation of the stock of some particular company that has done well by you if the fundamental or technical picture changes greatly?

DAT OL' DEBBIL MARGIN

IT IS certainly true that our friends can hurt us more than our enemies, for we are prepared to deal with enemies but we are easy
prey to the well-meant blunders of our friends.   And it is true, as we
have just seen, that the truth, if it is not the full and forthright truth,
can hurt us more than a lie.   For we can deal with lies by challenging
and disproving them.   But it is much harder to deal with a truth that
merely omits to state some essential facts in the case.

We are often told that trading on margin is an evil.   That is a
truth, too, in a way.   Plenty of people have lost their hard-earned
savings in margin accounts.   Perhaps you could say, with about the
same kind of truth, that automobiles are an evil, since every year
brings its thousands upon thousands of mangled bodies in the nation's
accident toll.

The "evil" in anything is, of course, an opinion or judgment.   It
is not, strictly speaking, in the thing at all, since it is of the nature
of a very high abstraction.   It is hard to "measure" evil since the
"amount of evil" in any situation would depend on the value system
of each particular observer.   Like other situations involving high abstractions it may be easier and more fruitful to ask the question in a
different form.

We could ask, "How is a margin account likely to lead to trouble?"
Or we could ask, "What is the nature of the trouble and what are
some of its principal causes?"   Then we might get an answer that would
help us to avoid these troubles, or at least to estimate the dangers.

Some of your friends will tell you they "pay cash for every stock they buy," and that "they wouldn't go on margin; not on your life!" They will remind you of "what happened in 1929." This last, by the way, is a simple matter of dating the map. For the 1929 margin picture is quite obsolete, and in order to talk intelligently about margin it is necessary to consider *today's* margin requirements, *today's* market action, and the rules and regulatory machinery of *today*.

Many of the very people who will scornfully reject any idea of trading on margin (making it quite clear that *you* are not better than a cheap tin-horn gambler), are setting aside a large part of their family earnings each week and each month to "keep up the payments" on their house, their washing machine, their TV, and practically every other major possession they have.

Except that we use different words, wherein is it basically different to buy a house on borrowed money or to buy stocks on borrowed money?

One could say that the purpose was different. The buyer of stocks on margin is putting up a smaller amount of money than he would if he bought the stocks outright, in the hope that with an advance in price he will make a correspondingly greater profit. But not the least of the arguments for buying a home is the feeling that "real estate values are increasing," so that the increment of speculative gain will more than offset the cost of interest and other charges on the mortgage.

People can kid themselves. Oh, *how* they can kid themselves. Call a purchase a "sound investment" and they will buy your house, your deep-freeze, or your forty volume set of The World's Great Literature. Call it a "speculation," and they will avoid it like the plague.

You see, we have "good" words, and "bad" words. As we abstract we lose the details, and in the highest echelons of abstraction we lose all details and often settle for a simple "either . . . or" orientation. It makes everything so simple if we have just a "good" and a "bad"; no in-between. Like the Westerns your children watch. No one has to be a very keen judge of human nature to detect the dangerous character of the slinking, leering, degenerate horse-thief. And no one needs to be very sharp to recognize the fine upstanding quality of the clean-shaven stranger from Montana.

Speculation is "bad" to most people because they have been

taught to attach a "bad" label to certain operations. Buying stock on margin is speculation. Therefore it must be "bad." But buying a color TV set on time is "an investment in family togetherness," therefore good.

There is no discrimination in this sort of thing. The labels tell the story. We don't have to look at the facts at all. And so, the most conservative financial operation involving margin will be automatically labelled "bad," and the over-extended purchase of the shoddiest piece of junk for the home will be labelled and considered "good" if the salesman can talk fast and smooth.

The fact is that "it all depends." Just as it is wise and practical for many families to buy their homes and perhaps some of their household equipment on borrowed money, it may be wise and practical to trade in stocks on margin. It is not in either case a matter of "either . . . or." It is a question of evaluating the relevant circumstances, and of striking a reasonable balance.

It is not necessary to go "out on a limb." That *would* be bad. But if we know what we are doing (and I am assuming that you are interested enough to do a little studying), and if we do not over-reach, there is no great danger in the operation of a margin account. It is, once again, a matter of "measuring in all things," and of "nothing in excess."

So far as outright ownership of stocks being safer than holding stocks on margin, that is one of those half-truths that can hurt you. For a great many people, who have never even thought of buying anything on margin, have lost a great deal, simply buying "good sound stocks" for cash and "putting them away in the box." These losses have been not only on account of the fluctuations in the stock market, but also, as we pointed out a few pages back, because of the fluctuations in the "dollar market."

QUESTIONS FOR CONSIDERATION

What happens when you buy an electric refrigerator "on time"? Do you borrow money from a finance company and pay interest on it in order to obtain the refrigerator now when you want it?

What happens when you buy stock "on margin"? Do you borrow money from a broker and pay interest on it in order to obtain the stock now when you want it?

278 GENERAL SEMANTICS OF WALL STREET

Did you ever hear of people who abused the use of instalment credit and got themselves into serious trouble because of it? Do you know any people who have used instalment credit for years without running into serious problems?

Did you ever hear of people who abused the use of margin by over-extending themselves and got into serious trouble because of it? Do you know any people who have maintained a margin account for years without ever being in difficulties?

Is it possible that many people who shun margin although they accept instalment buying, are projecting a "mental map" which they acquired second-hand by reading about the 1929 crash and stories of brokers jumping out of windows, customers wandering about in a dazed condition, etc., all linked with the word "margin"? Do you feel that these people necessarily have a "true" picture of the use of margin as it is practiced today?

NOT JUST A MARKET OF STOCKS

CASH itself is speculative. The value of cash, in relation to everything else, can change enormously.

You cannot hide from the reality of speculative fluctuation simply by pretending it isn't there. Your house, your stocks, even the cash money in your pocket fluctuates in value continually, if by "value" we mean, "what it will buy."

Of course, if you want to tie yourself up to a somewhat circular definition, and define a dollar as a dollar, without specifying the dates on your map, then you can achieve a purely verbal (and purely artificial) stability. Many Germans, during their disastrous inflation, stuck by the slogan "Mark bleibt Mark" until the whole house of cards came tumbling down.

But in any realistic sense, all the things that have monetary value are being continually revalued with respect to one another; and dollars also are in speculative flux with respect to their "purchasing power" or convertability into other goods or services.

Thus, it is an *artificial device* to measure everything of monetary value in terms of an undefined dollar. And by undefined, of course, we mean not freely convertible into a specified amount of a "standard" commodity, or index, composite, average, etc. which would represent the equivalent of a "dollar" in goods or services.

We use the artificial device of assuming a "real" dollar of fixed value. It is a convenient way to make stock charts for one thing; if the price scale was being continually adjusted for every jiggle in the supply of potatoes or fluctuation of electric power output it would be nearly impossible to keep a chart at all.

Everywhere we turn, there is, by implication, the idea of a fixed-value dollar. The Community Chest drive has a scale showing the number of dollars pledged each week. The corporation report shows the increase in "value of product" year by year as measured on a uniform (or perhaps logarithmic) scale of dollars. But nowhere is there a footnote to explain that when we speak of dollars we are not talking about a fixed and unchanging "thing." To be strictly accurate we would have to specify "dollar, 1948" or "dollar, 1958." Not the same. A matter of dating the maps.

Now, not all stocks move up or down at the same time. And the value of dollars is continually in flux with respect to stocks and to goods and services. The picture, then, like almost everything in "reality," is a lot more complicated than we like to think of it. But unless we can get some fairly solid contact with reality we can get badly set back on our heels when our high abstractions fail us.

When stock prices go up "generally," as they did in the years preceeding 1956, I wonder how many people make the mental reservation that at least some part of the advance must be considered as merely due to the shrinkage in the purchasing power of the dollar.

If this is true to a degree, then the lower the purchasing power of the dollar goes, the higher we may look for the stock averages to go. To a degree there is an inverse relation here: as stock prices go up, dollars "go down"; and vice versa to a degree: as stock prices come down, dollars "go up." This isn't just hypothesis; it is an observable fact.

There have been large fortunes made by certain men and women who have been sometimes referred to unkindly as "vultures," who "buy" their dollars when dollars are "very cheap"; that is, when one can get a great many dollars for a thousand shares of stock (when stock prices are high). Then, when the cold hand of depression squeezes the inflationary breath out of the economy, when the dollars are of such high value that just a few dollars will buy a lot of stock, then these "vultures" can take their dollars from the safe deposit boxes, or cash in their debentures and their bonds, and trade money for enormous quantities of the now-nearly-worthless stock. You could say that they sold stocks "near the top," and "bought them near the bottom." But I would rather that you would think of it in a little different light, since it is a matter of relativity anyway. Try to think of it that they "bought their dollars" when they were cheap, and "sold their dollars" when they were very dear.

It should be added that the designation "vulture" is a term having moral connotations. It is a label with a strong coloring of disapproval. It is metaphor, symbolical, a map. Also it may not be entirely a fair picture, certainly not if you assume that the free market is in any way desirable. And finally, it is nowhere near as easy to be a "vulture" of this sort as it might at first appear. One can lose one's shirt, and many do, in trying to foresee the speculative moves of dollars or of stocks. As Robert D. Edwards put it, "There is no Easy Money in Wall Street."

We are not endorsing or condemning "the vultures." The only purpose in mentioning them at all is to point up the fact that the market is one of fluctuating dollars as well as fluctuating stocks.

QUESTIONS FOR CONSIDERATION

"People are tall giants. Tables stand higher than one's head." True or false? (Probably false to you. True for a child or a midget.) (True for *you* at one time in your life.)

We had a kitten named Fatso. We built him a house of corrugated cardboard, about two feet high with windows, a door, and an upstairs and a downstairs. Fatso went in and out of the house, often through the windows; used to sleep inside. Why, after a time, did the windows "get too small" for Fatso to climb in and out of?

When I was a boy there were wonderful starfish and anenomes and big, big minnows in the rock pools at Aunt Hattie's place at Beverly Cove. Why were the minnows so much smaller when I last visited those pools?

We say, "Prices are going up. The cost of steak is terrible." Is this because steak is scarcer; is it because "dollars are smaller," or could it be partly on account of both of these factors? Is the price of steak or shoes or bourbon entirely dependent on the supply and demand of the commodity, or does it involve the *relative* value of dollars also?

When "stocks go up" could this be, at least in part, another way of saying "dollars are going down"?

CORRELATIONS AND CAUSES

THERE was a wonderful green-covered book when I was a boy. A book about mountainous tidal waves sweeping in a solid wall of water across whole villages. About the laying-down of the sediment over uncounted centuries, and how the rocks were formed from it, and raised and folded and twisted to make the hills. About volcanoes blasting cinders and flame, while rivers of lava swept down their sides to bury entire cities. Stories of how the earth was made, and of the sometimes delicate and often violent processes of nature.

The book was titled "Madam How and Lady Why." It was explained that in this book we would meet and come to know Madam How rather well. She was quite accessible; and if one would only take the time and trouble one could learn a great deal from Madam How.

But Lady Why was quite another sort of person. She was shy, and kept herself out of sight for the most part. Most people never saw her at all. Just occasionally someone who had learned to understand the ways of Madam How might briefly get a fleeting glimpse of Lady Why.

You remember some pages back we spoke about the attribution of qualities. How we project on reality the "maps" in our own head and "see" that "the book is red," or that "Sally is a pretty girl."

Among the high abstractions that we project on reality is the concept of "cause." The question "why" implies a cause. And we look for "causes" everywhere.

You can get into a good deal of trouble in trying to assign causes for everything. And as you know, once you begin tracing the sequence of causes and effects you can build up a chain proving very neatly that everything in the world is the result of a series of causes stretching back to the creation, and that the whole future of the universe, down to the smallest detail, is already determined by the present state of affairs.

This idea of predestination isn't quite as popular as it was back in the nineteenth century when it was a rallying point for what might be called the "cog-wheel materialists." Of course the universe was a lot simpler then than it is now, because people didn't know as much; and today serious scientists seem too busy finding out what is really going on to spend much time on what begins to look like a rather silly game of "playing with verbal maps."

Some people limit their choices. They set over-high standards for themselves. They expect the impossible from life. And they ask the wrong questions.

They ask: "Why was I born?" "Why am I unlucky?" "Why is Grandma so cranky?" "Why can't we ever save any money?" "Why is Bucyrus-Erie stock selling so low?" "Why did Soy Beans go up today?"

Some of the questions involving "why" that we ask others or ask ourselves aren't "proper questions" at all for the reason that they don't mean anything. "Why are there so many stars in the sky?" is a question so vague that there is considerable doubt whether it means anything at all. Certainly if an answer is expected, it would have to be re-phrased.

There are not only nonsense questions involving "why," but others where it would be necessary to specify the particular level or degree of "why."

For instance: Abigail asks me why the car slows down as we approach the Sumner Avenue railroad tracks. I could answer this "why" at several levels, which are similar to the various layers of the levels of abstraction we have discussed before.

Answer A: "Because the brakes tightened on the brake drum."

Answer B: "Because I pressed my foot down on the brake pedal."

Answer C: "Because I wanted to slow down the car."

Answer D: "Because it is safer to slow down when approaching a railroad track."

Answer E: "Because I want to drive safely at all times."

Answer F: "Because I love you and want to protect you."

You will notice that, just as in the other series of abstractions we have studied, the low level abstraction is specific, definite, and narrow. It covers very little ground, but like a close-up photograph it is sharp and clear: "Because the brakes tightened on the brake drum." That is why the car slowed down; that is true; that is a correct answer at a low level of abstraction.

Each of the other answers is also true, though at progressively higher levels of abstraction. Even the final answer of the series: "Because I love you and want to protect you," is true. But it is a much broader answer, in much more general terms. It covers more ground, but it is not nearly so definite, for it could include anything I might do to show my love and protect my child. It would cover teaching her how to cross streets safely, fighting off an attack by hoodlums, going out to the drug store to buy medicine when she was sick, earning money at my job; almost any of the hundreds of functions a father is supposed to perform.

The drawback of low abstractions is that they do not generalize and therefore do not point up the similarity of various different situations. You will notice that the highest-order answer, (F), does do just this; it includes and summarizes many of the duties of a father.

The drawback of the high abstractions, however, is that they are vague. If I tell my little girl that I have done something, "because I love her and want to protect her," that might mean any number of things. It doesn't particularize.

Now if you ask me why Soy Beans went up today I could tell you it was because the bidders in Soy Beans seemed more numerous and more anxious to trade than the sellers. A fairly low level answer. If I told you it was because the administration was believed to be leaning more toward firmer price supports, that would be a somewhat higher level answer. You will notice that here, as in the previous example, the first answer was a very earthy, specific hard look at what was observably happening. The second answer was a broad abstraction which, although it contained larger implications, was also considerably more vague as to its precise meaning. And of course the question "why" in regard to the Soy Beans could be answered in many other ways, each quite possibly correct at some level of abstraction.

As always (and as we have seen before) there is a place for high abstractions and for low abstractions, and all grades between. The important thing is to know what we are doing, and particularly, not to *confuse* the levels at which we are thinking or speaking.

And since the "causes" of things, as we understand them, very often represent the outcome of many stages of abstraction and logic, we should realize that these "causes" are not of themselves realities like the physical Soy Beans, but "maps" in our minds. We should understand this when we project these causes and attribute them to external reality.

As a matter of fact all of this business is part of the game of chasing the coy, evasive Lady Why. We are never going to catch up with her, not really, and we must be satisfied with the occasional flash of understanding, the fleeting glimpse. Like almost everything we have touched, we have got to settle for something less than 100%. In this case we have to settle for a great deal less.

It will probably be more productive to give your attention for the most part to Madam How. If you can establish that certain events have happened, and have happened in certain sequences, then you have the basic mechanism for a predictive method . . . and you can tell Lady Why to go hang.

Mariners certainly knew this, or at least acted on it, when they sailed the seas centuries ago. They set their courses by the stars. They did not know "why" the stars appeared to rise and revolve across the dome of the heavens. But they certainly knew "how." This was "the necessary and sufficient" data for them to plot their voyage. Yet the most persistent question one encounters in the board rooms of brokers is "Why?" "Why did Crucible Steel cut its dividend?" "Why doesn't New York Central advance?" "Why didn't the Rails confirm the industrials?"

If you will examine these "why" questions carefully you will see that there are many possible (and equally true) answers. Without meaning to exhaust the possibilities we could try re-stating the questions, or turning them into "how" questions.

We could ask, "How do stocks usually act when the dividend is cut?" We could ask, "How is New York Central acting now, and how has it acted for the past three weeks?" And we could ask, "How much would the Rails have to move to confirm the industrials; and how much significance could we attach to such a confirmation on the basis of past experience?"

You will see that the chances of getting a definite and useful answer to questions like these last are better than of getting any useful answer at all to the first series.

Also, consider this. When we shift from the "why" attitude to the "how," we begin to get away from the "cause-and-effect" idea. You will see, if you look back, that the last three questions, the "how" questions, do not require the attribution of *cause* at all. They simply ask for someone to take a hard look at a territory that can be inspected.

And because the "why" questions so often lead to nonsense, or confused levels of abstraction or vagueness, or to cause-and-effects answers, which concern the relation of maps to territories rather than the activities in the territories as such, we avoid the "why" type question whenever we can.

You see, it is possible to get into a good deal of trouble with "why" questions, especially if you don't understand the pitfalls of the cause-and-effect relation. I could take you out in the back yard and show you a pear tree, which blossoms gloriously quite early in the spring. Shortly after its blooming, for several years, a pair of robins has come and built a nest in a fork of that tree.

Now I could observe the flowering of the tree, and the subsequent building of the nest; and I might say "The robins come *because* the tree has bloomed." In other words, I have observed that repeatedly a certain kind of event follows another certain kind of event. And I draw the conclusion that one *causes* the other. *Post hoc, ergo propter hoc.*

A more scientific way to think about the tree-and-robin's-nest problem is to forget the "why" entirely, and simply accept the fact that one event is *correlated* with the other.

We can do this in many departments of life. We can do a good deal of useful predicting right at the operational level, that is, on the "how" level, without ever asking of nature or society the question "why."

"Why does she love me?" Or, for that matter, "Why doesn't she?"

"Why doesn't she?" What a question! How many lovesick teen-agers have nursed their aching hearts over that vague and perhaps unanswerable question. Of course, it might be because of halitosis (bad breath), or pimples; but then it might be because of hundreds of other embarrassing physical disabilities or personality shortcomings, too.

It could be that a smart teen-ager might win the lady if he would change his question and drop the "why." At any rate he would probably feel better. He could ask himself how she acted, what she did, what she said. For these are matters of observable fact. He could plan how he might act to please her more, how he could overcome his own awkwardness or acne or whatever. He could treat the problem tactically at the operational level, and not worry about the attribution of causes.

You will understand we are not thinking just of teen-agers and their girl friends. We are thinking of all the many different situations in life where people go around wringing their hands and asking "why," when they could often do so much better in meeting their real problems if they would start asking "how," and taking a look.

We are thinking about the market, which certainly embodies many of the problems we meet in other places. In the market you don't as a rule need to ask "why." Particularly if you are one who follows technical methods, you will not so often be looking for "reasons" as for "correlations."

If you find that certain kinds of stock, say gold mining stocks, or food stocks, or utility stocks tend to go up when the market averages are going sharply down, put that down in your note-book; make a map of that in your mind. Never mind "why" these stocks act in such-and-such a way. It is not necessary to know why, and except as a matter of "general interest" it can be just so much excess baggage to "know why."

What you do want to know is whether this tendency is a general one, one that has been observed on a number of previous occasions, and whether the evidence of the correlation is strong enough to justify you in acting on it. As a basis for the final judgment and decision, the material you need to answer your question can be obtained by checking the facts in external reality.

In technical analysis, as in many kinds of research in such varied fields as engineering, medicine, and sociology, it is possible to do a good deal of work by means of charts and diagrams. These are abstractions on paper; what we might call "externalized abstractions." The charts are not capable, in themselves, of answering questions that start with a "why." But they often can and do answer the sort of questions that begin with a "how." Charts will show you correlations that you might not see without them. They can help you to make your judgments as to the reliability of these correlations, the degree of dependability you can attach to them. And so again, our study calls for throwing out some very superfluous cargo. We can unload most of our "why's," and we can reduce the primary question-asking largely to matters of "how." We will look for correlations; and only after we have gathered our "how" data and established our correlations will we begin to exercise judgment in making the decision on whether to act on what we see.

QUESTIONS FOR CONSIDERATION

Which kind of question do you feel could be answered more specifically and definitely: "Why did Jack build the play house for the twins?" or, "How did Jack build the play house for the twins?" Does it appear that the first question might have several answers at different "levels," and also that it involves probing what is going on in Jack's mind? Would you say that an acceptable answer to the second question would be given in terms of the material used, masonry and carpentry operations performed, etc.?

When you see a flurry of activity in a certain stock do you rush to the news ticker to find out "why"? Do you think the news agencies, or the brokers, or your friends at the board room can always give you the correct answer? Is it necessary to know the "whys" of every situation in order to act intelligently?

If someone shouts at you, "Look out; the ceiling is coming down!" what do you do? Duck for cover, fast; or ask "why?" Wouldn't the really prudent man scram out of danger fast and save his "whys" for the investigation tomorrow?

When you can establish certain correlations you may be able to surmise the consequences likely to follow an event. Wouldn't you feel that a policeman, seeing six masked men with tommy guns going into a bank, might be justified in assuming "robbery" or at least "trouble," and would act on this opinion without, at that time, inquiring into the motives of the participants?

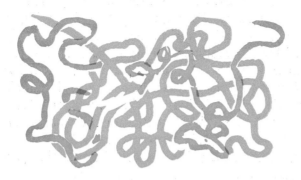

THE "FUNDAMENTALS"

THE great body of investors has always subscribed to the idea
that "by knowing all about the stock" they can make money in
the market, or at least protect their capital.

There are several things wrong with their expressed formula. In
the first place they are not going to know *all* about the stock. That
would simply be impossible. Certainly they are not going to know
"all" about a complicated situation like Gulf Oil or U. S. Steel
merely by thumbing through the Annual Report or by reading a few
news releases off the Broad Tape. They are not going to know "all"
by sitting around a broker's board room and exchanging opinions
with others of their ilk.

As a matter of fact they don't need to know "all." But whatever
they do know should be pertinent to the problem at hand.

Unfortunately, although they talk about "the stock," what they
study is "the company," as though, somehow, the company *was* the
stock. They pile up vast quantities of data pertaining to the corporate affairs, but seem to have very little interest in the stock in its
natural habitat, the market.

Such investors, and I am using the word here to include all traders,
speculators, etc. like to refer to themselves as students of "the fundamentals," no matter how superficial or irrelevant their agglomera-
tions of fact may be.

It should be plain enough that there are important factors that
affect the stock, which are not directly connected with the corporation's internal affairs.

The most important of these factors, perhaps, is the fluctuation in the value of dollars.   During the 1946 market collapse there was considerable consternation in the ranks because apparently there was "no reason" for the decline; in other words, there seemed to be no weakness in the business of the companies represented by many of the tumbling stocks that would account for the break in prices. But one of the most obvious weaknesses of the "fundamental" method is that it overlooks the action of the money market, of the political and psychological environment, and of all of the forces that may operate on the price of stocks beyond the specific records of the company whose stock is being studied.

Also, the "fundamentalist" is likely to pin his evaluation on the past records of the company's business, either under the assumption that things will continue as they have been, or that they will change in line with a "trend."   These assumptions are not entirely worthless.   They become dangerous only when we attribute an "absolute" quality to them and leave out entirely the possibility that things can change.   We have to *date* our maps.

We have seen how it is not possible to verify new features in today's territory by looking ever so carefully at yesterday's map. And yet we have all seen people, confronted by a tremendous breakout or collapse in a stock, rush to the Standard and Poor's data sheets to see what could account for the sudden change in value.   We must assume that the stock was competitively valued last week or last month, and if there is *now* a radical change in its behavior, this represents something that was not there or was not known before, and therefore we are not likely to find it by looking it up on "yesterday's map."   A more realistic way to go at this situation (if you must have "fundamental" reasons) would be to find out and evaluate what *new* factors have come into the picture.   And by the time you have found out what they are you may be reasonably sure that "the market" has found out, too, and has already revised its map . . . and its price ticket.

Not that these "fundamentals" are "all wrong."   Not that they are "without value."   The trouble comes in their inadequacy, and because people will attribute almost magical powers to a whispered rumor that "XYZ" is going to buy out "PQR" or that "TUV" has a new process for extracting gold from sea water.   After all, there have been some very successful men who operated largely on the strength of their understanding of "the fundamentals" and what they mean. But these men were not of the same breed as the average lunch-hour trader or board room hanger-on.

There is another word to be said about (and against) unqualified adherence to the "fundamentals." They seem to "explain" things.

You will remember the difficulties we had in seeking out Lady Why, and that it was often necessary to compromise on meeting Madam How.

For instance: We see a sudden whoop on the tape in "MNO," and as the stock pours across the Translux in thousand-share blocks we scurry for the Wall Street Journal (this morning's issue, which was prepared last night; the information is already out-dated to some extent) to see why "MNO" is going up. We know *how;* we can see that, right on the tape. But that is not enough. We have to find out *why.*

If you look diligently enough you can find out *why.* You can find reasons. If "MNO" goes up sharply today you will find "the reason" for the move in tomorrow's paper, in the columns of every commentator and analyst who mentions it. And if it goes down you will also find out "why."

Let us say that the Near East situation flares up today into a really threatening war-scare.

Now if the market should go down at the time of this news, to-morrow morning's papers will tell us *why.* Because a war would mean curtailment of consumer goods, the closing of many plants now making civilian products, shut-down periods for conversion to armament work, government restriction or control of profits, higher taxes, the danger of a physical attack on the country, etc.

But if the market should advance strongly at the time of the war-scare news, tomorrow's papers will also tell us *why.* Because the prospect of war would mean immediate stepping-up of military orders, the production of uniforms and equipment, full civilian employment to meet these new demands, an increase in rail traffic, government limitations on strikes or other work tie-ups.

Take it either way. You have your answer *why.* The Monday morning quarterback is never at a loss for reasons *why* State won the game, or lost, or tied.

Isn't this a sort of silly playing with facts? To take the truth and twist it around so it will tell you *why* something happened? Is it necessary to know *why?* You must realize that "why" refers to "causes," and "causes" can be taken at many levels of abstraction. We have to know just what level we are talking about if we want to get a useful answer.

It is often much more useful to study *What* is happening and *How*. And then we can very often ignore the question "why" entirely.

One danger of seeking out "the reason why," even supposing we have made a valid analysis of the case and have, in fact, come up with a sound reason, is that we then tend to close our eyes to all the other factors that may be operating in the same affair. There is no rule that says there must be "one" and "only one" reason for something happening, whether in the market or out of it. And more often than not there may be several, or many reasons, some of which we may not be able to discover, and which if known might not help us a great deal in deciding what to do next.

The methods of analysis that are known as "technical" are not concerned very much with the "whys." They do not look for "the reason" or even "the reasons." That accounts in large part for their effectiveness; and it certainly accounts for their unpopularity with a public which is continually asking the futile question "why."

QUESTIONS FOR CONSIDERATION

Are you fully aware of the effects of certain "good" words and certain "bad" words, as they may affect your attitude toward something? Would you feel different about George Washington if he had been presented to you not as an "American Patriot," but as a "British subject who was successful in High Treason"?

Would you say the word "fundamentals" was a "good" word or a "bad" word? Does it seem to connote good solid values, prudence, wise investment policy, etc.?

When you get the "fundamentals" does this suggest that you have "gotten to the bottom of it" and are therefore in possession of all the pertinent facts?

Is it possible that a man might have a great many "fundamentals" at his finger tips, but that some of these might be irrelevant or trivial, and that he might *not* be in possession of some other vital information?

Could we say that the word "fundamentals" is a multi-valued word in the sense that it can refer to many different things at different levels of abstraction? In a certain sense could we say that the "fundamentals" of a battle might be the record of troop disposition and movements. At another level, could we say the "fundamentals" might include the strategy of the generals planning the campaign. And at still another level might we include the "causes" of the conflict?

Is it possible to know "all" the fundamentals about anything? Does this make it "of no value" to know something of some fundamentals? Is it vitally important to know what kind of fundamentals one is talking about, and their limitations?

ACCRUED VERSUS REALIZED

SOME of the really serious barriers to an understanding of the market are so fragile one wonders that they can shut out so much insight. It would only take a couple of good hard looks and a little work with pencil and note paper to smash some of those barriers entirely.

One of the most formidable of these rice-paper screens is the matter of Realized Gains and Losses versus Accrued Gains and Losses. This question seems as baffling to the average investor as a kitchen chair upended at a berserk circus lion by his trainer. But it is no more difficult to figure out than a kitchen chair.

As you may know, there are two principal methods of business accounting, either of them acceptable in tax reports and other financial statements. In the "Cash" basis income and expenses, gains and losses are considered only as they are "realized," that is, at the time that money is received or paid out. In the "Accrued" basis, the unpaid bills and the uncollected accounts receivable are included. This basis takes note of the debts we would have to pay and the benefits we would receive if the business were to be entirely liquidated by settling all accounts.

If I buy 100 shares of a stock at 20 and it advances to 22, I have an "Accrued Gain" of two points or $200. If I sell it at 22, I will have a "Realized Gain" of $200 less commissions.

Now there is a certain school, which sometimes seems to include about 99.44% of the investors, which seems to believe, not only that there is something less tangible about the "Accrued Gain," but that it is purely imaginary, not to be given any serious weight or consideration at all. A disciple of this philosophy will tell you that the $200 is "only a paper profit," meaning, "no profit at all."

It all depends, of course, on what happens to meet the needs of his own ego; he will switch from "Accrued" to "Realized" and back again, or confuse the two, whatever will most effectively build up his self-esteem. If it is *your* stock, the Accrued gain is "no profit at all." If it is *his* stock he is likely to forget all that and tell you he "has a profit of two points on "XYZ." But if he has an Accrued *loss* he will revert to the view that it is "only a paper loss" and therefore "no loss at all."

Consider a case like this. Your friend has bought 100 shares of "ABC" at 20, and he has also bought 100 shares of "XYZ" at 20. The "ABC" has advanced to 23. The "XYZ" has declined to 17. Feeling, as he does, that the Accrued is not so genuine as the Realized, he can sell the "ABC" and take a profit of $300 less commissions. And if you ask him how he stands he can quite truthfully tell you that he had a nice gain in "ABC" and has no loss in "XYZ." This, of course, is true if we use his unconscious choice of the Realized method of accounting.

But this has in it some elements of high abstraction; and it is necessary to know, and most especially for your friend to know, just exactly what he is talking about, especially when he is talking to himself.

Otherwise he is headed for a peck of trouble; and this is a kind of trouble that has thrown many an investor for a fall.

Suppose that "ABC" had been sold, as we said before, at 23. He has a nice profit on it (Realized). And so far as "XYZ" is concerned, in the first place he doesn't recognize any loss in it, since Accrued losses mean nothing in his way of thinking; and in the second place because he is confident that "XYZ" will "come back." This is a "map," his judgment of "XYZ" made from whatever data he had at the time he purchased it. It may be, now, an out-of-date map, but it would be painful to think about, so he does not think of it. What he does, in fact, is to support his original judgment by every means he can. He will talk with his broker, who will as a rule reassure him that "XYZ" is a "good, sound stock." He will talk with friends or board room companions who may also own the stock; and they will strengthen one another's faith in the tottering stock through collective self-defense.   He will read whatever he can find that gives good news and promising predictions regarding "XYZ," but quite unconsciously he will not "see" anything of a pessimistic nature.   As a matter of fact he is not likely to encounter much that is pessimistic; the men who give out corporation news are not paid to give out gloomy statistics.

This leaves him feeling pretty good.   He will continue to feel good even if "XYZ" drops a point or two more.

Of course, if "XYZ" continues to slide, and reaches a soggy $5 a share, you and I know that he has a loss, whether he recognizes it or not.

And he will not, even then.   He will, very likely, have bought *more* of the stock on the way down; and now, with "XYZ" down to 25% of its original value, he will tell you seriously that he is "not a speculator," and is holding it for income because it is a "good, sound stock."

We will not ask the question, "How stupid can people get?" That would be unkind.   It would be unkind because this man did not ever have the training to see what he was doing to himself.

But the question is, "What can we do to prevent this kind of tragedy?"

In order to answer the question of how to prevent getting frozen into bad situations because of inability to recognize Accrued losses, we must take a little different view of the case.   Not greatly different. As we said at the beginning of this chapter, this difficulty is not insurmountable.

Let us take the liquidating value of the account as a whole, as it actually is at a given moment.   This is the Accrued basis of course. But it is not a move away from reality.   It is a facing up to the real facts.

If we take the case just given, where "ABC" had advanced from 20 to 23, and had been sold at 23, while "XYZ" is still held, having dropped from 20 to 17, then, except for commissions, your friend would come out just even if he closed his account at this moment.

If "XYZ" drops to 5, he must consider that the value of his account, if he should close it out, has shrunk, and he would then have a loss on the Accrued basis of $1500, less the net amount of the profit on the sold-out "ABC."

It certainly would have been better, in this view, if he had actually

sold the "XYZ" when it was at 17. Then he would have been somewhere near even. But if he is going to cling to an old and outdated
map of "what 'XYZ' is worth," right in the face of the hard facts,
then he is going to ride it down all the way. And unless he changes
his method of evaluation he will continue to accumulate losses which
will sooner or later have to be accepted as "real" and which will be
much larger than necessary. Unless, of course, his judgment is so
good that the stock he has ridden down from 20 to 5 actually justifies
his faith and does come back; and you know how often that particular
thing happens.

And even if his faith was entirely justified, would it not have been
better, far better, to have sold out the stock when it broke to 17,
and then bought it back at 5? In that way he could have bought more
than three times as many shares for the rise when it did come.

But people do not like to "take losses." They put so high a
premium on "being right" that they will be too seriously hurt by
even the smallest loss. They will ride a stock down the toboggan
for many, many points before they will admit to their broker (or to
themselves) that they were "wrong."

Great heavens! They don't even need to admit they were "wrong."
Their original judgment may have been quite correct. But the conditions may have changed. All that is necessary is to change the map
or make a new one on the basis of the present conditions. That
should not involve any loss of self-esteem; certainly not so much as
the ultimate loss of over $1000. But, as we have said before, nothing
takes precedence over the "self"; and a man will go down to ruin if
his value system is so poorly geared to reality that he cannot make a
slight adjustment in his opinions without feeling small, stupid, and
incompetent.

There was a man in a nearby city here in Massachusetts who went
into the commodity market for the first time a few years ago. He
started off, quite reasonably, by buying a contract of Wheat and a
contract of Onions. His hope was, of course, that both contracts
would advance and bring him a tidy profit. As a matter of fact the
Wheat did advance a few cents, and because he was timid and anxious
to bolster his unsteady confidence, he sold the Wheat, thereby taking
a "realized" profit. The Onions meanwhile, dropped a bit.

In the course of a few weeks Wheat advanced a few cents more.
The Onions, however slumped off a few points more.

298 GENERAL SEMANTICS OF WALL STREET

And a little later the Wheat shot up quite actively, while the Onions continued their downward course. The novice trader bought himself a second contract of Onions, in the pleasant hope that by "averaging" his cost he would be all right on the first substantial rally.

But the rally was not quite so substantial as he had expected. Onions broke down and made a new low. Wheat continued its advance.

Eventually there came the end of the contract, with Wheat soaring to the skies, but without our friend aboard, and Onions bumping along the bottom at giveaway prices.

The expiration of the contract caught this inexperienced trader unprepared. He was issued a "notice" calling for his acceptance of the onions: Onions standing by now, on car in a hot freight yard in Chicago; with many, many more fresh, juicy Onions pouring in constantly from the bumper crops of many farmers. He was, of course, forced to sell and sell at once. Either that or take a carload of Onions rapidly wilting in that freight yard. His loss was staggering.

I heard this true story from Victor C. Lea, Manager of the Commodity Department of Paine, Webber, Jackson & Curtis.

"Now where do you suppose this fellow made his big mistake?" Lea asked me. And then he answered his own question, though I knew the answer as you must, too. "Why, he made his mistake when he took his profit on the Wheat instead of taking his loss on the Onions."

This man sold out the contract that was doing well by him. He killed the goose that laid the golden eggs. He was "right" about Wheat, and sold it out. But he held onto the Onion contract, which was disappointing him from the start. He valued his "rightness" so much, his "perfect rightness" that is, that he refused even to consider changing his mind, and backed the losing contract all the way to the gutter.

What he had done was to set his "map" against the reality. He refused to date his map and revise it or make a new one. He had set so high a value on his ego that the loss of hundreds of dollars was as nothing compared to the hurt of making a slight concession.

"The science of commodity trading," Lea told me that same day, "is the science of taking losses." By this he meant that in order to prevent any such disaster as the one just described, a man must be able to keep an open mind. He must stand ready to throw the old map out the window as soon as it no longer represents the territory as it is today.

By thinking in terms of Accrual, rather than limiting one's point of view to the Realized, it is possible to see losses and gains in a different light. And when one can do this, he can take many small losses without fear or depression, if he has an overall plan that will give him the reasonable assurance of a few large gains.

In certain types of trading this is basic. A trader must take losses freely and often, perhaps as many as seven losses out of each ten transactions he enters. And if he tries to curtail or eliminate these relatively inconsequential losses, he may be heading toward a far more dangerous situation in which he could be crippled or wiped out by a single overwhelming adverse move.

QUESTIONS FOR CONSIDERATION

If you pin a label on your right hand trousers pocket marked "realized" and one on your left hand pocket marked "accrued," does it make any great difference in your financial status whether you put all your money in one pocket or the other, or take out some from the "accrued" pocket and transfer it to the "realized"?

When you call up your broker to know your "equity" or net worth, does he base his report on the "realized" gains and losses alone; or does he take into account also the "accrued" gains and losses?

If you wanted to borrow money from the broker on your holdings, would his decision to make the loan be based only on the "realized" gains and cash available? If your borrowing capacity and financial status are based on "accrued" gains as well as cash (including realized profits), then wouldn't you agree that the "accrued" part of your capital is "real" and important?

One of the basic requirements in setting up a mathematical system is that it be "consistent", that is, that it does not contradict itself. Is it consistent to consider only "realized" status at one time, and only "accrued" status at another, depending on which makes your operation look better? Would you say that this comes under the head of "kidding yourself"?

"UP" IS BETTER THAN "DOWN"

YOU may remember, some years ago, the movie "The Third Man," the picture in which Anton Karas made magic music with his zither.

In the early part of that picture there is a scene where an Austrian, trying to explain to an American who is looking for a friend, that the friend is no more: "He is gone . . . to Heaven" (pointing down) . . . "or to Hell" (pointing *up* dramatically).

This confusion with an unfamiliar language was good for a sure-fire laugh. Naturally. We all know where Heaven is. Heaven is *up*, and Hell is *down*.

Of course when we consider the nature of the physical universe it becomes a little difficult to make these stick. "Down" might mean in the interior of the earth, though that hardly seems remote enough for a truly cosmic Hell. "Up" must mean "in the direction of the sky"; but the sky is in *all* directions.

We could engage in heated discussions on this intriguing problem. And just how long would it take us, depending on our previous education and training, habits of perception, etc., to realize that this is just a game of playing with verbal maps, and has no more relation to physical realities than "How many angels can stand on the head of a pin?"

It is all right to assign directions to Heaven and Hell, such as "up" and "down," so long as we understand clearly that these are symbolic, that they pertain to the world of thought and not to the world of "things." It is when we confuse the high abstractions with physical observations that we begin to talk and think nonsense.

One of the most cogent comments on this tendency of people to confuse "things" with "ideas" is to be found in the twelfth chapter of the Book of Mark, where Jesus draws the line between the laws of the land and his ethical concepts: "Render to Caesar the things that are Caesar's, and to God the things that are God's."

The confusions we make! Consider the words we were discussing; "up" and "down." They have been clothed with symbolism and metaphor until we are not even aware of their implications.

In the ordinary sense, that is, the direct-observation low-abstractive down-to-earth sense, "up" can be defined as "in a direction contrary to that of gravity"; and "down" as "in the direction of gravity, or toward the center of the earth." These are primary definitions taken from Webster's New International Dictionary of the English Language, published by G. & C. Merriam Co. of Springfield, Massachusetts.

You will notice that "up" and "down" in these primary senses are purely geocentric terms, having no "meaning" with respect to the solar system, nor to "outer space," nor to the universe. Nor to man's destiny or aspirations, nor to moral values, nor to anything except to indicate a direction away from or towards the center of the earth. We must assume that this primary sense was the original meaning in which the words were used.

But "up" is generally toward the light, toward the great visible dome of the sky. "Down" leads to darkness and obscurity, yes, even to the grave. Stars are "on high," birds fly "aloft," clouds are "above us," the sky itself is "up"; while "down" suggests the dank miasma of caves, the unhealthy fungi of subterranean chasms, the fiery bowels of the mysterious underworld.

Man has "raised" himself from the quadrupedal posture. But he must sometimes walk carefully or he will have a "downfall."

Indeed, man was created "only a little lower than the angels," but mankind nevertheless did have a "fall," a fall from grace in the Garden of Eden.

Man tries to avoid "low" thoughts, and to concentrate on "higher" things. He "lifts up his eyes unto the hills." He "hitches his wagon to a star."

For every man wants to "rise" in the world. He hopes to have a "superior" record. He may be "elevated." He hopes "to get to the top." In that case we must consider he is a "high-grade" man; and we will "look up" to him.

We do not like to see a friend on the "downgrade." We hope he will avoid "low" companions, and will not "descend" to crime. For if he is "at the bottom of the heap," "downtrodden," an "underdog," he will be "depressed" and "downhearted." If he has "stooped" "too low," we may "look down on him."

A man who is "down at the heel" is not likely to be in "high spirits."

Does any of this sound familiar? Isn't this our old friend, "either . . . or" in another situation. The "up-and-down" dichotomy can be as damaging as the "success-failure" dichotomy; and in some ways perhaps even more so, for it is so often charged with emotion and relates to the most absolute, and at the same time the vaguest, of high abstractions.

As it so often happens with words that represent the extreme opposites of a scale of values, we simply wipe out everything in between and assign coefficients of either 100% or zero to any situation.

This is underscored by the adjectives and adverbs we use so often along with the "up-and-down" words.

We say he is "*utterly* downcast," "*absolutely* up in the clouds," "*completely* down in the dumps," or "*definitely* high-minded." If there was any doubt about what we meant, these italicized words make it clear that what we mean is "all-out." No measuring. No estimating of degree.

You will realize that a great many of the expressions quoted in the past few paragraphs, almost all of them in fact, do not refer to the "direction of something in relation to the center of the earth." We are talking in terms of symbols. And we must be careful not to carry symbolism too far. We must not mix things that do not belong together.

Notice the strong judgment content in so many of the "up-and-down" words. We have spoken before of the tendency we have to set up an "either . . . or" situation, and then reject one side, leaving us with only one acceptable choice.

It is the "down" words that represent what is "bad." And we reject them.

Nobody wants to "sink." Or to "go into a decline." Or to "fall down on the job."

But we do very much want to "be on the upgrade," to "move up in the world," and to be held in "high regard."

You will understand that the ideas that are so neatly represented by these up-and-down words would not in all cases be easy to describe directly. The metaphor is a sort of short-cut by which we can roughly get across to others (or even to ourselves) how we feel about the success or failure of someone, or about his social conduct or his physical condition. Just so long as we know what we are talking about, and realize that we are *not* talking about, "direction with relation to the center of the earth," we will be on fairly safe ground. But when we *forget* that these terms are not territories but only maps; when we use "up" and "down" symbolically without realizing that we are dealing with symbols; then we may look for trouble.

You may know that a great many men suffer from a variety of phobias, sometimes to a degree that can seriously interfere with their ordinary life and work. These phobias appear to be related to the confusion of verbal symbols (metaphors) with physical realities. They are very often connected with this particular metaphor, the "up-and-down" dichotomy. A man who is afraid of high places may be reacting to "high" in an entirely different sense; he may be shrinking from frustrations he has suffered in attempting to "make the grade" in reaching a "high place," perhaps in his business. Similarly, a man who feels "trapped," let us say by his job, or in his home life, may react with a fear of closed rooms, tunnels, caves, and the like.

We are not here primarily concerned with psychoneurotic symptoms. We are concerned with the market; but without this rather long discussion it would be hard to explain the peculiar attitude of 99 out of 100 investors towards short selling.

The short sale of a stock is, as you probably know, a transaction by which you borrow the stock from someone who owns it, and then sell it in the open market. This leaves you owing so many shares of the stock to the person who loaned you the stock.

Let us say you sold the stock at 50 dollars a share. 100 shares would come to $5000 (leaving out the cost of commissions).

Now if the price of the stock should drop to say, $40 a share in a few weeks or a few months, then you could buy back the stock at that price, at a cost of $4000, and return the stock to the person from whom you borrowed it.

Since you received $5000 when you sold the borrowed stock, and bought back the stock for $4000 when you returned it, you will have a profit of $1000 on the transaction.

The more the stock declines after you have sold it, the cheaper you can buy it back, and the more gain you will have.   And if the stock advances in price, you will eventually have to buy the stock to return to the owner who loaned it to you; and in that case you will have a loss.

In effect you have reversed the usual order of the dates of purchase and sale.   You have sold before you bought.   You are making a trade in which your objective (in the future) is not a higher price but a lower one.

The short sale is in almost every way the reverse of the purchase of stock on the long side.   When you are long of a stock you may receive dividends on it.   When you are short you must pay the dividends to the owner of the stock.

On the face of it there is no obvious moral angle.   Buying stock and selling stock short are both operations made in the ordinary course of business in a free competitive market.   They are part of the "speculative" or "evaluative" side of the market, regulated in much the same way by the rules of the exchanges and by the Securities and Exchange Commission (except that the regulations pertaining to short sales are somewhat stricter than those applying to long purchases), and the objective of the speculator in either case is to make a profit.

Then why is it that there is such general reluctance, even aversion, to selling short?

It might be because the market is generally a "Bull Market." (This is an extraordinary statement.   However, it has been true for over half a century and probably for longer.   It is also a somewhat misleading statement.)

If you examine the long term charts of the Dow Jones Industrial average you will see that since 1900 the "trend" or course of this average has been "upward" about two thirds of the time, and "downward" only about one third of the time.

Thus, followers of the Dow Theory or any other trend theory, if they neglect to take a look at what is happening, could easily say, "Well, if the market is going up two thirds of the time, then it would be smart for me to be always long of stocks; for the probabilities are in my favor.   I would not want to sell short since the odds against me would be two-to-one."

Unfortunately, during the one third of the time "the market" is declining, it tends to come down very fast, about twice as fast on average as it goes up. So while it is true that the trend is "up" most of the time, the slope on the relatively short down moves is much steeper than on the longer advances. In other words, the gains of a whole year can be wiped out in six months; and sometimes in six weeks.

Looking at this another way, if the down moves run much faster, it is possible to make money quicker on the short side, when these opportunities present themselves, than holding stocks long during the Bull Market periods.

Of course, actually, the stocks do not all move together. Some stocks have their Bull Market moves when most others are going down, as Lorillard and a number of other stocks did during the Bear Market in the summer and fall of 1957. But what we have said for the market-as-a-whole is also true of individual stocks. With all their irregularities of trend you can say, as a broad generality, "they come down faster than they go up."

However, to the average investor who has not looked at the chart records, it "seems" as if the sensible course was to buy stocks and hold them for the long-term advance. His faith in this advance allows for no interruptions, no exceptions. He has a one-way mind; he is thinking in line with the "good," or acceptable direction.

There is another reason people avoid short sales. They will tell you that it is more dangerous to sell short than to buy stocks "because a stock cannot go down below nothing and you can lose only the price of the stock; but there is no limit to how high it can go, so your risk of loss is unlimited." Bob Edwards answered that one some years ago when he said, "Nonsense. You can lose exactly the same amount either way; you can lose everything you've got and no more." If this statement is not precisely correct, it is at least approximately so. The margin clerk will see to it, for his own protection and the protection of his firm, that you are closed out when your losses have reached a certain point. And this would be true whether you were long or short. There is no "greater danger" in being short of a stock on margin than in owning a stock long on margin.

"Ah, yes," someone will say, "That is true, on *margin*. But I am not on margin. I buy only 'good, sound stocks,' and I do not have to sell them, no matter what happens. Now since you cannot sell stocks short 'outright' the way you can buy stocks, you could be frozen out, whereas I cannot be frozen out."

That argument sounds much better than it really is. The man who bought "SK" outright in February of 1953 at 43 or more, and saw his investment go down to 2-5/8 in December of 1957 still had his stock; he was not wiped out; but he was so seriously crippled that he might almost as well have been wiped out. He has a Pyrrhic victory, no more than that.

Actually, if he had gone heavily into "SK" when Studebaker was at the high levels, say investing all of his available capital in the stock, he would, at the end of 1953 be considerably worse off than a trader who had put only 20% of his capital into the stock and had been closed out with a total loss.

Suppose, for example, this trader had bought "SK" (on margin) at near the top, that is, above 43, and had sold it, or been forced to sell at around 25, at which point he had sold short. He would still have had the opportunity to profit greatly on the way down and might indeed have recouped most or all of his losses by 1957.

QUESTIONS FOR CONSIDERATION

When we say, "Ericson is going up in the world," is that a report of conditions in external reality? Does anyone expect to look out the window and see Ericson ballooning up into the sky? Is the statement, then, a report on external reality, or a rather high order abstraction; a map?

And when we say, "Sornberg has a low mind," that is metaphor, is it not? We cannot see, or point to the mind, nor observe with our eyes how low it is. What would you say of the man who "cannot rise to an occasion"? Of the person who "never gets anywhere"? Of someone who feels that parties are "a pain in the neck"? Of the girl with a "soft heart"? Or one with "her head in the clouds"?

Is it possible that these metaphors acquire too much "illusion of reality," so that we forget they are maps and treat them as if they were territories?

From what you know about high level abstractions, would you feel that the habitual use of metaphors in speech or thought would be more likely to lead to a factual and objective approach to life situations; or to highly colored snap judgments based on the literal interpretation of the metaphors?

Have you ever checked how you react to the words "up" and "down" in connection with market problems and matters outside of the market? Would it help if you could delay your reaction until you had examined the facts of the case?

THE UP-AND-DOWN OF IT

WE ARE accustomed to think of "up" as "good" and "down" as "bad." But we are not always consistent.

It is "good" for stock prices to go "up." But we overlook that this means that the exchange value of dollars is going "down"; though we know well enough that this may be a symptom of inflation; and that inflation is "bad."

It is "good" to buy things and have the prices go "up." We think of buying stocks and "sharing in the prosperity of a mighty America." Sometimes people buy Wheat and Potatoes and Soy Beans in the form of contracts for future delivery. Now when these prices go "up" it is not "good" in the same sense as industrial prosperity being "good." It can mean a disaster to the agriculture of the country. If the crop is blighted, destroyed by frost or flood or drought or insects, if a condition of scarcity threatens, that will be reflected in higher prices for commodities; a Bull Market, if you will. On the other hand if the heavens smile and the cornucopia of nature's bounty pours out a generous harvest, that is a Bear Market in commodities and prices tumble. But is this a "bad" condition?

Actually we might be much better off if we did not use the strongly colored and absolute words "good" and "bad" with respect to stock and commodity prices. The question is not one of "goodness" or "badness"; it is simply a matter of setting a fair value on what is being traded.

We have not quite finished the discussion in the previous chapter about short sales and why so many people avoid them like poison. There is another "up-and-down" angle to that question.

I would like to show you a photograph of a tank or boiler which has been hammered in several places to produce bumps raised on the surface, or dents sunk into the surface. This demonstration is most striking in the unretouched photo, but since this cannot be reproduced here, perhaps a drawing will convey the idea.

You will notice there are hammered places, two of which appear to be bumps raised on the outside of the tank, and three of which appear to be dents hammered in.

Now turn the page upside down and look at the tank again. How many bumps do you see; and how many dents?

Do you know why this is so?

Why do you see what were bumps as dents: and what were dents as bumps?

If you study the picture for a minute you will realize that the way you tell the bumps from the dents is by the shadows around and in them. And since the shadows are caused by the cutting off of the sunlight, the appearance of the bumps and dents depends on the position of the sun. Now the sun is ordinarily overhead, and the light comes either vertically or at some angle, from above.

When you turn the page upside down you see the bumps and dents in a "different light." If you assume (as we all do) that the sun is coming from "above," that is from position "X," it will reverse the appearance of bumps and dents and we will have the illusion that these have changed places. But the picture as originally shown was made with the sun in position "O"; and to give a fair representation of bumps and dents as before we would have to see the sunlight as still coming from position "O" after we turned the page around.

This we cannot do. We cannot easily picture the sunlight as coming from below. Therefore, since our mind cannot accept a sun "down there," we put it "up here" in position "X," and get a faulty interpretation of the hammer marks on the tank.

It is a typical case of how our old, learned habits of perception will over-ride our "intellectual" grasp of a situation. We "know better," but we still "see" it the old way.

This is very much the situation with short sales of stocks. When we buy stocks long, we exchange a certain number of dollars for a certain number of shares, which we intend to exchange again, if all goes well, for a greater number of dollars when stocks are worth more with respect to dollars.

To be consistent we should realize that when we sell stocks short we have exchanged a certain number of shares of stock for a certain number of dollars which we intend to exchange again, if all goes well, for a greater number of *shares of stock* when dollars are worth more with respect to stock.

In other words, to be quite consistent we should measure our gains on the long side, in "dollars," and on the short side in "number of shares of stock." But we forget to "turn the sun over," and so we measure *both longs and shorts* in terms of *dollars*, which leads to some of our inconsistencies and confusions regarding short sales.

For instance, consider a point that we touched on before; that one could only lose a definite amount in a long position, but there was no limit to the theoretical loss one could have on the short side. That argument does not hold water when you reverse the entire picture *including the sun.*

Look at it this way. If you buy a stock with dollars, the number of dollars you can receive for that stock when you close out the transaction is limited by zero at the bottom, and there is no definite limit at the top. The price *could not go* below zero dollars, and *could* go as high as any figure you wanted to name.

And when you sell a stock short (remembering to reverse everything in the picture), you have "bought" dollars with a certain number of shares of stock. The number of shares you can receive for those dollars when you close out the transaction is limited by zero at the bottom, and there is no definite limit at the top. The number of shares you could buy could *not* go below zero, and *could* go as high as any figure you wanted to name.

Now, if you have followed this, we have eliminated the paradoxes by looking at both purchases and short sales realistically; one being the opposite of the other.

And if you have trouble "seeing" this, please realize that it is not an easy thing to "turn the sun around." It takes more than logic alone to change the habits of many years; it calls for practice and the acquiring of new habits of perception.

Furthermore, the most difficult point in learning to accept and use the short sale is probably due to the powerful "set" which operates with so many people; that "Up is better than down." The prejudice of the perceived virtue in anything containing verbal "up-ness" as contrasted with the evils of anything containing verbal "down-ness" is so strong that it over-rides reason. And that is one reason so many people feel with regard to short sales that "high-minded men should not stoop so low."

QUESTIONS FOR CONSIDERATION

When we use the words "up" and "down" as metaphors, that is, as symbolic representations for something else, this may result in misunderstanding arising from a verbal confusion. In the case of the tank with dents and bumps would you say the confusion was of a verbal nature?

Would you consider the misunderstanding about the character of purchases versus that of short sales of stock was basically due to verbal confusion? Isn't there a non-verbal element, too, very similar to our failure to "turn the sun upside down."

Can you think of other paradoxes, illusions, deceptions, confusions, etc. in other phases of life where the source of the difficulty is not primarily due to the use or mis-use of words?

Have you been fooled by visual confusions at a magic show, where the magician may work the entire trick without using a word? Is it possible that you, through faulty perception, are fooling yourself about a number of things, both verbal and non-verbal?

POLITICS AND ECONOMICS

IT IS not the purpose of this chapter to start a Great American Movement to reform the tax structure. Anyone who has had much contact with politicians knows that any such campaign will run aground not only on the inherent economic stupidity of the breed, but also on the pressures that are brought to bear on these men by their own constituents. After all, politicians in our kind of democracy, are not selected by a winnowing of the most able citizens, but seem to attain their high offices too often by winning a sort of "popularity contest." Under these conditions, although you may occasionally get some kindly men, some able men in resolving human problems, you do not look for many who are strictly and dispassionately analytical. Almost everything in politics is compromise, and both the theory and the practice of politics require that the politician keep an ear tuned at all times to the rumblings and murmurings of his own constituency. If he hopes to be re-elected he had better listen carefully, and work toward legislation that will most nearly bridge the gaps between the various demands of the voters back home.

On certain subjects the politician is pressed very hard to conform to public opinion. As a rule he will yield easily enough, since as a rule he is "of the same culture" as his home environment and shares the general attitudes of his neighbors. You do not expect a Senator from Mississippi to take a strong stand against "white supremacy." You would not be surprised if a congressman from the corn raising states should come out for a more generous program of corn price

supports and aid for corn farmers. In our big cities a simple and
sure-fire campaign was always possible (this was some years ago)
on the promise of "a five cent fare."

Generally speaking, an attack on "the rich" is always in order,
and regardless of how well-heeled our representatives may be, or
how lush may be their private lives, it is often necessary for them to
appear in the raiment of the proletariat. You will see them at the
State Fair in their shirt-sleeves, munching hot dogs and throwing
rings to win a Kewpie doll. They will turn up in the picture section
of your newspaper pitching hay, wielding a riveting gun, or operating
a subway train. Just plain, ordinary guys, "no better than anybody else."

It is good politics to attack "the rich" from time to time. It
marks one as a friend of "the common man." And there are more
of *him*.

A good many of our tax policies seem to be framed in some such
atmosphere as this. Whether the indiscriminate bonuses and benefits to veterans (as opposed to really adequate help where it is badly
needed) come under the head of calculated exploitation or arise
simply because the politicos themselves share the same muddled
sentimentality they are appealing to in the constituents, is a moot
question. But the fact is that our elected representatives will necessarily represent the prejudices and partialities of the mass of voters.

You get echoes of these attitudes especially in tax matters. Sometimes it looks as though the tax program was framed more with an
eye to how it would look to the dullest-witted voter than to his real
welfare. Exemptions, deductions, special benefits, expenditures of
public funds, all seem slanted to "dressing up the package" so that
it will look much more generous to "the common man" than it may
really be; in fact sometimes the package is made to look better than
the budget or the facts could possibly substantiate.

There are just three of the many points concerning taxes that we
would touch on here. One of these is trivial, but revealing. It is
the manner in which dividends, capital gains, etc. are treated in
certain state tax returns, our own Massachusetts forms, for one. Any
income or gain derived from ownership in stocks is treated as "unearned" income, and is so designated. It is not permitted to claim
the ordinary personal and family exemptions, nor any of the customary
deductions, on such income. Neither is it permitted to charge against

it any of the expenses that might be incurred in securing income
from investments.   Furthermore it is taxed at a considerably higher
rate than "earned" income.   In spite of all the politicians' cant
about "free enterprise" and "the encouragement of private enterprise," and "sharing in the ownership of the tools of production,"
it is made quite clear that the owner of a single share of stock is,
to that extent and in that respect, a pariah, an "absentee landlord,"
a profiteer, and an oppressor of the poor.

We have seen in so many cases that a certain thing under one
name is "good," and under another name is "bad."   And it is particularly true in politics that we change labels very fast.   One moment "intrepid business initiative" is "good."   The next moment,
under the name "speculation," it is "bad."   As usual, the maps
are all anybody ever looks at; as usual, there are only two labels,
"good" and "bad."   And as usual, the territory may be quite different from the maps and labels, but the voters don't know that.

A second example of the political mind at work is the Capital
Gains Tax.   This tax is so set up that it benefits the long-term
investor, apparently on the assumption that one who buys a stock
and "puts it away in the box" is likely to be a hard-working, honest
citizen who is sharing in America's future by accumulating his savings in equities.   There is still, of course, the possibility that he
may share also in what politicians call "unearned increment,"
whether or not this may be merely the compensatory adjustment of
dollar values made necessary by the inflationary policies of the poli-
tico himself.   This "unearned increment" is, of course, looked at
somewhat disapprovingly, and also perhaps a bit greedily, but it is
a little hard to condemn it out of hand since it involves the port-
folios of too large a number of the constituency.   The hand of the
taxpayer falls lightly on the long-term investor.

But for the short-term speculator there can be no consideration.
To the politician, the assumption of purely speculative risks is merely
a form of gambling without the mitigating circumstances that make
"Beano" (for a worthy cause) a virtuous enterprise.   The very word
"speculation" is a powerful weapon that can be turned against an
opponent in a campaign.   It is a "bad" word; and taxing the hell
out of speculators is as much a part of the politician's credo as
"better schools" or investigating the local transit company.

This is the place where you and I should face this issue squarely.

Speculation is not incidental to the market; it is not a "fault" in the market. It is not something to apologize for and minimize. A free market is a speculative market, the one term implies the other; and the speculation is the process of evaluation by which the price of stocks or commodities or real estate is established between men. Without speculation there can be many types of economy. But it remains to be proved that any of the substitutes for a free competitive market can provide the type of economy which we feel has contributed to the health and growth of our nation.

You will understand that we are not speaking, here, of "manipulation," or "fraud." The word "speculation" has been applied to these, but we are not referring to these abuses. There is nothing inconsistent between a freely speculative market and one in which there is regulation to prevent the artificial moving or pegging of prices. In fact, in the sense in which we use the word, "speculation," to do its job in the public interest, must be policed against dishonest practices.

It is the free action of supply and demand in a speculative market that results in the democratic determination of price. Such a market will automatically take all the factors affecting price into consideration. It will weigh every report. It will consider every news item bearing on the situation. It will discount every foreseeable event in the future. No board, commission or commissariat, no matter how sincere or how able, could collect, compare, evaluate, and integrate all of the factors involved in a market situation as searchingly as the collective body of investors acting in a speculative market. And we, who profess to believe in Democracy, should realize that it is this mechanism of free evaluation that lies at the very heart of our economic freedom; even if our politicians do not realize it.

The third point in connection with the attitude of the political mind relates to short sales. This is another of the many verbal shibboleths the politician shares with his constituents.

So far as impartial studies can determine, there is no great depressing or inflationary effect on the market due to short selling. There are a good many serious students of the stock market who feel that short selling is a necessary and desirable function of the market as part of the evaluative process. And in commodity futures markets the short sale is simply and plainly "the other side of a long purchase," since for every purchase of a future contract there must be a precisely equal and opposite complement, that is to say, a short sale.

You would think that the politicians, if they were economists or "statesmen," would recognize this obvious fact and tax both sides of the transaction alike. But if you know the political mind you also know that it is often more concerned with maps than territories; and the label "short sale" on the map is a "bad" label.

Therefore you will find a most peculiar discrimination here. When two men meet through their respective brokers to conclude a transaction in commodities, one "buys for future acceptance," and the other "sells for future delivery." But the buyer and seller are not treated equally tax-wise. Apparently the "badness" of the word "sell" and the word "short" imposes a stigma which must be penalized.

Long contracts which are held for over six months are considered "Long Term Capital Gains," and taxed at the low rate. Short contracts which are held for over six months are not treated as "Long Term," but as "Short Term."

There is no particular reason for you to disturb yourself about this ridiculous situation. If you are a commodity trader you will be long part of the time and short part of the time, and your tax liabilities will average out. Besides, you will seldom have the opportunity to be continuously long or short of a contract for so long a period as six months.

The only reason we are mentioning this here, is to point up the predilection of people generally, and politicians in particular, to value the "map" or the "label" more than the "territory." If the facts are inconsistent with their opinions, they will not hesitate to throw away the facts and act on preconceived opinion alone. It is this habit and predilection that we are trying to overcome, not only in the market, but in every activity of life.

QUESTIONS FOR CONSIDERATION

Recognizing that there are certain activities in our community that seem to call for public ownership and administration, would you say that the overall interests of the public would be best served by a great extension of political control of our facilities, or by keeping these governmental operations at a minimum? (In answering this question be careful to consider the facts as you have actually observed them, not as you might hope or imagine they would be in an "enlightened state" in the future).

If you had to entrust a sum of money, say $1000, to each of ten persons you know, would you prefer to deal with ten professional politicians, or with ten business men?

Is it your impression that there has been more corruption in recent years in the stock market, or in politics? Can you specify cases to support your view, whichever it may be?

Do you feel that speculation is an essential part of our free evaluative market system? Do you believe that the public interest is served by "punishing," "abusing," or "restricting" speculators in such a market?

Do you feel that the politician generally is not entirely free to seek "objective truth," but is more or less bound to confirm and carry forward the prejudices of his constituents? Do you interpret certain laws and regulations pertaining to the market as measures intended to demonstrate that the politician is "against" the whole idea of the market?

A VARIETY OF DEVICES

THERE have been innumerable "systems" and mechanical methods proposed for "beating the market." It is true that few if any of them have consistently produced the profits hoped for. And it is not very surprising that they are so uniformly disappointing.

In the first place if there were a simple "system" for "beating the market," a plan that could be produced in printed form and advertised and sold at a modest price so that the "average man" could assure himself of big and reliable profits all the time, the thing would be a contradiction of itself from the start. If everybody knew what all stocks were certainly going to do all the time, their own actions in trying to take advantage of this knowledge would defeat their own end.

For example, if I knew, or had reasonably good ground for believing that "XYZ" would advance 25% in price in the next month I could buy some of that stock and make myself a tidy profit at the end of the month. But if "everybody," or nearly everybody had this same information and felt as I did, then there would be such a scramble to buy the stock that I could not buy it at the price I had hoped for and might have to pay nearly the ultimate price at which I had hoped to sell. Also, of course, those from whom I would have to buy the stock in order to gain any advantage from the move, would presumably also possess the valuable information, and would not want to part with their stock except at a price that would give them most of the hoped-for-profit.

Whatever is generally known or believed, whether good or bad, is discounted immediately in the price of the stock.

Therefore any method of dealing with the market successfully more or less presupposes some knowledge or some understanding or some device which is not the common property of "everybody."

Millions of sheets of paper and tens of millions of hours have gone into the study of the market in an attempt to discover some consistent and dependable relations that can be used to predict market value, and which have not already been entirely discounted by general use.

Some mechanical "systems" are almost obviously worthless. Others seem to have a certain limited usefulness. And others will show "flashes" of brilliant success at times, giving the illusion that they are, in very fact, the answer to all the market's problems. These last, however, can be especially dangerous, since the illusion of infallibility can lead to very serious losses when a series of adverse moves eventually comes to pass.

The market is probably too complex to yield its treasure to any simple formula or "system." It calls for experience covering many possible contingencies. To put it another way, it is doubtful whether there is any system that can guarantee that a fool cannot lose his money in the market, and doubtful whether there is any method that will automatically produce profits for the operator without any thought or study on his part.

On the other hand, if a man will use the experience and advice of others only to the extent that they check out in his own tests; if he will use his own eyes to make his own direct observations; and if he has the patience and imagination to abstract from these data some valid "meanings"; then he can hope to acquire the experience that can cope with this delicate and complicated mechanism.

"If a man would realize that this is a business and give it the same effort he would devote to any other business," (I am quoting Bob Edwards) "then he may reasonably expect to make for himself a fair return according to his ability."

And while I am inclined to be very skeptical about simple mechanical market "systems," I do believe that there is a great deal of value in studying the various factors that affect the market and the way these operate, alone and in combination.

It is not quite fair, and not quite realistic to raise the standard protests: "Well, if you're so smart, why haven't you got all the money in the world?" and "If a man knew a method of 'beating the market' he wouldn't be telling others about it; he'd be making money with it himself."

So far as the first of these is concerned, you don't really believe that all men value money beyond everything else in the world, do you? Granted that we all like to make money, and most of us would like to have more than we do; still, it is hard to believe that "everybody" wants "all the money in the world." There are other objectives, one of them being to have the regard and approval of others, and the most important of all being the possession of adequate "self"-esteem.

As to the second protest (and I think I can speak on this, for I have met a number of serious market students), it certainly isn't true in a good many cases, and I would suspect that it isn't true for most men who are really interested in this subject. There are, of course, all kinds of investors and traders. But the men who are doing the most constructive thinking are not concentrating on "beating the market" to the exclusion of everything else. Furthermore, many of them teach or lecture, some do advisory work, and in my experience they have few secrets, and in general are delighted to discuss the work they are doing quite freely and openly. Why? I suppose because they are men; because they are proud of their work; because they enjoy sharing the fun of their own work with others who are interested; because they like to display the results of their researches in the same way a sportsman likes to display his catch. And perhaps because they enjoy passing along something that may be a help to someone else. And, in general, because this market work is, for them, a great game, a game in which they can pit their minds against the mechanism of "the market" just as an engineer can match wits with the forces of nature, or a general with the complexities of a military campaign.

There are certain devices that have been used in various forms and in different combinations, with more or less success, to evaluate the market.

And . . . to repeat . . . we do not recommend adopting any simple, mechanical device as the beginning and end of market research. But this is not to say that these inventions are of no value.

One of the most important, because it opened up new lines of thinking about market problems, was The Dow Theory. This was probably the first thoroughly organized attempt to look at the market in terms of market action alone. Charles H. Dow did not actually complete the job, which William Peter Hamilton picked up and carried through.

According to Dow Theory, the averages of representative groups of stocks indicate the Major trend of the market. The presumption is that this Major trend will continue until a reversal has been signalled by the failure of rallies or declines in the trend.

There is not space here to outline the Dow Theory in detail. It has been explained in detail many times. Several chapters in the book, "Technical Analysis of Stock Trends," deal with Dow Theory.

Now the Dow Theory, in spite of its overall good record, is by no means one hundred percent satisfactory. There are a number of reasons why it is difficult or impossible, in practice, to obtain anything like the theoretical results it can show.

Nevertheless, like the pioneer work in any field, the Dow Theory served a purpose. It opened up the whole field of technical inquiry into the habits of stocks as they act in the market; a field in which Richard W. Schabacker extended the idea to the analysis of each particular stock as a separate entity. Schabacker, you might say, applied the principles which Dow had crystallized as a "high abstraction" to a more practical application as a "lower abstraction."

There have been a number of studies based on technical action or on some particular *angle* of technical study.

In connection with trend studies there have been "systems" developed by which stocks were purchased on moves up, and sold at pre-determined "objectives"; and there have been various methods of fixing such objectives, either in terms of percentage advances, projected distances as measured on charts, arrival at "resistance areas," etc.

And there have also been systems based on buying stocks on each decline, increasing the holdings as the price went further down and selling on the advance from the ultimate bottom.

Both of these systems contain something more than a grain of validity; but the half-truth can be dangerous, and the mechanical application of these methods has not been strikingly successful.

Various "timing" devices have been brought forward. Wave theories, cycle theories, etc. These methods, incidentally, include some of the best of the market studies; and some of the very worst.

Surely the worst are those studies which depend on pure astrology, in which investment is supposed to be conducted according to the various "aspects," "conjunctions," "oppositions," position in the various Houses of the Zodiac, and the like. Among the best are the studies of harmonic analysis such as those of Edward R. Dewey and his associates in the Foundation for the Study of Cycles.

Although there appears to be considerable theoretical validity to these mathematically-derived cycles as applied to the market, they are not easy to use as practical tools for profit. But there can be no question as to the integrity of the men who are doing research in this field; the work speaks for itself.

There are any number of methods of market operation based on various published data. Some of these use price action alone. Some consider volume. Others take into account the outstanding short interest, or the relations of round-lot and odd-lot short sales. The action of odd-lots in general has been studied with interesting results. Studies have been made of "new highs" and "new lows," and also of "advances and declines." Sometimes these data have been weighted and combined to produce indexes; or plotted against one another to show the relative action.

All sorts of graphic methods and statistical methods have been applied. We have moving averages and other "smoothing" devices. There are many different ways of charting market information, using arithmetic, logarithmic, square-root, and other scales.

Almost any of these methods, in intelligent hands, can be a help in "seeing" what is going on in the market.

But none of them can automatically take the place of intelligent observation and practical experience.

QUESTIONS FOR CONSIDERATION

Did you at one stage of your development cover reams of paper with figures and notes in an attempt to find a "sure" mechanical method of "beating the market." (If your answer to this question is "No," your experience has been very different from that of most of us.)

Did you ever find the "sure" mechanical method that takes the place of further effort on your part? (If your answer to this question is "No," your experience is like that of millions of others.)

Do you believe that anyone has found the "perfect" system of "beating the market" that any fool can operate safely and easily?

Do you believe that for $2.00 or $5.00 or $100.00 someone can show you the Magic Road to Fame and Fortune in Wall Street?

Does this mean that "nobody knows anything about Wall Street"? Because there is no "sure, easy" way, do we have to throw up our hands and say, "There is no way at all"?

Is money "everything" to you? Is money "nothing" to you? Do you have a pretty good idea of just where money fits into your needs and to what extent?

What is more important than making money? What is more important to you than "fame"; or "success"; or even "happiness"? (Suggestion: How important is the preservation and enhancement of your self-esteem; how you feel about yourself?)

CAN ANY MAN PREDICT THE FUTURE?

THERE is a question, implied in all of the attempts to analyze the market. Obviously, there is no need to find out what the "past" of any stock might be, since that is a matter of record, easily available. And we know the "present" price (or market value) of the various stocks. The only material gain one can look for in making a commitment in a stock lies in dividends to be paid in the "future," or in the price of the stock at some "future" date.

So the question of market study boils down to the larger question, "Can any man predict the future?"

I have tossed this question to a group in a classroom or during a lecture, right at the start of the discussion, and without any comment or explanation. Just the bare question, "Can any man predict the future?" Or, more operationally, "Do you know anyone who can successfully predict the future?"

This is not intended as a gag or cheap wise crack. It is a serious question, and a rather important one at that.

As a rule, when you ask this question, you will see heads shaking slowly from side to side. No one, it seems, knows anyone who can predict the future.

Very well. It just happens that I *do* know someone who can and does predict the future. *I* predict the future. Regularly, and successfully.

I know someone else who can and does predict the future, regularly and successfully. *You* do.

When you get up in the morning you go to the front door and open it. You expect to find something there. You have made a prediction, a prediction that the morning paper *will be* lying on the front steps, or at any rate within a certain radius of eight or ten feet depending on the throwing arm of the newsboy and the speed of his bike.

After breakfast you may go down to the corner and wait for a bus. Suppose a man from Mars came up to you and asked you what you were doing, standing there in the rain on a street corner at 8:15 in the morning. You could tell him that you were "waiting for a bus," and if he expressed some surprise, since no bus whatever was in sight you could explain to him patiently that "the bus was 'due' at 8:20."

What is this but a "prediction of the future"? Why, if you will check your activities through the day you will find that your "schedule" is nothing but one prediction after another; and all, of course, related to the "future." At nine-fifteen "the mail will arrive," at ten "there will be a meeting in Jones' office," at twelve thirty you "will meet Sanderson for lunch"; and so on. You know that next week your wife "will be going to a college reunion," and that in August you "will take a two week vacation in Maine." These are predictions . . . and like all predictions, they refer to future events.

You may even predict years ahead. Timothy is "going to go to Cornell and study engineering." You, yourself, are "going to retire on your fifty-eighth birthday."

These are all pretty good predictions. You expect they will "come true." If you predicted that you would win the Irish Sweep, or that Junior would eventually become President of the United States, or that your wife would have quintuplets in her next pregnancy, those also *might* "come true."

But you will realize that there are great differences in the *dependability* of various predictions. When we ask, "Can any man predict the future?" that isn't a very good way to ask the question. It is not an "either . . . or" situation. As in so many, so very many, of the problems of life, it is better to "measure" and evaluate as a matter of *degree* than to look for a snap "yes or no" answer.

Instead of saying "yes" or "no," we can begin to assign *values* to the predictions, not necessarily *precise* values, but at least indicative of the *order of reliability*, ranging from a value of close to zero for the prediction that you will be elected the next Pope, to a value of close to one hundred per cent that there will be a total eclipse of the sun, lasting 2.7 minutes, visible in Northeastern Asia and Northeastern America and over the Atlantic Ocean on July 10, 1972. There is, of course, the *possibility* that you will actually be elected Pope, though it is, perhaps, a remote one; and there is also the *possibility* that the eclipse will not come off as advertised, though that also seems a long chance.

In between, we have all degrees of reliability. The chances of the morning paper *not* being somewhere in the vicinity of the front steps might lie somewhere between "one in ten" and "one in a hundred." The prediction could fail because the newsboy was sick or because his bike had a flat tire, because the truck with the papers was delayed, because the heavy wind had blown the paper over in the next yard, or because the newsboy had chucked up the route entirely. The expected bus might not show for a variety of reasons; an accident, a traffic jam, a new operator on the bus, etc. etc. But the probability of the bus *not* arriving at approximately (note that "approximately") the right time, would probably lie between "one in ten" and "one in a hundred" in spite of the general opinion that buses *never* arrive anywhere on time.

If you had to make a "guess" whether the paper would be delivered or not, or whether the bus would arrive at "about" the time expected, or whether the mail would come in, or whether Jones would have his meeting, or whether Sanderson would meet you for lunch, your "best guess" would be that these things would occur. Or, to put it another way, if you took the opposite point of view you would be wrong more often than right. (Some of these seem so simple when we begin to talk about them, one has the feeling that it is all a waste of time. It is hard to realize that it is these "obvious" truisms that people will push past, like the elephant in the front hall, not seeing them. It is failure to understand and act on "simple points" like these that have led to financial ruin, family breakup, suicide, murder, war).

You noticed that we said probabilities may approach or "come close to" zero or one hundred per cent. Most of the predictive situations are "multi-valued" or "infinite-valued"; they do not ever attain the absoluteness of "impossible" or "certain."

However, if you pick up, say, a book, and let go of it about thirty inches above the floor, you will "predict" that it will fall to the floor. That is a prediction very *close* to "certainty." There are physicists who will explain to you that since the various molecules of which the material of the book consists are in motion, and not all moving in the same direction at any particular instant, some of the molecules are likely to be moving "up" or away from the floor at any moment. And if it should happen that at the instant you let go of the book, a majority of the molecules happened to be moving "up," it could be that the book would crash into the light fixture on the ceiling. This is not very likely to happen. It is vastly more probable that the book will "fall" to the floor.

Sir Arthur Eddington used as an example of the "near-infinite improbability" a room full of chimpanzees who have been trained to hit the keys of typewriters. It is quite possible to train chimpanzees to type, and it is also quite possible that in due course one of the apes would happen to type the word "go," or the word "we," or even a three-letter combination like "cat" or "boy." Perhaps now and then one of the apes would come up with five or six letters in succession that would make "sense." Eddington suggests, as a measure of improbability, the proposition that the apes might type, without error, all of the books in the British Museum. The New Yorker magazine, several years later, picked up this theme and ran a grand little sketch describing the laboratory with its rows of desks, each equipped with a typewriter and a stack of paper; and at each desk a chimp industriously working his way through Thackeray, Dickens, Trollope, and the Works of Sir Walter Scott.

We all can and do predict the future with varying degrees of success. A large part of our activities and all of our plans depend on these predictions.

The question, then, of prediction of the future resolves itself into evaluating the *degree of probability*, and this, of course, also involves *"evaluating our method of evaluation."*

You recall we mentioned two valuable questions to ask others or yourself regarding almost any statement. The questions, "Is that so?" and "How do you know that?" can go a long way toward weeding out nonsense and un-sanity from our daily lives.

Now we have to add another dimension to these questions. In considering predictive situations we must ask "What are the chances that it is so?" and "What is the evidence supporting your opinion as to the probabilities?"

This makes things a good deal more difficult; for we have to estimate not only the probability factors relating to the event itself, that is, the chances of its happening or not happening, but also we must weigh the dependability of the predictive method we are using.

Thus, we should be aware that in forecasting eclipses we are dealing with something much more precisely predictable than in the case of estimating next year's potato crop. Also we should know that even in the matter of the potato crop it makes a good deal of difference who is doing the guessing. The chances are that a man who has spent his life studying the agricultural economy of Aroostook County will give a better answer as to next year's potato crop than you or I.

This is important. The principle is broad and applies to many other cases besides potatoes. We have here a situation where the question, "How big will be the potato crop next year?" cannot be precisely answered nor with any great certainty. And so a good many people will throw up their hands (as they do about the stock market, about elections, about their own span of life, and other things) and will say, "Nobody knows." And if you must have an "either . . . or" answer, that is the right answer.

But we don't have to settle for an "either . . . or" answer. We can make some sort of estimate of the potato crop, or as to any of the other questions mentioned. The reliability of the opinion will depend, to a large degree, on the experience of the person making the evaluation. An expert on the economics of potato production does not "know all the answers"; but he can give an answer which will, year after year, come closer to the actual production than the estimate of someone who knows nothing about it.

You will notice that we are not talking about "being right" in any absolute sense. It is even possible that the stupidest dolt in the world may stumble on a "lucky guess" as to the potato crop or the score of Saturday's game, or the result of the election. But on balance, over the long pull, and in spite of inaccuracies and failures, the informed observer who has a systematic method of evaluation will average better on his predictions.

One of the very serious blocks to success in the market or elsewhere is the too-high value we put on "being right." If more attention were put on developing the basic method, we could afford to be "wrong" part of the time without any serious loss. The man who is going to change his method every time he has any degree of failure will be changing his method radically, or abandoning, it every few weeks. His wild "hunting" for a "perfect" method will prevent his ever arriving at a method that will stand up over the long pull. And the result, as you have seen it in everyday life, is the type of man who sends three dollars to some advisory service which is going to tell him how to "beat the market"; at the first failure he quits and sends another $3.00 to some other financial wizard for another system; and continues, perhaps for years, looking for something that is simply not possible. In the end, having an "either . . . or" point of view on most things, he will probably decide that "nobody knows anything about the stock market" . . . that it "is all luck," and that "nobody can predict the future." And of course, for all his trials and losses he has learned nothing, and is no closer to having a sound method of dealing with the market than he was in the first place. As a matter of fact he is discouraged and demoralized; not so much because of what the market has done to him, but because of his own lack of understanding.

There is no need to spend much time extending this point to other applications; the case of the psychoneurotic, shopping around from counsellor to counsellor, psychiatrist to psychiatrist; or the maladjusted businessman who tries every new course in "personality," and "inspiration," and "adaptation" in order to discover the magic formula for confidence, popularity, and the Big Job: these are all variations of the same pattern, and at the base of it is the inability to study the roots of a problem.

The difficulty here is not so much an inability to use the "low abstractions" of direct observation of a particular case, as an inability to generalize, to make higher abstractions. When we discussed the basic process of building up successive layers of abstraction we pointed out that while the lower abstractive levels provided specific detail about the "here and now," the higher abstractions made it possible to see the "relations" of things, and to get a generally broader, though less detailed, view. Also, it is only through these higher abstractions that we can arrive at "generalized conclusions." It is only by means of chains of logically structured chains of abstraction that we build a "method of evaluation."

Therefore we need both low level abstractions, high level abstractions, and a number of stages in between. But it is important to know what level of abstraction we are using.   We must not confuse ideas with things, maps with territories, symbols with facts.

QUESTIONS FOR CONSIDERATION

Have you ever tried to count the various predictions you make each day in your ordinary routine?   (Better stop when you reach 200.)

Do you realize how many of your predictions are made without any great conscious effort on your part; and how many of them are good predictions in terms of consistently satisfactory results?

Do you consciously weigh the "validity" of some important predictions so that you have some idea of how much uncertainty is involved?

Because it involves some (perhaps a good deal) of uncertainty, is a prediction therefore "worthless"?   Can you think of some very useful types of prediction that do involve considerable uncertainty?

Predictions are high level abstractions or maps pertaining to the future. Is it sometimes necessary to revise or discard a map in the light of changed conditions?   Do you do this with your predictions?

THE METHOD OF EVALUATION

THE *method* of evaluation, as distinguished from "situational" tactics, is the basic tool of prediction.

Unfortunately, people do use very high abstractions when they could more usefully "take a hard look at the facts," as, for example, when they talk about "juvenile delinquency," "sexual deviation," "political corruption," or "racial desegregation" in such general terms that it is hard to know just exactly what it is they are thinking about. And, on the other hand, they tend to look only at an isolated problem when they could more usefully tackle that problem by considering other problems having some essential similarities.

Thus, a man will worry himself sick about a bad personality clash with the boss, but will fail to see that this is only one case-in-point of his general inability to get along with people. In much the same way he will rack his brains to find a way to meet the instalment payments on the new car, but will not realize that his basic, generalized trouble is a lack of any financial plan; so that even if the payments on the car were taken care of, it would merely postpone trouble until the next crisis came up. Or again, he will lie awake nights wondering whether to sell his Lockheed or not, but will not even try to frame a policy that will help him next month with Socony Mobile, and next year with Chrysler.

There are times when we should look for *differences*, keeping in mind that everything and every event, in spite of similarities, is unique in some respects. There are other times when it is important to look for *similarities*. And so long as we do not make the mistake of considering "similar" as meaning "identical" we can draw some valid conclusions by means of these similarities.

This is the method of evaluation. It does not always give us the precise, exact, absolute, infallible answer to a question. Until we can recognize that precise, exact, absolute, and infallible answers are not possible in all matters, and that to attempt to operate as if they were is to court disaster, we cannot formulate a method of evaluation that is worth the name.

We are looking for something that will help us to make predictions on which we can base plans of operation that may be expected, on balance and in the long run, to be to our benefit.

You will notice that the last paragraph is rather carefully worded. We did not say that a good method of evaluation would give us predictions that would be "always" right. Nor did we even say that it would give us predictions that would be "usually" right.

Strange as it may seem there are cases where the optimum evaluative method gives a majority of "wrong" answers. For example, in commodity trading there have been a great many speculators who have lost heavily on balance or who have even been "wiped out," although a majority of their commitments were "right," that is to say, profitable. Conversely, there have been cases where a commodity operator has made net gains on balance year after year, in spite of taking losses on most of his trades. This, of course, is possible only if the average net gain of the profitable transactions is larger than the average net loss of the losing commitments. And it is possible that some successful traders in stocks may have methods which lead to a similar paradoxical proportion of gains and losses.

The point here is that the optimum method, the method that leads to the most generally beneficial result in the long run, is not necessarily the "obvious" choice.

Unless you are able to generalize at fairly high levels and then apply your conclusions systematically and with confidence that you have arrived at the best method you can find (until you develop a better one) you are going to be disappointed. And you will never feel any security in what you are doing, and you will never be able to accumulate any solid body of experience that can help you in the future, for you will be drifting from one "special situation" to another "special situation." In such a case, of course, a man is not seeing the similarities. He is not applying what he has seen previously, perhaps under somewhat different conditions, to a new situation where he is obliged to make a prediction. For such a man prediction means little. A blind guess is as good as anything. Or, as they say, "It's all a matter of luck."

You have probably had the feeling all the way through this book that we keep jumping from one stage setting to another. If only we could stick to Wall Street and talk about nothing but evaluating and predicting stock values! But the whole point of the "general" in "general semantics" is that we are hoping to learn, by means of higher abstractions, the similarities between quite different situations. Unless we can see that the reasons Sam cannot hold a job may be related to the reasons he can't quite get along with his wife and children, then we are missing the point. The factors that enter into politics may turn up in a little different shape in law; or in finance, or in religion, or in mathematics.

I believe it was Bertrand Russell who said something to the effect that it was centuries before men learned to recognize the common factor (or similarity) in a brace of pheasants, a pair of gloves, and a fortnight. All, of course, are examples of the number *two*.

When you have worked out rather *general* methods of evaluation you will find they can be applied to many different kinds of problems. You will not, of course, overlook the particular circumstances, and you will take these particular circumstances into account in applying the method. But the method is of far-reaching importance. Without it, you have nothing solid on which to build.

QUESTIONS FOR CONSIDERATION

The value of looking closely at an individual situation or a single thing (low order abstraction) is that in this way you can see the particular characteristics that make it different from all others. What is the value of "taking a broad view" at a high level of abstraction?

Are you able to see the similarities between problems in different parts of your life? Can you generalize your semantics? Can you see how you may be making the same *kind* of mistakes in your market operation that you have made in your home life? Or your social life? Or your business life? Can you see where these are different, and still see the common factors that relate them?

Is it possible that some of your problems may stem, not so much from particular events and crises, as from a basic lack of a general method of evaluation?

Can you recall and list a number of cases from your own experience where your faulty evaluative habits have caused you unnecessary trouble?

BUILDING THE METHOD

G O BACK in your mind to what we discussed in the early chapters on abstraction. The camera, when it is moved back, away from the scene, takes in more territory, but shows less detail.

In order to see the broad outlines of problems in a general way, we must move back. We must be prepared to sacrifice some of the detail. We have already spoken of one detail we must discard; the attempt to make "perfect" predictions. We must give up absolute "rightness," absolute "success," and absolute "knowledge." In return we will get a panoramic view in which we can see the *relations* of things to one another. But before we get done we may have to throw out a lot more than we have so far.

Talk to the average board room trader about Baltimore and Ohio and he will produce from the files of memory quite a lot of specific material, much of it, no doubt, true. He can tell you the present price of the stock, the price at the 1957 low, also the 1957 high, the earnings trend for the last year or so, the dividend situation, and probably quite a lot of assorted data and scuttlebutt about the management of the company, the effect of present and projected taxation, the prospects for the next five years under present trends in transportation, the proportion of gross business coming from freight and passenger traffic respectively, etc. etc.

If you should happen to mention that the 1958 market situation in Baltimore and Ohio seemed very similar to that, say in Loew's, Inc. in 1946, our trader might look startled, might express himself pretty strongly to the effect that there is no similarity between Baltimore and Ohio and Loew's, Inc. Of course, you could knock this down at once with a very high abstraction, namely that they are both American corporations.

But there are more definite (lower level) abstractions than that, which show similarities. The two stocks have about the same number of outstanding shares. They have sold at these dates in about the same price range. They both had a big advance a year or so previous to these dates, made rather similar top formations, and declined very rapidly. Both showed signs of recovery as of the respective dates given. Our friend, in short, has overlooked some quite obvious similarities. Or if he has noticed them at all he has brushed them aside as having no significance.

If we draw the daily charts of Baltimore and Ohio and Loew's (and keep in mind that a chart is a map, an abstraction), we can show our friend at a glance the very similar market action in these two stocks during a two year period. He is practically wrestling with the elephant now, for it is right square in the doorway and he can't get around it. But he squeezes under it, and fails to notice it. "So what?" may be the reaction. "So what, if a movie stock twelve years ago had the same shape chart as a railroad today? Does that make Loew's the same as Baltimore and Ohio? Are you trying to tell me that because you have a pattern of marks on a sheet of paper I ought to buy or sell stocks the way you read those marks? Look, mister, I am going to stick to studying the Rails, and I'm going to find out what gives with Baltimore and Ohio. And I don't want any part of your charts."

But . . . if we want to find out what *will happen in a certain situation in the future*, we can look at situations in the past which have some relevant similarities and see *what has happened*. Sometimes it helps.

If we compare the records of various events in the past and we find certain consistent similarities between them we may be able to extract some general principles that will help us to frame an estimate of probabilities in the future.

We are not speaking of "causes" now. Not the "why" of things. Just the "how." We are talking about *correlations*.

Let us suppose that you are wistfully looking at some stock "QRS" which has run up in price from, say eight dollars a share to around fifty, all in the course of less than six months. There is not much use in nursing your regrets or asking "why" didn't you buy it when it was selling at eight. And it may be a little late to buy the stock now, at least unless you know exactly what you are up to.

But you can ask yourself, "*How* did this stock get to fifty from a price of eight?" You can draw a chart of the price action, showing the time on the horizontal scale and the price level on the vertical scale; and you will have a picture of the advance in "QRS." It is not a picture of the business of the "QRS" company, and it tells nothing whatever about the products of that company, the make-up of its board of directors, or the prospects of a 3-for-1 split in July. It is simply a record of the price advance plotted against time.

If we kept daily chart records of several hundred stocks, as some do, we could compare these charts, and we might find several cases where a spectacular advance like the one in "QRS" had occurred. These might be in the stocks of very different sorts of companies. They might be in stocks of widely different price range. And they might be taken from the records of various years.

But if we took the charts having the similarity of "a sharp move up," we could look for correlations. Instead of standing at the brink of the future trying to peer ahead into the darkness, we would be able, through the magic of map-making, to look back at the *origins* of these stock advances. Then we could, in effect, put ourselves back in time and stand at the brink of the future *then*, when these moves started, and we could trace clearly what happened from *then* to *now*. We could check whether there were any conspicuous similarities in the chart pictures as of the time these big moves started.

If we found that a considerable number of sharp, spectacular moves had sprouted from a long period of dullness, perhaps several years of inactivity when the price did not move very much one way or the other, then we might check further.

We might make a predictive guess. We could guess, for instance, that when a stock that has been inactive for several years, suddenly sprouts into great activity, moving up slightly on big volume, this is "the *kind* of situation" from which a number of big, spectacular moves have emerged.

This is not really a finished prediction, let alone a predictive method. It is just a guess, based on a few observations. It remains to check other charts including some that are *now* making this sort of move; and to watch these and see whether any of these do follow through in patterns similar to the older examples we had observed first.   If they do, and if there is a profitable degree of correlation, on balance, in buying these "early breakouts," then we have a rough predictive method.

Note several points here.   The charts do not tell us "why" any of these moves take place.   The charts on which we based the original "guess" may have been taken from a number of different years.   Therefore, assuming we will check the "guess" to be sure the conditions still apply, we may strike the dates off the charts. The charts may represent the stocks of many different kinds of business.   Therefore we may strike the names of the companies off the charts.   The stocks may have been selling at widely different price ranges.   Therefore we can strike the price range off the charts. The stocks may have had greatly different capitalizations, and so some of them may have shown much more volume than others.   We are interested in the *relative* activity, day by day and week by week, but we can strike the absolute numerical scale off the chart.

In order to cover more ground, in order to see more clearly the *similarities*, we have in this case deliberately abstracted to a point where our chart now shows no date, no corporate name, no price, no numerical volume scale.   We have reduced the situation we are studying to its bare bones.

QUESTIONS FOR CONSIDERATION

Are you able to "move back" far enough to see the similarities between quite different things (like moving back with a camera to get a more inclusive view)?

Are you able to see the similarities between stocks of companies in very different lines of business, at different price levels, of different degrees of market activity?

Do you feel that if you can establish certain similar patterns of past performance between these diverse stocks, you may be able to proceed to form some general conclusions as to their typical habits?

If you do this, will you be able to keep in mind, always, that you are dealing with a generality, a high order abstraction, and be ready to check the facts in any individual case to see how it fits the broad generality?

THE METHOD IS BUILT FROM THE BARE BONES

WHEN we first started discussing "relevant" data it may have bothered you that we made such a point of discarding extraneous facts, keeping just what was "necessary and sufficient."

Now you can see how important this is. Unless we are able to abstract, to strip the facts of everything except precisely what will help us to make a simplified, generalized "guess", we are going to be confused and bogged down in a morass of detail.

The question we took up concerning stocks breaking out of inactivity is just one possible study. There are hundreds or thousands of similar questions, as many as you want, that can be put to the test. But before you can set up any predictive mechanism you must scrape away and discard everything that is not needed.

We can use charts (or diagrams, or tables) to answer a great many questions. But the first step, and a most important one, in setting up each question, is to decide just what it is we are going to look at, and to limit the data to be collected accordingly. We can inquire what happens after a stock is split, whether there are any observable relations between dividend rates and stock prices, how the Rail stocks in general compare with the Utilities in general. We can investigate the action of low-priced stocks as compared with high-priced stocks. We can look at the action of certain stocks during times of market panic. We can analyze what happened to various stocks in the period of 1929-1932.

But in each case it is necessary to "strip away" extraneous material so that we can see clearly the thing we are studying.

This type of "technical" study is quite different from the kind of "statistical analysis" in which the main purpose of the charts, tables, etc. is historical and is intended to fill in the detail for a comprehensive examination of each particular situation. One of the reasons it is so hard for those who are not familiar with technical method to understand the high value given to charts by technicians is that they do not understand the purpose of the charts as high level abstractions.

Sometimes "the thing we are studying" is only a small part of a larger picture; then we may have to build up a collection of "parts" and construct a highly abstract organism. (As artificial, if you will, as Frankenstein's monster, but much more useful.)

The picture we have of "economic man" is such a robot. Hans Vaihinger has written about the "as if" situations, where we habitually use a fiction "as if" it were the truth, knowing full well that it is fiction all the time. We know, for instance, that men do not act precisely the way we would expect them to act according to classical economics. This is partly because every man is different from every other man, and partly because the economic forces are not operating in a vacuum. There are family ties, personal loyalties, individual ambitions, etc. that do not tie in, always, with the motivations of classic economics. But "economic man," though he doesn't "really" exist, does have a "reality." The reality is that in certain situations segments of mankind collectively tend to act "as if" the picture of "economic man" were "real."

In law we have a counterpart to "economic man." We have "the prudent man," an extraordinarily stuffy phantasm, but no doubt a creation that suffices as a substitute for reality in certain "as if" situations encountered in legal matters connected with banking and finance.

We have many such "as if" setups in scientific work. And we have many cases where certain known and admitted facts of reality are deliberately disregarded in order to study certain other facts. We sometimes assume a "constant temperature" or "constant pressure" when we know these are not really constant under the conditions of an experiment. We disregard friction, or back-lash or any number of other inconvenient factors in order to get at the bones of some *particular aspect* of nature.

And so, we collect these abstract, over-simplified pictures of "idealized" portions of reality, and we construct methods based on what we can deduce from what we have seen.

The conclusions will be tentative, subject to re-examination, revision, or rejection. They will be "partial" rather than absolute, and will express predictions in terms of probabilities rather than certainties. The conclusions will be as free as we can make them from highly colored or absolute "judgments."

Thus, if somebody should ask me, "What is most likely to happen in the case of a stock whose chart has been making the kind of formation we call an Ascending Triangle?" I would say, "It is most likely to break out and move up substantially, probably at least a distance equal to the open side of the Triangle." If they ask whether this "will surely happen," I would have to answer, "No; not 'surely.' Just probably." And if they ask if this is "good" or "bad," I would have no answer, for such a question has no meaning at all in this case; we would have to know "good for whom" or "bad for what."

In stripping extraneous matter from our studies and reducing everything to a few simple and answerable questions which we have selected as a basis for our inquiry, you will notice we have left behind a good deal of trouble. We have chucked out our absolute ambitions and ideals. We have tossed away the goal of perfect results. Instead of storming the gates of Valhalla we have settled for a very ordinary kind of success, in a limited degree, and in a narrowly bounded area.

If we can do this, we can eliminate a good deal of the unnecessary strains and tensions of life. We know there are going to be problems. There are going to be losses. There may even be some downright defeats. But if we can stop worrying about impossible objectives and vague aspirations, and about conflicts that have no existence save in our own minds, we will usually be able to handle the "real" problems.

And this is true in many areas of life besides the stock market.

QUESTIONS FOR CONSIDERATION

Are you able to "see" the generalized meaning in a chart, diagram, map, etc.? That is to say, do you understand the advantages (of simplicity, of reducing a problem to simple terms) in such high abstractions?

Do you understand the limitations of charts, diagrams, maps, etc. (due to their showing only certain elements of the territory)?

Do you see how the study of maps of quite different territories may help you in perceiving certain typical features that may be likely to occur in other territories?

PUTTING THE METHOD TO WORK

STORED up in our minds there is a vast, yes vast, collection of information; what we have seen or experienced, what we have read, what we have been told, and then all the logical combinations we have made, resulting in attitudes, opinions, prejudices, judgments, etc.

There are people who seem to carry around a great deal of pure information in a rather unorganized form, so that they are full of facts but don't have very much ability to predict. And there are others whose abstracting at higher levels has gone on for years without much comparison with reality, so that while they can voice predictions on almost any subject (often loudly and vehemently), the results of these predictions don't check out too well in reality.

The discipline which has become known as General Semantics is concerned with organizing the factual material and its derivative higher abstractions in such a way that the relation between "in here" and "out there" is continually maintained on a "current" basis. The "raw material" of knowledge is consciously organized and the relevant portion of it can be focussed on whatever particular problem concerns us. We know what happened in the past, we have noted certain correlations, we draw some conclusions, and then we can make an "informed guess" on the probable outcome of some new situation with an enormously better chance of success than someone who has not organized his mind in this way.

When a patient recites his symptoms to a doctor, there is a process

of "re-call" going on in the doctor's mind.   He brings into consciousness some of the things he learned in medical school bearing on cases
with these symptoms; and he remembers articles on the subject he
has read lately, and he recalls some of his own cases that seem similar.
He considers the history of other cases like this, and their outcome;
the kinds of treatment that seemed to benefit them; and on the basis
of all these, plus his observation as to the condition of this particular
patient here and now he makes his diagnosis, prescribes treatment,
and makes a prediction or prognosis, at least to himself, as to the
probable course and duration of the ailment.

Change a few words and this is exactly what a lawyer does for
his client.   It is what an engineer does in solving a problem.   In
practically everything we do we take the stored-up data from the
past, and apply the conclusions we can make from it to a problem
in the future.   Our solution is a form of prediction, whether it is
that an action for damages of $5,000 will probably be successful, or
that a cantilever bridge built according to such-and-such specifications will stand any storm likely to hit this county.

QUESTIONS FOR CONSIDERATION

Are you aware of how you re-call from your mind the particular memories,
opinions, judgments, etc. that may seem to apply to a case-at-hand?

Do you realize how your perception of the new case-at-hand may be
affected by what you have stored up in the past?   Do you realize how you
will tend to see "what you expect to see," and may overlook something quite
important because you were not "set" to recognize it?   (This is what we
mean by failing to see an elephant that is standing in the front hall; and
this is hardly an exaggeration; it is amazing what can be overlooked.)

Do you see how important it is, after you "re-call" and "recognize"
the situation, to take time to examine the *new* case-at-hand and note the
important differences, thus bringing your previous "maps" up to date,
and adding to your store of information?

HABIT CAN BE A PITFALL

THERE was a story about a woman who visited a fortress in Spain. It was a large establishment complete with park and shaded walks, and with benches along the walks. At the main gate to the grounds and at each of the other gates there was a sentry; in front of the administration building, the armory, and the powder magazine. The lady visitor noticed that there was a sentry pacing a short post along one of the walks, back and forth in front of one of the benches. As she watched, another soldier appeared, saluted and relieved him, continuing to walk the same post before the bench. The visitor asked the lieutenant who was guiding her over the grounds just why a sentry had been placed at this spot, which was not near any of the buildings nor any of the entrances. The lieutenant explained that this was one of the regular posts and so far as he could remember there had always been a sentry at this spot. However, he would be glad to check the orders at the main office.

On checking these it appeared that the original order had been issued several years earlier at the time a new commandant had been appointed. It was merely a copy of a previous standing order calling for a sentry at Bench Number 23. A further search of the records carried back five years more, when the previous order had been issued. And this order had been made out to replace a previous one, since the old commandant had been taken suddenly ill and had been replaced by another. It was only a day or two before this illness that the original order had been placed; an order calling for a sentry at Bench Number 23, "which has just been painted."

Through the accident of a new commandant coming in, all orders, including this one, were re-issued; and inadvertently, this particular temporary order was then issued without qualification and became a permanent standing order. For over ten years a sentry had marched back and forth in front of Bench Number 23, and there was no machinery to cancel it. The soldiers who marched asked no questions. The superiors in charge merely followed their standing orders. The clerks simply carried forward the standing instructions. The commandant had other matters to think about. This thing, once useful, had long outlived its usefulness; but there was no one to spot the anachronism.

We do this sort of thing, you know; to ourselves.

This sort of situation comes up in business all the time. Somebody starts a system, say taking off the subtotals of expenses for Department 16 and carrying them in a special file. Perhaps somebody was making a special study at one time, or maybe the government had called for a detailed report on this department. But in the course of months and years the old clerks would teach the new clerks, and the old managers would train the new ones. And this would become just part of the routine, somebody's job; and the blue cards and the green cards would pile up in the files and nobody would ever use them. They were just part of the overhead, and as fixed as the laws of the Medes and Persians. Just a sentry marching back and forth in front of a park bench.

If you think this is a stupid exaggeration, permit me to give an actual example. Some years ago I served on a municipal committee in charge of Public Relations for the City of Springfield. Under our jurisdiction came the annual Municipal Register. On investigation it turned out that this large volume of some four hundred pages of small type and tables of figures was produced at a cost of over ten dollars a copy, and ran the city a few thousand dollars each year for its printing and binding. It also turned out that there was no law that required any such report to be printed, although the Municipal Register had actually been issued each year for nearly a century.

On checking the various departments it was found that although each department of the city government had a file of these reports, none of them ever used them for any purpose, since the particular records of each department were kept in the department's own files. Neither the mayor, nor any member of the Board of Aldermen nor the Common Council (Springfield has a bicameral system of city government) ever consulted the book, although each of them received a copy. The public library reported that no one ever requested to see the Mnuicipal Register either at the Main Library or at any of the six branches. The local newspaper reporters covering city hall said that they got their material from their own files, or from the particular departments as needed. A number of copies of the report were sent, each year, to the City Clerks of other municipalities; but it is hard to believe that these City Clerks were any more anxious to plow through the deadly pages of these reports than the people in our own town.

As a matter of fact no one could read the report intelligently even if he tried. Tables of figures often carried headings like "Committed during the year: Sewer Construction—1935—Docket Mass. 1242R." Since the only way to get any further light on this would be to go to a department head, who might or might not see fit to explain, the information hardly contributed much toward the enlightenment of the citizenry or toward a more economical city government.

In a city of 150,000 our committee was able to find just one person who had ever looked at the book; a reporter who said he had "once or twice" looked up some figure in it. The Springfield Municipal Register was, by any standard, one of the most completely unreadable and unread books ever published.

The happy ending to the story seemed to come when the committee substituted a controlled-free-circulation book titled "Our Home Town" which reported city affairs in such manner that citizens lined up in queues two blocks long to get their copy, and which won a lead editorial, "A Bell for Springfield," in the Ladies Home Journal. The citizens were hungry for information; hungry for bread instead of stones from the City Fathers. The cost of the new book was just under fifty cents a copy as against ten dollars for the Municipal Register.

But, believe it or not, after two years of "Our Home Town," it was replaced by the Municipal Register in its old form, and the old-style register has been published regularly every year since then as the city's contribution to public enlightenment.

This is the sentry again, of course, with a new quirk, the reversion to the old habit even after a definite break has been made.

You'll find Spanish sentries in the Army and in the Navy. You

will encounter them, many of them, in the courthouse and wherever
else legal business is transacted.   And if you ever have dealings with
the Post Office you will run into battalions of them patrolling the
dark corridors of the Postal Laws and Regulations.   There is very
likely more than one Spanish sentry guarding the routine of your
family life.   And in the inner fortress of our own minds these senti-
nels police our thoughts with the authority of yellowing orders from
a long-dead past.

Don't under-estimate habit.   And don't under-estimate the power
of directives handed down from long ago, however irrational or
obsolete they may be today.

Let us say we have a method of evaluation, based on a new look
at current facts.   And then comes the opportunity to act, in the
stock market or in some other area of life.   And what do we do?
Do we follow the conclusions of our method?   No!   Too often, after
having gone through all the intellectual labor of setting up a good
method, we revert to something out of the long-ago.   Something
we "have always done," something "father told us," something we
"learned in school," something, we don't know where it came from;
but when we are forced to make a fast decision under pressure we are
very likely to revert to our habitual responses, inculcated years ago.
And often our action will be diametrically opposite to what our
considered reason would indicate we should do.

This is what people mean when they say "you can't change
human nature."   You can!   You can change your own human nature
and to your great advantage, but you should know that after you
have thoroughly absorbed all the arguments, and feel that you
"know" how to tackle a problem, "those little devils start creeping
back in again."   And unless you watch yourself, you are back doing
it the old way all over.

Hence the familiar wail, "How could I have been so stupid as to
buy that stock?"

QUESTIONS FOR CONSIDERATION

Do you feel that "habits are bad"?   Doesn't it all depend on what the
habits are and whether they lead to satisfactory outcomes?

Would it make for an easier life if you had to "think" consciously about
every single action you take all day, every day?   If you had to "consider"

every minor decision, such as which button of your shirt to button up first, or whether to put the tooth paste on the top shelf instead of the second shelf, would this make your life simpler and easier, or otherwise? Would you go completely stark raving mad if you had to "think out" each little thing all day long?

Would you say that *all* habits are useful? Would you say that *all* habits are harmless?

Isn't it a question of whether a habit represents a routine action or series of actions which can "take a load off your mind," and which can be "taped in," so that thereafter it will operate for the most part without your conscious attention?

When a habit turns out to be harmful, or interferes with your efficiency, then shouldn't you check back to find the origin of that habit, see what usefulness it may have had for you originally, and whether the circumstances have changed significantly since then?

Would you say that one could gain great benefits by re-examining his habits, breaking or changing those that are "working against" his interests, and establishing new habits that will serve a more useful purpose?

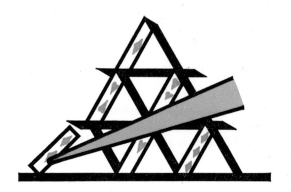

CHAIN AND FLASH REACTIONS

YOU may have known some anxious mother who seemed able to build a catastrophe out of the simplest and most ready-to-hand materials. If she went to the store and left the front door open, the children might wander into the house for a drink of water. And then they might want to explore the medicine cabinet above the wash basin. And there might be some of those pills Uncle Henry took the time he had the spasms. And if they took those pills it might make them sick. And if she didn't get home in time they would be dead. The poor woman could have them all dead and buried before she'd walked a single block.

One thing associates with another. If I say "pen" you may think of "ink." If you say "cat" I think of "dog." Things and events we have seen or heard at the same time, or in the same place, or which have the same names, "go together." Past experience and habit build up chains of associations. You can go from one to another like chain lightning. The squeak of a door in a dark room in an unfamiliar house may suggest a sinister creeping figure. The intruder has a knife. He is coming across the room to where you lie. He is about to plunge the knife into your ribs! You break out in a cold sweat and get up quickly to turn on the lights and see . . . and of course there is no marauder there at all. Just a door that squeaked a little and started a chain of associations in your mind.

People can become panicked when a chain reaction leads to the possibility of a disastrous outcome. They can become overwhelmed with greed or lust or envy when such a chain races from some simple fact through a chain of associated abstractions to some very high order conclusion. The thing can all happen in a flash. In fact if it did not happen in a flash it probably wouldn't happen at all; for very often the chain will break down under any close and leisurely examination.

You can be panicked out of stocks you may have bought; and then a day or so later wonder "just what got into you." People will "lose their nerve." People "go to pieces." And when they look back at the awful Thing that threatened them, it wasn't really very awful at all.

The way to protect one's self from being stampeded by a chain or flash reaction is to delay your response. That is not an easy thing to do without training and practice; not when you so easily "jump to the conclusion" and feel confronted by an immediate and present danger. But the habit of delay can be learned. You are already familiar with the old formula for controlling your temper. You just "count to ten." Sometimes it may not work, you may have good reason for your anger even then; but sometimes it can save you from an unjustified outbreak. Certainly the principle is good. If you will just take a few moments to examine the territory before acting on the maps alone you will often save yourself a good deal of trouble.

It may be that the reaction is one that brings on fear. It may cause anger. It may lead in other directions. But the few seconds you may take to ask yourself, "Is this really what it seems to be, or is it largely a big build-up in my mind?" can pay you rich dividends.

The man who hesitates is not so often "lost" as the one who does not hesitate. When the salesman's voice on the telephone suggests that you "act at once" so as to get these "fast, enormous profits," it will be worth your while to take a little time to look at the facts. Otherwise the high order "hope" of quick, easy money may stampede you into very heavy losses.

QUESTIONS FOR CONSIDERATION

Can you think of ten times in the past month when you have "blown your top" about some crisis at home, on the road, or at the office? Would you have "lost" anything by weighing the circumstances before letting fly? Would you have been better off in some of these cases if you had investigated or considered first; that is, if you had "delayed your reaction"?

NUMBERS CAN BE PITFALLS

TAKE a paper napkin. Lay it on the floor in the corner of the room. Tomorrow morning lay another one on top of it. The next day, two on top of that. The following day, four; and so on, doubling the number each day for just thirty days.

How high a pile? A foot? A hundred feet? Fifty miles? Figure it out. If you are not familiar with geometric progressions you may be surprised.

Then try this. You have $3500 in the bank. I also have $3500 in the bank. You tell me you have drawn your money out of the bank and used it to buy a certain stock at $5, which you feel will be worth more soon. I do not take the tip at once, but several weeks later, with the stock selling at $7, I take my money out of the bank and invest it in the stock. Three months later, the stock happily having advanced to $12, we both sell out.

Since you bought yours first at $5, and I paid $7, you have more profit than I do. How much more? Would you say it was 20% more, or 30% more, or 50% more, or 100% more? Would it surprise you to find that it was very close to 100%? That you had made practically twice the profit I had made? Figure it out. But don't feel too chagrined. The treasurer of one of our important corporations gave me the answer 30%. Almost everyone will underestimate.

What happens in these cases? How can figures play such dirty tricks on us?

Of course, like all other errors where our maps tell us one thing and the territory turns out to be something different, it is not the territory that is "wrong." Somehow we have learned some things that aren't always "true." Isn't it amazing when you begin to look around *how much* of what we have learned has to be revised, re-dated, or re-specified?

In this case of the two stocks, what we are bucking is the logarithmic nature of the real world around us, as opposed to the arithmetic world we learned about in school. We still think, for the most part, with arithmetic "maps."

The difficulty here probably comes from at least two sources. In the first place, there are, of course, many instances where things appear in arithmetic relations. If we count the houses along the street it is a matter of "one, two, three, four." In fact all the counting we do is arithmetic. We count money. We count the days. We count the number of stocks that have made new highs for the year.

And this leads to a second point. Because so many of the simple transactions we use in early childhood are arithmetic in nature, and involve positive whole numbers, that is the kind of mathematics we are taught in school. We learn that John has seven apples and in an outburst of generosity gives Charley two of them and Andrew one. Mary gets an allowance of fifteen cents and earns twenty cents more delivering a package. And so on.

The result is, we become accustomed to regarding the world as being made up of things that can be expressed in positive whole numbers. The intervals between two consecutive whole numbers are equal. The difference between six and seven is exactly the same as the difference between sixteen and seventeen.

What we learn early we learn well. Fortunately, before it is too late, we learn about negative whole numbers, and about fractions both as ratios and as decimals. But unfortunately, by the time we begin to study proportion and percentage and matters like that we have become pretty well bored with the whole subject of "math" (which is not exactly taught along inspired lines in most schools), so we stop learning and go forth in life to seek our fortune, and we really haven't very much except the "two-plus-two-equals-four" type of figgering.

There is nothing wrong with this; in its place. It is "valid" in many situations, and in dealing with "counting" problems it permits of "exact" answers.

It works out well for keeping a cash account, taking an inventory of countable things, and a great many other problems in life.

But it does not take in a whole "other" aspect of the world that is quite as important. We grow up without any deep, basic, untuitive, "second nature" grasp of the logarithmic relation, which is another mathematical way to look at the world; not the only "other way," either, but it is so important that we are bound to suffer if we do not have the use of it . . . we are like one-eyed men, having only a limited sense of perspective.

If the abacus, or counting frame is the prototype of "counting" (or digital) mathematics, then the slide rule can be considered the prototype of "measuring" (or analogue) mathematics.

The first obvious difference between "counting" and "measuring" is that counting seems *absolutely* exact, whereas measuring is at best no better than the marks on the measure and the keenness of eye of the measurer.

This difference is more apparent than real, however, since outside of accounting work the great majority of practical problems do not call for "absolutely exact" answers, but only reasonably close approximations. Furthermore, where the figures are very large, or involve operations with long decimals it is not actually feasible to get the "absolutely exact" answer even where a digital method is used.

The big difference in the two approaches to calculation is in the "point of view."

We said that the difference between six and seven was "the same" as the difference between sixteen and seventeen. In one sense that is true. In another sense no. If you buy 100 shares of a stock at six and it advances to seven you have made $100. If you buy 100 shares of another stock at sixteen and it advances to seventeen you have made $100.

But the profit in the first case amounts to about 17%. In the second case it is only about 6%. And if the stock was bought at one hundred and six and advanced to one hundred and seven, then the profit would be less than 1%.

If you had put a thousand dollars into the stock at six, you would have had a gain of $167. With the stock at 16, it would have been $62; and at 106, $9.

Thus, as a stock moves up, each point becomes a smaller percentage, and therefore less important. And as it declines, the percentage becomes larger; and more important.

There are any number of traps in life and in the market that center around the differences between logarithmic and arithmetic viewpoints. These confusions do not arise from mixing up different levels of abstractions. They are due to faulty identifications between two sets of high level abstractions. It is very easy to make these identifications unconsciously.

A very typical confusion of this sort comes up in connection with "averaging" stock purchases. Joe Frazer has bought 100 shares of "JKL" at 20. If the stock goes down to 10 he can put in another $2000, purchasing 200 shares, making his average cost for the 300 shares about 13⅜, so that a three and three-eighth point rise will wipe out his entire loss. And if the stock runs down to 5, then he can buy 400 additional shares for another $2000, and this will give him a total of 700 shares on which he will have an average cost of about 8⅝; so that even at this juncture a three and five-eighth point rise will wipe out all of his losses. This looks like such an easy, sure, and simple way to recoup.

Joe will tell you (and he is right) that it is extremely unlikely that the stock will go to "nothing". He has firmly etched in his mind a whole system of maps pertaining to arithmetic computation. "Obviously," he feels, the stock, in declining from 20 to 5, has come down "three quarters of the way."

Therefore, he believes, and believes very firmly, "It can't go down more than five points more, and is not likely to do that."

This is true in a way. He is making the not-altogether-unreasonable assumption that the declines from 20 to 15, 15 to 10, and 10 to 5, are equal, and that the decline from 5 to 0 is also equal to these others. He is wrong, however, when he tells you, as he will, that "JKL" has already had its "down" move; that it *can't go down* much more.

Joe is so sure of this that he will give you quite a battle if you so much as question him. For it "stands to reason" that the stock having dropped 15 points from 20 to 5 cannot go down another 15 points. And it is true, arithmetically speaking, that "JKL" is approaching "the bottom area." But this is definitely *not* true in the world of ratios.

If you were to tell Joe that the stock could go down just as much if he bought it at 5, as if he bought it at 20, he would think you were crazy. And if you told him the stock could go right on down without any limit, he would *know* you were crazy.

But look! If I buy "JKL" or any other stock at 20 and it goes down to 10, the value of what I own has diminished by 50%. If I had bought 100 shares, it would have cost me $2000 at 20; and would be worth $1000 at 10.

Now if I should buy $2000 worth of the stock at 10, and it goes down to 5, what is my stock worth? It is worth $1000, and the value of my investment has diminished by 50%.

Suppose I buy $2000 worth at 5. A decline to 2½ slices 50% from the market value; my stock is worth only $1000.

Name your own figure. Buy the stock at $1. It can go down to 50¢. Buy it at 10¢. It can go to 5¢. And at any price, no matter how low, the stock could slide another 50% and cut your capital by 50%.

Not only that. We have only used the figure 50% as a convenient example. If a stock can decline 50%, it can decline 90%; and it can make this decline from any point, no matter how low.

Among the "Famous Last Words" of the market, one of the most famous is the line, "They *can't* go much lower!"

QUESTIONS FOR CONSIDERATION

Are you aware that numbers are abstractions, that is to say, "mental maps"?

Do you realize that there are different ways of looking at things, and that the way you learned in school may not be "the only correct way"?

Are you fully conscious of the great gulf between arithmetic computation and the logarithmic (or ratio, or proportion) way of viewing things?

Do you know that the word "average" as it is used by most people is a very loose word which can be interpreted in various ways? (Arithmetic mean, median, mode, etc.)

Do you understand that, for all their usefulness, there are many situations in nature that cannot be described in "numbers"? That our education in arithmetic has given us a useful "set of maps," but we have not all learned that there are a number of branches of modern mathematics which go far beyond the realm of numerical computation?

THE WONDERFUL CURVES

WHAT we have been talking about in the past chapter is the "logarithmic relation." It is a matter of ratios rather than ordinary addition. It is the basic pattern of growth for many things in nature, and for some things in finance.

The logarithmic relation operates all around us every day in plain sight, but if we have been trained only to "additive" relations we do not perceive it. We are like color-blind people, seeing only certain parts of the scene and missing the beauty of chromatic harmony.

For the logarithmic aspect of nature is as beautiful as the bright colors of spring or the crystal etchings of frost in winter.

The principle of logarithmic growth is so simple that it is hard to understand why we so persistently overlook it. It is simply the very usual way in which capital at interest, many plants, and some animals increase by adding a certain proportion of their present size during each successive interval of time.

A hundred dollars, placed at interest computed annually at ten per cent, will grow to $110.00 in a year. At the end of the second year it will have added ten per cent to the new total of $110, and so will have grown by $11, and will amount to $121. At the end of the third year the total will have been increased by ten per cent of $121, or $12.10, and will come to $133.10. The fourth year will make it $146.41, and so on.

You will notice that as the principal increases, the increment, figured as a constant percentage will also increase in numerical value.

357

And this will be true whether the growth rate is ten per cent or thirty per cent, or ninety per cent. It will also be true whether the growth is "compounded" every year, or semi-annually, or on a weekly or daily basis; or whether it is computed as an infinite convergent series to show the "continuous" rate of growth if we assume that growth is being added in every tiniest instant of time.

And because the size of the increment is proportional to the size of the "principal" at any particular time, we can say that the "*rate* of growth is proportional to the *state* of growth" (where "rate" is considered to mean the added quantity of dollars, inches, pounds or whatever is the unit of growth).

This is the primary law of growth for many things. Not only money in the bank, but many organisms in nature: pine cones, and snail shells, and the twigs on trees, and sunflowers, to name just a few examples of this law in operation.

If you were to mark off a snail shell into sections covering the same angular distance you would see that each segment of the snail's house is the same *shape*, though they are much smaller near the center and become larger as you progress outward from the center. Any one of the sections would look very much like any other section if you magnified or shrunk it. If you assume that the snail will add one of these sections each month you will see that with each successive month he is adding a larger extension to his house; but each new addition represents *the same percentage increase.*

And because of this constant *percentage* change, the snail shell presents a curve which is *the same shape in any stage of growth.* A baby snail will resemble a grandfather snail, only in miniature.

Leaving out practical matters of getting enough food, and maintaining structural strength, there is no limit to the size the curve of the snail's house could be carried to. Look at it as a mathematical curve. It could continue adding constant percentage increments indefinitely; it could be drawn as large as you wanted it. And conversely, there is no limit to how far back you could run it, going in toward the center. Theoretically the segments go on getting smaller and smaller, but there is no end to the mathematical series, nor to the curve.

You may recognize at this point the similarity between the snail's house and Joe Frazer's stock as discussed in the previous chapter. There is no limit at either end. Here is a similarity between two abstractions; the behavior of a stock chart and the shape of the snail's house, which is of tremendous practical importance. For both the stock price and snail's house are essentially logarithmic functions.

A good many stock analysts now use a type of paper known as "semi-logarithmic," meaning that the price scale is logarithmic but the time scale is linear. Some years ago I designed such a paper especially planned for stock analysis. This *"TEKNIPLAT"* charting paper is laid out on a scale that is similar to the scale on a slide rule. The spaces on it are numbered, but they are not equal spaces. They are so ruled that two equal vertical distances on the paper always represent the same *percentage* change. When a stock advances 10% from 20 to 22 it moves up the same distance as another stock which has advanced 10% from 60 to 66, or from 100 to 110. And when a stock declines 10% from 100 to 90, or from 30 to 27, or from 10 to 9, it is possible to compare the action of stocks at different prices more fairly than by the arithmetic scale.

You can see how this explains Joe Frazer's problem. If a constant percentage decline is always represented by the same distance on the paper, then in a decline of 50%, the distance from 200 to 100 is the same as from 50 to 25, and this is the same as from 4 to 2, or from 1/2 to 1/4, or from 1/256 to 1/512. A 50% decline is always possible from any price, however low. A 50% decline will always have the same effect, that is, it will cut your capital in half. And therefore there is no "zero" on the logarithmic scale. It extends from the infinitesimally small to the infinitely large.

The logarithmic spiral, which is the curve we saw in the snail's house, is of course the visible expression of the logarithmic relation we have discussed in connection with stocks. The slide rule and the snail shell express the same mathematical pattern.

It is not only the property of the snail and of stock prices and bank interest and other business functions. It is also visibly expressed in many forms in nature, as we suggested earlier. If you examine the arrangement of the seeds in a sunflower head you will see that there are *two* logarithmic spirals, one having a rather sharp pitch to the center, the other taking a more leisurely course at a more oblique angle.

A pine cone also shows two intersecting series of logarithmic spirals running at different pitches. And although it is not quite so easy to see, the angular spacing of the small twigs as they grow from the branch of a tree or shrub is also a logarithmic sequence.

From the purely practical point of view of understanding how stocks move it will be important to observe and absorb these logarithmic relations until it is second nature to think of things in terms of "percentage" or "ratio" changes.

But aside from the business of making money, the wonderful world of the logarithmic spirals contains so much of beauty and so much of the sheer wonder of pattern and rhythm (and I should add here, "as I see it," though I feel sure you will too, when you look into it) that it seems a pity our children are not schooled from the very start to see the world in broader terms than the "true" but sometimes terribly misleading "arithmetic" relations.

There are logarithmic spirals that generate the most interesting designs. As Jay Hambidge pointed out in a study of "Dynamic Symmetry; The Grecian Vase," the harmonies that emerge from the properties of the logarithmic spiral were at the root of much of the greatest of the architecture, sculpture and painting of the ancient Greeks. Some of the spirals are close relatives of other forms. There is, for example, a "root three" logarithmic spiral which is all tied up with the 30°–60° triangle, the "root three" rectangle, the hexagon, etc., and which is a joy to experiment with. And there are others, too, which have almost magical qualities in their various relations.

If this is a digression it is a deliberate one. I would like to feel that you want to know more about the "wonderful curves," for they are among the great beauties of nature.

QUESTIONS FOR CONSIDERATION

Is there anything about the series: 1, 3, 9, 27, 81, 243 . . . , which seems "less reasonable" to you than the series: 1, 2, 3, 4, 5 . . . ? Do you realize that there are other kinds of series also having an orderly arrangement and progression, such as 2, 4, 16, 256, 65,536 . . . ? Are you aware that the arithmetic series: 1, 2, 3, 4, 5 . . . , is not the only one observable in nature, and in fact is not the most common?

Have you ever, yourself, personally studied the beautiful logarithmic curves of a sea shell? Compared the different kinds of logarithmic spirals in various types of shell? Have you looked at the symmetrical arrangement of the petals or the seeds in certain flowers? Have you examined a pine cone in order to see the double channels of logarithmic spirals on its sides? Can you think of any other natural phenomena that assume the logarithmic form?

In your investing program are you chained to the additive philosophy of the counting house, or are you conscious of the "ratio" methods of engineering? Do you think only of "points gained or lost," or do you keep in mind always the "percentage gains and losses"?

LOSSES CAN BE PITFALLS

THIS is a sad subject and we will make this chapter a short one. But a few words on the subject of losses are in order.

Nobody really likes to take losses. Losses represent "hurts." And much earlier in this book we showed how people will feel badly "hurt" by experiences that would not be so terribly painful if their outlook was just a bit different; for example, the hurt of being *second* in a competitive examination, out of a hundred and thirty-five students.

Since the worst hurt of all is an injury or humiliation to the self-esteem it is not surprising that a good many investors will take some rather terrible monetary beatings before they will admit to their brokers, their friends and most especially to themselves, that they have made a mistake. Of course if they "saw things a little differently," making a mistake might not loom so large or so shamefully in their perception. And very often, too, it might not be really a matter of "making a mistake" at all. It could be that conditions had changed; and a new territory calls for a new map. But, as you know, some of our friends will defend the map as if it were a matter of sacred honor, regardless of whether it still represents the territory or not. And a defense of obsolete maps can lead to terribly heavy losses; in the market and elsewhere.

What constitutes a loss depends very largely on your value system. What may be a matter of "worse than death" to one individual may be no more than a "pain in the neck" to someone else. A matter of *degree*.

362

Furthermore there is a matter of level involved here, that is, the level of abstraction. Suppose that I enter into a series of trades, say in commodities, and the results of these trades are something like this: Loss $150; loss, $75; loss, $225; gain, $1500; loss, $180; loss, $50. It is perfectly true, at the level of individual study of each transaction, that I have had five losses and only one gain. But at the slightly higher level of abstraction where we combine the operations to get a net result, it becomes clear that I have profited considerably on the series as a whole.

It seems childish and silly to bring up such a simple and obvious point. Yet, so inflexible is some people's aversion to "loss" (*any* "loss"), that such a series of transactions is an abhorrent nightmare. They literally cannot stand it. And I have personally known traders in both stocks and commodities, who, although they were making profits "on balance," were so upset, so badly "hurt" by the incidental losses, that they quit the market entirely. It would be hard to understand how people can ignore or jeopardize their own material interests, as many do, unless we understood how important it is to them to protect their self-esteem, their self-regard; the way they feel about themselves. And you will realize that it is possible to learn to see things in a different light so that some of the terrifying losses and threats of loss do not seem so horrible.

We can take a lot of losses if we know what we are doing, and if we can see and fully appreciate that the losses are not "unbearable." And in many cases we may find that the losses are an essential part of the "means" which is justified by the "end."

One habit, which tends to distort perception and to increase nervous tension about accrued losses, is the practice of comparing every quotation with the price at which a stock was bought (or in the case of short sales, at which it was sold).

Harry will come in and tell you that "MNO" is now selling at 23. "But I paid 28 for it, and if it gets back there I'm going to sell and get my money back."

Why 28? The market doesn't know and doesn't care what you paid for a stock. There are times when the smart course would be to buy more stock at 23; and to hold when the stock advanced to 28, to 35, to 60. There are other times when the best action would be to sell the stock immediately at 23 or whatever you could get for it. Unless you have some very good technical reason or fundamental reason why the stock should be sold at 28 there is no reason you should make that particular price a "sacred cow."

Wouldn't it be better to forget the price you paid and just take it from there on its own merits. If the stock is acting all right, hold it, regardless of what you paid for it. And if it is not acting all right, sell it and be rid of it.

QUESTIONS FOR CONSIDERATION

Which would you consider a better basis for selling out a stock you own: "I paid $22 for it, and the price is now $32, so I have a good profit," or, "The action of the stock during the past weeks suggests that now it can no longer be considered strong; so I will sell"?

If the stock looks as if it had "turned the corner" and was no longer strong, would you sell it regardless of whether you had bought it for $22 or $42?

Does the taking of a loss in a stock necessarily mean that you were "wrong" in your original decision? Isn't it possible that the conditions have changed, and you must revise your mental map of the situation?

Which is more important to the progress of an account; the number of times you were "right," or the overall net gains? Does it matter how many losses you take if the net result is satisfactory? Would you feel that in some drastic reversals the man who might take a net loss, but who could keep this loss relatively small, would be doing a constructive job by protecting his capital to use in future opportunities?

Is it really the money losses, as such, that hurt and depress investors so much, or do you feel they are hurt because they believe they have "not done as well as they expected of themselves"? Is it really principally money at the heart of this feeling, or is the concern with maintaining "self-regard"? Is it possible that these people have an unrealistic view of what they should expect from themselves, and that they feel hurt too much by matters in which others might not feel "inferior"?

PROFITS CAN BE PITFALLS

ALMOST everything we have said about losses can be applied, sometimes with a reverse twist, to profits.

The same type of individual who is so badly hurt by a small loss will become very nervous when he has a profit. In fact it is hard to say which is more painful to him; to be losing money, or to be making accrued gains but dreading the possibility of a reversal that will wipe them out.

It hardly seems necessary to point up the fact that there is a good deal of "either . . . or" in this. The implication is very strong that unless one makes profits *all* the time and has no losses, he is "no good." And, as usual, there is no in-between in the mind of such a man.

Anxiety holds back the nervous trader from taking his losses early. He dreads them so much. He hopes to avoid them entirely by waiting. And it is also anxiety that forces his hand when he has a profit. It is not exactly "greed," it is really anxiety, something akin to fear. And so, all a-tremble lest his two or three points of gain be swallowed up in a reaction, he "takes his profit," prematurely. This ensures good commissions for his broker; but it also effectively cuts out the chances for him ever to make a substantial gain.

As we saw in the case of losses, part of the blame for this premature selling should be laid to the habit of comparing the price of a stock with "what I paid for it." And it won't hurt to repeat, here, that the market is not interested in what you or anybody else paid for a stock. You can see this very clearly if you realize that investors and traders are buying stocks at every fraction of a point up and down the scale; and it does not make sense to say that your best policy is to sell at "ten points higher than your cost," or "on an advance of 15%," since then each buyer at a different price would have a different objective, and some indeed would have as their selling point the very price at which you might be buying. The continual reference to a "cost price," especially if it is coupled with an objective based in some way on that cost price, simply leads to a mechanical "system," something like the systems that are hopefully tried out each season against the wheels at Monte Carlo. That kind of system does not lead to success.

We mentioned anxiety as a reason the nervous traders sell out prematurely to take a profit. But the major "fear" may not be fear of monetary loss. It may be something quite different. It may be, in fact you must know from your own experience that it often is, a fear of "not catching the top."

They want "the top" so badly. Superiority; being on the up-and-up; there is so much metaphor in these up-and-down words!

And "the top" is pretty absolute. "Half-way" is not the top. "Eighty per cent" is not the top. It is "either . . . or."

The unhappy part of this reaching for the top is that the nervous trader seldom gets it. He will almost invariably reach out too soon, and pluck his budding profit before it has really blossomed at all.

In a way he will be less badly hurt by taking the profit prematurely than he would if he allowed the gains to run and eventually sold out *after* the top, on the way down.

This should be underscored. He will buy a stock at 26 and sell it at 30, to take a four point profit; and if the stock then advances to 40 he will not feel too seriously injured, for he can comfort his tender ego with the soothing thought, "I realized a good profit; now I don't care where it goes." But one has the feeling that if he *had* continued to hold his stock, saw it go to 40 and then break down to 34, he would not be nearly so happy. For it will be much easier for him to rationalize the taking of the four point profit *on the way up*, than to justify his action in selling *on the way down* even although his profit might be twice as large.

Although profits and losses make up the story of market success and failure, it is probably a good thing not to concentrate on the detailed record of these profits and losses. It is not possible to fret oneself into opulence by torturing some sort of victory or make-believe victory out of every single trade.

What will be far more productive in the end, is to formulate a method of evaluation (which becomes, in effect, a method of prediction), test it, revise it continually as necessary, and then give it your full confidence, letting profits and losses fall where they may.

QUESTIONS FOR CONSIDERATION

Have you felt the strain that often goes with a very profitable stock position, when you wonder, "Should I sell out now, and then perhaps lose a much bigger profit to come?" Does this kind of tension suggest that perhaps you need a basic method or policy so that each decision will not be a new worry to you?

What is it in these cases that lies at the bottom of the anxiety? Is it entirely the money itself? Or would you say it involved the feeling of "having to be right," of having to prove something"?

Have you ever checked the results of your own trading, for say the past three years, from the standpoint of whether your sales in profitable positions were necessary and justified; and whether you might have done better on balance if you had held these positions until you felt they had definitely shown signs of reversal?

Do you know that there are many inexperienced traders who take a profit on a majority of their trades and still lose money on balance? Do you know that there are successful traders who actually take losses on a majority of their commitments and still make a net profit on their total operation?

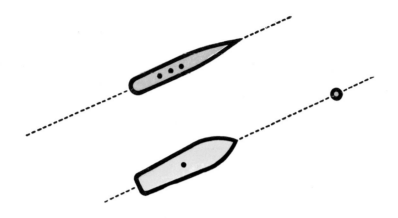

COMMON SENSE CAN BE A PITFALL

SUPPOSE that in some sort of naval maneuvers an oil tanker is ordered to take a course parallel to that of a destroyer, the course to pass through a specified buoy or marker. Common sense tells us that there can be one, and only one course that fills these requirements, since one and only one parallel line can be drawn to a given line, passing through a specified point not on the given line.

We learned this in school. We also learned that parallel lines are lines which never meet, however far extended, and which are in all parts equally distant.

By "line" we meant "straight line." And since a "straight line is the shortest path between two points," we could define a straight line on a surface as the path of a tightly stretched string that lay entirely on that surface.

Now if the captain of the oil tanker has put his ship on the course "parallel" to the destroyer and pointing in the direction of the buoy, we could check the accuracy of his navigation if it were possible to stretch tightly a string along the line of the destroyer's course, and along the tanker's course, and then check whether these lines were in fact "equally distant in all parts." We could do this, at least theoretically, by setting out lines supported by cork floats along each of the courses.

As a matter of fact this will probably not be necessary. For if you consider the matter, you will see that no matter *what* course the tanker sets, it will intersect the course of the destroyer if extended far enough.

You can verify this by marking "straight lines" on an orange; and by "straight lines" we would mean, of course, lines that are the shortest distance between two points; in other words, "great circles." And any two great circles will intersect.

Therefore, there is no such thing as lines being "parallel" on the surface of a sphere. Any two great circles, which are the closest thing to straight lines here, will always intersect.

And so, it is not possible for the tanker to take the course ordered. It cannot be done on the surface of the sea.

Common sense in a case like this would trick a landlubber because he would not realize that the surface of the sea is not a plane, and the laws of Euclidean plane geometry do not apply on any large area of the ocean. He must use a "non-Euclidean" geometry.

So often people will vehemently, angrily insist that what they have learned is "common sense." They will shout at you and snarl at you and tell you that what they believe "stands to reason." And so it does. It stands to reason in terms of the data they have abstracted and the methods they have been taught. But they should realize that there may be some conditions where a new way of looking at things is called for.

Time was when "it stood to reason" that a flying machine couldn't get off the ground. "Common sense," more recently, would show that man couldn't expect to fly faster than the speed of sound, and live. "Common sense" told grandfather to plant his crops only in the light of the full moon. "Common sense" provided and still does provide a good many remedies and health measures, from avoiding drafts and keeping our feet dry to taking daily sun-baths in ultra-violet light.

"Common sense" tells us that the Republican point of view, or the Democratic point of view, as the case may be, will save the country. "Common sense" tells us that negroes are inferior people who cannot "rise" to equality with the Master Race. "Common sense" tells us the way to solve our social and political problems is to turn to the wisdom of our forefathers.

And "common sense" warns us against selling stocks short, *ever*. And against buying stocks which are not earning and paying good dividends. And against trading on margin. "Common sense" tells us "no man ever went broke taking a profit," and leads us to take our profits quickly. "Common sense" suggests that we buy stocks which have declined greatly and are now at their eight-year lows.

In short, "common sense" often seems to approve opinions and actions which do not stand up under scientific examination. What we call "common sense" appears to be a kind of intuition. It is derived, of course, from what we have previously learned; but it often perpetuates obsolete ideas, false theories, superstitions, prejudices, hopes, and desires; in short a hodgepodge of undigested and inadequate concepts.

This of course is not entirely fair. Not all of the opinions that we call "common sense" are faulty, or inadequate, or obsolete. In fact it may be *because* so much of our "common sense" is very good sense and very useful in making valid predictions that a "faulty" common sense can be so very dangerous.

We might compare it to a system of coinage. Where there is only an *occasional* counterfeit, it is likely to sneak unnoticed into circulation.

It is certainly not necessary to reject all that passes as "common sense." But we can avoid losses by testing and checking wherever we can. And as we have suggested before, we can start by asking the questions, "Is that so?" and "How do you know that?"

QUESTIONS FOR CONSIDERATION

Do you feel that your "common sense" must be a collection of "maps" you have learned by observing, reading, or hearing, in the past, and which you have accepted so strongly that they now operate at the unconscious level, requiring no detailed "reasoning" by you?

Are you familiar with the fact that in some perfectly rational and often highly practical mathematical systems the ordinary "common sense" rules, such as the "commutative" and "associative" rules by which we relate numbers in arithmetic or algebra, simply do not apply and are not "valid"?

Is it possible that some of the precepts, rules of conduct, etc. you learned at home, or in school, or at Sunday School, and which seem to be so obviously part of the "eternal verities," may not stand up under close examination in the world as we know it?

Do you think it might pay, when you make a decision because it is "obviously common sense," to take a good hard look at it anyhow, and see whether perhaps you are dealing with an old map, or a faulty map? Does this mean that you expect "all common sense" to turn out to be faulty? Do you have to reject "all" merely because "some" may be out of line with the facts?

Is there any great virtue in refusing to look at the facts to see whether the "common sense" you take for granted really "makes sense"?

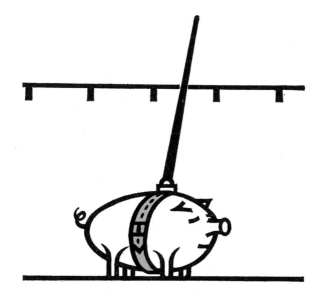

THE PIG-WATCHERS

THIS chapter is utterly mad and I hesitate to bring it into the orbit of this book at all. However, I can do so without too much loss of face by giving full credit to my brother, Beverly Magee, who first outlined this outlandish analogy to me several years ago.

You may be familiar with Wendell Johnson's discussion of "reality" as he presents it in his fine book, "People in Quandaries." He points out that beyond the system of abstractions and symbols which constitute our perception we have no knowledge of "reality." We can explain the "how" of things from what we observe, as we might examine a sealed watch and then construct theories of what was inside of it and what made it go, but we cannot get inside the watchcase of reality and find out "why" and "all about it."

Bev suggested, during a coffee-and-beer session after one of our school evenings, that the "reality" in the market was largely unknown, like most realities. He reviewed the facts that we see only "part" of the "end results" of what is going on, and that while we may abstract some data and come to some valid conclusions that have prediction-value, we are not ever going to know all the details, and we are never going to lay hands on the ultimate "why" of most market phenomena.

"It is like a pig in a barn," he said. "One of these big barns, all closed up on the ground floor, but with a hayloft above, with a large open door.

"On the ground floor there may be various animals, their food, bedding straw, watering troughs, etc.   We have been given to understand that there is a pig in there.   He has a wide leather belt or harness around his body, and on the top of it there is a ball-and-socket joint.   A long pole is attached to this joint; and the pole extends up through a small hole in the center of the ceiling so that the top of the pole is visible through the hayloft door.   The pole comes up through the floor and stands four or five feet high above the surface.

"Now, when the pig moves about, the pole will be moved also. It will move to the left as seen through the hayloft door when the pig moves to the right.   It will move to the right when the pig moves to the left.   It will rise higher from the floor when the pig is near the center of the barn, and it will move lower when the pig goes off to the sides of the barn."

Actually, to us as "pig-watchers," the question of what kind of pig, or what size or color, or for that matter whether it is a pig at all, is not important.   We are perched in a nearby tree watching the motion of the upper part of the pole, the only part we can see, and we are going to make observations and deductions and perhaps predictions concerning the situation below.   Some of the watchers who are not comfortable with highly abstract symbols will assign "meanings" to the pole's movements.   They will try to "interpret" these movements as corresponding to various assimilative, combative, copulative, etc., actions of the pig.   Others, who might consider themselves "pure technicians," will watch the pole, and work entirely on the basis of what the pole has done, is doing, or might be expected to do according to trends, repetitive motions, extrapolations, etc.

This, as we said, is all utterly mad, especially if one adds, as my brother did, that the view into the hayloft is not complete and continuous; for we must assume that all this goes on during a dark and rainy night, so that the end of the pole is observable only from time to time in the intermittent illumination of lightning.

And there was more.   Quite a bit about the shouting crowd of us "speculators" in the tree, betting on each next move of the pole, even selling each other pole sheets and pig forms.

Mad it may be.   But in observing whatever they can of the motions of the visible end of the pole, the pig-watchers are abstracting from a directly visible external reality, at a low level.   They have established certain facts, and from these facts they may be able to come to some valid and useful conclusions. And it could be questioned whether the attempts of others who may try to predict the motions of the pig by reading up on pigs, and by "thinking about" pigs, and by asking their friends how they feel about pigs, and by following the latest statistics on pig production and the visible supply of corn, will, in the end, lead to better predictions.

The technical method in the market is concerned with high level abstractions. We are dealing with "facts" that are already some steps away from the ultimate underlying reality. But we are dealing with facts, and we are dealing with a simple, straightforward body of information, limited as it may be; and what we lose in detail we may gain in not being burdened by the crushing load of extraneous and irrelevant data.

QUESTIONS FOR CONSIDERATION

In studying the market action of a stock is it of vital importance to you to know the color of the directors' hair, the number of acres the factory occupies, or the date of incorporation of the company?

If it is market action you are interested in (and if you are interested in buying or selling the stock it is the market that will determine the prices you pay or receive), isn't it rather more important to watch what the market is doing than to try to understand all the surrounding circumstances?

If the pig-pole makes certain motions in definite series or cycles, is it necessary to know all about the pig in order to correlate and study these past motions, and thus predict the expected motions of the pole?

Do you feel that watching the bare end of a pole in a barn, or watching the motions of a stock as it moves on a chart, is too "cold," too "abstract"? Do you feel you want something more visibly "tangible" to observe?

Are you familiar with the work of engineers, research students in medicine, physicists, and others who deliberately strip from the external realities the particular abstractions that concern them in a certain problem, disregarding extraneous matters, and disregarding the "reasons" that may lie back of the phenomena so far as the problem-at-hand is concerned?

NOTE: The pig used as a model for the illustration in this chapter was not, of course, a flesh-and-blood porker. This pig, actually, was a large piggy-bank, the property of Louisy Magee, who graciously loaned him for this pose.

THE LIMITS OF PREDICTION

SO FAR as the stock market is concerned, the use we will make of all the study and observation we may do is largely to anticipate and predict the probable future course of market values. To a very large degree the value of all study and experience in any of life's activities is a matter of predicting probable future events. Certainly all planning, anticipating, budgeting, organizing, preparing, etc. relates to the future and involves considerable prediction or expectation of things to come.

There is not space in this study to go into the detail of technical market analysis which is one of the methods of market prediction, and the one with which I am most familiar. This subject has been taken up in some detail in another volume, "Technical Analysis of Stock Trends" by Robert D. Edwards and John Magee.

However, in a few words, one could say that the technical method, like any method of prediction, involves looking at the past, checking whether the present conditions are greatly different and if so making allowances for the differences, and then making certain conclusions based on these studies, as to what seems most likely to happen in the future.

This is not a particularly mysterious process although in its details it may involve a tremendous amount of sheer labor. The principles involved are simple enough.

For example, if I have the past record of a series of numbers and the series runs as follows; 7, 7, 7, 7, 7, 7, 7, 7; and the present term of the series is 7, I would predict, with some confidence that the next (future) term will be 7.

If the past series runs; 3, 4, 5, 6, 7, 8, 9, 10; and the present term of the series is 11, I would predict that the next term will be 12.

If the past series runs; 3, 6, 12, 24, 48, 96, and the present term is 192, I would predict that the next term will be 384.

Depending on the total picture one has, one may look for a continuation of a constant number, or an arithmetic progression, a geometric progression, an exponential progression, a cyclic or wave-like rhythm, or any form that seems to fit the past and present facts, projected in the future, as if we were continuing some sort of "orderly" pattern.

The trick, of course, is to find the "orderly pattern," which may not be a simple function but may be a combination of several quite different functions.

Also, one must be careful not to let one's enthusiasm run wild to a point where one "sees" patterns and rhythms where none actually exist.

And of course it is necessary to be on guard all the time against the various "pitfalls" we have discussed, the prejudices and attitudes that are so ingrained in us that they may distort our vision and "slant" our evaluation.

It is because these "ingrained" opinions are so deeply a part of our value systems that they can be so damaging if they are distorting our perception of the facts. That may be why it is almost impossible to "learn" stock trading or commodity trading solely from reading a book or attending a class. It requires days, weeks, months, sometimes years of personal close observation and experience to implement the reading or the classroom study. It takes that time and that experience to revise the old and sometimes faulty concepts. For they are not going to erase themselves or amend themselves just on the strength of your intellectual acceptance of a new viewpoint alone. The new ideas must be developed until they become the "habitual" responses.

One of the "old" tendencies that can be a dangerous pitfall is to predict in terms of a change in the Major trend. This probably comes out of a whole complicated evaluation in which we appraise a stock according to certain "fundamental" facts about the company it represents. Such an attitude can lead to a frame of mind where any considerable advance in the price of a stock leads to a certain habitual response; namely that the stock is "over-valued" in the market. The conclusion, of course, is that eventually the stock will "find its 'true' value"; and the prediction from all of this will be that the stock should be sold.

The same situation in reverse occurs when a stock has declined sharply. The tendency is to "feel" that the stock "is priced too low," is "under-valued," "can't go much lower," etc. And, these reactions lead to a prediction that the stock will shortly advance in price, and therefore that it should be bought.

Sometimes this type of prediction (that the trend will reverse itself) will be confirmed in the future action of the stock. However, before pinning too much confidence in this particular method it would be well to check the record of past predictions made on this basis. You may find that it is much harder than you thought to predict even approximately when or where the turning point will come.

For myself, I would prefer to make exactly the opposite prediction. If I had only the choice of predicting a *reversal* of the Major trend, or a *continuation* of the Major trend, I would have to choose the continuation. As Robert D. Edwards has put it, I would agree that "A trend should be assumed to continue in effect until such time as its reversal has been definitely signaled."

However, what we are talking about here is not the detail of prediction, not the application of technical methods. It is something much more basic; the limits of prediction. If you consider the question of whether the trend or direction of a stock's price should be predicted in the expectation of a reversal of the Major trend, or in the expectation of a continuation, you will see that we are once again talking about an "either . . . or" situation. And, wherever we can, we try to frame the problem so that we can change the "either . . . or" into a matter of *degree*. Then we will be able to answer the question in several, or many, ways, and not in just two ways.

Sometimes, as in this case, we cannot exactly change the "either . . . or" question to one of degree; but we can do something that serves much the same purpose. We can reduce it to a "probability."

If you say U. S. Rubber is "going to go up," and I say U. S. Rubber is "going to go down," then in a month or after whatever time we agree on, you can take a look at it, and say, "You were right," or "I was right." If the stock has gone up you would be *right*, in this situation; and if it has gone down, then I would be *right*.

And this, again, is the two-valued situation, the "either . . . or." Which is what we are trying to avoid.

You see, in this view, if your predictive method is "right" it will give you the "right" result. If the stock goes up in price, then you are "right," and your prediction is "right," and your predictive method is "right." But if the stock goes down, then you are "wrong," your prediction is "wrong," and your predictive method is "wrong."

This leads to trouble. You might be quite "right" about U. S. Rubber this month. You might be "right" about Granite City Steel next month. And about Northern Pacific the following month. But sooner or later you will be "wrong" on one. This, almost by definition, makes your method itself "wrong," at least in that particular case. It either discredits your method entirely, or it casts a shadow and a doubt on it. At the very least it destroys your confidence.

(And let me interrupt here to suggest that you consider for a moment *other* kinds of prediction, outside of the market. You will see how this same failure and demoralization can occur wherever you attempt to set up a "perfect" "either . . . or" predictive method.)

But we don't have to do it in a two-valued, absolute way! We can recognize certain limits of predictive expectation in terms of probabilities; and then we will not continually be afraid to use our method because of our lack of confidence in it. We will not be expecting more from our method than we can reasonably hope for. And we will not be basing our method on a few accidental "successes."

Is this clear? Do you see that a very stupid method of prediction (such as betting even money that one can draw a Spade from an ordinary deck of cards) could at times produce a succession of "wins." If you should see someone make such a bet over and over again, would you feel it was a "right" method of prediction; even if he won eight times in succession?

Or, to put it another way; suppose you were to have the chance of betting even money you would *not* draw a Spade from the deck. Every time you drew a Heart or a Diamond, or a Club you would win. Only when you drew a Spade would you lose.

Under these conditions, if you were to lose several times in a row on this bet, would you discard your method as "wrong"? Would you *reverse* your method and bet that you *would* draw a Spade, merely because of a run of luck against you?

Isn't is possible to say that, providing the deck of cards is an honest one, containing the usual cards and properly shuffled, it makes *no difference* how many times you "win" or how many times you "lose." This does not affect the "rightness" or "wrongness" of your method of evaluation. And your best policy is to continue to use your evaluative method so long as you are convinced that it is based on adequate data and valid reasoning.

Of course you know this. You know this from what you have previously abstracted from your experience in drawing cards from decks. It seems terribly redundant to have to go through this long discussion of something (perhaps an elephant stuck in your front entry) so obvious, so plain. You know that neither the roulette croupier nor the owners of the casino care very much whether you or any other player wins or loses. If the casino's bank is well-heeled, the "method of evaluation" will wear down the string of luck or the "system" of any roulette player, as every professional gambler knows. And the method of evaluation used by the professional gambler is *not* based on being "absolutely right" on any particular play or series of plays, but on a prediction as to the "most probable outcome of a long series of plays taken as a whole."

Then why is it that so many people either have no real evaluative method at all, or follow one which represents so little first-hand checking and verifying that it may be worse than useless? Could it be that because they are so deeply trained in "either . . . or" and "right and wrong" they cannot habituate themselves to a method based on *uncertainty?*

If we know that on the basis of past experience and in view of the present outlook we may expect to "win seven times out of ten, in an even-money series of bets," we can accept this seven-out-of-ten probability as something akin to what would be a "measure" or "degree" in some other types of problem. With certain reservations and precautions we can accept this as the measure of our expectation; and by continually re-checking and verifying we can adjust and refine this until it becomes a highly dependable tool so long as the basic conditions of the contest do not change materially.

We can operate on this basis with considerable confidence. And with this foundation for our confidence we will not "need to be right" all the time.

Think what this means? Consider the nights you have lain awake and worried about what "the market" would do tomorrow, or whether "XYZ" would go up or down before the end of the week. You will not be able to eliminate *all* anxiety about the market. But you will be able to reduce greatly the amount of your tension and worry since you will not feel threatened with a "total failure" of your method every time a stock moves a point or so "against" you.

What we have done here is to set some limits on the predictive science. The average man seems to recognize no limits whatever. What he so often seeks and demands is an *infallible* method of reading the future. And he is so sure that, if he only keeps trying and searching, he will come up with the "right" method, that charlatans mulct him of millions of dollars every year by supplying spurious "perfect systems." (And this also is true in many other streets besides Wall Street.)

We have set limits. We have stopped short of the "100%" upper limit, representing infallibility, and we have set our goal considerably above the "0" of the thoroughly discouraged cynic who feels it is "all just luck."

By observing the results of a method as applied in the past, and noting the number of successes and failures, we can gauge the (past) success of the method. We can then project these results into the future as a probability, and say, "I believe, on the basis of the past records, this method will probably produce an average net return of between 20% and 30% per year."

That statement isn't nearly positive enough to satisfy the man trained to think in absolute terms. Neither is the expected return anywhere near as large as such a man would expect (on the basis that he will be "always right"). Neither is it definite enough; for the man we are speaking of does not think in terms of "somewhere between." He wants it right out plain and sharp.

Of course the chances of our being "totally defeated" are much less than his. But for him it is necessary to "reach the top" and that means shooting at nothing short of perfection.

QUESTIONS FOR CONSIDERATION

Do you expect a fortune teller to tell you that, "In view of the overall situation and the probabilities, you might expect perhaps to meet someone friendly to you who had a good deal of money"? Or would you expect something more like, "In three weeks you will meet a tall dark millionaire, who will fall madly in love with you"? Which prediction seems to carry more assurance? Which seems more positive and more specific? Which one is probably the better prediction?

If you should consult an eminent medical specialist would you expect him to give you a prognosis in absolutely definite, positive terms? Or would you consider that with the best information he can get, his opinion will be tentative, stated cautiously, and without too specific predictions? What would you think of a doctor who told you that "You will die in six weeks unless you get treatment, but I can cure you in three weeks?" Doesn't the charlatan capitalize on the insecurity of frightened patients by giving them assurance in very authoritative terms? Would you consider this a good predictive method? Do you think, in the end, this operates to the best interests of the patients?

When you see a stock adviser advertising that "This Bull Market will reach 800 in the Dow Jones Industrial Averages before the end of the year," would you feel that this was a considered and scientific prediction? Or would you put it down as a typical charlatan's come-on designed to give you a false sense of security? Do you expect a financial analyst to "know all the answers" about the future? Or do you look for a reasonably correct estimate of the probable developments most of the time? Which kind of counsellor would you feel is more likely to be of most value to you in protecting and enhancing your capital?

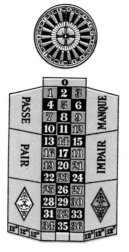

IS THE MARKET A "GAME"?

WE HAVE spoken of flipping coins and drawing cards in connection with predictive methods. We have mentioned "bets" on the outcome of these operations.

Since what we are interested in is the development of predictive methods that can be applied to market situations, the question arises, "Is the market, then, simply a gambling game?"

If by a "gambling game" we mean a contest in which the sole purpose is the gaming itself, and in which the result is determined largely by "luck," then the market is not "simply a gambling game." Under the conditions of fairly free competition which is an essential part of the democratic way of life as we know it, we must have some means of determining the exchange value of goods and money. The market is the means of this evaluation.

It does, however, have some of the features we associate with gambling. It involves "winnings" and "losings," although it is certainly not "merely" the transfer of gains and losses from one participant to another as in a poker game since it is tied up with many basic economic and monetary factors. If one regarded the market as a "poker game" one of several factors he would have to consider is that it is a game in which the value of the chips is continually changing. Viewed as a game it is more like poker than it is like shooting craps or tossing coins, since it involves not only "pure luck," but a considerable degree of strategy.

But where a crap game, or a poker game, or a horse race serves no

381

"real" purpose other than to provide a means for gambling (leaving out the somewhat thin claim that horse racing contributes to "the improvement of the breed"), the gambling aspect of the market is incidental to its evaluative function, just as the gambling element in insurance is incidental to its protective purpose.

But there is another sense in which the market can be considered a "game." The word has been used to designate any situation in which a stake is put at risk on the outcome of a future event. This would include not only all pure gambling games, but also any speculative business enterprises, such as the opening of a store, the purchase of a stock of materials, the agreement to perform certain work according to the terms of a contract and within a definite time limit. The term "game," in this sense, would also involve other questions where future events may decide the outcome of a present decision. For example, it could be considered "a game" whether to buy personal liability insurance or to take one's chances without it. Or whether to go into business after gaining a B.A. degree or continue one's studies toward an M.A.

We could even consider some situations as "games" where the stake to be put at risk was not expressed in money or goods, though we are not going to go into these fields in detail here. But you know that the game-like problems of evaluating the probable future are present in almost every decision of life. We sometimes speak of "the game of love," and certainly the weighing of values between solitary independence and the mingled joys and burdens of a shared life has something of the nature of a "game." Even in questions of ethics and morals, there is a game-like element of prediction and of evaluation. For example; what might be the expected advantages and disadvantages of attempting to cut down a rival for an important job; including one's possible monetary gain, increase of importance in the company, etc., on the one hand, and contempt for one's self and feelings of guilt on the other. It would be interesting to frame a number of such situations in terms of "game problems," but that is beyond the scope of this book.

In the sense in which "games" are being studied there is a stake, not necessarily monetary, which is risked against certain known or unknown odds, and against certain known, or unknown, or *partially* known strategy. Such games would include various forms of gambling; they would include markets, insurance operations, military and naval campaigns, and a great many problems that come up in engineering, sociology, medicine, and many other fields.

In going into such a game there are three principal factors to be studied.

1. The purely mathematical odds.
2. The "strategy" of your opponent, who may be a person, a group, or "nature."
3. The payoff on each of the available choices.

QUESTIONS FOR CONSIDERATION

Do you consider "tennis," "golf," "draw poker," "contract bridge," etc. to be games? Do you see how "politics," "a love affair," "setting up a new business," and "the market," have some of the same characteristics as games? (Suggestion: these situations cover certain campaigns involving strategy, uncertainty, imperfect information, etc., and in which these factors must be evaluated in order to make predictions that will result in the greatest overall probability of the most generally advantageous expectations for the player.)

Would you say that a great many, perhaps a majority of the decisions one has to make involve some of these "game" features?

In view of the complexity of many life problems would you expect that it is always possible to resolve these questions to a perfectly definite and complete mathematical formula? Is it possible, however, that "half a loaf is better than none" and that some consideration of the various elements of a problem, seen as a "game," might be of practical help in arriving at a decision likely to produce a satisfactory result?

THE PURELY MATHEMATICAL ODDS

IF SOMEONE produces a pair of dice and sets one of them on the table in front of you, what predictions can you make about the result of a toss?

If you assume that the die is honest and that all faces are as nearly alike as they can be made you would not be able to favor the chances of one side coming up over any other; so by a sort of negative reasoning you would be forced to give each of the six sides an equal chance and you would probably say "the chances of throwing any particular number (from one to six) is one out of six; and the 'correct' odds for a bet on any selected number should be five-to-one." This would mean that your best prediction would be that if repeated bets were made on a single number at five-to-one odds, the net result would tend to be fairly even; neither you nor your opponent would have an "expectation of advantage."

If you chose two numbers, the chances of throwing one of the two in a single throw of the die would be predicted at one out of three, and the correct odds to make the game even would be two-to-one. If you chose three numbers, the expectation would be one "win" out of two throws, and the odds for an even game would be one-to-one, or even money.

Any of these three situations is what has been called a "fair" game; that is to say neither you nor your opponent have any predictable advantage.

In such a game the result must be "pure luck" on any throw.   No

384

positive or absolute prediction as to the outcome of the next throw will be valid. But the expectations are even, meaning that since it is not possible to give one number a specific higher expectation than any other, we must assume the chances are equal for each.

This does not mean, however, that the results will actually be "even," for although it is not possible to predict which player in a "fair" game of pure luck will come out ahead, the chances are very high that one will win and one will lose, and it may be definitely predicted that there will be "runs of luck" of various degree.

The more throws that are made the smaller will be the expected difference between the winner's hoard and the loser's in *terms of the percentage of the total* money wagered. But the difference *in terms of number of dollars* may be expected to increase. And with a greater number of throws we may expect a greater number of "runs" of four "wins" in a row, five "wins" in a row, etc. Also with more throws we may expect to encounter a longer *maximum* "run," say a run of fifteen "wins" in a row, or twenty "wins" in a row. And the distribution of these differences and these "runs" can be plotted in terms of expectancy and distribution.

It is not our intenton to go very deeply into probability studies here. But there are one or two important points that can apply to dealings in markets and in other problems of life.

One is that it is not good tactics to enter a game situation in which pure chance is the major factor, and in which the expectation of winning is less than even.

Thus, with the single die we would make a single number bet if we were given odds of six-to-one; we would be "indifferent" to such a bet with odds of five-to-one, and we would not make any bet if we were offered odds of four-to-one or less.

Furthermore, we would have a clear understanding that even with the favorable odds of six-to-one, we might experience a "run" of "bad luck" in which we could lose many times in succession; and while this would not affect the validity of our decision to play, it could deplete our capital or wipe us out entirely unless we took steps to protect ourself.

It is this particular "trap" that has caused the downfall of so many players in games like Red Dog, where a player holding say, an Ace of Spades, Ace of Hearts, King of Diamonds and King of Clubs, could be beaten only if the next card turned happened to be the Ace of

Diamonds or Ace of Clubs.   Any other card would give him a "win,"
and if, as sometimes happens in Red Dog, the pot was enormously
swollen, the player might be tempted to bet the entire pot, perhaps
hundreds or even thousands of dollars on the "nearly sure thing."
This would be a case where the mathematical odds of winning were
overwhelmingly in the player's favor; and yet it might be bad tactics
for him to risk perhaps a year's pay on the outcome of what is still an
"unknown" future event.   Many a Red Dog player has rushed in to
such a play to his sorrow, not realizing that in spite of extraordinarily
good odds, the one-to-twenty-three chance of ruin is too large to
justify risking "everything."

We would safely make a bet of any amount, we could stake everything we owned and our life itself that two of the Navy's rocket
satellites will not collide in outer space.   That is of a degree of improbability that "approaches the infinite."   But you cannot, without proper safeguards which we will discuss a few chapters further
along, risk your entire fortune on "just a little better than even odds"
or even "a good deal better than even odds."

There is one point we did not even consider in connection with the
die.   Before it is thrown we can look it over as it lies on the table.
But we have no way of telling whether it is actually an honest die.
It might be weighted somehow inside, so as to favor one number and
make that number come up more often than the others.   Suppose
that we were told by a trustworthy informant that the die was loaded
in this way; but we were not told which number would be favored by
the loading.

In this case we would know before the die was thrown that the
expectation for each of the sides was not "equal."   We could no
longer make the prediction that "the chances" were the same for
each number, for we would know that they were definitely *not* the
same and that in a long series of throws one of the numbers would
tend to pile up a much larger number of "hits" than the others.

However, in this case (not knowing the favored number) we
would not be any better off than in the first case where presumably
the die was fair and all numbers had an equal expectation.   For we
could not assign the higher expectation, which we know will apply
for one of the numbers, to any particular one.   Therefore, if we are
required to lay out our tactics and place our bets in advance we would
have to proceed "as if" each of the numbers had an equal expectation.

It would be a perfectly justifiable assumption under these conditions, and would give us the chance to make the best "plan" possible with the data we had.

As soon as the die is actually thrown, however, we can begin to collect "statistical" information to supplement the "theoretical" predictions we had made. If the die is a "fair" one, we will find that after a number of throws have been made the distribution pattern will begin to show the *tendency* for the numbers to come up in approximately equal ratios; and the deviations from equal distribution will show "normal" variations. Given a large number of throws a trained statistician could detect the effect of any loading, not only as to which was the favored number, but to what *degree* this number was favored.

Thus we can take our theoretical "guess" (this is a high abstraction) and use it as a prediction. But as the play progresses we can take the *actual observed results* (and these are abstractions of much lower order), and feed them back in order to check, and if necessary correct our original "guess." In this way we have a continually self-adjusting predictive method; and this is the process we outlined some chapters previously as the basic method of evaluation.

And so, even in matters of "pure luck," such as the drawing of cards, the turn of a roulette wheel, or the toss of a die, we do not need to depend wholly on what we have concluded by logical deduction, nor by what we have been told or what we have read; for by using our experience as it unfolds to give us a statistical check, we can correct our appraisals to take care of any error or omission in the original theory, or to allow for new or changed conditions.

QUESTIONS FOR CONSIDERATION

If Lucky Joe has flipped a coin and has come up with Heads seven times in a row, would you give better than even money against his getting Heads on the next toss? Would you give better than even money that he *would* get Heads on the next throw? Would you feel that his past records, assuming that the coin is "fair" and that the toss itself was also "fair," had any significant bearing on the *next* toss?

Suppose you are allowed to reach into a box and draw out a numbered card. If it has an even number you win $1. If it is an odd number you lose $1. What are the odds; that is, what is your "expectation"? Would you be willing to risk $1 on this game? Would you be willing to play if the ante were raised to $1000? If the odds are the same, then what is the essential difference between these two situations. Would you be as willing to enter the second contest as the first, and if not why not? Is it enough, merely to know the mathematical odds in a "game"?

Do you see a basic difference between drawing cards from a deck, one at a time, until the deck is exhausted; and drawing a single card and then shuffling it back into the deck and drawing again?

Do you feel that there are basic differences between predictions that relate to events that can be or have been repeated many times, and those relating to events that cannot be repeated at will or are unique?

What processes seem to go on in your mind when you have to "weigh the probabilities" in a situation?

THE STRATEGY OF YOUR OPPONENT

B Y "STRATEGY" we do not mean doctoring the dice or marking the cards. We mean a considered plan of action within the "rules" of a game or contest by which one opponent pits his intelligence against another's.

In the case of flipping coins, tossing dice, drawing cards, etc. there is no "strategy" in this sense. The game is decided in terms of the odds, and of course, on the outcome of the flip, toss, or draw, which would be a matter of "pure chance."

There has been a vast amount of study put into "systems" of winning against games of pure chance, usually games in which the odds or payoff are loaded against the player to start with. It is true that even in a "loaded" game such as the commercial games in any gambling casino, where the house takes a constant percentage, the outsider sometimes wins quite heavily and for an extended period of time. But except for these fortuitous runs of luck, the "system player" in such games usually comes out poorer than he went in; and no one yet has devised a "system" that will ensure an expectation of winning against such games.

In the games of "pure chance," whether or not they are loaded against the outside player, it is possible to make a reasonable estimate of the mathematical probabilities as well as the normal random deviations to be expected from the "ideal" distributions. And once you have made these estimates there isn't anything *you* can do by "planning" to increase the mathematical expectation of winning.

But the situation is quite different when we come to games of "strategy." These games may or may not involve "pure chance" as a factor. But they also involve, as a rule, the intelligent planning of an opponent. This complicates things enormously.

The game of Paper, Scissors, and Stone is a case where "pure chance" doesn't enter at all. Scissors can cut Paper, Stone can break Scissors, and Paper can wrap up Stone. Therefore Scissors "win" over Paper, Stone over Scissors, and Paper over Stone. If your opponent chooses Paper and you choose Scissors, you win. If he chooses Scissors and you choose Paper, he wins. If he chooses Paper and you choose Stone, he wins. Since each choice is made simultaneously, it becomes a contest in which each tries to "read the other's mind."

Poker, on the other hand, is a game which combines "pure chance" as represented by the deal and the draw of the cards, *plus* the planning of a campaign in which the opponent tries to "read your mind" and if possible to mislead you into *mis*-reading *his* mind.

Poker is a type of game that can be used as a sort of simplified map (an abstraction) of certain other types of contest. Or rather, certain aspects of the game of poker are similar to some aspects of other kinds of contest. For this reason poker provides a good analogy for clinical study where the "game" we may be interested in might be something far more complex, such as the market.

You may not recognize the stock market or the commodity market as very close counterparts of the game of poker. And in truth they are not very close counterparts. Neither is a guinea pig a close counterpart to a man, but the guinea pig can be used to study certain physical conditions which may have similarities to those in men. For that matter a water pipe is not very much like an electric wire, but it sometimes helps in teaching elementary science classes to understand how electricity on a wire acts, in some ways, like water in a pipe.

You may not recognize in the market your "opponent" in the contest or game. Keeping in mind what we said about this analogy being a generality it may not surprise you to know that "the opponent" is not ordinarily to be considered the person from whom you buy stock or to whom you sell it, nor even the "class" of those who buy and sell stocks. Your opponent in this case is "the market itself." It is not specific and certainly not personalized. You are playing in this contest against a high abstraction rather than "a person" or "people." Like playing a game of tennis against a high cement wall.

While many games of strategy do involve human opponents in situations very much like a poker game (as in an auction, at a directors' meeting, in election campaigns, etc.), there are many other "games," especially in scientific and economic work where the opponent is so vaguely defined that he appears mainly as "the other side of your transactions." In such a "game" your "winnings" or "losings" would not be transferred from the opponent's tank into yours (assuming the unit of value in the game was measured as a liquid), but you might consider that your "winnings" were pumped into your measuring tank from a large lake, and your "losses" drained from your tank back into the lake. You would be measuring the degree of your success or failure not in terms of the gains or losses of a particular other person, but as affecting you only, the "opponent" being considered to be an infinite "bank."

In such cases, we could speak of our opponent as "nature." This is not a very good choice of a word, but since we have explained what is meant, you will understand.

Thus, if I were to buy 5000 shares of Central Violeta Sugar, I could consider not only the effect of the acquisition on me and my affairs, but also the effect of my purchase on the "floating supply" of the stock. But if I were to buy 5000 shares of General Motors, while this might have a large effect on my own affairs, the reducing of the "floating supply" in "GM" would not have any visible effect. This is because, unlike a "thin" stock such as Central Violeta Sugar, there is a tremendous "lake" or floating supply of shares in General Motors.

Similarly, when you are buying a very "thin" commodity you must consider not only your own side of the transactions, but its effect on the "supply side"; but if you should be buying one of the big commodities like Wheat you would be dealing with a supply so vast that your purchases could have no substantial effect on it.

And since, in general, we avoid the "thin" situations where even a moderate amount of trading tends to create severe strains in the supply-demand balance, we will normally be dealing with stocks and commodities that do not have the specific "human" quality of a personal contest.

There are traders today, and there have been many in the past, who enjoy the matching of wits in what amounts to a man-to-man contest. Very often market commentators, market advisers, or investment brokers will promote and feature some situation where a very small number of shares of a stock may be available; a small issue, an issue in which many shares are tied up or closely held; a situation in which the key to the problem is a policy of inter-personal strategy.

This is quite different from the cases where the supply is so large as to be virtually unlimited. The whole strategic problem becomes quite different when it is possible to buy or sell in any amount at any time without visibly affecting the market.

Actually, of course, *any* purchase or *any* sale, however small, is going to have some effect on the supply, just as taking a teaspoonful of water from the ocean will, to some degree, lower the level of that ocean. And it is also true that under certain conditions of panic or boom the status of even the large stocks can be affected. For instance, if a popular radio commentator were to tout a particular stock, even a fairly large issue, he could temporarily distort the normal "supply reservoir" by creating an artificial demand.

But in the main, where we are dealing with the important stocks listed on the big exchanges, we can assume that our transactions will not materially affect the supply. We can assume that for all practical purposes it is "unlimited," and we can assume a certain continuity and stability to that supply. We can consider it, collectively as a unit, "as if" *it* were an opponent in the "game" of our market operation; and we can assign certain habits and characteristics to "it" and deal with it "as if" it were, in a sense, a person.

This does not eliminate the need for strategy on our part. "The supply" of the stock, or the "open interest" of a commodity is not really a personality; but it can be considered to represent the collective personalities of all of those who are concerned with it.

We have set up an imaginary "person" who combines the hopes and fears and expectations of all the individuals who are involved in the stock or the commodity. It is, in a way, as though the stockholders or commodity traders had elected in a democratic way a representative or champion to handle their interests.

And it is this imaginary person who faces us across the table as our "opponent."

During the past ten years a great deal of research has been done on "Game Theory." This subject has tremendous implications in military and scientific work. Much of this theory involves new and difficult mathematics. Fortunately some of the basic principles are not too hard to understand, and have practical applications in stock and commodity market study.

Pure "probability mechanics" are not enough when you are dealing with strategy situations, which these are, where underneath all the vast complexities of the seething markets there lie the intelligent plans and tactics of individual human beings. In collectivizing them all as an abstraction we must not lose track of the fact that the problem still involves matters of human intelligences competitively engaged in a contest of evaluation. And there is a great deal more to this than "pure chance."

QUESTIONS FOR CONSIDERATION

Are you fully aware that where a "game" is not a matter of "pure luck" a great deal depends on what your opponent decides to do?

If your opponent has, to some extent, "figured out" your own strategy, or anticipated what he feels you would do to promote your own interest, wouldn't you assume that he will use this belief to plan his own strategy so as to defeat you and ensure a "win" for himself?

Can you assume that your opponent is so stupid that he will not be able to figure out your strategy or part of your strategy?

Suppose, then, you assume that your opponent has indeed figured out your strategy. Can you plan your own moves in such a way that even if he makes the most effective plays against you, you will be protected to the greatest possible extent?

Would it make any difference, from your own point of view, whether you were operating in a "game" where your opponent was an individual, a coalition, a team, an aggregation, or a large impersonal opponent which you might designate "the market," or "society," or "nature"? Would you not still have the problem of determining your course of action so as to defend yourself most effectively against whatever counterplays might occur against you?

Which is more important to you: To "win," or "to protect yourself from total loss"?

THE PAYOFF

YOU remember when radio giveaways started. First it was a box of soap flakes. Then it was a fur coat. Pretty soon the sponsors were offering trips to Bermuda or Hawaii, then cash prizes and bigger cash prizes, and then as the TV age came into its own, great bundles of big money, with Cadillac convertibles to the losers for consolation prizes. What more could anyone ask? Big, showy prizes, lots of money, and no work. Something for nothing in a big way.

Lotteries have always been popular. In some countries a few pennies will get you a chance to win a huge fortune. Not much of a chance, but something to pin one's dreamiest hopes to, especially if one needs so badly to dream and has so very little in reality.

We have lotteries in the United States, too. At least I suppose you can still go into a cigar store or lunch room and buy a ticket on the treasury balance or the day's take at Pimlico and on the remote chance that your number, in full, might come up, your fifty cents stands to win you five thousand dollars. And we have "The Numbers" for the very poor and very stupid.

No! Stupid is too strong a word. Uninformed, yes. Ignorant of the true odds against them, yes. But when you are low enough in the economic peck-order you *need* something to buck up your frustrated spirits. It is the old story; a man's self-esteem is his most valuable possession; and while he may be on half-time at the shop and have a sick wife at home, if he carries in his pocket the magic Number that *might* produce the big payoff this very afternoon, who

394

can say that he is not getting full value for his money? What price self-esteem?

Whether a "game" is a matter of pure chance or involves strategy angles, you will find that most people will look for the big payoff. After all the big prize is not the money. It is the winning of it. It is blowing it in and the feeling of "being on top" of things. It is telling the neighbors about winning the Chevrolet grand prize at the Beano game. It is that feeling that "I *do* amount to something after all," that counts.

If it were not for that it would be hard to explain why people do play gambling games. Most often they cannot "afford" to play them, in terms of ordinary "common-sense" economics. The odds in all commercial gambling schemes are shamelessly loaded against the customers.

But they don't seem to care much about the odds. This may not be entirely because they don't understand or can't figure the odds. It is more that they don't seem interested. As if the odds were not really the most important angle. And psychologically, from their own point of view, perhaps they *are not* so important.

What does seem important is to "maximize" one's gains. It is not much fun to play the odds-on favorite. Not much of a victory to take a small niggling profit on what is almost a sure thing. This is not going to soothe anybody's aching ego. What will make the skies light up and the bells to ring, is to walk up to the window with a fifty dollar win on a two dollar ticket. It's the long shots that pay off in thrills and satisfaction. It's the big payoff that you can talk up at the bar.

Not because you need the money! But because it shows how "right" you were. A very smart Joe! Picks 'em right! Not just lucky: cagey, too!

This all involves . . . well, it involves a good many of the faulty or absolute evaluations we have analyzed before. The need to be "right" is evidence of the "either . . . or" dichotomy in action. The acceptance of a money prize, whether earned or merely the result of pure chance, as a sign of importance and success. The general attitude of inferiority. The inability to evaluate the real chances of winning, and of course, the extreme view that the biggest prize is the only one worth going for.

People like big payoffs. One of the most typical human traits in market operations, or for that matter in any "game" operation, is the desire to "make a killing." Unfortunately it is too often the player himself who gets "killed."

Just how far people can go in pursuing the payoff regardless of consequences appears in the almost daily headlines reporting the passing of some poor devil who tried his hand at the good old game of Russian Roulette. We don't know the details of the wagers involved in these games, but whether the nominal prize was measured in hundreds of dollars or in thousands, it seems clear that the *real* prize was something else. For a man does not bet his life against a hundred dollars or against ten thousand dollars; not even at five-to-one odds. The *real* prize must appear to be vastly more valuable.

And the only prize that could warrant the risking of life itself in a deliberate wager would be the preservation or enhancement of self-esteem.

So the real expected payoff in a game of Russian roulette is not the stake that lies on the table, but the intangible payoff of glorifying the ego. And a man with an adequate feeling of security and self-esteem would not *need* to take such desperate measures to win such a prize. This is the psycho-pathology of the gambler in which money, property, even life itself are wagered against an intangible abstraction.

The whole viewpoint of the habitual gambler (and in this sense we must now include a good many of the market traders) is defensive. He is trying to bolster up his finances and his self-esteem. Too often he succeeds in doing neither. Worse than that; the very methods by which he tries to help himself contribute to his further demoralization.

If he were able to stand back away from himself and look at himself from a distance as if he were someone else, he might see that he would have a lot more to talk about and feel good about if he could protect and build up a solid backlog, than he can by "plunging" for the big payoff . . . even if he should *win*. For one thing, if he could somewhat reduce his demands to be "top dog," he might be able to settle for something less than the top payoff without feeling humiliated.

But as things are he is not willing, in fact he is not able, to make any compromises. You cannot talk with him about "safety" of principal because his whole idea of "the game" (whatever game it may be) is to plunge, and plunge, and plunge, and hope that he doesn't get wiped out, and hope that he will make the big killing.

Since we cannot reach *him* in his present frame of mind, let *us* talk over the problem a bit.

Suppose we forget the big payoff for a moment, and consider the other side of the picture entirely. Not how much you are going to win *if* you win. But how much you stand to lose *if* you lose. You will certainly agree that you expect sometimes to lose, and, of course, you hope sometimes to win.

If the game is one of pure chance and if the probabilities are heavily loaded against you, wouldn't it be a good idea not to get into it at all? Not unless (without kidding yourself) you can go into the game just for the fun of it, playing pennies or nickels or dimes, and not caring whether you win or lose. Certainly you are not going to buck a percentage game that is unbeatable on the long term, with any sizable amount of money, regardless of how big the top payoff may be.

But if the game is one where strategy enters into it materially, you may feel that you can cope with your opponent on his own terms. You may feel that you can out-smart him.

Assuming that the mathematical odds are not so heavily against you that your strategy would not have much chance, figure out what strategies you might use.

And then consider the various courses you might take, and then put yourself in your opponent's shoes to see what he could do to you in each case. You may find that his *best* reply to certain of your available plays could be extremely damaging to you. In certain other plays you might make, the very *worst* he could do to you would not cause you too serious a loss.

True, in these latter cases you might not stand to win the biggest payoff. But if you plan out and carry through a strategy that will make sure that your losses are held to a minimum *regardless* of how intelligently your opponent attacks you, your winnings may ultimately amount to more than you could expect by shooting continually for the "Big" payoff.

In theory and in actual application this process of evaluating a "game situation" is rather complicated. It is not possible here to go into the details of it. As a matter of fact it is not necessary to go into great detail, for if you can simply grasp the big fact that the big payoff is not always the most profitable goal in the long run; and the fact that before counting unhatched profits one should allow for the possibility of the most serious loss that may be incurred; then you will have the rough outline of a most practical method of dealing with strategy problems.

QUESTIONS FOR CONSIDERATION

When you play a pinball game or a beano game, or take a chance on a Pontiac sedan, do you feel that you are entering a contest in which you have a "fair" chance? Then why do you do this, beyond the natural desire to help some worthy charitable cause? Do you realize to what extent the "odds" are loaded against you?

Why will so many people venture a small amount in a big lottery; for example, why will they risk a nickel or a dime in a drawing where they may win $100,000? Would you say the mathematical odds are likely to be "fair" in such a game? Would you feel that these people are entirely foolish, or that they cannot in any way justify their need to gamble for the big payoff? What is it worth to feel that for a small sum one has a ticket on romance, and fame, and wealth, and Success? Is it barely possible that certain sinister operators take advantage of these great needs and feather their own nests exceedingly softly thereby?

Is there some essential difference between venturing a nickel at a lawn party in the hope of a big payoff (Pontiac sedan), and laying out a sizeable part of one's life savings in a business venture or market operation on a long-shot gamble in the hope of a huge clean-up? In the latter case isn't it rather important to know what the real odds are against one, so as to evaluate the dangers and opportunities of the gamble realistically?

How much, roughly, is it worth to the chance-taker to win the Pontiac sedan; and how much to gain a feeling of participation, opportunity, hope, excitement, and the thrill of a great stimulus to the ego?

FRACTIONIZING VERSUS MAXIMIZING

W HEN we spoke about predictions and the "degrees" of predictability, ranging from the "nearly certain" to the "almost impossible," we outlined the problem of everyone who has to make some sort of decisions on a hundred and one matters concerning the "unknown future" every day of his life.

But to the man who is dedicated to "absolute rightness," any method of making these decisions on a "maybe" basis leaves a great deal to be desired. And therefore, as long as he is so dedicated, he is going to batter his brains against the unattainable, in the hope that if only he can know "enough" or "all" about it, he can come up with the right answers all the time. His intellect may tell him that this is not a reasonable hope, and in actual experience he knows that not *all* of his predictions come out as he anticipates. But since he has no other method of dealing with the situation he goes right on looking for perfection; and being continually frustrated, he becomes discouraged.

He will tell you with a good deal of bitterness that, "It's all right to talk about 'probabilities,' but what about the market right now? What about U. S. Steel right now? Is it a buy or is it a sell? Is it going to go up or going to go down? The wrong answer is going to mean a loss. What to do about it?"

He knows, part of him knows, that even if U. S. Steel looks like a buy according to the very best and most complete information he can get today, tomorrow there may be a shake-up in the company's direc-

torate, or an adverse court decision, or a general smash in the market-
as-a-whole due to some scare or national disaster that nobody could
foresee. And yet, if he is going to deal in stocks he has to make decisions and face these unpredictable future events.

What steps can he take to protect himself against the unpredictable?

He could take one big step if he would use the method that any
insurance company uses to protect itself. He could diversify his
holdings. The Travelers Insurance Company doesn't know whether
Aunt Matilda will break her arm tomorrow or not, and certainly the
company is not going to study Aunt Matilda's personal life in every
detail and follow her around all day to guard against a claim on her
accident policy.

The insurance company doesn't worry much about Aunt Matilda,
for it has thousands of policies covering many other Aunts and Uncles
and Cousins in every part of the country. It has not even tried
to make any precise and absolute predictions about what will happen
to any one of them. But the company does have a method of evaluation, based on a good deal of past experience. Their own records will
show about how many policy holders will probably break an arm in
the next six weeks, give or take a reasonable margin of error. And
while this doesn't help very much in telling Aunt Matilda's particular fortune, it does make possible extremely precise predictions as to
the whole group.

You and I cannot do exactly what the insurance company does.
We do not have the capital to invest in thousands of different stock
situations. It would not be a practical way to invest in any case.

However, we can study the record of hundreds or thousands of
stocks in their past actions; we can note certain sequences of events,
and we can establish certain correlations. We cannot tell what any
particular stock will do or when. But we can learn to foresee the
"probable" action of any stock with a good deal of success. That
is to say, our prediction, if carried forward in the record of several
hundred stocks, will be valid within the reasonable limits of expected
error, as long as the general patterns of stock behavior do not change
radically and suddenly.

Over the entire period in which records of market action have been
kept, the basic behavior of stocks has changed very little. Such
minor changes in the typical habits of stocks as have occurred can be

allowed for, that is to say, if we have formed certain opinions as to how stocks "will probably act," we can revise and bring up to date this overall map from time to time to meet any new conditions.

This is the method of evaluation and prediction for stocks. Not necessarily the only method, but typical of evaluative methods in many lines of study. We look at the past and extract the generalized patterns, similarities, correlations; and project these into the future as a basis for prediction.

Being an abstraction this method deliberately ignores much detail (it doesn't care to know too much about Aunt Matilda's affairs). Being a high abstraction with the conclusions expressed only as "probabilities," it assumes from the start that some of the decisions made on this method will turn out "wrong." But there is also the big assumption that if the method is valid and the probabilities assigned are reasonably correct, the results, applied to a number of decisions, will be correct within the expected limits.

Notice "within the expected limits." When the insurance company writes an accident policy for Aunt Matilda, the "expected limits" of its prediction, for all the accident policies they may have are very narrow. It can tell you down to several decimal places what the annual total of claims will come to. With the man who buys a *single* stock or makes any single decision on a matter involving uncertainty, the expected limits of success or failure are much wider; in fact he may be little better off than if he flipped a coin so far as the expected outcome of his single prediction.

But you and I can take a point somewhere between the fine precision of a big insurance operation and the out-and-out gamble of the plunger. Assuming that we have some idea what to expect "in the long run," based on careful study and observation, we can avoid the extreme risk of "bad luck" by making *several* commitments.

We will not make any commitments unless we feel the probabilities "favor" our success. That is, we won't take a chance on something in which the probabilities are "loaded" against us.

Now how would this work? Let us assume that we have developed certain evaluative methods. We have spent some weeks or months or years observing past history. We have made our tables and charts and breakdowns, and we feel that we have abstracted certain factors, which, if they occur together, point to a probability of say 55% that certain consequences will follow. For instance, we may find that a particular type of breakout from a long-term formation in a stock, accompanied by a certain volume of activity, seems to lead to a substantial up-trend in 55% of the cases over a period of years and in many different types of stock.

If we used $20,000 capital to enter twenty situations having this probability, using $1000 in each, we could assume that as long as this probability held true, our "expectation" of the result would be eleven "wins" and nine "losses." Let us, for the moment assume also that the "wins" would each give us $1000 profit, and the "losses" would each involve the total loss of the $1000 put up. Then we might expect a theoretical result of eleven wins in which we would make $11,000 profit, and nine losses in which we would lose $9,000. We would then have a net profit of $2000, or 10% of our capital.

It would be a little easier to study the effect of diversification if we change the terms of the problem slightly. Instead of winning "even money" eleven times out of twenty, we might expect to win exactly half the time, but each "win" would give us $1200 instead of $1000. Thus, in twenty commitments we could expect to win ten at $1200 each, or $12,000, and to lose ten at $1000 each, or $10,000. This would give us a net profit of $2000 for the twenty trials, as above, or 10% of the total capital, the same as before.

This is, in effect, a "percentage game," in the same sense that the business of an insurance company is a "percentage game." You (or the insurance company) is counting on the relatively small expectation of a percentage gain in each transaction to give protection to capital over the long run, and to compensate for the taking of risk (which is the business of both speculators and insurance companies).

In order to gain any real protection, however, you must diversify your holdings in such a way that you do not stand to lose everything on one single disaster. You may have an expectancy of gain amounting to 10% on each transaction. At these odds, your "mathematical expectancy" would be a gain of $2000 on an investment of $20,000.

But if you were to wager your $20,000 in one plunge on the even-money chance of recovering either $22,000 or being wiped out, you would still be risking your entire fortune on a fifty per cent chance of total loss.

On the other hand, if you were to make twenty successive wagers of $1000 each on the same terms (in each individual transaction you would stand to recover either $1200 or nothing), your chances of total loss in the entire series would be less than one in a million.

It is true you could and would have some losses. But they would not take everything you had and wipe you out. The chances of losing even half your capital would be something less than one out of eight, and this would leave you still with a stake for a come-back.

In fact, one could say that the probabilities of fulfilling the mathematical "expectation" of ultimate profit in a "game" such as we have described, where only a small portion of the capital was used in any one commitment, and where there was a constant favorable percentage, are astronomical. At any rate the chances of ultimate success are tremendously greater than those in say, the opening of a new store or establishment of a law firm.

It is not necessary, of course, that the twenty "partial" commitments be made in sequence, one at a time. All of the capital can be used at the same time if desired, with the same results. The great difference between this method and the usual way of "shooting the works" is that you will not have all the eggs in one basket, for each separate unit will be invested on its own merits and in various types of situation. Some of these may be in railroads, some in aircraft, others in motors, or utilities or building materials; and some may be long and some short. It is variety that gives strength to the method, just as a fagot of small sticks may be much stronger than a single log of wood.

This method, which we have outlined in very general terms, can be applied in many ways to almost any market operation. It will not appeal to the out-and-out "gambler," since it is not spectacular. The nervous and insecure gambler does not have either the patience or the confidence to wait out a method which is almost sure to produce a moderate gain over the long pull while giving him an enormous degree of protection. He wants to dash in quickly and grab a fat profit; then stand back and wait for another opportunity to grab and run.

However, by "fractionizing" instead of "maximizing" profits the investor who can follow through on a balanced and diversified program will stand to gain not only greater profits in the long run, but peace of mind as well.

An essential part of this whole thing is the acceptance of the probability of some losses, which we mentioned briefly in passing. Since the losses are expected in advance and have been already considered and discounted, they cannot hurt too badly. Whereas the plunger is out on a limb, completely at the mercy of whatever unpredictable reversal may strike, the balanced and diversified investor cannot be hurt badly by an adverse move for he has already taken it into account as a possibility, and part of his holdings are so placed that they will act as "insurance" against any collapse or runaway inflation in the market.

The method of designing a "balanced and diversified" program is taken up in some detail in Chapter XXXVII of "Technical Analysis of Stock Trends." Essentially it is a matter of studying the individual trends of particular stocks and, instead of plunging all-out on the "long" side or the "short" side, taking a position in which the strongest-appearing securities are held "long" and the weakest "short" in a ratio corresponding approximately to the ratio of the number of "strong-looking" stocks to the number of "weak-looking" stocks in the whole market, or at least in the group of stocks one has under study.

What we are talking about here is not some one unique and "magic" way of dealing with the market. The point of this book does not lie in some formula or system at all. The big point is the acceptance of a new outlook. And it is this new outlook that provides the tools for coping with the unpredictable future.

The devices we use for handling this problem in stocks are much the same as those we can use in other problems. We give up the attempt to be "perfect." We stop trying to "maximize" our gains. We settle for a great number of small satisfactions and victories instead of the big showy "killing." We plan to take small losses in stride. We follow a carefully worked-out method of evaluation and prediction, and we stand ready to change it as new conditions require. Change the terms slightly and this formula will apply to business problems generally, to family problems, and to personal conflicts and tensions. It is simply the scientific process applied to every-day life.

QUESTIONS FOR CONSIDERATION

Do you see how the average gambler, or the average business man, or the average investor is led into taking unwarranted chances in his efforts to maximize his possible profits? Do you see the dangers in this?

Would you try to pick out the "one best" situation from a number of possible commitments, and then plunge heavily into this in the hope of "winning" a large reward? Or would you divide your commitments between a number of situations that looked good, with the expectation that some of these might eventually result in losses? Would you, in this second case, stand to make the big, spectacular profit? Would you stand to get hit by the big, spectacular ruin?

Are you familiar with the type of all-outer who wants to stake his "all" on some "one sure thing"? Does such a course sound like the policy of a confident and well-balanced investor?

ACCENTUATE THE NEGATIVE

ONE of the ways we are educated for failure and despair is the training we get to "think" positively.

The man who uses the word "perhaps" very often is not considered a "dynamic" thinker. We have been given the idea that it is better to come right out with a strong opinion than to be, as they say, "wishy-washy."

Read the editorials in your paper. Listen to the political speeches and sermons. Go over the "letters to the editor." You will find a great deal of "absolutely loyal," "utterly depraved," "100% American," "completely ruined," "supreme happiness," etc. These are not "measured" words. They are absolute, hard, unyielding words. They are words likely to be colored with emotion, in fact they seem more like rallying cries to a "cause" than considered statements of thinking men and women.

In developing methods of evaluation, in prediction, and in any analytical work you will find it more useful to use a less dynamic, one might even say negative, approach.

There are times when "I don't know" is the best answer to a question. "Perhaps," "Maybe," "Sometimes," "To a degree," "Up to a point," "For some people," "Under these conditions," "As I see it," "So far as I know," "Probably," "Unless the conditions have changed"; all these are good honest phrases expressing doubt or limiting the area covered by accompanying statements.

Use them! Learn to think in negative terms! You will not be

disappointed so often because you will not have "claimed" so much. And you will not be crowding yourself to *believe more than you know*.

Coupled with statements as to the probability of predictions "coming true," these negative and doubt-expressing phrases can give you a realistic idea of just how far the limits of your knowledge of a situation really go.

The questioning phrases also underscore the possibility that a change in your expectations can occur, either due to the strategic operations of a personal opponent, or due to some basic change in the market, commodity, economy, or whatever you are evaluating.

Very often the best protection against defeat is to make one's plans on the assumption that one's opponent has "found out" one's own strategy, and similarly the best protection against total ruin can be to assume that some part of one's predictions are going to be "wrong."

Since if we take the extreme point of view on every part of our program we will be exposed to crippling losses on even a moderate set-back (for instance, if we went 100% "bullish" to the extreme limit of our resources), it will be safer to "expect" some degree of set-back, and to assume the possibility of a serious reversal. We can protect ourselves against these eventualities by deliberately "damping" our enthusiasm. Instead of going "100% bullish," we can take a predominantly bullish position but cushion it with a few short sales in weak-looking stocks. In this case we do not really expect to take a profit on these short sales. We may expect, in advance, to have some moderate loss on them if all turns out as we hope it will. The small losses will be the premium we have paid for protection. And in case of a real collapse, our "insurance short sales" will soften the blow and greatly reduce our losses.

What we have outlined above is a deliberate policy of "expecting" certain losses; of planning to take them as part of the cost of protection. It is a studied policy of avoiding the attempt to make a perfect score. It is an example of hedging which could be extended in principle to other market problems; and to problems not connected with the market including some of those in our personal lives.

By accentuating the negative we can avoid the pain of complete disappointment when a completely optimistic plan falls flat.

In effect what we are doing is to trade some part of the shining opportunity for a considerable portion of solid security. We can take the job we are sure of instead of gambling for the Big Opening.

We can settle for Jane next door, instead of seeking the Fairy Princess. We can buy insurance and pay premiums for protection we hope we will never have to cash in on. We can, by hedging and compromising, reduce our "demands" and step up our "accomplishments," and in this way narrow the frustrating gap between our aspirations and our performance.

QUESTIONS FOR CONSIDERATION

In some ways isn't our habit of always trying to see the "positive" side of things somewhat similar to the old "either . . . or" dichotomy? Aren't we limiting our view to one thing or its opposite, and then ruling out the forbidden side so that we end up with a single-valued outlook? Would you say that a one-valued outlook in a multi-valued world might restrict one's views and cramp one's style? Isn't it somewhat *unrealistic?*

Do you see how, by admitting more than "one side" of a question you can increase your understanding of the problem, and that this may save you from being swept away by your own enthusiasm and that of others?

Would you feel that if, when you entered into a "stock transaction," "business venture," "love affair," "card game," or other enterprise, you had already considered and allowed for the possibility of failure or partial failure, you might be better able to prepare for such a reverse, and you might be able to protect yourself in large degree from its effects?

NET LONG TERM GAINS

PERHAPS you, like so many of us, were trained in the hard tradition that if you want to amount to anything you have to strive for perfection. Parents and teachers have held up before us the ideal of making every moment count, and hitching one's wagon to a star, and getting to the top. Congressmen have sounded off about the indomitable spirit of enterprise. We have been exposed to directives and precepts about how to do something called "succeed."

Since we never had it quite straight just what was meant by "success," and since the details of how the indicated power drives were supposed to get us into orbit have not been precisely delineated, it is no great wonder that a good many of us try to play it safe by going all-out all the time. We don't exactly know where we're headed or what is the prize, but we feel we can't afford to lose it, whatever it is. We want all the money we can lay hands on, we want all the power we can grab, we want everybody to love and admire us, we want to be good, and pure, and generous. We want all there is of whatever has the seal of approval of our culture; anything that has a good label, regardless of whether it is what we really need or want and regardless of whether it is compatible with some of the other things with "good" labels.

Since for so many of us it must be either "this" or "that" and no "in-between," we have to go all-out in a blind and desperate competitive race with no one to tell us when we have crossed the finish line, and no idea whether we are really on the course. So we just go like hell until we drop in our tracks.

And if the race looks hopeless, if we feel we cannot expect to come in first, then all is lost, for second is no better than last in an "either . . . or" world; and then we drop out of the race and don't even try any more.   Perhaps we turn to liquor in a serious way to cover up the hurt of "losing."   Or shut ourselves up tight in a little world of small routines and time-consuming rituals, so that we can justify our feeling that we are "above" the grab for status, or wealth, or fame. This is the other side of the "either . . . or"; the demoralization, when "nothing matters any more."

But you don't have to own the New York Central, or be President of the United States, or marry the richest girl in the world, to live a happy life.   And if you can get away from the symbols of power, wealth, and approval and take a hard look at the particular facts in your particular life, you may find that what you really need and want isn't nearly so hard to get as the concept of "success" that has been subliminally impressed on your value system.

If you haven't been so blinded and so conditioned to conformity that you cannot feel any desires outside of the standard symbols, then you can make your own deal with the world on *your* terms and not on *its* terms.   You can set your sights on a goal that meets your "necessary and sufficient" specifications of a full and adequately successful life.

What does this mean?   Why, in material matters it means that not every woman would actually sell her soul for a mink coat; she might want a pair of field glasses or a new electric stove much more. Not every man would need a Cadillac to set the hall mark of success on his career.   He might, actually, get a lot more fun out of a small sailboat, or a new high-fi sound system.   Not every male would respond to the sexual appeal of the cow-like breasts so insistently advertised as "top priority."   There are other fetishes that can be quite as interesting.   And of course, most of us "know," even though we don't act accordingly, that piling up money is not the first and last end of a business or professional career.   It is possible to get a lot of satisfaction and a lot of prestige along with a moderate salary.

Perhaps the slogan, "Take it easy," would come nearest to explaining the different viewpoint we are suggesting in this book.   All the discussion of "measuring" and of "infinite-valued orientation" amounts to an argument for moderation.   All the study of hedging and "partial" commitments in the market, comes to much the same.

In line with this new (and perhaps radical thought), we try to find the *easiest* way to do things, not the *hardest*. We don't necessarily shoot for the "top," we just try to make a passing grade. We don't necessarily go for "millions"; perhaps tens of thousands or hundreds of thousands will buy us all we can ever want. We don't grit our teeth and decide "always to be right in our judgments; and never to take a loss." It is amazing how many losses a man can take, if he knows what he is doing, and still come up with a net profit.

By deliberately putting aside the mantle of the saint, the robe of the dictator, the silk hat of the tycoon, we can go about the business of getting ourselves "enough" virtue, "enough" power, "enough" wealth, "enough" love, etc. with a great deal better expectation of reaching our goal, and a lot less anxiety.

It is possible, under these conditions to "take it easy" to a degree most people would hardly believe. By cutting down one's over-high aspirations they become much, much easier to achieve. This leads to self-confidence, to a feeling of accomplishment, to security, and very likely to more effective efforts since there is not the continual worry and tension that goes with trying to earn more or achieve more than is humanly possible.

Thus, a man who is willing to settle for the girl next door instead of the story-book princess will increase his chances of success in the field of romance and save himself a great deal of heartache.

In the market it is very much the same story. You have watched the nervous, jittery men who pace around the back of the brokers' board rooms, suffering with every tick of the ticker, uncertain, irritable, and anxious. With their absolute standards they cannot afford to be "wrong," and to be "right" they must make a profit on every trade and they must buy near the bottom and sell near the top. In order not to feel they have failed, they must literally do the impossible.

It isn't necessary. If a small part of the energy that goes into the fruitless, unplanned drive for "absolute" success could be used to observe the market as it really is, and to develop a basic method of evaluation, these poor harried souls could rest so much easier. They could go a day, or a week if need be, without ever looking at the tape. They could afford to be "wrong" quite often; they could take quite a lot of small losses. And still do very well in their market operations, possibly better than they are now doing.

They could, if they were willing to give up the all-out drive to "win all," operate in Bull Markets and Bear Markets, in stocks or in commodities, without ever having the feeling that a slight mistake on their part or some event entirely beyond their control could "wipe them out."

It is just a matter of being willing to open one's eyes and see not just one side, but "many" sides of a question. To be willing to diversify. To be willing to "hedge." To be willing to sell short. To be willing at times to take three small losses in order to get one substantial gain.

The prize? One would not look for "the top." One would not pile up a collossal fortune for one's heirs and the tax authorities to wrangle over. One would not ever become a "wizard of Wall Street." One would not feel that he was "the master" of the market.

But what would it be worth to feel secure, and reasonably protected because one had a "moderate" position? What would it be worth to avoid the headaches, the threat of ulcers or of heart failure? What would it be worth to be able to *think* serenely and enjoyably about the market, instead of *fighting* it like a cornered animal?

What would it be worth to have peace of mind and a better chance for steady, reasonable profits? What would it be worth to have time to read, to fish, to take pictures, to be with one's family, to sit on the bank of a quiet pond and watch the clouds float by in a blue, blue sky? What would it be worth to have the time to do the experiments and carry out the projects one has been planning to do all these years and never got around to?

These are the *kinds* of values we are thinking of. By eliminating the "unnecessary" worries and tensions of life, general semantics can make it possible for us to realize our potentialities in our own right and in our own way to a much greater degree than most of us can do under the distorted and unrealistic value concepts we have acquired from the culture in which we live.

As you may have gathered, all of this is a "non-social" point of view. That is to say it calls for a sharp and drastic break with much of the tradition and custom of our environment. It calls for a new point of view, not only in the market, but in matters of politics, the law, religion, family life, social ambitions, and most especially in the aims and goals we set for ourselves and how we regard ourselves in relation to the world around us.

It is "non-social" in that sense. It is not, however, "un-social," and certainly not "anti-social." It is not a move *against* one's fellow men to want to take a hard look at one's own real needs and aspirations. It is not *against* society to repudiate folkways, creeds, superstitions, pre-scientific theories, and obsolete directives that no longer fit the facts. It is not *against* people to chuck out all the nonsense and unsanity that has kept men ignorant, hostile and worried.

The purpose of general semantics is to keep up-to-date the maps by which men live. We have today the physical machinery to make a world where more people can be healthy, and well-fed, freer from hostility and freer for the "pursuit of happiness" than at any time in the history of the world. We are not doing a very good job of putting this machinery to work. There is not too much time left.

It is time to put away childish things and become men.

QUESTIONS FOR CONSIDERATION

Has this book touched on some of the problems and difficulties you have experienced in the market?

Does it touch on some other problems in other phases of your life quite unconnected with the market?

Do you feel that by a more thorough understanding of the forces that operate within each of us, and the mechanisms by which "we know what we know," we can learn better how to cope with and/or adapt to the conditions of the world we live in?

Are you aware of certain "feelings," "beliefs," "convictions," "faiths," "attitudes," "opinions," "prejudices," etc. that seem to operate in you without conscious thought on your part?

Have you ever examined these thoughtfully in line with the observed facts in your environment to check how effectively they represent the actual present conditions in the world around you?

Particularly, have you examined your habitual reactions and responses to various questions in the fields of: the stock market; the ethics and philosophy of business; morality, sexual and otherwise; politics; religion; racial attitudes; personal antipathies and preferences?

Do you feel that if you could bring your "mental maps" up to date and sharpen your appraisals of the external world of tangible reality you would be in a stronger position to deal with the problems of your life?

Do you feel that this kind of self-re-education cannot fail to give you a more sympathetic understanding of the problems of others; and in the long run to prepare you for a more useful, more successful, and happier way of living?

INDEX

INDEX

Principal references are given in italic type